THE PROTESTANT BISHOP

Henry Compton, Bishop of London,
from a portrait by Sir Godfrey Kneller in the National Portrait
Gallery

THE PROTESTANT BISHOP

BEING THE LIFE OF
HENRY COMPTON, 1632-1713
BISHOP OF LONDON

BY

EDWARD CARPENTER
CANON OF WESTMINSTER

LONGMANS, GREEN AND CO
LONDON · NEW YORK · TORONTO

LONGMANS, GREEN AND CO LTD
6 & 7 CLIFFORD STREET LONDON W I
BOSTON HOUSE STRAND STREET CAPE TOWN
531 LITTLE COLLINS STREET MELBOURNE

LONGMANS, GREEN AND CO INC
55 FIFTH AVENUE NEW YORK 3

LONGMANS, GREEN AND CO
20 CRANFIELD ROAD TORONTO 16

ORIENT LONGMANS LTD
CALCUTTA BOMBAY MADRAS
DELHI VIJAYAWADA DACCA

First published 1956

PRINTED IN GREAT BRITAIN AT
THE UNIVERSITY PRESS
ABERDEEN

CONIUGI DILECTISSIMAE

CUIUS CURA

HOC MEA MANU SCRIPTUM OPUS

SI INCURIOSE PERDIDISSEM

SEMEL ET SAEPIUS RECIPERABAT

Note

The spelling of many original letters has been modernised for the benefit of the general reader.

FOREWORD

THE name of Henry Compton, Bishop of London, is almost unknown to the general reader, and is familiar to the historical student only in connection with the Revolution of 1688. The first biography of him appeared in 1713, and was almost certainly written by one of the tory clergy whom the Bishop attracted around him in his later years. It is, in the main, a piece of tory propaganda, so much so that the writer found the Bishop's activities before and at the Revolution somewhat of an embarrassment. It is from this work, together with three funeral sermons preached in London in the year of his death and later published, that subsequent notices of Henry Compton in Granger, *Biographical History*, Kippis, *Biographia Britannica*, Chalmers, *Biographical Dictionary*, Cunningham, *Lives of Eminent Englishmen*, and *The Universal Magazine*, June 1740, have been drawn. The article in the *Dictionary of National Biography* also uses these sources, supplemented by contemporary histories and diaries.

The following study, based largely upon manuscript sources and contemporary pamphlets, is the first full length biography. Amongst such material, the Tanner and Rawlinson MSS. in the Bodleian Library, the Fulham MSS. at present with the Church Commissioners, the State Papers Domestic (cited as *S.P.D.*) at the Record Office, and the numerous publications of the Historical Manuscript Commission (cited as *H.M.C.*) have proved most valuable. Without such first-hand sources, a biography of this kind could not have been attempted. In addition, contemporary diaries, such as Edward Lake's, and histories, such as Burnet's, and the many biographies of statesmen and ecclesiastics which have appeared in recent years, have been found most helpful, both in themselves and in suggesting material which I could not otherwise have known. As too often happens, however, sources which I had expected to find particularly fruitful (e.g. the Danby Papers) proved perversely silent.

As to the subject of this biography, I hope I have outgrown the enthusiasm which persuades the biographer that he has unearthed some long neglected hero whose major contribution to the life of his time has been unaccountably overlooked. I

cannot honestly put forward any such claim on behalf of Henry
Compton, yet it may be modestly asserted that his championship
of the cause of English liberty, and his zeal as a reforming
bishop, have not received quite the attention which they deserve.

The reader will notice, when he leaves the section headed 'A
Political Bishop', that the nature of the interest changes, and that
the story in some respects loses momentum. Regrettable though
this may be, it is I fear inevitable. Compton's political career,
till the time of the Revolution, has (I think) real dramatic interest
and for this reason I felt it unwise to interrupt the flow of
events with other material, although I realised that this must
mean a marked change in the character of the work in the second
half. Though in some ways the discharge of his diocesan administration, his care of the American Plantations, his efforts on behalf
of French and Scottish refugees, and his relations with foreign
churches are perhaps more important than his political career,
they lack the same continuity of interest and read more
slowly. Yet this contrast is not without significance, for the
more colourful aspects of his life do not always represent the
Bishop at his best. It would indeed be a very unbalanced (and
untrue) portrait of Henry Compton which neglected, or hurried
over, the enormous and routine labour which he devoted to his
ecclesiastical responsibilities. The day to day oversight of his large
diocese, his concern to help his fellow Protestants in America, in
Scotland and in France—these were preoccupations which the
Bishop never treated in a cavalier or light-hearted manner. If he
could, in a crisis, perjure himself to James II, ride off with Princess
Anne, and sulk after being passed over for the Archbishopric, he
could yet also apply himself with equal diligence to less exciting
though in the last resort more rewarding activities. Such aspects
of his career can be brought out only by a rather factual and
detailed examination.

The reader may also reflect, when he arrives at the end of this
book, that though he has read much *about* Compton, he yet still
finds him a somewhat shadowy figure. The reasons for this are
not far to seek. No personal letters of the Bishop survive. I doubt
myself whether he wrote many. Though passionate, and liable to
sudden enthusiasms, he never found self-expression easy, nor did
he wish to indulge in it. His extant official letters are terse, to the
point, but not personally revealing. I should have rejoiced to

discover a letter written by him to an intimate friend—assuming he had one—when William III appointed Tillotson Archbishop ; or to learn what really happened when, as contemporary gossip reported, a nephew tried to poison him; but in neither case was I so rewarded.

Thus the following portrait of Henry Compton must be, of necessity, largely an objective one. Perhaps this is as it should be, in the case of a man whose contribution to the life of his time was pre-eminently practical.

The kind people whom I ought to thank are too numerous for me to mention by name. It must suffice if I express my appreciation to the Reverend Professor Norman Sykes who first suggested Henry Compton to me; to the Marquess of Northampton for allowing me to consult his *History of the Comptons of Compton Wynyates*, and to reproduce the portrait of the Bishop as a young man; to the Bishop of London for his permission to inspect the Fulham Papers, and the Reverend W. M. Atkins for introducing me to the diocesan records at St. Paul's Cathedral; to the incumbents of the various livings which Compton held; to the Master of St. Cross at Winchester; to Dr. Geoffrey Nuttall and Mr. Harold Goodwin for reading the book in manuscript; to Mr. Robert Lee for helpful suggestions; to Brother George Every; and to the officials of the British Museum, the Record Office, and the Bodleian Library for their constant courtesy.

CONTENTS

Part III. A Universal Bishop

PLATES

PART I

A POLITICAL BISHOP

PROLOGUE

Wʜᴇɴ King Charles I raised his standard at Nottingham in enemy country on 22 August, 1642, he was soon forced to retire to Shrewsbury in order that he might gather recruits from Wales, and from the loyal counties of Cheshire and Shropshire. He managed to muster some 15,000, and his intention was to out-march the Parliamentarians, under the command of Robert Devereux, Earl of Essex (whose forces were roughly equal to his own) and then to seize London. After a little skirmish outside the ancient city of Worcester, the two armies confronted one another on Sunday, 2 October, 1642, at Edgehill on the borders of Oxfordshire. Whatever advantage the Royalists might have gained from their position on a steep hill facing west was largely lost through the wise prescience of Essex in refusing to advance, and the rash impetuosity of Prince Rupert, who leading the King's cavalry down the hill with his accustomed fire, rushed furiously to the attack. Sir Jacob Astley, surveying the scene of battle, prayed fervently: 'O Lord, thou knowest how busy I must be this day; if I forget Thee, do not Thou forget me.'

The Royalist horse, as so often, swept all before them, but their very success prevented them from using this ad-vantage with restraint and caution. The struggle between the infantry on both sides was terrible. It was grim hand-to-hand fighting, in which the royal standard bearer, Sir Edmund Verney, perished. The numbers killed, writes Clarendon, were 'prodigious'. If there were a victor it was Charles, for he was able to push on to Oxford, but it was a victory almost as costly as defeat. Thus was fought the first great battle of the Civil War.

Present in the Royalist camp was a young boy, not yet eleven years of age, whose father and four brothers took part in the charge. His name was Henry Compton, and in later life, looking back on this and other days of battle, he delighted to relate, with pardonable exaggeration, that 'he had formerly drawn his sword in defence of the Constitution'. The boy's father was Spencer Compton, the second Earl of Northampton, soon destined to give his life in the cause of the King, to whom he gallantly devoted his whole family and fortune.

The life of this young boy forms the subject of the following biography.

CHAPTER ONE

YEARS OF UNSETTLEMENT

IT was not until 1618 that the Compton family, which still bears the title, was honoured with the Earldom of Northampton. The Comptons were an old Warwickshire family who took their surname originally from the Lordship of Compton in that county, anciently distinguished by the appellation of Compton at the Vineyard. As early as the reign of Henry II, there were some of this name flourishing in that part of the country; but they first stepped onto the wider stage of national history when 'Will Compton' (1482?-1528) gained the favour of Henry VIII. This young man acted as page to his imperious master when Henry was yet Duke of York, and he was present with him in France on that colourful, if somewhat revivalist, Field of Cloth of Gold. William Compton was knighted at Tournay in 1513; was created Chancellor of Ireland (1513-16); and proved his military valour in the Scottish wars. His son Peter, and his grandson Henry—the latter was summoned to Parliament in the fourteenth year of Elizabeth, and was afterwards one of the Peers for the trial of Mary Queen of Scots, being created Baron Compton—consolidated the family fortunes, albeit in a less dangerous and spectacular manner. This growing wealth and prestige at last brought a more exalted reward when William Compton (d. 1630) became Lord President of the Marches, and was created first Earl of Northampton by James I in 1618. He made a lucrative choice in selecting for his bride Elizabeth, daughter and heiress of Sir John Spencer, Lord Mayor of London, who, however, by no means at first gave the match his approval. Of this marriage came Spencer Compton, father of the subject of this biography, whose career it will be necessary to follow in somewhat greater detail.

Spencer Compton was educated at St. John's College, Cambridge, and was created a Knight of the Bath on 3 November, 1616. He was early introduced to affairs of state through the family influence, and became a member of Parliament for

Ludlow in 1621-2. It was about this time that he married Mary, daughter of Sir Francis Beaumont, Knight of Cole Orton, Leicestershire, a family which claimed descent in the direct paternal line from Louis VIII of France.[1] Spencer Compton was now a rising favourite at Court, particularly with the younger set, and in March 1622 he was appointed Master of the Robes to Prince Charles, and in this capacity accompanied him next year on his quixotic journey to Spain. The intention was that Charles, handsome, twenty-three, and infatuated for the time being with the brilliant but shallow Charles Villiers, Duke of Buckingham, should travel incognito to Madrid, win the good will of the King of Spain, woo the Infanta, and like a knight of old romance, bring her back to England. At 8 p.m. on 7 March, 1623, the Prince reached Madrid, having ridden across France—but Spencer Compton was not with him, for he had been taken ill at Bruges and had had to be left behind.

When Prince Charles succeeded to the throne, Compton was re-appointed Master of the Robes, and he was summoned to the House of Lords as Baron Compton on 1 April, 1626. On his father's death, 14 June, 1630, he became second Earl of Northampton.

The constitutional struggle between Charles and his Parliament, increasingly a part of the religious conflict between high Church Anglicanism and Puritanism, was becoming more and more the great issue, particularly as the King was faced with a growing financial problem which made it difficult for him altogether to dispense with the House of Commons. Spencer Compton, by habit and conviction, was a Royalist through and through, but he was not without a shrewd natural common-sense, which it is one of the tragedies of history that Charles so singularly lacked. He supported the King enthusiastically in the two Scottish wars, but definitely advised his royal master to summon Parliament. That word of four syllables, he declared, was 'like the dew of heaven'.[2] When the Civil War broke out, so Clarendon, the veteran Royalist, wrote later with admiration, 'he entirely dedicated all his children to the

[1] Sir Francis Beaumont was brother to the Countess of Buckingham, who had married Lord Compton's uncle, Sir Thomas Compton. See William Bingham Compton, 6th Marquis of Northampton, *History of the Comptons of Compton Wynyates*, p. 75 (privately printed and circulated).

[2] Hardwicke, *State Papers*, ii. 210.

quarrel'.[1] In September, 1640, he wrote to his son James, in the Low Countries, urging him to return home, and asking him to 'get into contact with all the gentlemen in the county in whom I have any interest'.[2]

Spencer Compton himself followed the King to York, and 'was entrusted with the execution of the commission of array in Warwickshire, in which county his family interests were dominant'.[3] He tried with courage, but without success, to surprise Warwick Castle, which was heavily defended, and on 23 September he was defeated by Hampden and Ballard at Southam. He fought with Rupert in a little skirmish outside Worcester, and (as we have seen) he took part in the charge at Edgehill. His tested loyalty and undoubted capacity caused the King to place more responsibility on his shoulders, and in November 1642, after Charles's return to Oxford, he was entrusted with the supervision of Banbury and the surrounding countryside, at the same time being ordered to raise a troop of horse. The holding of this part of England for the King became almost a family affair. Lord James Compton, his eldest son, was made lieutenant-colonel: Sir William, his third son, was put in charge of the castle at Banbury, at the capture of which he had displayed outstanding courage.

On 19 March—it was a Sunday afternoon—the Earl, with three of his sons, marched out to do battle with the Parliamentarians on Hopton Heath, the enemy forces being double his own and under the command of Sir William Bruereton and Sir John Gell, whose regiment was notorious for its plundering. The Earl successfully routed the enemy's cavalry and captured eight guns, but the Parliamentary infantry stood firm. Flushed with victory, and following the fatal habit of too many Royalist commanders, he carried his charge too far and found himself surrounded. His position was hopeless. He was offered mercy but with characteristic pride he answered that 'he scorned to take quarter from such base rogues and rebels as they were'. It was a magnificent gesture, but the Earl of Northampton paid for it with his life, being dispatched by a blow on the head.[4] Of his

---

[1] Clarendon, *The History of the Rebellion and Civil Wars in England* (Oxford, 1826), iv. 460.

[2] *S.P.D.* Car. II, 29 Sept., 1640, 468, no. 87.   [3] *D.N.B.* xl. 449.

[4] Writing to his mother, the third Earl relates: 'His armour was so good that they could not hurt him till he was down and had undone his headpiece.' See pamphlet, *The Battle of Hopton Heath*. B.M.

death, Clarendon writes with measured dignity: 'The truth is a greater victory had been an unequal recompense for such a loss. He was a person of great courage, honour and fidelity, and not well known till his evening; having in the ease and plenty and luxury of that too happy time indulged to himself with that licence which was then thought necessary to great fortune.'[1]

The Earl of Northampton seems to have been a devoted parent. A brief note to his wife, Countess Mary, from York, sent to her in the midst of the struggle, and not many months before his death, says much in a little space. 'I dare not write so large as I would, but I dare write that I long much to be with you. P.S. My blessing to the children.'[2]

Henry Compton, his sixth and youngest son,[3] was thus left fatherless at the age of eleven, at a time, moreover, when the growing superiority of the Parliamentary forces was making life increasingly difficult for the members of his family. His brother, Sir William, who gallantly defended Banbury against eleven attacks of the enemy, was forced to surrender it in 1646; and suffered imprisonment on three separate occasions during the years of the Commonwealth.

But it is time that we turn to the subject of this biography.

Henry Compton was born in 1632[4] at Compton Wynyates, a sleepy little hamlet set in the green fields and quiet countryside of Warwickshire, some five miles from Shipston. Its population was only forty-six in 1800, and it is unlikely to have been much greater some two centuries earlier. In this remote hamlet Sir William Compton built a manor house in the reign of Henry VIII, and was honoured by a royal visit. Spencer Compton, the second Earl of Northampton, made this country seat his home, (hence Henry's birth here) but on 12 June, 1644, after his death, it suffered the indignity of being garrisoned by the Parliamentary forces, in which year the village church was

---

[1] Clarendon, *op. cit.,* iii. 459.

[2] *S.P.D.* Car. I, 14 June, 1642, 468, no. 87.

[3] The names and dates of birth of the children are as follows: James, 19 Aug., 1622; Charles, 1623; William, 1625 (Lloyd, in his *Memorials of those that suffered,* 1668, mistakenly states that Charles and William were twins); Spencer, 1629; Francis, 1629; Henry, 1632. There were also two daughters, Anne, 1638 and Penelope. See William Bingham Compton, *op. cit.,* p. 76.

[4] Wood, *Athenae Oxonienses,* 1721, ii. 968. Compton died on 7 July, 1713, and his age on his tombstone in Fulham churchyard is given as 81. The existing registers at Compton Wynyates do not commence till 1683.

reduced to ruins, and the baptismal register, containing almost certainly the entry of Henry Compton's birth, was destroyed. Dugdale in his *Diary* writes: 'The rebels with 400 foot and 300 horse drove the Park and killed all the deer, and defaced the monuments in the Church.'[1] They are said to have captured in the house the Earl of Northampton's brother, some 14 officers, and 120 common soldiers.[2]

Where Lady Northampton and her young sons and daughters lived during the troubled years that followed we can only suggest in barest outline. In 1645 she was almost certainly in or near Banbury, but finding her situation dangerous she moved to the Royalist headquarters at Oxford. For this indiscretion she was forced to compound her estates for alleged delinquency and was fined £990. In her petition against this heavy exaction, she complained bitterly that she 'had not contributed to this unhappy war'. At the beginning of 'these sad distractions', she said, she had lived not far from Oxford, but 'the outrage of the soldiers in these parts grew so high that your petitioner being a woman and destitute of former friends, with four small children[3] conceived herself not to be safe . . . whereupon she was necessitated to take up her abode in Oxford'.[4] Perhaps it was some satisfaction to her that the fine was reduced on her agreeing to settle a sum of money for the establishment of a Puritan minister.

She then went to live in retirement at Grendon Manor House, which was the property of her son Charles, and situated near the Northampton's family home at Castle Ashby. The Lady Dowager also owned a house in London, 'one of the new built in Queen Street', where she died on 18 March, 1657, though it is unlikely that she was often in residence there during the early years of the Commonwealth.[5]

Henry's presence at Edgehill might suggest that he was in the care of his soldier brothers and moved with them from camp to camp. More probably, however, he spent most of the time at school, and passed his holidays with his mother. His early biographer—not, however, always a reliable authority—tells us that

[1] Quoted Compton, *History of the Comptons*, p. 90.
[2] *Letter Book of Sir Samuel Luke*, vol. 1, B.M. Egerton MSS. 785.
[3] 'Four small children' is perhaps a pardonable feminine exaggeration.
[4] Compton, *History of the Comptons*, p. 103.
[5] *Ibid.*

'he received an Education in his tender years suitable to his Quality'.[1]

From a letter written years afterwards, it seems that he attended for a time the Grammar School at Uppingham, where Francis Meres, a Trinity College man, was headmaster. The young scholar long remembered his former preceptor with affection, and as Bishop of London he petitioned Charles II to give him a prebend of Lichfield. 'He is old but deserving', he wrote, 'being a good scholar and well principled. He was once my schoolmaster and I would present him with this, more to show my good will than that I can imagine he will ever receive any advantage of it.'[2]

Henry Compton's subsequent movements during the period of the Commonwealth are as uncertain as those of the rest of his family, particularly in those years which saw the execution of Charles, the final defeat of the Scots at Worcester, and the assumption by Cromwell of supreme executive responsibility. Two facts about him, however, we do know—that he travelled extensively abroad, and that he entered Queen's College, Oxford, as a nobleman.

On 9 February, 1652, he secured a licence from the Council of State granting him permission to journey beyond the seas, but he was soon back in England for he went up to Queen's College in 1654, where he matriculated on 12 December.[3] The present College buildings date from the Restoration, so that they are not those with which Compton first became familiar, nor was the library in his day yet enriched with the large and unique collection of books which it owes to the munificence of Thomas Barlow—a great scholar but a thoroughly bad bishop.

It is unlikely that Henry Compton proved himself a very serious student. The unsettled political circumstances of the day, the enthusiastic loyalty to the exiled House of Stuart which he shared with the rest of his family, and his own practical tempera-

---

[1] *The Life of Dr. Henry Compton*, 1713, p. 2.

[2] Compton to Williamson, 23 July, 1678, *S.P.D.* Car. II, 405, no. 131. Compton does not seem to have been successful, for some three months later he was again writing to Williamson to secure for Meres the living of Lutterworth (*S.P.D.* Car. II, 407, no. 14). This request was equally unfruitful, but the next year Meres became a prebendary of Lincoln. (See *Alumni Oxonienses*.)

[3] *S.P.D.*, 9 Feb., 1652, 311. 1. 111, vol. 18. A. Kippis, *Biographia Britannica*, i. 53, and other authorities who have followed him, are in error in saying that he went up to Queen's College in 1649. See Foster, *Alumni Oxonienses*.

ment, hardly predisposed him, we suspect, to prolonged study. The time came when he grew weary of Oxford, and he decided, once again, to quit his native land, defiled as it was for him by the major generals of the Protector and the Puritan domination.

Until the Restoration—a considerable period during a most important phase in his spiritual and mental development—Henry was for the most part abroad, though his exact movements are again unknown. He certainly was in England, however, in 1657, possibly on account of his mother's death, for in a letter to her daughter who was married to James, third Earl of Northampton, Lady Dorset writes: 'James, Isabella, little William and Uncle Mr. Henry Compton went to Skipton Castle for four nights returning again to Castle Ashby on July 4.'[1] A friend later said of these years abroad: 'The better to prepare him for that Figure He was afterwards to make, he spent some years in Travelling: not to suck in the Maxims of Foreign States, or to try the Vices of Foreign Courts: Nor before he knew our Constitution in Church and State, was able to defend it, and [was] sure to stick to it.[2] He observ'd and examin'd the Civil and Ecclesiastical Polities abroad; he made them his Study but not his Rule. The more he stayed in France and Italy the more English-Man he was.'[3]

It is a pity that we have no details of Henry Compton's travels during these formative years.[4] In France he must have seen something of the Fronde, that unsuccessful effort, first by the Parliament of Paris and then by certain discontented nobles under the Prince of Condé, to curb the power of the French monarchy, whose policy was in the hands of Cardinal Mazarin. The Bourbons, however, unlike the Stuarts did not (as yet) succumb, but making an unnatural alliance with Cromwell, they triumphed over their adversaries. James, Duke of York, himself an exile,

[1] Family documents at Castle Ashby, 1186, 1, quoted Compton, *History of the Comptons*, p. 111.

[2] This is a curious statement since he left England when its constitution in Church and State was overthrown.

[3] T. Gooch, *A Sermon preached before the Lord Mayor*, 1713, p. 7.

[4] The movements of the rest of the family are equally obscure. The sixth Marquis of Northampton writes (*History of the Comptons*, p. 104): 'Of Henry's brother Francis, who was three years Henry's senior, and of his two sisters, we know nothing before the Restoration; but we may assume that except for periods of the boy's absence at school they all lived quietly with their mother. They had no part in the wars and apparently they took no part during the Commonwealth in plotting for the Restoration. Their names do not appear amongst those constrained to live abroad.'

entered the French service as a volunteer, and Compton is said to have 'trailed a pike in Flanders' under him.[1] If so, this unattractive Prince does not seem to have been very grateful in later years.

In Italy our young exile must have seen many signs of obvious decline in what has been called 'an inglorious and passive chapter in Italian history.' Venice was suffering sadly from its prolonged warfare with the Turks, which had led to the sealing off of Egypt from the Levant. This, together with the discovery of America and the opening up of the sea routes to the Indies, had injured her trade beyond hope of recovery. The city states had now their days of greatness behind them; their governments were often corrupt, and an enervating apathy seized many of their citizens.

Such a long stay abroad, and at such an impressionable age, could not fail to exert a strong influence upon the young refugee. Not only did he return master of the French and Italian tongues,[2] but if we may judge from his character later in life, with a considerable knowledge of men and affairs, and an outlook genuinely cosmopolitan. Henry Compton was never a scholar and Burnet properly complains that he had not gone through his studies with the necessary 'exactness';[3] but he was always sensitive to people and moved easily in society.

Maybe it was his sojourn in Italy which did so much to engender a lifelong animosity against the Roman Catholics, a hostility so extreme that at one crisis in his career he cast aside the traditional Royalism of his family, and took the lead in exiling from the kingdom the son of that monarch for whom his father had died.

[1] A. Kippis, *op. cit.*, i. 53.
[2] J. Cockburne, *The Blessedness of Christians after Death*, 1713, p. 25.
[3] G. Burnet, *History of My Own Times*, ed. Dartmouth, 1823, ii. 88.

CHAPTER TWO

A LAX CLERIC

ON 26 May, 1660, Charles II returned to his native land, after many years of vicissitudes which left their permanent (but not always happy) marks on his character. Macaulay has vividly described the scene. 'When he landed, the cliffs of Dover were covered by thousands of gazers, among whom scarcely one could be found who was not weeping with delight. The journey to London was a continued triumph. The whole road from Rochester was bordered by booths and tents and looked like an interminable fair. Everywhere flags were flying, bells and music sounding, wine and ale flowing in rivers to the health of him whose return was the return of peace, law and freedom.'[1]

On 29 May, the King in magnificent estate marched through the city of London. The young Earl of Northampton, as was fitting, 'led a troop of 200 gentlemen in grey and blue', and on 21 June he presented to the returned monarch at Whitehall a congratulatory address from the gentlemen of Warwickshire.[2] It was but justice that the Earl should be made lieutenant of this county.[3]

In the train of the King during the weeks that followed, there hurried back to their native land those who had suffered and endured in the royal cause, who had had their family estates despoiled, and the traditional pattern of their life destroyed. They returned eager again to tread their ancestral halls, to atone for the years that were lost, and to wreak vengeance. For the most part they were to be bitterly disappointed.

Among those who came back, though the precise date of his return is unknown, was Henry Compton. His brothers were already in England when he arrived, and in fact Henry was the only one not to sit in the Parliament of 1661. As a youngest son he had no estate to lose, but his family had suffered cruelly, and

[1] Macaulay, *History of England* (Everyman Library), i. 121.
[2] Compton, *History of the Comptons*, p. 11.
[3] *Ibid.*, quoting family documents, no. 974.

it was necessary for him to decide upon a profession. Circumstances, or what he himself later called 'Hobson's choice', pointed to a career in the army,[1] for, as he wrote to Sir Robert Southwell, clerk to the Council: 'I find that preferment like other things, is more easily imagined than compassed.'[2] Was he not, anyhow, an old campaigner, who had already seen service on the battlefields of Flanders?

It so happened at this time that the Earl of Oxford's 'Blues' was in process of being revived as a regiment of the King's body-guard, and the Compton family undertook to officer one troop. The first muster of what became the Royal Horse Guards was held in Westminster on 16 February, 1661, and present at it were Sir Charles Compton in command of a troop, Francis as lieutenant and Henry as cornet.[3] In November, Henry was made lieutenant on the death of Sir Charles.

But Henry soon decided to transfer himself from the camp to the University, and he went up to Cambridge and was admitted a Master of Arts in 1661, without, however, resigning his commission in the Blues.[4] How far this University, still under the spell of More, Whichcote and Cudworth, those germinal thinkers who approached the revelation of Christ in the philosophic spirit of Plato, influenced the soldier student we cannot tell. Their effect upon him was probably not very profound, and it is doubtful whether he was long in residence. His past life had not been such as to incline him to pursue the academic way, nor did his temperament lead him in that direction.

Henry's brother, Sir William, was now rapidly becoming a person of note in national affairs. In 1660 he had been admitted a member of the Privy Council, and in June of that year he was appointed Master General of the King's Ordnance. On 3 July, 1662, Pepys records that he 'dined with the officers of the Ordnance; where Sir W[illiam].... and other great persons were. After dinner, was brought to Sir W[illiam] Compton a gun to discharge seven times; the best of all devices that I ever saw.'[5]

---

[1] Compton, *History of the Comptons*, p. 123.

[2] Quoted E. Packe, *An Historical Record of the Royal Regiment of Horse Guards*, 1834, p. 16 n.   [3] E. Packe, *op. cit.*, p. 5.

[4] J. and J. A. Venn, *Alumni Cantabrigienses*, 1922, p.378. Compton's biographer seems to have been perplexed that Henry did not return to Oxford which he had left without taking a degree.

[5] *The Diary of Samuel Pepys*, (Everyman), i. 263.

In the last month of the same year, Sir William was made a Commissioner for Tangiers, which possession had come to the English Crown as the dowry of Charles's Queen, Catherine of Braganza.[1] But Henry had preceded him there, being sent out in August for six months on full pay in the King's service, with permission to take with him two servants and a horse.[2]

It is quite clear that Henry Compton was finding it difficult to settle down after his early years of wandering, and on his return home from Tangiers, disappointed with his slow rate of promotion, his active soldiering seems to have ceased. Yet even this short period of military service (with his 'campaigning' on the Continent) left their permanent marks upon him. Later in many of his talks to his clergy he introduced the metaphor of the camp, and James II reproached him—they became bitter enemies—because he spoke 'more like a colonel than a bishop'. Perhaps, even more significant, Henry Compton was to appear again in arms—the last of the soldier-bishops—on an occasion momentous in English history.

Of his career during the next few years no continuous narrative is possible, and we must be content with catching a glimpse of him from time to time: but these glimpses suggest the same unsettlement that we have already noticed. His years of camp and travel had bred habits which were not easily thrown aside. Perhaps that was why, late in life, he advised Sir Robert Southwell against sending his son abroad as part of his education, since it might give him 'a tincture of such principles as would not suit well with our climate'.[3]

On 25 February, 1664, Compton was granted a pass for himself and four horses to cross over to France,[4] and he seems to have stayed in Paris for some months. Certainly he was there in July, for he wrote to Sheldon, Archbishop of Canterbury, giving him an account of the Church in France, which, he said, was oppressed at home by the King and from abroad by the Pope. Compton was undoubtedly enjoying himself, despite lack of funds—a constant problem throughout life—and he asked the Archbishop to intercede with the King that he might remain a

---

[1] Compton, *History of the Comptons*, p. 120. Sir William died very suddenly in Drury Lane on 18 Oct., 1663. He was buried in the north aisle of Compton Church.　　　　[2] *Ibid.*, p. 123.

[3] *H.M.C.*, App. ix, Report II, p. 460 n.

[4] *S.P.D.* Car. II, 25 Feb., 1664, Minute Book E.B., p. 43.

few months longer, since 'it may conduce to confirm my health'.[1]
If possible, he added, he hoped to proceed to Rome.

It is probable that he remained on the Continent for some
considerable time, though he was in England in March 1666, for
in this month Dr. Fell wrote to a friend that he was 'glad' Mr.
Compton had returned home, and he was looking forward to
seeing him.[2]

Dr. Fell's acquaintance was to prove valuable. This learned
Vice-Chancellor, who did so much for his University, is chiefly
remembered to posterity as one of the founders of the Oxford
University Press, and also, perhaps unfortunately, through the
cruel lines of Tom Browne:

> I do not love thee, Dr. Fell,
> The reason why I cannot tell;
> But this alone I know full well,
> I do not love thee, Dr. Fell.

Dr. Fell advised Compton to enter Christ Church as a
canon commoner, and on 7 July, 1666, he was incorporated
Master of Arts at Oxford.[3] Again following Dr. Fell's advice,
he decided to seek ordination. We need not assume any profound sense of vocation, for this was hardly thought necessary
in those days. It was not often that a nobleman's son wished
to enter the ministry. We may reasonably suppose, however,
that hatred for the Commonwealth régime had bred in Henry
Compton not only a deep affection for the monarchy, but
also an enthusiastic loyalty to the Church of England. Under
the date 2 May, 1666, in the Act Book of the Archbishop
of Canterbury, there is recorded: 'Henry Compton, M[aste]r
of Arts and Brother to the Right Hon. the Earl of Northampton, Petitions his Grace for a Faculty to receive both
the Orders of Deacon and Priest (extra tempora).[4] The Person
being examined and approved, a Fiat was passed upon his
Petition directed to the M[aste]r of the Faculties.'[5]

---

[1] Compton to Sheldon, 23 July, 1664, Bod. Tanner MSS. 47, fo. 184.

[2] Fell to Williamson, 5 Mar., 1666, S.P.D. Car. II, vol. 40.

[3] Foster, *Alumni Oxonienses*, i. 314. The cost of his journey from Compton
Wynyates to Oxford (Nov. and Dec. 1667 and Mar. and Apr. 1667) is entered
in the account books of the Northampton family (F.D. 1001/19).

[4] I.e. outside 'the times appointed in the canons' (Canon 31)—that is the
Ember seasons.

[5] Lambeth, *Act Books of the Archbishop of Canterbury.*

The immediate result of Compton's ordination was the grant of a reversion to the next vacant canonry at Christ Church. A man with such powerful connections did not have to wait long for ecclesiastical preferment, though a writer in the *Universal Magazine* later said of him that 'he might have made high demands upon the Court, and raised himself at once to the greatest dignities, yet he chose to make a gradual and regular advance'.[1] Promotion came in a very attractive form from the King in the Mastership of St. Cross at Winchester (vacant through the death of Dr. William Lewis, in his early years chaplain to Lord Chancellor Bacon), 'fit preferment', so comments a friend, 'for Him whose House was always a constant Hospital'.[2]

The Hospital at St. Cross owed its foundation to Henry de Blois, brother to King Stephen, and was afterwards further endowed by Henry de Beaufort, whose Chapel in the Cathedral is one of its great glories. To Compton, whose financial anxieties were at this time particularly acute, the income from this preferment, some £500 per annum, must have been very acceptable, and he was instituted by Bishop Morley to the Mastership on 18 November, 1667.[3] The new Master, it is not surprising, undoubtedly developed a great affection for the old Hospital, and like many men of affairs 'in his after life, which was one continued Scene of Business (and sometimes of Disturbance) He often thought how much happier he had been if He had continued there'.[4]

The visitor to St. Cross (after he has refreshed himself with the beer which is provided there *gratis*) may still see signs of Compton's residence. His name appears in more than one place on the walls: and it is generally supposed, from the position of his initials, that he rebuilt the outer gateway, the ambulatory and the infirmary.[5] A generous inclination to help the poor was always one of his most endearing characteristics. Often in fact his charities landed him in debt.

Richard Heylin, Canon of Christ Church, died in April, 1669, and Henry Compton, who had been disappointed of a former vacancy,[6] was now to reap the reward of his influence at Court

---

[1] *Universal Magazine*, June 1770, p. 337. He was in fact made a bishop eight years after his ordination.   [2] T. Gooch, *op. cit.*, 1713, p. 8.
[3] Records of St. Cross.   [4] T. Gooch, *op. cit.*, 1713, p. 8.
[5] Records of St. Cross.   [6] *H. M.C.* Finch MSS. i. 443.

and his friendship with Dr. Fell. Lord Arlington, Secretary of State, who was one of the most powerful figures in the Government, wrote to Sir Joseph Williamson at Newmarket, where the King was taking his pleasures sadly by reason of a cold, 'to put His Majesty in mind of his promise to Compton of a Canonry in Christ Church'.[1] Charles was not unkindly when it demanded no sacrifice from himself and on 27 April the grant was issued. Two days later Henry Compton received his warrant.[2]

His new dignity did not immediately alter his manner of life, though it introduced him to Dr. Richard Allestree (1619–81), Regius Professor of Divinity, who seems to have had a great influence upon him, particularly through his 'Whole Duty of Man', which 'always attended him',—that is, if we assume him to be the author. Doubtless its practical wisdom, not unmixed with devotion, appealed to the young man of affairs.[3]

On 25 May, 1669, Henry Compton became a bachelor, and a month later a doctor, of divinity.[4] This short interval of time does not suggest a very exacting theological discipline, but we must remember that he was a nobleman's son. He was next appointed Sub-Dean of Christ Church, an office which he doubtless secured through the good offices of Dr. Fell, and in this capacity he was called upon to take part in an event unique in the history of the University. The circumstances arose out of the imagination of the Vice-Chancellor, and the generosity of the Archbishop of Canterbury. Dr. Fell had long deplored the use of St. Mary's Church (where the trial of Thomas Cranmer had taken place) for secular business in connection with the University, and he encouraged the Archbishop in the splendid conception of what has now adorned the University for nearly three hundred years —the Sheldonian Theatre. Christopher Wren was called in as architect. The cost of the building came to nearly £25,000—an enormous sum for those days—and Dr. Fell was made treasurer. It was fitting that he should preside over the formal opening on 9 July, 1669. The occasion was magnificent, with celebrations lasting throughout the day, though not even this air of rejoicing could prevent the bad tempered Dr. South, the University

---

[1] Arlington to Williamson, 27 Apr., 1669, *S.P.D.* Car. II, 259, no. 55.
[2] *S.P.D.* Car. II, E.B. 19, p. 102.
[3] W. Whitfield, *A Sermon on the late Lord Bishop of London.* 1713, p. 11.
[4] Foster, *op. cit.*, i. 314.

orator, from indulging in some unnecessarily 'malicious and indecent reflections on the Royal Society as underminers of the University'. John Evelyn, who was present, was quite shocked at this wanton indiscretion.[1]

On the following day the inceptors of theology made brief orations, and it was generally agreed that Dr. Henry Compton, 'being junior', performed his task efficiently and with great dignity. Dr. Thomas Lamplugh, later to become Archbishop of York in 1688, informed the Secretary of State that 'Dr. Compton performed his part so well that he came off with great applause, gaining reputation to himself, and did the University a great deal of honour'.[2] Evelyn found nothing to take exception to in what the Sub-Dean said: 'He began with great modesty and applause', he wrote.[3]

The diarist, it may be convenient to notice here, regarded Compton with respect, though he did not know him intimately. After hearing him preach some four years later, in April 1673, he wrote: 'This worthy person's talent is not preaching, but he is like to make a grave and serious divine.'[4] Later when he dined with him in 1676 he commented: 'He had once been a soldier, had also travelled in Italy and became a most sober, grave and excellent prelate.'[5] It was something to win the respect of such a man. Another contemporary wrote later that as Sub-Dean, Compton 'moderated in the Divinity Disputations with such Gravity and Wisdom, as made these Exercises both reputable and instructive'.[6] Doubtless what he lacked in theological learning he made up in commonsense.

But this gravity of demeanour was not suddenly acquired. In 1670 Compton was deeply in debt, very largely brought about by his personal extravagance, and his desire to help others. The executors of a certain Dr. Povey seem to have come down upon him for the repayment of a loan, and Compton after admitting that the profits from St. Cross were disappointing and not sufficient for him to discharge his obligations, confessed ingenuously that he had no option but to go back on his word, 'a thing I abhor'.[7] In March, he was begging Williamson, who

[1] *Diary and Correspondence of John Evelyn*, 1850, ii. 41.
[2] Lamplugh to Williamson, 13 July, 1669, *S.P.D.* Car. II, 216, no. 174.
[3] Evelyn, *op. cit.*, ii. 41.   [4] Evelyn, *Ibid.*, ii. 83.
[5] *Ibid.*, ii. 107.   [6] Gooch, *op. cit.*, 1713, p. 8.
[7] Compton to Williamson, 17 May, 1670, *S.P.D.* Car. II, 275, no. 141.

became involved in this unhappy business, not to press him for a sum of £200 till Easter. Towards the end of the next year, he missed a preferment that might have made him better off. On 24 September, a grant was issued to him from the Crown to hold the Deanery of Winchester 'void by the promotion of Dr. Clerke'.[1] But for some reason or other, Dr. Clerke did not move (maybe on second thoughts he preferred to stay where he was) and Compton in consequence did not become Dean. Thus his financial embarrassments continued, as the following extract from a letter of Crosse to Williamson, written in April 1672, from Oxford, makes evident. 'I told you Dr. Compton would wait this month as chaplain, and so you might have opportunities of discourse with him. I shall not scruple to let fall words whereby he may understand you expect full interest. I believe he does not suspect me to know him so engaged to you for so great a sum; however I will do as you appoint. He cannot break his word to pay less than £200, if not more next month.'[2]

But Henry Compton did, apparently, break his word, for he was quite unable to live within his means, let alone save enough to discharge his obligations. It is not possible to state exactly what form his extravagance took, though it is not difficult to read between the lines of the following letter sent to Williamson who was acting for the creditors: 'Expensive Dr. C[ompton], I hear, is now in Paris. I shall not fail to solicit him when he returns. He wrote to me before he went, that he would not fail of the whole at Christmas.'[3]

As late as 31 January, 1674, Crosse was still pressing Compton for payment and in the process making many embarrassing calls. 'I cannot have Dr. Compton in that esteem I wish', he wrote complainingly, 'for I am ashamed a person of that quality should forget his word so often as he has to me, and besides he puts me to make so many visits to him as I have already done in vain.'[4]

If Henry Compton's financial position was bad, it would have been far worse had it not been for his parochial preferments. His first living came in his presentation, by the Crown, to the

---

[1] *S.P.D.* Car. II, 24 Sept., 1671, E.B. 35 B, fo. 16.
[2] Crosse to Williamson, 23 Apr., 1672, *ibid.* Car. II, 306, no. 52.
[3] Same to same 9 Oct., 1673, *ibid.* Car. II, 337, no. 92.
[4] Crosse to Williamson, 31 Jan., 1674, *ibid.* Car. II, 360, no. 106.

Rectory of Llandynam in the County of Montgomeryshire.[1] The records of this parish are obstinately silent as to his labours, and it is most unlikely that Compton attended personally on this cure, or even visited it on a single occasion, unless he was presented to it soon after his ordination, in which case a journey to Wales in 1666 may have been for that purpose.[2] As it was, a curate doubtless shepherded the flock for a consideration. Compton held this living till he became Bishop of Oxford in December 1674.[3]

His next preferment was to the Rectory of Cottenham, upon the nomination of Archbishop Sheldon, on 15 April, 1671.[4] Cottenham is a small village in the fen district of Cambridgeshire, and is now remembered as the original home of the Pepys family. Archbishop Tenison was born there in 1636, and long retained an affection for his birthplace. The parochial registers, again, do not suggest that Compton was ever resident in the village, or attempted a personal ministry. They show, however, that Thomas Brett, father of the nonjuring Bishop, did duty for him during part of his brief incumbency, which lasted only until the end of 1674. The records are complete,[5] in duplicate, for this period, but Compton's name does not appear once in the register, not even as a counter-signature under the curate's, as was often the case with many other absentee rectors of Cottenham.

Compton resigned both his livings when he became Bishop of Oxford in December 1674, but this did not signify that he had finished with parochial preferment.[6] On 25 November of this year, he had been presented by the patron, George Morley, Bishop of Winchester, whom he had doubtless come to know intimately while living at St. Cross, to the Rectory of Witney in Oxfordshire. The records of this parish are unfortunately

---

[1] *S.P.D.* Car. II, E.B. 47, p. 3. Compton's biographer knows nothing of Llandynam and confesses (*Life*, p. 3) 'I know not whether I am right in the order of his preferments'. Kippis, however, (*op. cit.*, p. 53), writes: '. . . before that (i.e. his preferment to Cottenham) he had a smaller benefice'.

[2] Compton to Williamson, 2 Oct., 1666, *S.P.D.* Car. II, vol. 174.

[3] *Ibid.* Car. II, E.B. 47, p. 3.   [4] Cottenham Parish Records.

[5] Perhaps one copy was sent to Compton as often happened with absentee rectors.

[6] It is significant that in the Act Books of the Archbishop of Canterbury there is no grant of a dispensation to Compton to hold Cottenham with Llandynam; yet he certainly held them together, as he did later Witney and Llandynam, also without a grant. He was therefore an illegal pluralist. As the livings were more than thirty miles apart, the Archbishop could not have granted a dispensation even if applied to, except on a royal warrant.

defective, and so completely has Compton's name been forgotten, that it does not even appear on the list of rectors which
hangs in the Church.[1] True his incumbency was very short,
for he held the living only till he became Bishop of London
in November, 1675.

It is impossible, unfortunately, to extol Compton's parochial
ministry, and we cannot accept the verdict of Kippis that in
Cottenham and his other livings 'he showed great concern for the
souls of men'.[2] Absenteeism and pluralism were of course common
at the time, and even reformers were forced to recognise the sad
necessity for at least some measure of them (as we are forced to
do reluctantly again today and for the same reasons); but such
men as Thomas Tenison, White Kennett and Simon Patrick were
at this very time setting a high standard of pastoral care. Doubtless
Compton's Mastership of St. Cross and his Canonry at Christ
Church provided more attractive places of residence, with
congenial companionship. But it must be admitted that Compton
had not yet developed that conscientious application to his
spiritual calling as a minister of religion which was certainly one
of the marked characteristics of his later years as a bishop. We
are led to conclude that he regarded his early preferment as
primarily a financial asset, though he may have demanded of his
curates some account of their stewardship.

But more exalted office was in store for this rather lax cleric.
On 15 January, 1672, John Cosin, Bishop of Durham, an earnest
disciple of Archbishop Laud, died in London. For two years the
See was kept vacant—a shocking scandal—but in 1674 Nathaniel
Crewe, Bishop of Oxford, was translated to this prince-bishopric,
and thus embarked on a very undistinguished—Macaulay says a
'prostituted'—episcopate which lasted no less than forty-eight
years. The result of this translation was to create a vacancy in the
See of Oxford, and in March 1674, a news-letter of the day
reported 'that the Bishop of Oxford is to be moved to Durham,
and Dr. Compton will succeed him'.[3]

This information (as was by no means always the case with
news-letters) proved to be correct. The Earl of Danby, anti-Papal
and anti-French, had had his way with the King.[4] On 24 August,

---

[1] Parish Records. [2] Kippis, *op. cit.*, i. 53.
[3] *H.M.C.* App. vii, Report XII, p. 108 (Le Fleming MSS.).
[4] Burnet, *History of My Own Times*, ii. 88.

1674, a warrant for a *congé d'élire* was issued to the Dean and Chapter of Oxford, and this document, together with the letters missive, nominating Compton as Bishop of that See,[1] were dispatched on 1 November.[2] On 10 November, the Dean and Chapter met and carried the election in due form.[3] On 20 November the royal assent was given.[4]

It is clear that the expense of setting up in his new bishopric —there is still extant in his own handwriting a detailed list of the charges which he incurred[5]—together with his debts not yet discharged, pressed heavily upon him. This was almost certainly the reason for a royal warrant issued to the Archbishop of Canterbury by which Compton was allowed to hold *in commendam* with the bishopric, his Canonry of Christ Church, the Mastership of St. Cross, and the Rectory of Witney.[6] The Bishopric of Oxford, in Compton's day, was one of the most poorly endowed, its annual income, to quote his own estimate, being only £343 7s. 1¼d. [sic].[7] His biographer tells us frankly that 'the Income indeed of this Bishoprick was by much too narrow for his Charitable and Liberal Hands'.[8]

Financial anxiety, however, did not prevent Compton from holding what may appear an extravagant confirmation dinner in the Goldsmiths' Hall on 2 December, 1674.[9] Certainly the meal, costing the equivalent in modern money of at least £400, was an excellent one, and conviviality must have been assured. Beef, veal, mutton, poultry, brawn, fish, fruit, a little tobacco, and wines for which three serving men were required—all these doubtless kept the guests in a good humour. Parson Woodforde would have been very much at home.

An additional expense which Compton had to bear arose out of the old custom of presenting to each person at the dinner a pair of gloves—a charge which Charles II by an Order in Council,

---

[1] *S.P.D.* Car. II, 24 Aug., 1674, E.B. 3513, fo. 31.
[2] *Ibid.*, Car. II, 1 Nov., 1674, E.B. 47, p. 1.
[3] *Ibid.*, Car. II, 10 Nov., 1674, Case F, no. 62.
[4] *Ibid.*, Car. II, 20 Nov., 1674, E.B. 47, p. 2.
[5] Bod. Rawlinson MSS. 984 C, fo. 7.
[6] *S.P.D.* Car. II, 30 Nov., 1674, E.B. 47, p. 2: see also Bod. Tanner MSS. 147, fo. 67.   [7] See Bod. Rawlinson MSS. 983 C, fo. 16.
[8] *The Life of Dr. Henry Compton*, p. 4.
[9] Bod. Rawlinson MSS. 984 C, fo. 17. This is here wrongly described as celebrating his confirmation to the See of London, but the date, 2 Dec., 1674, makes this impossible.

dated 23 October, 1678, later declared an 'unnecessary burden', and commanded that it should be replaced by a gift of £50 towards the rebuilding of St. Paul's Cathedral.[1]

Four days after the dinner (6 December, 1674) Henry Compton, at the age of forty-three, was consecrated a Bishop in Lambeth Chapel by the Archbishop of Canterbury, assisted by his brethren of Winchester, Salisbury, Rochester and Chichester. Of these bishops perhaps the most distinguished was Seth Ward (1617-89) of Salisbury, a mathematician and astronomer of considerable ability, and equally to his credit, a conscientious diocesan Bishop.

The new Bishop chose for his preacher William Jane (1645-1707), student of Christ Church and newly made his chaplain, but the nomination was not a happy one, for Jane (or 'Janus' as some preferred to call him) was an ambitious clergyman of a rather low type. In his sermon, which extended a full clock hour, he traced the origin of episcopacy back to apostolic days (he was a high churchman) and then proceeded to express sentiments, which in common with many a preacher, he might himself have taken more to heart. 'Let Socinus go on with as much scorn as he pleases', he said, '. . . a true Catholic Bishop that knows that it cost more to redeem a soul will hence take an argument that his watchfulness over his Flock ought to rise in some proportion to that esteem and value which his Lord and Master hath set upon it. He will not forget or betray his trust, for the sake of silver and gold, and those other corruptible things which he well knows were utterly unable to redeem it.'[2]

Of Compton's tenure of this episcopate, there is, in fact, nothing to tell, for he was only in this office a matter of some twelve months when he left it to become Bishop of London—a rapid promotion which shows he had by now become a national figure with powerful friends.[3] It is necessary, therefore, at this turning point in his career, to take a glance at the political situation in England at this time, particularly as Henry Compton was destined to play a prominent part in it.

[1] Bod. Tanner MSS. 282, fo. 74. The Archbishop was not to proceed to the consecration until he was given a receipt from the treasurer of the rebuilding fund.

[2] W. Jane, *A Sermon Preached at the Consecration of, etc.*, 1675, p. 15.

[3] Thomas Gooch said later that the Bishopric of Oxford 'did not give him a sphere extensive enough to act in'. (*op. cit.*, p. 8).

CHAPTER THREE

ALLY TO THE EARL OF DANBY

NEVER before, perhaps, was a monarch so popular as Charles II when he stepped ashore at Dover on 26 May, 1660. His journey to London, as we have already noted, was a triumphal progress, during which the pent up emotions of his long tried people found almost hysterical expression.

The King was recalled to his native land by a coalition of Presbyterians and Cavaliers, for it is not surprising that throughout the country there should have been a reaction against the Puritanism of the Commonwealth. It almost seemed (though this was not in fact the case) as if that which Archbishop Laud had unsuccessfully endeavoured to secure through the prerogative of the Crown was now to be granted spontaneously by the Restoration Parliament.[1] The Corporation Act purged the civic authorities of all those who held the Covenant[2] in veneration, or thought that rebellion might ever be lawful. The Act of Uniformity turned out of their benefices those who would not subscribe to the Book of Common Prayer as revised in 1662, or submit to episcopal ordination.

Yet this exaggerated display of loyalty to the throne, so marked a feature of the early years of the Restoration, was in many respects more vocal than sincere. It was born of a nostalgic devotion to a known pattern of life made up of King, Church and Parliament, and also of a fanatical hatred for the efficient but severe government of the Protector with its major generals and its standing army. 'Non-resistance' was in fact a weapon of offence to thrust in the side of Dissenters rather than a garment of humility. The Stuarts were later to learn this to their cost.

The intentions of Charles II have provided a fruitful field of enquiry for the more imaginative historian. Certainly he was

[1] An interesting study as to why this should have been the case may be found in R. S. Bosher, *The Making of the Restoration Settlement*, 1951.

[2] I.e. The Solemn League and Covenant which laid down the principles of Presbyterianism.

determined not to go on his travels again, and by refraining from illegal taxation he avoided some of the worst mistakes of his father. He was also determined (as Clarendon found) not to allow any minister to interfere with his private immoralities—an expensive luxury which necessitated his using public money for domestic purposes. In so far as Charles had any religion, his sympathies were with Rome, as Henry Compton knew only too well,[1] and in so far as he had political ambitions, it was the pattern of kingship so magnificently displayed by Louis XIV which he admired and wished to emulate. To assert the power of the Crown, and to remove the disabilities from Roman Catholics —these were the wishes, next to his own pleasures, which were nearest his dissolute heart. But ever skilful and adroit, ever cynical and selfish, he knew when to go forward, and when to retreat.

For the early years of his reign, the Earl of Clarendon (1609–74) was in fact Charles's first minister. He was a member of the old school, firm and fixed in his loyalty to Church and Crown but personally obnoxious to Charles because he stood for the stricter morality of an older generation. Though Clarendon has given his name to the statutes which re-established the supremacy of the Church of England and excluded Dissenters from local government, he himself would almost certainly have preferred less extreme measures.

The English people (that is, of course, those who were politically conscious) desired at this time two things in their relations with the powers on the Continent, but they did not always realise that these were incompatible. They wished to cripple the Dutch, their commercial rivals, and at the same time to break the power of Louis XIV, the embodiment of personal despotism and aggressive nationalism. Foreign policy, therefore, hovered fitfully between alliance with the Dutch against Louis, and alliance with Louis against the Dutch, depending on many factors—on the military situation at the moment, and the King's relations with his ministers and Parliament. The situation was made more complex by the tortuous policy of Charles II and the cunning of Louis XIV, who took full advantage of the confused constitutional 'milieu' in England. The French monarch bribed both King and Parliament in turn, in order to strengthen

[1] J. Cockburne, *The Blessedness of Christians after Death*, p. 18.

the hand of Charles or secure support for a pro-French policy in the House of Commons.

The suspicions which the Lower House, in spite of its Royalism, entertained for the intentions of Charles, were reflected in a growing insistence that it must superintend the expenditure of money allocated for specific purposes, and in particular that grants made for the war against the Dutch must not find their way into the pockets of the King's mistresses. In May 1667, the anger of Parliament vented itself against Clarendon, when, to quote Macaulay, 'the roar of foreign guns was heard for the first and last time by the citizens of London'. Lord Arlington needed a scapegoat. The Commons thirsted for blood and Clarendon thought it prudent to accept the King's advice and to withdraw to France.

The fall of Clarendon marked the end of the first period of Charles's reign, and it was followed by a ministry (notable for the signing of the Triple Alliance in January 1668) which included Arlington and Buckingham. Towards the end of 1670 there began to emerge the Cabal, under which Charles was guided by no single person, but was advised by a changing group of five ministers, who it has been often said, 'had only one thing in common, namely, that they were none of them attached to the Church of England'. It was during their tenure of office that the King sought to make himself financially independent of Parliament. The Treaty of Dover between himself and Louis, by which Charles was to declare himself a Roman Catholic in return for support against the constitutional opposition at home—its complete text was known only to the two Roman Catholic members of the Cabal—encouraged him to issue a Declaration of Indulgence in March 1672 under which, equally with the Roman Catholics, the Dissenters were to receive civic liberty. Though Anthony Cooper (1621-85), soon to be made Earl of Shaftesbury, supported the King at this time, the Dissenters, in a world increasingly dominated by the aggression of Louis XIV, were not prepared to purchase even liberty on these terms. Instead, Parliament took fright and passed the Test Act (1673) which made the reception of the Sacrament in the Church of England, together with a declaration against all distinctive Roman Catholic doctrine, a condition of holding office under the Crown.

The Test Act was the beginning of a new phase in the struggle
for power. James, Duke of York, the King's brother, was forced
to come out into the open and resign the office of Lord High
Admiral, in which capacity he had certainly done good work;
and Clifford likewise had to retire from the Treasurership. It was
the end of the Cabal, and the Earl of Shaftesbury now passed over
into irresponsible and dangerous opposition to the Crown. The
Whig party was thus born, and its strength lay in the English-
man's fear of Rome, and his suspicion of the real constitutional
intentions of Charles.

The King, unlike his brother, knew how to bide his time,
and his concern to 'Catholicise' England, never strong, largely
disappeared after 1670. He now turned to Sir Thomas Osborne
(1631-1712) whom he made Treasurer and created Earl of Danby
in June 1674. The Earl was another Clarendon but brought up to
date; for he shared most of the instinctive loyalties and prejudices of politically conscious Englishmen. He was a Tory (if
we may yet use this term) and a supporter of the monarchy—
provided that it did not assert its power too far—and his policy
was to seek an alliance with the Dutch against the power of
Catholic Louis whom he dreaded and despised. As Treasurer,
Danby showed conspicuous ability, and although, according to
his enemies, he was without friends or scruples, 'except his own
impudence',[1] he began, by means of a cynical and systematic
bribery, to build up in the House of Commons an opposition
to the more irresponsible of the Whigs. He was a strong supporter of the Church of England, and his policy was to protect
it from two enemies at once, from the Dissenters on the one side
and the Roman Catholics on the other, which latter attack was
generally believed to be growing more serious as a result of
Charles's flirtation with Louis and the undisguised Romanism of
James, Duke of York. Danby even endeavoured to secure by
Act of Parliament (he was unsuccessful, however) that every
magistrate, public servant and member of Parliament should
swear 'never to endeavour any alteration in the Government in
Church or State as it is by law established'.

[1] As a matter of fact, Danby did refuse French bribes in 1678, and could at
other times have had French money 'but unlike many of his opponents he never
stooped to receive bribes from the enemies of his country'. See Andrew
Browning, *Life of Thomas, Earl of Danby*, 1944, 51, i. 259 n.

To further his ends, Danby was particularly anxious to secure the co-operation of the Church, especially the bishops (who sat in the House of Lords) and to use them in support of a policy which it was equally in their interests to pursue. He looked around the bench, made a shrewd judgment of character, and chose Henry Compton as his ally and at times his instrument. They had much in common. Both were Tories: both were ambitious: both were strongly anti-French and alive to the Roman Catholic menace: both were devoted to the interests of the Church of England.

The result of this alliance was very soon seen in Compton's more intimate introduction to Court life. On 15 July, 1675, on the death of Dr. Blandford, Bishop of Worcester, he was made Dean of the Chapels Royal, an office of considerable political importance, particularly at this time, because it gave him a decisive influence on the education of the young princesses, the daughters of James, Duke of York.[1]

But a greater honour awaited him. On 7 October, 1675, Humphrey Henchman, Bishop of London, died in his eighty-third year. The appointment to this diocese, where was situated the seat of government, was of great political and ecclesiastical significance. Danby became active, and on 2 December the King declared his pleasure that the Bishop of Oxford should be translated to London.[2] On the same day a *congé d'élire* was issued to the Dean and Chapter of St. Paul's Cathedral, with a letter missive nominating Henry Compton.[3] On 10 December the Dean and Chapter met to elect,[4] and the royal assent and confirmation were given on 13 December.[5] It was not until February next year, however, that the Bishop performed his homage.[6]

Nomination to London meant that Compton must shed his other preferments (he could not decently do otherwise) though he did secure a dispensation from the Archbishop of Canterbury, upon a royal warrant, which enabled him to hold St. Cross for a short time.[7] His financial difficulties were not yet over (they

---

[1] *S.P.D.* Car. II, 15 July, 1675, Precedents 1, fo. 85.

[2] *Ibid.*, Car. II, 2 Dec., 1675, E.B. 43, p. 64.

[3] *Ibid.*, Car. II, 2 Dec., 1675, E.B. 47, p. 18.

[4] *Ibid.*, Car. II, 10 Dec., 1675, Case F, no. 70.

[5] *Ibid.*, Car. II, 13 Dec., 1675, E.B. 47, p. 19.

[6] *Ibid.*, Car. II, Feb., 1676, Case F, no. 75.

[7] Act Books of the Archbishop of Canterbury, iii. 273. Also, *S.P.D.* Car. II, 6 Dec., 1675, E.B. 47, p. 19.

never were!) and he managed to obtain a grant (29 May, 1676)
which enabled him to spread the payment of his first fruits[1] (a
sum of £1,019 8s. 4d.) over a period of four years.[2]

It soon became common knowledge that this promotion was
engineered by Danby and that it represented a concession by the
King to the anti-Roman-Catholic sentiment of the nation.
Burnet, who was never a friend of the Bishop and as a consequence found it difficult to be fair to him, writes that at this time
Compton was 'a property and tool to the Earl of Danby', and
that the Earl managed to persuade Charles that Compton's
elevation to London would 'do no great harm to any person' and
would make the King popular with the clergy.[3] On 7 January,
Danby secured the dismissal of Halifax and Holles from the
Council, and a fortnight later the nomination to this body of
the Bishop of London.[4]

Certainly Compton's translation was very acceptable to his
brethren in the London diocese 'because they knew him to be a
bold man, an enemy to the Papists, and one that would act and
speak freely what they would put him upon which they themselves would not be seen in'.[5]

Dr. Samuel Speed, Canon of Christ Church, who during his
varied career was buccaneer and naval chaplain, expressed
himself almost (but not quite) lyrically on the appointment:

> Illustrious Prelate! whom the World must own
> A Father of the Church, a Martyr's Son.
> May thy bright Fame outshine the Morning Star
> As Prince, a Prelate and a Batchelor.[6]

We may well think such sentiments excessive, but it was
in fact surprising how soon Compton grew in stature to
match his new office. Particularly was his translation to London
important in view of the advanced age of the Primate
and his declining health. Compton's thrustful personality made
it inevitable that in these circumstances he would take the
lead, and his few extant letters to Archbishop Sheldon, not

---

[1] The first fruits was a fee payable to the crown out of the first year's income
by a new holder of an ecclesiastical office.
[2] *S.P.D.* Car. II, 29 May, 1676, E.B. 47, p. 27.
[3] Burnet, *op. cit.*, ii. 89.
[4] P.C. Reg., 21 Jan., 1676, 65, p. 102.
[5] Burnet, *op. cit.*, ii. 89.
[6] Samuel Speed, *Prison Pietie*, 1677, p. 186.

important in themselves, suggest this kind of relationship.[1] A notable illustration comes immediately to mind.

One of the difficulties confronting Danby in endeavouring to commend his strong 'Anglican policy' to the King was the criticism that it would have the effect of bringing all the Nonconformists together into a common interest, and that their strength would then prove 'too formidable to be suppressed'.[2] Such arguments could not be ignored if Danby were to build up a powerful party in the House of Commons and secure the support of Charles. The Earl rightly felt that the only effective reply to such criticisms was to illustrate how small, numerically, the Nonconformists actually were. He determined, therefore, in the spring of 1676, to conduct a census of the whole population, and he approached the aged Archbishop Sheldon for this purpose. The task was—and was known to be—quite beyond him, and to Danby's satisfaction, and probably at his instigation, he entrusted it to Compton, asking him (we quote the Archbishop's own letter to the Bishop of London) to make enquiry concerning: 'First, What number of persons or at least families are by common account and estimation inhabiting within each parish subject under them [i.e. the Bishops]. Secondly, what number of Popish recusants, or such as are suspected of recusancy, are there among such inhabitants at present? Thirdly, what number of other Dissenters are resident in such parishes, which either obstinately refuse, or wholly absent themselves from, the Communion of the Church of England at such times as by law they are required?'[3]

It was a piece of work after the Bishop of London's own heart, and under the guiding hand of Danby, he set about it with zest. The machinery for making the enquiries lay ready to hand in the incumbent of the parish with his churchwardens, the archdeacon and the bishop. Compton therefore instructed them to begin their task after the Easter Visitation.

The returns which Compton finally received from the bishops, and which he himself conflated, were certainly revealing. Their precise degree of accuracy can hardly be assessed for a

[1] See Compton to Sheldon, 15 Jan., 1677, Bod. Tanner MSS. 40, fo. 44, in which letter the Bishop of London takes the initiative in arranging the bishops' proxies for the ensuing parliament.

[2] See Morley to Danby, 10 June, 1676, *Leeds Papers*, p. 14.

[3] Sancroft's letter is reproduced in Wilkins, *Concilia Magnae Britanniae*, 1737, iv. 598.

variety of reasons.[1] The mere fact of a census frightened some 'weaklings' back into the Church: Presbyterians were usually accounted as Conformists: and since the census was generally understood to be for the purpose of testing the strength of the Nonconformists, it was only natural that many incumbents tended to interpret doubtful cases in accordance with their own wishes. It must be added that no exact census was taken of the Province of York, but that its population was assumed to be one-sixth of that of the Southern Province, with the same relative proportions of Conformists to Nonconformists—an assumption which hardly suggests a very scientific approach to statistics. Still the overall totals may be taken as giving a rough impression of the relative strengths of the religious 'denominations' in 1676.

From the returns, Compton estimated that the proportion of Conformists to Nonconformists throughout the country was 23 to 1: Conformists to Papists 179 to 1: Nonconformists and Conformists to Papists 187 to 1. The figures for the Province of Canterbury (they refer only to those over sixteen years of age) were as follows: Conformists 2,123,362; Nonconformists 93,151: Papists 11,878. In view of Compton's specific responsibilities it is interesting to notice the relative figures for the diocese of London which were: Conformists 263,385; Nonconformists 2,089; Papists 2,069. In other words, nearly a quarter of the whole Nonconformist population of the Province, and a fifth of the Roman Catholic, were concentrated in the diocese of London.

The figures were certainly satisfying to Danby, for no matter how inaccurate in detail, they clearly indicated that the Nonconformist population was not numerically very strong; and that the Roman Catholic population was minute. The political implications of the census were cynically illustrated by a statement in the official return that 'there remain therefore in the Province of Canterbury fit to bear arms 4,239 Papists', and in the Province of York only 711. If the immediate purpose was to test the relative strengths of the Conformist and Nonconformists popu-

---

[1] A copy of this return is to be found (not in its rightful place) in *S.P.D.* Will. and Mary, 1693, pp. 448-50. It is also printed in Dalrymple, App. ii, pp. 11-15; and summaries are in Leeds MSS. pp. 14-15: and Leeds MSS. Packet 7. See also Reynolds to Compton, 28 Jan., 1675/6, Bod. Tanner MSS. 42, fo. 219.

lation, it is clear that Compton was thinking in terms of possible political and religious developments.

Yet though the returns of the census were reassuring the first result of the Bishop of London's increased responsibilities was to make him more militant in his Protestantism than hitherto, and particularly was this the case in his relations with the Court.

Here there was a great deal to make him uneasy. His chief and immediate concern was the growth of Roman Catholic sympathies within the Royal family, and it was a situation for which, as Dean of the Chapels Royal, he felt a particular responsibility. Charles's leanings, in so far as religion played any part in his dissolute life, were generally known to be Catholic rather than Protestant. James, Duke of York, had now openly declared himself a Roman Catholic, and had married for his second wife the beautiful Mary of Modena, a member of that Church. Between James and Henry Compton there developed a deep personal hostility, and it was common knowledge that the Duke had opposed the Bishop's advancement to London. Already the question of the succession to the throne, and fears as to what would happen if England were governed by a Prince who was a convinced Roman Catholic, made many thoughtful citizens uneasy, and were later to find expression in an Exclusion Bill.

James was, of course, heir to the throne, but next in succession after him came the Lady Mary, and then the Lady Anne, both daughters of his first marriage to Anne Hyde, daughter of the Earl of Clarendon. The education of these young ladies was, therefore, a matter of prime constitutional importance—more important, so it was to prove later, than could possibly have been foreseen at the time—particularly at a Court where the *laissez faire* morality of Charles tended to conceal the serious religious interests of more responsible people. In the eyes of convinced Protestants it was imperative that these Princesses should be brought up as sincere members of the Church of England, and it was to this delicate task that the soldier-bishop now addressed himself.

His approach to the problem was typically forthright, for he proceeded to confront James in person. The interview proved embarrassing, since the Duke's temper was at the best of times erratic. Compton introduced the subject by observing, perhaps a little ingenuously, that James's daughter, the Lady Mary, 'was now of an age' to think of preparing herself to receive the Sacrament according to the rubrics of the Church of England. Might he have permission, he asked, to confirm her?

The Bishop knew well, of course, that the Duke was not able to give such permission consistently with his own religious allegiance, and it could not, therefore, have come as a surprise when James replied firmly that since his conscience did not permit him to communicate with the Church of England in any religious function, so for the same reason he could never give his consent for his daughter to do so. It had been much against his will, he added, that his daughters had been bred Protestants at all, and the reason why he had not endeavoured to have them instructed in his own faith was simply that, had he attempted to do so, they would almost certainly have been entirely removed from him.

Compton, however, was neither overawed nor dismayed. 'I hope', he said, 'that you will not take it ill if I do the duty of my function and confirm your daughter.' 'I cannot give my consent to it', James replied sternly as he brought the interview to an end.[1]

But James was not always without tact, and happening to meet the Bishop next day he advised him to inform the King of what had passed between them. Thus encouraged, Compton went immediately to Charles and forthwith received the royal command to confirm his nieces. The Duke of York later confessed that he knew this to be inevitable and therefore preferred that it should be done on the King's express authority, and without his own consent, rather than on the sole initiative of the Bishop.

The confirmation of both Princesses on 23 January, 1676, by the Bishop, was a victory for the national Protestant feeling, and a personal triumph for Compton.[2]

The education of these two young ladies was thenceforward the special care of the Bishop in virtue of his office as Dean of the Chapels Royal. Thus was begun a relationship between him and the Princesses which was to last the rest of their lives. It is therefore important to notice that both of them came to cherish a genuine affection for the Church of England. Mary's stock of theological knowledge grew to be considerable, as her father later discovered,

---

[1] J. S. Clarke, *The Life of James the Second*, 1816, i. 502.
[2] *Continuation of Roger Coke's 'Detection'*, 1718, iii. 117.

Compton Wynyates, the birthplace of Henry Compton

and her influence upon ecclesiastical appointments, during her few years as Queen, was always salutary. Anne's name has become almost a household word through her Bounty which was a real gift of love.[1] In most difficult days, though Mary may have attended Brownist meetings in Holland, neither of them faltered in their allegiance to the 'Ecclesia Anglicana', despite the un-doubted pull of family affection. For this firmness, which has left its mark upon English history, Compton must be given a share of the praise.

Behind the Bishop in this policy of upholding the rights of the Church of England in Whitehall was, of course, the Earl of Danby, who, being well aware of the duplicity of Charles and the Romanist fervour of James, was particularly anxious to remove the Princesses from the Court atmosphere. Marriage was the obvious way of escape. But the Earl's own position was now by no means secure. He stood, as it were, between two hostile armies, and both might close in upon him; between Charles, on the one side, pursuing an anti-Parliament and pro-French policy, and the opposition factions led, amongst others, by Shaftesbury and Buckingham, on the other side, whose rallying cry was soon to be the exclusion of James from the succession. Perhaps Danby's greatest achievement—and in this respect he builded better than he knew—was his persuading the King to agree to the marriage of Princess Mary with William, Prince of Orange, the implacable enemy of Louis XIV, and the courageous upholder of Dutch independence. William was suddenly invited to England in 1677, and preparations for the marriage set in hand.

Danby seems to have convinced even James that the wedding would be to his advantage, for the Duke sensibly told the Council that he hoped his acquiescing in it would satisfy the nation that his religion was a purely private affair. But Charles, in his heart, could not really have welcomed it, despite the fact that it increased his bargaining power with Louis. Yet the King's unfailing 'bonhomie' came to his rescue, and he was the life and soul of the wedding party. Dr. Lake, Chaplain to Princess Anne, has left behind an entertaining account of the celebrations. The King's sister-in-law was expecting a baby at any moment, and Charles was particularly anxious that his niece should be married before this

---

[1] It is perhaps a pity that Queen Anne's name should be lost under the more comprehensive title 'Church Commissioners'.

event.[1] Thus the marriage was somewhat hastily solemnised in Princess Mary's bedroom by Compton at nine o'clock in the evening of 4 November, the Prince's birthday.[2] Charles gave his niece away, and when the taciturn bridegroom came to that part of the service at which he endowed his beloved with all his worldly goods, the King was heard to remark that he 'would to put all up in her pocket for 'twas clear gain'. The ceremony was not, of course, complete until the guests, following the custom of those days, had attended the bridal couple to bed, which they did at eleven. Surely no man was better qualified to pull the curtains than the King himself, and as he did so he was heard by Dr. Lake to remark reassuringly to the rather frigid husband: 'Now nephew to your Work! Hey! St. George for England.'[3]

This marriage was destined to change the course of English history, but that was still in the future. For the present it was a great grief to the Princess to leave her native England and she departed in tears with her undemonstrative husband. It says much for her devotion and intelligence that she later won even his cold heart.

Compton's vigilance in protecting his remaining royal charge from the corrupting influence of Rome was constant. A small instance will suffice.

The day after the wedding, Princess Anne fell sick—perhaps it was the fare or the result of genuine sorrow at losing her sister—and it was feared that she might be developing smallpox. Dr. Lake, her Chaplain, accordingly received orders—they came from James—not to visit her to say prayers, because of the risk of infection. The Chaplain, however, suspicious of the Duke's real motive, was consequently much 'troubled' in his conscience as to whether he ought to obey, particularly since he knew that Anne's nurse, who took the opportunity of being constantly in attendance, was 'a very busy zealous Roman Catholic and would probably discompose her if she had an opportunity'.[4] Such was the state of suspicion at the Court in matters religious!

Dr. Lake, therefore, unburdened himself to the Princess's

---

[1] James's wife gave birth to a son on 7 November, who was baptised, not by Compton but by the Bishop of Durham. *Diary of Edward Lake*, Camden Society, 1846, ed. G. P. Elliott, p. 6.

[2] Sandford and Stebbing, *Genealogical History of the Kings and Queens of England*, 1707, p. 679.

[3] *Diary of Edward Lake*, p. 61.   [4] *Ibid.*, p. 7.

governess, the Lady Frances Villiers, who advised him to discuss the matter with the Bishop of London. Compton proved to be in no two minds as to what ought to be done. He peremptorily ordered the Chaplain 'to wait constantly on her Highness, and to do all suitable offices ministerial which were incumbent on him'. He did so, and was in daily attendance on the Princess during what turned out to be a mild attack of smallpox. By 29 November, she had fully recovered and ordered Dr. Lake to render thanks in her chamber, while at the same time she gave him two guineas for distribution to the poor.[1]

Compton has been blamed by at least one contemporary for this 'very extraordinary degree of interference'[2] in what was said to be a purely domestic affair. Perhaps the Bishop did take things a little too seriously at times, particularly where the Roman scare was concerned. But the criticism is naïve and unrealistic, for what might well be regarded as of family interest only in a private citizen assumed (at this date) a far different significance in a royal household.

Yet the Bishop of London was beginning to have other things on his mind, for he was already becoming preoccupied—perhaps a little unhealthily—with another matter which concerned him more closely.

In October, 1677, the aged Archbishop Sheldon was taken seriously ill. His own physician gave up the case as beyond remedy. Hope revived, however, when a German doctor prescribed his 'aurum potabile' which when first applied 'had wonderful effects and gives a fair promise of recovery'.[3] But such hopes did not prevent speculation as to who his successor would be—in fact, such speculation had been rife as early as the summer of '76. One candidate, in the eyes of most contemporaries, seemed to stand head and shoulders above the rest. The Bishop of London owing to his position at Court, his intimacy with the Earl of Danby, his family connections, and his militant Protestantism, was the popular favourite, though more informed people immediately recognised that he would encounter deadly opposition from at least one quarter. Some three weeks before Sheldon's death, Sir Robert Southwell, in a letter to the Duke of Ormonde in Ireland, reported that Nathaniel Crewe,

---

[1] *Diary of Edward Lake*, p. 11.   [2] *Ibid.*, p. 7 n.
[3] *H.M.C.* App. vii, Report XIV, p. 381 (Ormonde MSS., vol. 1).

Bishop of Durham, had come to London, and enjoyed 'particular favour' (i.e. with James) just where Compton was 'greatly in want of it'. The Bishop of London, so Southwell rambled on, seemed to have resigned himself to the fact that his 'pull' with Danby could not counterbalance Crewe's favour with the Duke. In these circumstances, with almost diabolical cunning, he was now doing all he could to advance the claims of his former tutor, Richard Sterne, Archbishop of York, solely because he was older than the dying Sheldon, and thus if appointed could not hold the office long.[1] The Bishop of London would soon have a second chance!

On 9 November, Sheldon died, despite his German physician. It was a break with the past, for the old man had often attended the King's father during the Civil War.

Who was to succeed him? In Whitehall and in the coffee-houses many a tongue wagged. We can recapture some of the excitement (though not necessarily the facts) in the entertaining despatches which Southwell sent to Ormonde, from one of which we have already quoted. The Duke doubtless read them the more eagerly since there were aspirants for Lambeth even in Ireland.

On 13 November, Southwell reported that he was still without any definite news, though 'the Bishop of London seemed to have more voices in public discourse than any other'.[2] The Duke of York, however, was wholeheartedly for the Dean of St. Paul's, William Sancroft. On 20 November the situation was about the same. 'The general vogue runs for my Lord of London, and the more so for the opposition that is said to be against him in one place.'[3] A week later the Bishop's supporters were not so confident. 'He takes it not upon himself but many are so zealous for him that 'tis said whoever carries it, yet he will be at the head of the Church.'[4] Yet some were so certain of the Bishop of London's final success that they began to solicit his favour. Herbert Aubrey wrote asking that he might serve in the new Archbishop's household,[5] and John Fisher sought his help for his studies.[6]

[1] Southwell to Ormonde, 16 Oct., 1677, *H.M.C.* App. xiv, Report VII, p. 381.   [2] Same to same, 13 Nov., 1677 *ibid.*, p. 385.
[3] Same to same, 20 Nov., 1677, *ibid.*, p. 386.
[4] Same to same, 27 Nov., 1677, *ibid.*, p. 388.
[5] Aubrey to Williamson, 24 Nov., 1677, *S.P.D.* Car. II, 397, no. 204.
[6] Fisher to Williamson, 14 Dec., 1677, *ibid.* Car. II, 398, no. 90.

So December came, and still no Archbishop was appointed. It seemed that strong opposition to Compton from the King's brother was holding up any nomination. All kinds of rumours, therefore, began to circulate, and more claimants came into the field. It was said that the Lord Chancellor of Ireland had landed in England and that his claims were being supported both by Ormonde and James.[1] Others reported that there would be no appointment at all, but that the Archbishopric would be put into the hands of a commission of three people—Compton, Dolben of Rochester, and Fell of Oxford—for a number of years and that the revenue thus saved would be devoted to the building of Wren's masterpiece on Ludgate Hill.[2]

Many still felt, however, and Southwell seems to have come round to this point of view, that in the end the King would 'suddenly declare' Compton Archbishop, because in a crisis he usually had the good sense to respond to the popular will, and there could be no doubt that 'the general vogue of all Churchmen was with him'.[3] As late as 22 December, Southwell wrote that 'the vote abroad was still for the Bishop of London, though it is affirmed his Majesty had long since declared for the Dean of St. Paul's had he not been extremely pressed to avoid the mortification it must be to so many prelates that none of their whole order should be thought competent to that dignity'.[4]

Interested in all this chatter, because in the thick of it, was Dr. Edward Lake, who was in a privileged position to hear the tittle-tattle of the Court. One of James's servants, *rara avis* in that royal household since he was a zealous Protestant, told the Chaplain confidently in the middle of December, on the authority of Edward Coleman, a Roman Catholic conspirator intimate with the Duke, that Henry Compton would not be Archbishop 'because of his forwardness in persecuting Roman Catholics particularly the Portuguese ambassador and himself'. At the moment, Coleman said, 'the scales were equally pois'd and in one of them was the Dean of St. Paul's, and in the other the Bishop of Oxford.[5] . . . one of them would certainly be Archbishop; and without all question the Bishop of London

[1] Southwell to Ormonde, 4 Dec., 1677, *H.M.C.* App. vii, Report XIV, p. 388.
[2] *Diary of Edward Lake*, p. 11.
[3] Southwell to Ormonde, 4 Dec., 1677, *H.M.C.* App. vii, Report XIV, p. 388.
[4] Same to same, 22 Dec., 1677, *ibid.* App. vii, Report XIV, p. 390.
[5] I.e. Dr. Fell.

might with his interests have turned the scales for the Bishop of
Oxford, did not my Lord Treasurer[1] all along caress him as
secure of it for himself '.[2]

But the end of this period of waiting and growing tension
was at last in sight, and Dr. Lake brings it to a climax (in his
Diary) with a real dramatic flourish. The King had finally made
up his mind (it seems to have been his real intention all the time)
to appoint William Sancroft, Dean of St. Paul's—in many ways
a surprising choice since he was not even in episcopal orders.
On 29 December, therefore, he sent Mr. Chiffinch, his 'closet
keeper', to bring him to Whitehall. But Sancroft could not be
found. Intensive search was made, until he was finally run to
earth where any good story-teller must inevitably place him—at
Fulham with the Bishop of London. Mr. Chiffinch tactfully drew
the reverend Dean aside, and whispered that the King wished to
see him. 'What have I now done', he cried in dismay, 'since his
Majesty hath now sent for me.' At five o'clock that evening, in
Mr. Chiffinch's lodgings, Sancroft was ushered into the royal
presence, and Charles without more ado offered him the Archbishopric. In words which we may do the saintly Dean the honour
of regarding as sincere, and which were not without some degree
of truth as later events showed, he protested 'that he was very
unfitt for it thro' his solitary life which he had a long time led',
and he therefore 'fervently desired his Majesty to recommend to
it some bishop more worthy of it'.[3]

The King had made up his mind, however, and he replied
lightheartedly that whether Sancroft accepted or not, he had
already disposed of his Deanery to Dr. Stillingfleet. Thus it was
settled and Dr. Lake records in his *Diary*, under 30 December:
'This day Dr. William Sancroft, Dean of St. Paul's, was declared
Archbishop of Canterbury, contrary to the expectations of all
the Court; and the dissatisfaction of many bishops, who resented
the leap from the Deanery of St. Paul's over their heads into the
Primacy.'[4] The news-letters were full of it next day.[5]

Why was the Dean of St. Paul's thus promoted, and Compton

[1] I.e. The Earl of Danby.   [2] *Diary of Dr. Lake*, p. 19.
[3] *Diary of Edward Lake*, p. 19. It is true that at the Revolution Sancroft did
show a lack of public ability, and withdrew from affairs when he ought rather
to have tried to commend his point of view to his countrymen.
[4] *Ibid.*, p. 19.
[5] *H.M.C.* App. vii, Report XII, p. 141 (Le Fleming MSS.).

passed over? The question is, perhaps, not difficult to answer. In one of those rare moments of intuition which now and again descend upon the rake, Charles recognised in Sancroft a man of God, who stood outside much of the religious and political strife of the day. In this negative sense it was a non-political appointment, though of course it represented politically the defeat of the militant Protestant party. Dr. Lake points out that Charles had always entertained 'a particular esteem and kindness' for Sancroft, and had been heard to remark, in Oxford, during the plague, when the Archbishop of Canterbury fell ill: 'I know no person more fit to succeed him than the Dean of St. Paul's.'[1]

Compton, on the other hand, had drawn upon himself the implacable hostility of James who 'gladly submitted' to Sancroft's elevation 'willing that anybody should be Archbishop than the Bishop of London'.[2] The Bishop's aggressive Protestantism in the day-to-day administration of his diocese,[3] his interference in the religious education of the Duke's own daughters, and his political alliance with the Earl of Danby—these all fanned a personal resentment which was to become still more acute as the years went on. The Bishop of London's only real chance of going to Lambeth lay in the Protestant sentiment which supported him being so strong that Charles dare not resist it. So far as the King was concerned, Compton was tolerated rather than regarded as personally agreeable. He was certainly not unhappy to pass the Bishop over and his popularity with the rank-and-file of the London clergy was not sufficient to offset this royal dislike.

Nor was the Earl of Danby anxious to press Compton's claims very forcibly, since he was particularly concerned not to spoil his relations with James—and James had set his face against such an appointment. With the typical duplicity of political life at the Restoration, he therefore played a double game. While assuring Compton until within three days of Sancroft's elevation that 'he might set his heart at rest, for he would certainly be Archbishop', yet on the other hand he 'clandestinely supported the rise of Sancroft'.[4] Burnet suggests that Danby 'never intended' that the Bishop of London should go to Lambeth.[5] Perhaps it is fairer to say that he recognised from the outset

---

[1] *Diary of Edward Lake*, p. 18. [2] *Ibid.* [3] See chap. V.
[4] *Diary of Edward Lake*, p. 18. [5] Burnet, *op. cit.*, ii. 89.

that such promotion would not come Compton's way, but that he weakly buoyed up the Bishop with false hopes. As he could not secure Lambeth for Compton, why not be 'in' with Sancroft?

To Compton his being passed over was a sad disappointment. Though mercifully hidden from him at the time, it was an experience which he was to undergo later in an even more bitter form. The immediate effect upon him was undoubtedly to increase his opposition to the Court, and to make even more difficult his relations with James, Duke of York.

It is, perhaps, to the Bishop of London's credit that even to win the Archbishopric he would make no effort to placate James, for while the appointment was still pending, he was using all his influence to secure the dismissal of Edward Coleman, private secretary to the Duchess of York—a man whom Macaulay is not far wrong in describing as 'a very busy and not very honest Roman Catholic intriguer'. The Bishop went so far as to bring his complaint before the Council with the result that the King privately advised his brother to have him dismissed.[1] Also, in the interests of Sarah Churchill, later Duchess of Marlborough, Compton managed to secure the banishment of Mrs. Cornwallis —a fervent Roman Catholic—from personal attendance upon the Princess Anne.[2]

At least the Bishop did not try to win favour by soft-pedalling his Protestantism. In fact his anti-Roman-Catholic vigour was particularly noticeable at this time, as a later chapter will show. He was constantly securing the suppression of Popish books, urging the dismissal of Roman Catholics from Court, receiving converts from Rome, and encouraging the writing of Protestant pamphlets.

Such activities may serve to introduce that extraordinary chapter in English history known as the Popish plot.

That there was some movement on foot by the Jesuits for the more active proselytisation of England at this time is certain from the correspondence of Edward Coleman, and it was upon such a slender substance of fact that the notorious Titus Oates, with other equally irresponsible and unscrupulous rogues, based their fabrications.

[1] *Correspondence of the Family of Hatton*, ed. E. M. Thompson, 1878, i. 137.
[2] Burnet, *op. cit.*, ii. 89.

The career of Titus Oates reads more strangely than fiction. Not even his greatest enemy could call his religion static, for he was in turn Anglican vicar, naval chaplain, Roman Catholic student, embryonic Jesuit, Government pensioner, and finally a zealous Baptist. One thing he certainly possessed—an amazing resilience. From the little that he had heard when studying in the Jesuit College in Valladolid (until expelled) he concocted a story (in collaboration with a companion, one Tonge, as unscrupulous as himself) which contained the alarming intelligence that Charles was to be murdered, and the country put under the government of the Jesuits. This vile plot, Titus Oates was able to reveal, had been drawn up in the White Horse Tavern in Fleet Street at a 'general consult' in April 1678. With superb effrontery—it was a lifelong characteristic—he laid this information before Sir Edmund Berry Godfrey, a justice of the peace for Westminster and a zealous Protestant. A month later Godfrey was found cruelly murdered in a ditch.

The sorely tried emotions of the English people now found expression in a welter of unreason. Hidden fears which Charles's policy engendered were brought into the open. Oates became a national hero, received a pension from the Government, and was royally entertained. It is not surprising that more informers (such as Bedloe) soon came forward to share the profits of this lucrative mendacity. As a result, thirty-four Roman Catholics (including Coleman) were judicially murdered for their share in a plot, which existed for the most part only in the fertile imagination of Titus Oates and others like him. The temper of England at this time may be seen in that one fervent Protestant wrote to Henry Compton suggesting that the Protestant powers of Europe should declare war on the Pope and set out to capture the Vatican library, where they would find evidence for the most blood-curdling papal machinations against this country. Some people, the writer ingenuously confessed, might regard such a military operation as 'a little dishonourable', but think how wicked the Pope was![1]

The Bishop of London was one of a Committee of the Privy Council which met to interrogate Oates, and to make the preliminary investigations.[2] In fact he seems to have played a

[1] Vanbrugh to Compton, 28 Dec., 1678, *S.P.D.* Car. II, 408, no. 106.
[2] *H.M.C.* App. vii, Report XIV, p. 457 (Ormonde MSS., vol. 4).

prominent part in this witch-hunt and to have followed consistently the lead of Danby. On 1 November, we find him writing to Henry Coventry, one of the Secretaries of State, insisting that as the investigations had been referred to a Committee, so its members must have 'all the evidences as are taken in the case', particularly the testimony of the three informers, the brothers Atkins and John Childs.[1] In view of his militant Protestantism, it is not likely that Compton was very 'objective' in his examination of evidence: but in this respect he was representative of most Englishmen of his age, some of whom in their excessive zeal began to suspect even Danby of having concealed the extent of this Popish plot although at first many thought he had invented the whole thing to prevent his own fall.

The Earl of Shaftesbury, one of the most remarkable men of any age, whose frail emaciated frame ('a running sore') housed a spirit which was coldly calculating and restlessly ambitious, saw immediately the possibility of using this Popish scare for his own purposes, though he himself was almost certainly not taken in by the 'plot'. This irresponsible statesman had come to the fore as the opponent of Clarendon and the 'friend of toleration'. He had been a member of the Cabal (though the secret clauses of the Treaty of Dover were not revealed to him), but because of his strong Protestant sympathies he had been dismissed from the Chancellorship by Charles in September 1673. He had then given vent to his resentment by becoming the militant leader of the opposition party, successfully blocking Danby's famous 'Non-Resistance' Test Bill of 1675. Imprisoned in the Tower in 1677, he had been released in time to use with cunning and great skill the vast possibilities of the Popish plot. By sheer force of character, he persuaded the opposition to make an alliance with Louis against Charles, a manoeuvre which he artfully foresaw would inevitably lead to the ruin of Danby.

The impending fall of this statesman, coming at a time when Compton had already suffered a bitter disappointment at the hands of the Court, could not but be without its effects on the Bishop's own fortunes. Early in February 1678, he confessed to a friend 'with a heavy heart' that the Lord Treasurer 'was looked upon as a lost man'. This was due, he explained (how often are we content with secondary causes!) to Danby's remonstrating

[1] Compton to Coventry, 1 Nov., 1678, B.M. Add. MSS. 32095, fo. 123.

with the King in September 1677 on the evils of 'those entertainments' at Nelly's and the 'scenes of abuse' which inevitably accompanied them; to which Charles had gaily replied that 'he would not deny himself an hour's divertissement for the sake of any man'.[1]

Nor was Danby's warning to the King on this subject a lone voice. The Bishop of London felt a greater responsibility and, preaching before the King in February of this year, 'he did particularly explain the dangers of ill conversation, or the showing any degree of countenance or delight in those who were under marks or blemishes of an evil life'—a sermon which was regarded as 'a loyal effort to save his patron' (i.e. Danby).[2] The Earl of Arran, who was a member of the congregation, noted 'that the meaning was very visible to all'.[3]

These endeavours to secure a moral purge were certainly distasteful to the King (he had had enough lectures from Clarendon to last a lifetime) but they were not in themselves the cause of Danby's fall. This was immediately due to the malevolence of Shaftesbury and the treachery of Ralph Montague, who made public the letters, which to humour Charles and against his better judgment, Danby had sent to Louis in connection with the royal pension. Everyone knew that the Lord Treasurer was notoriously anti-French, yet he was made the scapegoat. Compton himself did not entirely avoid the general suspicion which was directed towards this minister on the eve of his fall. In former days people would cry in the streets as the Bishop of London passed by: 'Make room for a Protestant bishop'; now they were silent and a few began to whisper that even he was a concealed Papist.[4]

To Charles this unpopularity of a Bishop he disliked was not unwelcome, and he used the opportunity to remove Compton from the Council on 13 January, 1679.[5] It is true that Compton had been deliberately provocative of late—or at least that was how the King chose to interpret his actions. On the Council he

[1] Arran to Ormonde, 9 Feb., 1678, *H.M.C.* App. vii, Report XIV, p. 106 (Ormonde MSS., vol. 1).

[2] Barrillon to Louis XIV, 17 Feb., 1678.

[3] Arran to Ormonde 16 Feb., 1678, *H.M.C.* App. vii, Report XIV, p. 401 (Ormonde MSS. vol. 4).

[4] *Ibid.* App. vii, Report XIV, p. 470 (Ormonde MSS. vol. 5).

[5] *S.P.D.* Car. II, 13 Jan., 1679.

had supported orders to disarm all Papists,[1] to confine them to their houses within five miles of London,[2] to search Whitehall and Somerset House[3] and to interrogate the Roman Catholic servants of the Queen and the Duchess of York.[4] In his own diocese he had issued an order that persons attending Mass at ambassadors' houses, other of course than those who could claim diplomatic privilege, should be arrested.[5] Also he had joined in controversy with the Lord Chamberlain, Arlington—a Roman Catholic—upon the latter's claiming that he had the right to appoint the Lent preachers to the royal household.[6] To fill up the sum of his misdeeds, Compton absented himself, out of private pique, from paying his normal respects to the King.[7]

But Charles's sudden displeasure took the Bishop by surprise, and he begged William Sancroft, his successful rival for Canterbury, to intercede for him. It was a 'grievous thing' he wrote to the Archbishop, 'for a loyal person to lie under the displeasure of his Prince', and equally intolerable 'to be careless of such misfortune'.[8]

Tittle-tattle and malicious gossip now began to say that the Bishop was so disgruntled with his removal from office that he 'was stuck into close counsels with the Earl of Shaftesbury who is like to be in top and already courted by all accordingly'.[9] If this were true (it is extremely unlikely) such a wooing did not last very long, for the same gossips were reporting not long afterwards that 'in all things concerning the Lord Treasurer [i.e. Danby] the Bishop of London hath forsaken Shaftesbury'.[10]

The anti-Popish scare, the fulminations of Shaftesbury, who secured the passing of a bill excluding Roman Catholics from Parliament (James was exempted from its terms), and the attack on Danby, made Charles realise that for the time being at least he must bow before the storm. Parliament was dissolved in accordance with an agreement into which Charles had entered

---

[1] Record Office: *Council Register of Charles II*, vol. 13, 409.
[2] *Ibid.*, 444.   [3] *Ibid.*, 469.   [4] *Ibid.*, 442.
[5] S.P.D. Car. II, 6 Dec., 1678, 408, no. 50.
[6] *Ibid.*, no. 208. The appointment of such preachers was, as a compromise, entrusted to the Archbishop of Canterbury.
[7] Compton to Sancroft, 14 Jan., 1679, Bod. Tanner MSS. 39, fo. 155.
[8] *Ibid.*
[9] H.M.C. App. vii, Report XIV, p. 470 (Ormonde MSS. vol. I).
[10] *Ibid.* App. vii, Report XIV, p. 496 (Ormonde MSS., vol. 4).

with the Presbyterian group led by Holles, and when it met again in March 1679, Danby was dismissed and lodged in the Tower. He pleaded the King's pardon, but this did not prevent an impeachment being brought against him; though Charles was anxious in his own interest (he was not particularly concerned with the fate of the former Lord Treasurer) that this should not be proceeded with. Thus in the Tower Danby remained, and could not secure a temporary release even when his wife was seriously injured in a street accident.[1] It is to the credit of Compton that he used his influence—true it was not very great at the time—on his old ally's behalf.[2]

Everything now seemed to be working out as Shaftesbury desired. The King artfully called Temple as an 'elder statesman' from the Hague, and accepted his doctrinaire proposals for a Cabinet Council of thirty members. On this large and unwieldy body of which Shaftesbury became President, Compton was unexpectedly included and with the Archbishop of Canterbury represented the Church. Had the Country Party under Shaftesbury's leadership now pursued a moderate policy it might well have swept all before it. But divided counsels, and his own fanaticism, finally played into the hands of the astute Charles.

Men's thoughts turned, meanwhile, to what became the burning question of the day—the succession to the throne. James's uneasy situation while this grave matter was being agitated may be seen in his frequent exile—once to Brussels and twice to Scotland. To Charles, James's presence in England was often an embarrassment, and the matter was frequently brought up to the Council. Particularly in October 1680, with Parliament due to meet soon, did the Duke find himself in a dilemma. The Lord Chancellor Sunderland, and nine others on the Council, were for his returning to the Continent. Compton—we might not have expected it of him, unless he thought that James was less dangerous present (because so unpopular) than absent—in company with Lords Clarendon and Worcester, voted for his remaining in England.[3] Finally the King made up his own mind, and James was packed off to Scotland.

---

[1] *H.M.C.* App. vii, Report IV, p. 357. (Ormonde MSS., vol. 6).
[2] *Ibid.* 1913.   Finch MSS., vol. I, p. 51.
[3] *H.M.C.* App. vii, Report XIV, p. 459 (Ormonde MSS. Vol. 5).

But the Duke of York's removal to Scotland did not solve the problem of the succession or make it any less urgent in men's minds. At first Charles was prepared to accept some compromise, and he agreed that certain limitations in respect of Church preferment and in the appointment to some state offices should be imposed on the sovereignty of a Roman Catholic monarch: but Shaftesbury was determined on nothing less than total exclusion. Even in this he might well have carried responsible opinion with him, had he not gone further and made his cardinal mistake. If James were to be excluded, in whom was the succession to be placed? To most sensible people the answer was obvious—in Mary, daughter of James, and wife of William of Orange. Shaftesbury, with incredible folly, turned to the Duke of Monmouth, the handsome but politically incompetent natural son of Charles. In making this fatal choice, Shaftesbury divided his own party, lost respect among more sober people, particularly in the Church, and thereby played into Charles's hands. Not even his fanning the dying embers of the papal scare, or his proceeding against James as a Popish recusant, could prevail. Charles was astute enough to see that Shaftesbury had dug a pit and could soon be pushed into it—and that there was room in it to engulf his allies. When the Exclusion Bill came up to the Lords, Halifax, 'the Trimmer', spoke with real force against it. All the bishops present, including Compton, voted against the Bill,[1] and it was rejected by 63 votes to 30.[2]

The Bishop of London, in fact, had no sympathy with the claims of Monmouth, and brought before the Council the case of one Standen, who expressed himself very violently in November 1680, while the debates on Exclusion were occupying the attention of Parliament. 'What need they make such ado about the Succession', Standen protested, 'when there was a lawful heir to the Throne already, the Duke of Monmouth.' Mrs. Standen seems to have given vent to her feelings in an even more forthright manner. 'If the Duke of York ever came to town again and I see him', she cried in a rage, 'if there are either dirt or stones in the way, I will fling them in his way. He is a rogue and a traitor.'[3]

---

[1] The Earl of Dartmouth is in error (Burnet, ii. 246) in suggesting that Compton, with Bishop, Pearson and Lamplugh, voted for it.

[2] Burnet, *op. cit.*, ii. 246.   [3] S.P.D. Car. II, 24 Dec., 1680, 414, no. 159.

Events were now rapidly moving towards a climax, and the King skilfully called his next Parliament, in March 1681, to meet at Oxford. The choice of place seemed to imply that London was no longer safe, and that the country was on the verge of civil war. With equal cunning, Charles resumed his role of pensioner to Louis XIV, thus becoming, for the time being at least, more or less financially independent of the House of Commons.

The Parliament at Oxford proved as intractable to the King as his earlier ones. Yet Charles could see that the opportunity for which he had waited so long had at last come. He dissolved Parliament suddenly in April. The Church, Universities, and the people as a whole (except in London) were thoroughly frightened, and as a result rallied round the throne. Shaftesbury avoided arrest by escaping to Holland. The Duke of York returned and the Duke of Monmouth departed. Lord Essex committed suicide in the Tower some two years later, and Lord William Russell and Algernon Sidney were beheaded.

For the rest of his reign, Charles for most practical purposes was supreme. Though he took care not to repeat the grosser mistakes of his father, yet 'he moved coolly and resolutely forward on the path of despotism'. Parliament, in defiance of the Triennial Act, was not summoned. James, in equal defiance of statutes, was readmitted to the Council and to the office of Lord High Admiral. Towns were bullied into surrendering their charters, by which manoeuvre the King secured control over their corporations.

The Bishop of London's Protestant zeal during this period grew to match the pace of events, though this did not prevent Charles, in February 1681, constituting him and Sancroft a small committee to advise on ecclesiastical preferment.[1] Recommendations, both in Church and Universities, were first to come before this small body which would then offer its advice to the King. In July, three more members, Halifax, Hyde and Seymour, were added;[2] but it does not seem that this experiment was any more successful than a similar device proved to be in the reign of William III. Preferment meant power, a means of rewarding friends and sometimes of bribing enemies, and no King was prepared entirely to part with it. The probability is

---

[1] *S.P.D.* Car. II, 27 Feb., 1681, 415, no. 58.
[2] *ibid.* Car. II, 21 July, E.B. 53, p. 61.

that this committee, in so far as it functioned, did some useful work in respect of routine preferment.[1]

And so Charles's reign drew to its close. It could not have given James much satisfaction when the Bishop of London on 16 August, 1682, as Dean of the Chapels Royal, baptised his third daughter Charlotte Maria; and on the evening of 28 July, 1683, married his second daughter Anne to George, Prince of Denmark, in the Chapel of St. James's.[2]

Early in the latter year there had been talk of the Crown proceeding against the Bishop in King's Bench for 'issuing processes out of the ecclesiastical courts in his diocese in his own name and not in his Majesty's,' but the King wisely entered a *nolle prosequi* to the indictment.[3]

James was now soon to change his whole status, for Charles did not live long to enjoy his despotic triumph. The King was blessed with a magnificent physique which allowed him to indulge in a life of excess which would have killed any less virile person. Yet despite this, his health on the whole was good. True he had had one dangerous illness, when Sancroft took alarm, and contemplated drawing up special prayers for the Kings' recovery, but was deterred from doing so by the Bishop of London. Explaining his position in a letter to the Archbishop, Compton said that, though confident 'no sincere Protestant or good subject but offers up prayers continually for his health and safety', he yet thought that to draw up special prayers might well cause a crisis by 'making an extraordinary impression upon the minds of men.' Also the consent both of the King and Council must first be obtained. As for himself, said the Bishop, he would instruct his clergy to remember his Majesty in the prayers before the sermon.[4] But Charles recovered.

In the spring of 1685 he was taken ill again, and many hoped that he might once again recover. People thronged to the churches to pray for his him—a thorough rake usually has his following—fearful of the shape of things to come. Round the bedside of the dying King there hovered the Bishops, and Compton offered words of consolation to the royal master with

[1] See Bod. Tanner MSS. 282, fo. 81.

[2] Stebbing and Sandford, *op. cit.*, p. 758. See also Luttrell, *A Brief Historical Relation*, i. 272; and *The Life of Dr. Henry Compton*, p. 14.

[3] *S.P.D. Car. II*, 7 Feb., 1683, E.B. 68, p. 204.

[4] Bod. Tanner MSS. 37, fo. 25.

whom his relations had never really been cordial. But Charles did not respond and remained silent, a fact which Burnet ascribes 'to the Bishop's cold way of speaking and to the ill opinion they had of him at Court as too busy in his opposition to popery'. James alone (egged on by the French ambassador Barrillon) seems to have sensed his brother's one remaining anxiety—if we except his concern for Nelly and his regret that he was an 'unconscionable time a-dying'—and Father Huddlestone, who had saved Charles's life after the Battle of Worcester many years before, was ushered into the bed-chamber. Charles was then hastily received into the only Church which he seems to have regarded with any respect.

James had not long performed this last act of brotherly regard before he himself became King.

CHAPTER FOUR

PRACTICAL RELIGION

IF we are to understand the relations between Henry Compton and the new King, we must look a little closer at the Bishop's impact on the spiritual life of the nation, remembering of course that we cannot at this time separate the religious from the political.

Both Gilbert Burnet and John Evelyn agree that Compton was not a great preacher. The former regarded his sermons as deficient in theological learning, a shortcoming which he ascribes to his not having pursued his studies with the necessary 'exactness'. The latter was not impressed when he heard him in the pulpit, though he was pleased to say of him that he was 'grave and pious'. Certainly the Bishop had not the scholar's temperament. He was essentially a practical man, concerned with the vital religious and constitutional problems of his day. Not one of his sermons was published during his lifetime, nor were any of them 'collected' after his death—perhaps a unique distinction for such a prominent ecclesiastic of that age who had preached on so many important national occasions.

But strange as it may seem, this very lack of literary skill and theological scholarship which made his preaching so inelegant to the refined taste of contemporaries, nurtured on the conceits of more polished performers, makes what remains of his Charges and 'Conferences' more palatable and comprehensible to us today. Gifted with a shrewd commonsense, sharpened by a wide experience of men and manners both at home and abroad, he usually managed to distil a great deal of practical wisdom into whatever he said, particularly in the 'Conferences' with his clergy which were such a marked feature of the first half of his episcopate. The dust has deservedly settled on the massive volumes of sermons which it was the ambition of distinguished ecclesiastics to leave behind them in those days. Compton, however, wisely realised his own limitations, and did not affect to play the scholar. In his addresses he seldom attempted to split nice theological hairs, but was more concerned with reminding his brethren how best to discharge their parochial duties; with rallying them to resist the attack from the Church of Rome; and with urging Dissenters to forget their scruples, and to stand with the Church of England against a common foe. In some respects Compton remained in temperament a layman (he was over thirty when he was ordained) for his travels in Europe, together with his military training, scanty though it may have been, undoubtedly left their permanent marks upon him.

Before we turn to his work as a bishop, we shall be wise to glance rapidly at his theological 'point of view', which, despite the fact that his political and ecclesiastical loyalties were subject to change, in its essentials remained with him throughout life. Here his outlook was neither speculative nor sceptical. His beliefs were clear cut, definite, and simple, and on occasions he could express them with vigour. It was the influence of religion on human conduct which was his prime concern, and he had little interest in the nice discussion of abstract theological problems.

So far as the Christian Mysteries [1] were concerned, the Bishop accepted them as authoritatively revealed by the Word of God in the Bible. The more such truths were called in question, and made the subject of popular discussion, the more such controversy, so he maintained, degenerated into 'endless Disputes about Words without ever coming to the Question'.[2] The Bible was the textbook of the devout Anglican Churchman, in contrast with the Roman Catholic who set up the authority of the Pope, the Quaker who bowed down before the 'inner light',[3] and the Deist who trusted the guidance of his own reason. The doctrine of the Holy Trinity, for example, 'begins and ends in the Word of God. We believe it because God has said it.'[4]

It was understandable that Compton, in a world of competing faiths, should want to find authority somewhere, but he was too intelligent not to realise that there were difficulties in this simple position in respect of the Scriptures. If the Bible is the textbook, it seems to teach a bewildering variety of lessons, for not all those

---

[1] *I.e.* doctrinal truths such as the Atonement.

[2] *The Bishop of London's Tenth Conference with his Clergy*, 1701, p. 1.

[3] Compton had little sympathy with the Quakers. In a charge to his clergy he spoke of their 'horrid blasphemous Invectives against the whole Institution of Christianity'.

[4] *The Bishop of London's Tenth Conference, etc.*, p. 21.

who admit the unique claim of the Scriptures come away from them with the same conclusions. James Nayler and William Laud, for example, both accepted the Bible as authoritative, but no two persons could have drawn more different conclusions from it. Certainly the Bible does not always shine with its own light. Yet though the Bishop recognises the problem he has really no answer to it except to assert dogmatically that the Bible is authoritatively interpreted in the Creeds and the Thirty-nine Articles. In other words, he finds his authority in the particular communion to which he belongs.

In all these matters, Compton protests (with the usual impatience of the man of affairs) we must not be too curious but rather concentrate on the practical side of religion. He never seems to have realised that a great deal of religious controversy (or at least some of it) and much unbelief do in fact result from genuine concern with, and often bewilderment at, the nature of the subject matter discussed. 'It were an indignity offered to the Truth of God', the Bishop writes, 'to expect an Account how such a thing can be, to which He has already given His Testimony that it is. . . . For the secret things belong to our Lord God. The Reason and Account of things are many times, as in the Particulars, of so absolute a Nature, and so foreign to the Constitution of Flesh and Blood, that to search after them were but lost Labour, in confounding our Understanding about things which are infinitely too high for us.'[1] One of the signs of the times which he particularly deplored was the 'proud conceit' which too many people had of the 'Power and Sufficiency of their own Faculties', which encouraged them not to allow that God could 'reveal anything beyond the reach of their own understanding. If He declare the Mystery of His divinity, He must also explain the Reason and Manner of [it].'[2]

Yet if the Mysteries of the Christian faith are dark and known to us only because God has revealed them, the everyday duties of the follower of Jesus are perfectly clear and plain. 'The End of all Religion is to eschew evil and do good, that we may glorify God in our Souls and in our Bodies which are the Lord's.'[3] The Bishop never tired of exhorting both clergy and laity to a life of active virtue, and to avoid all occasion of sin: certainly

---

[1] *The Bishop of London's Tenth Conference, etc.*, p. 4.
[2] *Ibid.*, p. 8.   [3] *The Bishop of London's Seventh Letter*, p. 7.

there was a great need for exhortation of this kind in days of such moral laxity.

But an obvious question presented itself. If the Mysteries of the Christian faith are unfathomable and known to us only on the authority of the Bible, while the rules of morality are so easily discoverable by the reason—as the Bishop seems to suggest —why then bother about the former at all? Are they not seen to be simply irrelevant? If it is good conduct that matters, and we are simply to accept difficult Mysteries without enquiry, is there any real need to concern ourselves with them?

It was to the negative conclusion that the Deists felt themselves led. Compton's answer to such scruples is emphatic: 'The Book of Nature [i.e. reason] may tell us our Duty but we also read in it our own Shame and Confusion, for want of Power to fulfill the Dictates of it.'[1] Mankind, because of the Fall, 'is in a miserable and corrupt State', and it is to this desperate human situation that the Christian Mysteries direct themselves. They represent the power of God to rescue man out of his helpless condition of sin. 'We are absolutely dependent', the Bishop writes, 'upon the righteousness of Christ for our justification: and for getting out of our state of corruption into the glorious liberty of the children of God.' On this subject, he speaks with genuine feeling:

> Where are those Incentives to an exalted life if Christ died not for our sins, and rose not again for our justification in a direct and plain sense? Indeed, where is the Reliance of our Faith? Where is the Foundation for our Hopes? When a poor Sinner laden with Transgressions comes to cast his Burden before the Throne of Grace, finding his Spirit overpowered by the Flesh, what means can a Socinian propose to him for his Relief? He can only tell him that a great Prophet has revealed wonderful means for leading a good life: but that he must pluck up his Spirits and set to work, for that he has natural Strength to deliver him from this Thraldom if he please. And what a miserable Comfort must this be to a languishing Sinner, that finds he has no Strength to deliver himself. Therefore he must not, neither will he, when he has looked into the Gospel promises, take the Word of these Men. There he has a powerful Redeemer, God as well as Man, making Intercession and giving full satisfaction for the Sins of the whole World?[2]

---

[1] *The Bishop of London's Tenth Conference*, p. 31.   [2] *Ibid.*, p. 38.

Compton, therefore, regards deism and rationalism as unrealistic: they cannot deal effectively with the real condition in which man finds himself: they require bricks without providing straw, as St. Paul discovered when he tried, by his own efforts, to keep the law.

There is no need to doubt the reality of the Bishop's conviction as to this distinction between religion and ethics. Though he did not realise that his theological position, in the form he stated it, was untenable, and needed the treatment which Butler later gave to it, he was yet right in maintaining a difference between the Christian faith and a self-sufficient Renaissance humanism. True, he separated reason and faith by a great divide which on his own presuppositions he could not cross, yet there was relevance in the judgment which he passed on his own age that 'the Root of all Bitterness proceeds from the circumscribing the Authority of Revelation within the Compass of our own Reason whereby God's determinations are subjected to our own Judgment'.[1]

When Compton turns from such difficult questions of theological belief to the Church and its ministry, he presents a strange amalgam of the Laudian high Churchman and the practical, almost latitudinarian, bishop. There can be no question, as this biography will show, but that contemporary events often conditioned the Bishop's thinking, and that sometimes his principles were not easily brought into harmony with his practice. This may have been due both to the scanty nature of his theological studies and the pragmatic cast of his mind. Unfortunately, opponents were apt to suggest low motives for what appeared as glaring inconsistencies.

The Church of God, Compton never tired of repeating, was like an army in its need for unity and discipline; and it derived its authority and title deeds from the commission of Christ handed down from the Apostles. The history of the Church fell into two periods. During the first, it possessed infallibility and the power to work miracles. When such exceptional endowments were no longer necessary, they were withdrawn.[2] During the second period, its permanent expression lay in the commission to preach the Gospel, and to administer the sacraments through an ordained priesthood.

---

[1] *The Bishop of London's Tenth Conference*, p. 38.
[2] William Paley (1743-1805) held a similar view.

Yet within this army, there was room for a certain diversity of belief provided that discipline was maintained in the ranks. 'Not every Article in the Thirty-nine', the Bishop is prepared to allow, 'obliges to an explicit belief. It is enough for many of them that they are not opposed.' The ceremonies of the Church, and the manner of their performance, are not in themselves important. They are significant 'only relatively'. They conduce to discipline, and it 'is purely in obedience to our Superiors, and to avoid the Scandal of Irregularity that the Duty of the Observation' is incumbent upon us.[1] 'There is a just and decent Liberty', he told his clergy in 1693, 'due to all Christians whereby to judge for themselves in the Essentials of Religion'; though it was their duty to be prudent in the exercise of this freedom, lest in avoiding 'that Popish Extream to take away all Liberty by an absolutely blind Obedience and implicit Faith . . . we with the Fanaticks assume to ourselves an unlimited Power of following the Wild-Goose Chase of our wanton and uncertain Imaginations'.[2]

The mean between these two extremes, the Bishop asserted, was to be found in the Church of England. 'The outward Adornment of this Doctrine is to have all things done decently and in order: the world is constituted and governed by Order, and God is the God of it. This is the Discipline contained in our Canons which adds strength to our Faith, and Life to our Charity.'[3]

This insistence on discipline is one of the Bishop's most oft-repeated themes. In an army (how often the metaphor is introduced) 'the least lack of it is punished because of the Enemy', and where religion is concerned, 'if nothing is ordained contrary to the will of God, we should be obedient for the sake of peace'—'it is enough for many doctrines that they are not opposed.'

Such an ecclesiastical position failed to commend itself to the majority of Nonconformists for the perfectly obvious reason that what Compton could lightly dismiss as matters of indifference were to them grave and serious problems in which their consciences were involved.

[1] *The Bishop of London's Charge*, 1696, p. 8.
[2] *Ibid.*, p. 17.
[3] *The Bishop of London's Seventh Letter*, p. 12.

From this short sketch of Compton's theological position, we may notice three things. First, an almost complete lack of interest in theological discussion for its own sake; second, a real concern for the practical expression of religion in a good life; and third, a convinced attachment to the *via media* of the Church of England.

CHAPTER FIVE

DEFENDER OF THE 'ECCLESIA ANGLICANA'

WHEN Henry Compton became Bishop of London in 1675 there were two problems exercising the minds of most thoughtful Englishmen, which they themselves regarded as real and urgent.

There was first the undoubted attack on parliamentary government which lay behind Charles's domestic and foreign policy, and which appeared to have triumphed in 1681 with the collapse of the constitutional opposition. Owing to the King's cunning, and a caution begotten of his determination not to go on his travels again, the danger was not always realised, but it was in fact very real. It became more apparent as Charles's reign drew to its close, and a scandal under James.

Secondly, there was the attack on the Church of England and its status in the national life which was thought to result from Charles's own leanings towards the Roman Catholic faith, and James's conversion.

We need to remember that it was the Court of Versailles which set the pattern of kingship for the age, and that in the eyes of those who admired Louis XIV, parliaments seemed relics of a feudal and barbaric past. Such institutions were in fact fast disappearing over Europe, and the Renaissance monarch, himself symbolising the unity of his people, seemed to be a more efficient guarantor of law and order—and it was law and order which most people wanted. But the prestige and policy of the French monarchy seemed to support the argument that the new pattern of kingship needed the Roman Catholic religion, perhaps in a Gallican form, for its support. Protestantism (this may well appear strange in view of the subsequent history of Germany) was regarded as being 'insolent to princes', and to have been nurtured in rebellion.

In England the national Church was inextricably interwoven with the whole legal and constitutional machinery of government. Its bishops sat in the House of Lords: its Prayer Book was sanctioned by Act of Parliament: its clergy were protected in

their freehold by common law. In spite of the Laudian respect
for the Crown (Charles I had a deep affection for the Church)
and the preaching of non-resistance from many an Anglican
pulpit (by men who ought to have known better), it yet remained
true that any attack by a 'would-be absolute monarch' on the
laws of the land was bound to involve the Church, particularly
when the monarch, who claimed to be *legibus solutus*, was a
convinced Roman Catholic.

Henry Compton's hostility to Rome was due to an instinctive
fear that she was un-English, alien to the whole national way of
life, and the handmaid of continental despotism. His Toryism, in
spite of his travels abroad and his great sympathy for French
refugees, was essentially insular in outlook. To keep England
Protestant—which meant to maintain the rights and liberties of
the *Ecclesia Anglicana* and to persuade the more amenable of the
Dissenters to conform—this was the wish dearest to his heart.
To achieve it, at a crisis in the history of England, he departed
from the traditional Toryism of the family, though he never
became a consistent or doctrinaire whig. When the danger from
Rome was removed, and personal disappointment soured him,
then his loyalty to the Church of England became more narrow,
and he grew less tolerant of those outside it.

His fear of Rome began early and it was undoubtedly fostered
by his travels abroad. In 1667 he felt strongly enough to publish
anonymously in London his own translation from the Italian of
a work which he had come across on one of his visits to Paris,
The Life of Donna Olympia Maldalchini, a lady who was alleged
to have governed the Church of Rome, during the pontificate of
Innocent X (1644-55).[1] Some two years later he printed, again
anonymously, his own translation, this time from the French, of
*The Jesuites' Intrigues; with the private Instructions of that Society
to their Emissaries*, a work which purported to have been found
'in manuscript in a Jesuit's closet after his death . . . and sent
from a Gentleman in Paris to his friend in London'.[2] Compton's
intention in translating these two books was obvious: it was to

---

[1] *A Translation from the Italian of* 'The Life of Donna Olympia Maldalchini',
who governed the Church during the Time of Innocent X, which was from the year
1644 *to* 1655, London, 1667, written originally by Abbot Gualdi and printed
privately at Paris.

[2] *The Jesuites Intrigues; with the private Instructions of that Society to their
Emissaries*, 1669.

make the Roman Catholic Church appear in as odious a light as possible to his own countrymen, and thereby to put them on their guard.

The latter part of Charles's reign, and the three crowded years of his brother's, were the golden age of Roman Catholic controversy in England. Sermons, public debates, popular songs, pamphlets and lampoons—all discussed authority in religion, what this Father had said or that Pope had done. As we turn over such compositions today, and disturb the dust which has settled on their pages, we wonder how they could ever have been read with such avidity, and become the talk of the town. The reason, however, is not far to seek. It was the power with which Roman Catholicism was armed at Versailles, and the aggression of the French army, which gave to the controversy such a living interest. What happened to Protestants in France, might it not later happen here? Perhaps the fear was irrational, but it was none the less real.

Immediately after his enthronement as Bishop of London, Henry Compton embarked upon a deliberate anti-Roman Catholic policy along several fronts.[1] He placed himself at the head of his clergy as their natural leader, and met personally a large number of them. To do this he started a practice (which it is, perhaps, a pity his successors abandoned) of calling together for regular consultations the clergy of the cities of London and Westminster in what he called his 'Conferences'. At these meetings it was his custom to address his brethren on some subject of immediate or pastoral interest and then to throw the subject open for general discussion, he himself presiding. Each clergyman present was invited to express his opinion, and at the end the Bishop summed up the debate 'with that accuracy and faithful memory, that the ablest and most celebrated of our learned judges have not been thought to excell him in that Talent'.[2] After the Conference, the Bishop summarised their common deliberations in a letter to his brethren.

Not all the clergy of his large diocese were able or required to attend these central Conferences.[3] For those distant from

---

[1] T. Gooch, *A Sermon, etc.*, p. 10.

[2] W. Whitfield, *A Sermon, etc.*, p. 8.

[3] A list of the subjects discussed at the Conferences, together with the dates of meeting, is to be found in chap. 12, p. 208.

London there were local gatherings called together by the rural deans on the instructions of the Bishop. Such occasions were undoubtedly welcomed by the majority of country incumbents, if for no other reason than that they gave them an opportunity to meet each other, and to realise that they were facing common problems. Such meetings usually began with a service in Church, at which the preacher was appointed by the Bishop, and concluded with a discussion, usually at a local inn, when the episcopal letter was read. A report of the proceedings, with a list of absentees, was then sent by the rural dean to the Bishop.

These Conferences undoubtedly provided Compton with an opportunity of taking the clergy into his confidence, and becoming sensitive to their thoughts. It was inevitable that most of these meetings, during the troubled years which immediately followed his translation to London, should deal with the Romanist controversy, because it was uppermost in everyone's mind.

We propose to look at a few typical gatherings in London and also in some of the country deaneries.

The subjects chosen for discussion in the three Conferences held in 1679 were the with-holding of the cup from the laity ('Half Communion'), 'Prayers in an Unknown Tongue', and 'Prayers to the Saints'.

As to the first of these, Compton said firmly that the Council of Constance, in laying down this prohibition because of the 'dangers and probable scandals that may happen', was acting clean contrary to the teaching and example of Jesus. Surely, he asked, and the question was typical of his practical outlook on matters religious, our Lord knew full well the possibility of spilling the wine. In fact it was a Pope, Gelasius, who maintained that the faithful 'should receive the Sacrament entire or be entirely rejected; the separating the one and the same Mystery could not be done without gross sacrilege.'[1]

Concerning 'Prayers in an Unknown Tongue', the Bishop remarked that such a custom could not exist where 'Scripture and Reason prevailed'. It was expressly forbidden by St. Paul, because it prevented the unlearned from understanding and therefore they could not conscientiously say 'Amen'. God had given us minds to think with, and 'how can it be imagined that God should expect less than the offering up to Him what He

[1] S. W. Cornish, *Episcopalia*, p. 17.

has given, not to talk like Parrots but with our Understanding and reasonable Service'.[1]

As to 'Prayers to the Saints', the Bishop claimed that this offended against both the first and second commandments.[2]

So far as the Conferences in London are concerned, we have no further details of them except this summary of what the Bishop said, but we are fortunately able to eavesdrop at the discussion of the same subjects in some of the country deaneries. Reports from twelve such meetings for the year 1679, all of them sent in to the Bishop by the rural deans, are still extant. They throw an interesting light on the preoccupation of the country clergy with the threat from Rome.

On 2 June, the clergy of the deaneries of Ongar and Harlow (it seems to have been the practice in certain parts of the diocese for two deaneries to meet together) assembled at Theydon Mount to discuss 'Half Communion'. They began with a service in the Church, and papers (subsequently sent to the Bishop) were given by two local clergy. A letter from Compton was then read, but no general discussion followed, because, as the rural dean reported, he 'found none of them prepared to discourse upon that subject as supposing that no more was expected of them than to disavow the Popish doctrine.'

On the whole the rural dean was very pleased with the proceedings—it was something of an experiment—and he reported that everything had gone off very well, the sermon and papers being 'inoffensive and as befitting scholars'. In dismissing his clergy, he reminded them that their next meeting, in accordance with the Bishop's summons, would be on 13 June, when they were to discuss 'Prayers in an Unknown Tongue'.[3]

We have no record of this next meeting, but on 14 July the two deaneries of Harlow and Ongar came together again, this time to concern themselves with the alleged Roman practice of giving worship to saints and angels.[4]

We have seen that at their first Conference these country clergy were reluctant to embark upon discussion. They had now overcome their initial shyness of each other, and there was a real spate of words. Mr. Butler of Bobbingworth—one of those

---

[1] S. W. Cornish, *Episcopalia*, p. 18.　　　　[2] *Ibid.*
[3] Hall to Compton, 2 June, 1679, Bod. Rawlinson MSS. 983 C., fo. 42.
[4] Same to same, 14 July, 1679, *ibid.*, 984 C., fo. 192.

naturally voluble people who are the embarrassment of every deanery meeting—led off in a long and rambling oration in which he condemned the worship of the saints as unscriptural and opposed to the practice of the primitive church. Mr. Dod of Chigwell followed, discoursing 'very large': Dr. Walker then delved into the mysteries of Muezzin in Daniel: Mr. Horton was dull and factual: Mr. Arrowsmith of Northweald spoke 'very particularly in detestation': and Mr. Alchorne of High Ongar entered upon a learned exegesis of 1 Timothy iv. 1.[1] The other clergy were put on their mettle and they all added their voices to the general condemnation—discussion we can hardly call it for there was no minority opinion. One speaker made the interesting point that angels and saints were a historical legacy of the old *daimonia*, the 'middle powers', which were half way between the celestial beings above and the *baals* below. Such an argument shows the beginning of an historical approach to religion such as Dr. Spencer (1630–93) attempted in his *De Legibus Hebraeorum*.

Some eleven clergy were absent, two on 'necessary business', four through illness, and the others for no reason that the rural dean knew of.

The deaneries of Colchester and Tendring met at Colchester on 22 May, 1679, in response to the Bishop's commands, and their subject again was 'Half Communion'. They assembled in the Parish Church, and the Reverend Powell preached a learnedly apposite, if dull, sermon. Afterwards they adjourned to an inn, 'from which we parted in good time,' so the rural dean, William Skelton, hastened to assure the Bishop.[2]

The discussion followed closely the lines of the sermon, and the general conclusion was that the real cause for the Roman Catholics denying the cup to the laity lay in the doctrine of transubstantiation, with its effect of exalting the status of the priesthood. The arguments advanced in its support—the dearness of wine, and the danger of spilling it—were 'frivolous and weak', especially when we remember that it was our Lord who had instituted the Communion in two kinds.

As a result of the meeting an agreed report was sent to Compton, in which the rural dean assured him that the atmo-

---

[1] 'Now the devil spirit speaketh expressly, that in the latter times some shall depart from the faith, giving heed to seducing spirits, and doctrines of devils.'
[2] Skelton to Compton, 22 May, 1679, Bod. Rawlinson MSS. 984 C., fo. 180*b*.

sphere of the gathering had been 'friendly and fair', both in Church and afterwards, and that all the brethren had been unanimous in opposing papal claims. The harmonious nature of the proceedings doubtless came as a relief to the Bishop for in Colchester there lived one of his most bitter opponents, Edmund Hickeringill, Vicar of All Saints, whose Church had been a centre of disturbance for many years. Hickeringill attended the service, but did not proceed to the inn afterwards, though he gave to the rural dean a curious document which he insisted should be forwarded to the Bishop. This paper contained the eccentric Vicar's opinions, in metre, on matters theological—some thirteen stanzas of wretched doggerel from which we quote the following:

> Christ and Paul gave bread and wine
> To these the Greek Church doth incline
> And we with them therein combine
> But they water mix with wine.

The rural dean felt diffident as to the propriety of sending such nonsense to the Bishop. 'Your Lordship will be pleased to hear from me', he wrote, 'an account of Mr. Hickeringill's reasons for what he thus sends . . . he was solicitous it should be sent and under his own name.'[1]

But Henry Compton was to hear much more of Hickeringill during the coming years.

On 18 June, the Deaneries of Colchester and Tendring met again to wrestle this time with the well-worn theme of 'Prayer in an Unknown Tongue'. Unfortunately the preacher whom the Bishop had nominated 'made so many excuses about loss of books' that the rural dean was forced to find a substitute which he did by 'prevailing' upon Mr. Witham of Manningtree. The general discussion which followed does not seem to have been very exciting—the subject hardly lent itself to controversy among Protestants—and the rural dean followed the usual practice of drawing up an agreed summary. They were unanimous that in prayer man acknowledges his dependence upon God, intercedes for His help, and eases his own conscience, none of which can effectively be done in an 'unknown tongue'.

[1] Skelton to Compton, 22 May, 1679, Bod. Rawlinson *MSS.*, 983 C., fo. 15.

Mr. Hickeringill and seven others were absent on this occasion, and failed to send any explanation. In addition three sent excuses —a funeral, illness, and a visit to Suffolk, though in the last case the absentee sent his curate.

The rural deanery of Witham in Essex met in July 1679, and as a result thirteen clergy signed a paper declaring that the worship of saints and angels had no foundation in Scripture, and was utterly at variance with the practice of the early church.[1] At another meeting they protested against 'prayers in an Unknown Tongue'. 'We unanimously declare', so ran their condemnation, 'that the Doctrine and Custom of the present Roman Church concerning the Liturgy and private prayers for the ignorant in an unknown tongue is not only not agreeable, but plainly opposed to the Doctrine and Practice of the truly ancient Catholic Church, and also the custom of other Churches which are not absolute Protestants.'[2]

It would be tedious, however, to continue this round of the deaneries, particularly as the account of their proceedings presents a monotonous similarity. That they were appreciated, however, is clear from the numbers who attended, and the reports of the rural deans, who stressed 'the great advantage' which the clergy received from them. They certainly gave the brethren throughout the diocese a sense of unity springing from a personal loyalty to the Bishop and a common determination to resist Roman Catholic encroachment. They also encouraged the clergy to discuss their problems together. The letters which Compton himself wrote enabled him to take his own clergy into his confidence; and the reports which he received from the rural deans, with their summary of discussion and list of absentees, enabled him to make some assessment of how far his brethren were behind him. Particularly did these Conferences keep the clergy alive to their responsibilities as members of Church and State, and thus help to build up in London and throughout the diocese a solid core of resistance to the policy of James when he later ascended the throne. The clergy, themselves stimulated at these meetings, undoubtedly passed on to their congregations, not perhaps so much the substance of their deliberations, as the spirit which animated them.

[1] Browning to Compton, 17 May, 1679, Bod. Rawlinson MSS., 983 C., fo. 20.
[2] Browning to Compton (undated), *ibid.*, 984 C., fo. 177.

Yet these Conferences were but one means of opposing the claims of Rome. At the same time the Bishop was constant in his anti-papal activities on the Council, so much so that he incurred the anger not only of James but of the less zealous Charles. A few typical instances of Compton's vigilance must suffice.

In July 1676, the Bishop was particularly concerned at the increase in Roman Catholic literature, and he drew the attention of the Council to the publication, by an obscure printer, one Anthony Lawrence, of a book entitled *The Great Sacrifice of the New Law*, written by James Dymock. Through the Bishop's initiative, the unhappy man was brought before the Council, and Compton secured an order, dated 21 July, empowering the Wardens of the Stationers Company to search Lawrence's premises for any Roman Catholic books and report back to him.[1]

In matters of this kind, Compton, in company with liberal minded opinion of the day, did not believe in freedom, and would most certainly not have subscribed to Milton's noble plea for the liberty of the press. Quite the reverse. The Bishop of London was prepared to do everything in his power to prevent by law the dissemination of Roman Catholic propaganda. In August 1676, there were rumours that 'divers Popish and un-licensed Books were lodged in three warehouses over the stables in Somerset House'. The Council, again egged on by the Bishop of London, took the matter very seriously, and the clerk was instructed to go in person with the Vice-Chamberlain, to make a thorough investigation, and to send whatever books they found to the Bishop.[2] On 18 September, of the same year, a similar order was given to search the houses of a number of printers and a bookseller. In January 1679, when the religious atmosphere was becoming more tense, the Bishop took the responsibility of ordering the Customs House to seize all copies of a book written by Dr. Moore *Of the Increase and Growth of the Popish Religion in England since 158-*, and only later did he inform the Council of what he had done.[3]

Nor were books the Bishop's only preoccupation, as we have seen in a former chapter. In 1680 he was complaining to the

---

[1] *S.P.D.* Car. II, 21 July, 1676, 383, no. 136.
[2] *Ibid.* Car. II, 9 Aug., 1676, 384, no. 1113.
[3] *Ibid.* Car. II, 3 Jan., 1679, 411, no. 6.

Council that from information he had received it was clear that the power of the Jesuits in England was increasing.

The University of Oxford also came under his protestant scrutiny, for it was important that young and impressionable students should not be led into temptation. Sometimes he had real grounds for anxiety. During the summer of 1680, a member of University College preached a sermon in St. Mary's which was judged by some members of the congregation to be 'contrived in a Popish style from the beginning to the end'. It was not so much what the preacher directly affirmed, but that the use of such phrases as 'infallibility of the Church Catholic', 'counsels of perfection', and 'merit' seemed to suggest 'inclinations towards Popery'. True the sermon was doctrinally unimpeachable, the preacher cunningly constructing it so as 'to be capable of being eluded by an equivocal interpretation'. In due course he was brought before the Heads of Houses, when he cleverly asked whether he was being charged with having contravened any particular article of the Church of England. Much to the relief of the Bishop of London, who was kept in touch with these proceedings through William Jane, prudence asserted itself, and the offending clergyman agreed to sign a recantation.[1]

In 1684, the Bishop of London had his attention drawn to things nearer home. The Parish of St. Martin in the Fields was at this time in the care of a very vigorous Protestant, Thomas Tenison, who informed Compton 'that the Florentine Resident in Leicester Fields has for the last six months permitted a priest to preach and catechise in English in his house day by day to the enticing of men to resort thither'. Compton immediately wrote a strong letter of protest to the Earl of Sunderland, one of the secretaries of state.[2] Such an abuse of diplomatic privilege was by no means uncommon, for some eight years earlier Compton had vigorously complained to the Council against the Portuguese Ambassador licensing a translation of the Mass for the Queen's household.[3]

Yet it was not enough, so the Bishop felt, to oppose Roman Catholic assertion when it came into the open. It was equally

[1] Jane to Compton, 18 July, 1680, Bod. Tanner MSS. 37, fo. 71.
[2] *S.P.D.* Car. II, 1684, 438, no. 112.
[3] *Correspondence of the Family of Hatton*, i. 137.

necessary, so far as possible, to secure a measure of unity among all Protestants so that their collective strength might act as a deterrent. There could be no greater invitation to Papal aggression than internal division. Tory and fervent champion of the Church of England as Compton undoubtedly was, it was yet his consistent policy at this time, by means of a conciliatory approach, to induce the more amenable of the Dissenters to conform to the established Church. We need to remember that Dissent had not yet come to be finally accepted as the inevitable accompaniment of a national church. Certainly the growing menace of a resurgent Roman Catholicism did in fact bring Nonconformists and members of the Church of England closer together in heart and mind than they had been since the breakaway under Elizabeth. Exposed to a common attack they were prepared to forget some at least of their differences and to stand together to defend a common liberty. So much was this the case, that though as a body the Dissenters suffered under the so-called Clarendon Code, they preferred (with some exceptions of course) not to accept emancipation through the Declarations of Indulgence which both Charles and James issued. They did not want to be unconstitutionally exempted even from statutes which they regarded as tyrannical.

To place the Church of England in as favourable a light as possible in the eyes of the Dissenters, the Bishop did his best to encourage the writing of books which might predispose some of them to overcome their scruples. 'He put others upon writing', a contemporary explained, 'not because he could not do it but because he had no leisure himself; for by his several Charges to his Clergy and his Conferences with them, it appears that if he would he could write on any Subject as learnedly and effectually as any.'[1]

The Bishop's expectations did not appear unreasonable during these years, particularly if the Church of England were prepared, by a charitable gesture of Prayer Book revision, to meet the Dissenters half way. At least that was how Compton thought right up to the Convocation of 1689, though by that time he had unfortunately allowed personal disappointment to cloud his public policy. It is one of the tragedies of English religious history that the favourable opportunity provided by a common

[1] John Cockburne, *The Blessedness of Christians after Death*, p. 20.

hostility to James was not used with more wisdom and charity.

The Bishop of London in this respect also adopted an interesting method of commending the Church of England to those outside it.

The sympathy of all English Protestants—and particularly of the Dissenters—went out to their brethren on the Continent, many of whom were undergoing cruel persecution. No man did more to help them than Henry Compton, as a later chapter will show. He decided, therefore, to ask some of the best known of these continental Protestants what they thought of the Church of England. Did they themselves feel that they could honestly join in its worship, and were the Dissenters justified in making separation a point of conscience? Letters were dispatched along these lines to three learned continental divines, all of whom the Bishop had met during his travels in France.

The first to answer the Bishop, on 3 September, 1680, was Monsieur le Moyne, Professor of Divinity at Leiden, who was not without some knowledge of the religious life of this country having spent some time here in 1675. His letter left no doubt that he regarded the Church of England as a truly Protestant Church. 'If your Confession of Faith be pure and innocent', he wrote, 'your Divine Service is so too; for no one can discover anything at all in it that tends to Idolatry; this were to make Profession of a terrible kind of Deity to believe that they are able to destroy those eternally that are willing to submit themselves unto this.'

As to episcopal government, of which the Dissenters in England so bitterly complained, 'what is there in it', he asked, 'that is dangerous, and may reasonably alarm men's conscience?' Was it not the bishops at the Reformation 'who delivered England from the error in which she was enveloped?' Surely this service by itself 'ought to oblige all good men not to separate from it; but to look up to the Church of England as a very orthodox Church'. Such was the opinion, he writes, of Protestants in France, Switzerland, Germany and Holland. It was the more surprising, therefore, in fact 'a horrible Impudence', that 'some Englishmen themselves had so ill an opinion of her at present and divide rashly from her as they do'. Some kind of union, which accepted a form of episcopacy, was an obvious necessity, though it must naturally be approached with tact and understanding. 'It looks as if it were a Design reserved for your great Wisdom', he wrote to the Bishop, 'and if you do not succeed it is clear that all others will labour but in vain.'[1]

The second reply, written on 31 October, 1680, came from Monsieur de l'Angle, one of the preachers of the reformed Church at Charenton. He again had visited England some two years previously, and while in this country had preached to a congregation under the jurisdiction of the Church of England. His general attitude was very much the same as the Professor at Leiden. 'I cannot express to you with how much grief I understand that your divisions continue', he began, 'at a time in which there are such pressing reasons for being Reunited. Above all, that which you tell me of the writings that are at this time published to make men believe that Communion with the Church of England is unlawful, and that the Ministers cannot permit it to private Persons without sinning, seems to me a thing so unreasonable in itself, and so very unreasonable now, that I could scarce believe it, if it were not attested by a person of your merit and consideration.' The Church of England was a true Church of our Lord: its worship and doctrine were pure, with nothing in them contrary to the Word of God. 'It is without doubt', he wrote, emphatically, 'the duty of all the Reformed of your Realm to keep themselves inseparably united to this Church': and if, 'there were nothing wanting to cure it but the abstaining from some expressions, the quitting some Ceremonies, and the Changing the Colour of some Habits', then he was sure the Bishops would be willing to countenance such reform.[2]

The third letter came from Monsieur Claude, also formerly a minister at Charenton, who after the Revocation of the Edict of Nantes had fled into Holland, where Prince William commissioned him to write an account of the sufferings of his fellow religionists. It was this rather harrowing narrative which Thomas Tenison, then Vicar of St. Martin's, later translated into English for the benefit of his countrymen.[3]

We are not surprised that Monsieur Claude's letter ran very much as the other two. So far as episcopacy was concerned, he

[1] Stillingfleet, *The Unreasonableness of Separation*, 1681, p. 410.
[2] *Ibid.*, p. 423. That Compton allowed this last conciliatory sentence to be published shows his own feelings at the time.
[3] See E. Carpenter, *The Life and Times of Thomas Tenison*, p. 323.

stated definitely that he did not 'blame those that observe it as a thing very ancient, and I would not that anyone should make it an occasion of quarrel in those places where it is established'. He himself and other French Protestant ministers made no difficulty in committing their flocks to ministers ordained by bishops in the Church of England. Ceremonies which were matters of indifference were not an adequate cause for separation. He himself had always regarded the Church of England as 'an elder sister for which we ought to have a kindness accompanied with respect and veneration'. Whereas the Divine Providence had placed some Churches at the time of the Reformation under a Presbytery, it had placed the Church of England under episcopacy. He therefore hoped that the Dissenters would reconsider their position, since 'to imagine that we cannot with a good conscience be present at Assemblies but only when we do fully and generally approve of all things in them is certainly not to know either the use of Charity or the law of Christian society'.[1]

The replies of these divines certainly bear witness to a large and liberal spirit, though it is not improbable that their attitude was affected, perhaps almost unconsciously, by the sad plight of so many continental Protestants and their need for English help. These theologians clearly regard episcopacy as but one among many possible patterns—a view held by a large number of 'latitudinarians'[2] in the Church of England, and going right back to the Reformation—though they come near to suggesting that the Reformation would have been more perfect had it been abolished. Compton, however, was at this time concerned with practical problems, and he was not primarily interested in questions relating to the *esse*, *bene esse*, or *melius esse* of episcopacy. His main preoccupation was to secure greater unity among Protestants in England, and he hoped that this exchange of letters might help to bring it about.

At one with him in this desire was Edward Stillingfleet, who made it the theme of his book *The Unreasonableness of Separation* (1681) which, as its title suggests, was an appeal to the Dissenters to see the danger of their isolation. It was fitting that the replies of the continental divines to the Bishop of London's inquiry should be included in this work as an appendix.

[1] Stillingfleet, *op. cit.*, p. 449.
[2] And not only latitudinarians!

The scruples entertained by some more rigid churchmen at the feelers which Compton was putting out to Protestants abroad may be seen in the misgivings of Thomas Ken, when Chaplain to Princess Mary in Holland.

In July or August 1680, the Bishop of London wrote to The Hague, asking Ken whether he would sound the Dutch divines as to their opinions concerning the points of difference between the Church of England and the Dissenters. His reply was not encouraging, for Ken suggested that whatever their opinion, it would not be of much value. 'The Generality of Dutch Divines despised Ecclesiastical Antiquity', he wrote. They thought the Church of England half papist, and quoted as their authorities the writings of the English Nonconformists. If any reported favourably, they would at least expect a deanery in reward.[1]

We can see here the inevitable tension between the practical bishop faced with an urgent problem at home, and the more theologically minded divine abroad, thinking in terms of principles and living in an environment where his Anglicanism was sharpened by contrast. Ken may well have read a short book which had appeared in England some six years previously: *The Peaceable Design; or an Account of the Nonconformist Meetings*, in which John Humfrey, an ejected minister, asked what the Church of England could say to the Papists, if in order to accommodate Dissenters it should loosen its hold on the essential nature of episcopacy.

We can already hear in the distance the rumbles of the South Indian controversy.

The difficulty, of course, was a real one, for to those who held episcopacy to be of the *esse* of the Church, absolute surrender on this point must be the condition of re-entry for the Dissenters, no matter what efforts might be made at conciliation on other and minor matters. It was this problem which later wrecked the Comprehension Scheme of 1689, and has often frustrated the hopes of the liberal school within the Church of England. 'You seem to have forgot one main thing', a pamphleteer of the time wrote, 'and that was to make up your Chancel Door; for it may so happen that more Conformists may go out at that, than grave Dissenters go in at the other.'[2]

---

[1] Ken to Compton, 19 Aug., 1680, Bod. Rawlinson MSS. 983 c., fo. 55.
[2] *To the Reverend and Merry Answerer of Vox Cleri*, 1689, p. 10.

Whatever the Bishop's own feelings, Ken's letter certainly had the effect of persuading him not to solicit the opinions of the Dutch divines.

The fact that Compton would not have regarded himself as a 'latitudinarian' may serve to remind us that the desire to effect some kind of accommodation with the Dissenters was not at this time solely the concern of one party within the Church. Sancroft was equally devoted to the same cause.[1] Nice distinctions of theology which in more placid days might seem important appeared in a different light against the background of a major menace. And this fact, many Churchmen felt, applied equally to the Dissenters. If Anglicans were willing to embark on some measure of Prayer Book reform, particularly in respect of the 'controverted ceremonies', then surely the Dissenters must recognise that, by allowing their scruples on episcopacy to perpetuate a schism, they were in fact imperilling the very Protestantism which they were seeking to uphold. Writing in July 1683, Thomas Tenison, then Vicar of St. Martin's, made a bold appeal to the more responsible Dissenters to forget their difficulties and to re-enter the Church of their forefathers. 'I beseech you', he pleaded, 'make such advantage of this juncture. Sit down and think once more of the Nature of this Church. Confer with the Guides of this National Religion, read without Prejudice the Books commended by them to you. Peruse seriously the Books which Authority hath set forth. . . . Do as the Antient Non-Conformists did who would not separate though they feared to subscribe.'[2]

But if the Dissenters were to be wooed, the Court determined to woo them in its own way. Both Charles and James preferred that they should owe their freedom to Declarations of Indulgence issued by the Crown, rather than by their making common cause with the Church of England. In June 1683, there was a rumour going the rounds of the diocese that the Bishop of London, in company with Stillingfleet, Tillotson, Sharp and Burnet, had fallen under the King's displeasure, and that they were all to be 'suspended', 'because they were not so violent against the Dissenters'.[3] Only the Crown was to show them favour.

---

[1] R. Masters, *History of Corpus Christi*, p. 393.
[2] Quoted E. Carpenter, *op. cit.*, p. 94.
[3] Luttrell, *A Brief Historical Relation*, i. 246.

Compton was to move a long way from this position in later years, so much so that John Cockburne, a high Churchman, preaching the Bishop's funeral sermon in 1713, stated, though erroneously, that his Lordship had consistently 'opposed the Dissenters'.[1]

Whatever may have been Compton's policy during the reigns of Charles and James so far as a united Protestant front against the Roman Catholics was concerned, there could be no denying that the Dissenters often constituted a pastoral problem to many incumbents in the diocese of London. The clergy in Colchester, for example, where the eccentric Edmund Hickeringill professed as extreme a sympathy for Nonconformists as he did aversion to his diocesan, found relations with them difficult indeed. In 1682 Sir John Shaw, the Recorder of Colchester, complained bitterly to the Bishop 'of the great heat and zeal of some men, dissenters from the Church of England', whom he had hoped 'might have been very well content with that liberty which they had too long enjoyed without interruption'. In company with the former Mayor, he had embarked upon a visitation of all the conventicles in the city, and in one of them, so he told the Bishop, he found over five hundred persons present, though most of them were 'silly women and children'.[2]

The Vicar of Windsor, John Barrow, was undoubtedly disturbed at the activities of the Dissenters in his town, and sent a complaint to the Bishop of London. They had abandoned a meeting place on the outskirts of the city, he wrote, because it was too large and proposed now to adapt a barn right in the centre of the town, 'which being so near the Court must be most provoking'. ''Tis a great discouragement to myself,' the Vicar confessed to Compton, though he was convinced that 'the least stop put by authority in the building of the conventicle would in a short time reduce the whole town.' 'But our magistrates here', so he commented, 'live by their trades, and will not lose a customer to execute a law. If by your Lordship's means his Majesty were acquainted with what they are doing, it is possible he might think it for his own and the Church's service to give order to suppress it.'[3]

[1] *The Blessedness of Christians after Death*, p. 20.
[2] Shaw to Compton, 2 Oct., 1682, Bod. Rawlinson MSS. 983 C., fo. 59.
[3] *S.P.D.* Car. II, 15 Dec., 1681, 417, no. 274.

The Bishop was probably sympathetic, but perhaps not over energetic on the Vicar's behalf, a fact which may be inferred from Compton's later complaining to Dr. Fowler, Vicar of Cripplegate, that far too many incumbents in London presented Dissenters before the magistrates for no other reason than 'to make them odious'.[1]

The Bishop's practical dilemma in his dealings with Non-conformists—a dilemma resulting from a general desire to maintain a united Protestant front by being friendly, while at the same time not upsetting his own clergy—may be seen in his rather ambiguous relations with the saintly Richard Baxter, most reasonable and most loveable of Nonconformists.

Richard Baxter, though himself episcopally ordained, felt himself unable to identify himself fully with the Church of England after the failure of the Savoy Conference in 1662 to secure a comprehension. From then on till 1687 he suffered from a great deal of persecution. He was denied the use of the Chapel, which he himself had built in Oxenden Street in London, whereupon he bravely transferred himself to a Chapel in SwallowStreet, situated in a large and poor parish. Even here, however, he was not allowed to preach in peace. A local justice, one Parry, took out a warrant to apprehend him, and when Baxter arrived at the Chapel on 6 November, 1676, he found himself confronted by six constables and four beadles. He wisely decided not to attempt an entry; but instead consulted the Duke of Lauderdale, who advised him to approach the Bishop of London. Compton received Baxter kindly, and according to the latter's account, 'spake very fairly and with peaceable words'.[2] But news of this interview soon went the rounds, and opponents of the Bishop at Court—and they were many—'contrived that a noise was raised, that he was treating a Peace with the Presbyterians'.[3] Compton was on the horns of a dilemma, and as nothing happened, Baxter paid him a second visit. One word from the Bishop to Justice Parry, Baxter pointed out, would secure the removal of the constables from the chapel door, and the cancelling of the warrant. Thus entreated Compton 'did as good as promise . . . that he did not doubt to do it'. Such fair words, however,

---

[1] *S.P.D.* Car. II, 21 Apr. 1683, 423, no. 118.
[2] *Reliquiae Baxterianae*, 1696, Lib. i, Part iii, 178.
[3] *Ibid.*, Lib. i, Part iii, 178.

were not followed by any practical action. The constables continued at the Chapel door, and Baxter concludes his narrative of this sad story as follows: 'I came near the Bishop no more when I had so tried what their [*sic*] Kindnesses and Promises signifie.'[1]

Yet such an unhappy incident did not prevent Richard Baxter from naming Compton among the six moderate bishops to whom he dedicated his 'Apology for the Nonconformists' Ministry' (1681).

We need to remember, of course, that these years of the Exclusion Bill and the militant opposition of Shaftesbury were years of promise for the Dissenters. Thus they may be pardoned for not always seeing the contemporary scene through the eyes of a zealous Anglican. Certainly they were very active at this time. In July 1681, Josiah Ricraft, a magistrate of Middlesex,[2] wrote to the Bishop asking his guidance. 'Our Non-Conformists are building several new meeting houses', he complained, 'and since last Friday that the grand jury acquitted College,[3] they grow impudent, and unless the laws be put in execution against conventicles, I fear things will be worse.' Unfortunately, the justices themselves were divided as to what action ought to be taken. The Lieutenant of the Tower (Sir William Gulstone) agreed with the writer of the letter in wishing to put the law in execution, but the three 'new made justices' were apathetic. If only the Bishop would speak his mind strongly, Ricraft would try to overcome the scruples of his more luke-warm colleagues and begin straightway 'by convicting some of Meade's [4] proselytes and try what effects it will work'.[5]

Though Compton would not actively champion the rights of Baxter, it is unlikely that he gave a strong lead in supporting Josiah Ricraft.

[1] *Reliquiae Baxterianae*, 1696, Lib. i, Part iii, 178.

[2] Joseph Ricraft was formerly a prominent Presbyterian, but changed his principles at the time of the Restoration.

[3] Stephen College (1635?-81), 'the protestant joiner', began life as a Presbyterian but conformed at the Restoration. A virulent opponent of the Church of Rome, he appeared in arms at Oxford in 1681. He was arrested in London but a Bill against him was thrown out by the grand jury in July. He was, however, later executed in Oxford.

[4] Matthew Meade (1630?-99) was an independent divine in Stepney.

[5] Ricraft to Compton, 11 July, 1681, *S.P.D.* Car. II, 416, no. 49.

CHAPTER SIX

SUSPENSION

JAMES II came to the throne at a time which appeared most propitious for his designs. Following the collapse of the constitutional opposition, the last year of Charles's reign had been one of quiet and increasing loyalty to the Crown. The new monarch, therefore, entered his inheritance with the good wishes of his people. It throws much light on his unhappy genius that he should have forfeited them so completely that within a few years he was in exile.

The new King was known to be a fervent Roman Catholic, and to be inclined to despotism. What was not known, except to a few which included the Bishop of London, was that he entirely lacked that instinctive commonsense which frequently had saved his brother from disaster. Of more serious purpose than Charles, it was his firm intention both to increase the power of the Crown, and to foster the Roman Catholic religion by raising his fellow believers to full political status despite the laws of the realm. It was the conjunction of both these policies, and the pursuit of them together, without discretion, which finally spelt the ruin of both. Compromise was abhorrent to his kingly make-up (it was compromise, so he was convinced, which had brought his father to the block) and a vein of cruelty disinclined him to show mercy.

The first public impression, however, which James made on his subjects was a good one. A contemporary writes: 'All was serene and calm at first.'[1] His declaration to the Privy Council was sensible and restrained—so unlike his later harangues—and it was particularly acceptable to the bishops and their clergy. 'Since it had pleased God to place me', he said, 'in that Station to succeed so good and gracious a King, as well as so kind a Brother, I will endeavour to follow my Brother's Example, more especially in that of his great Clemency and Tenderness to his People. I have been accounted to be a man for Arbitrary Power, but that is not the only Story which has been made of me, and I shall

[1] *The Life of Dr. Henry Compton*, p. 14.

make it my Endeavours to preserve the Government both in Church and State, as it is by Law Established; and as I shall never depart from the just Rights and Prerogatives of the Crown, so I will never invade any Man's Property.'[1]

Had James remained true to this solemn promise, his destiny, and that of his royal House, would almost certainly have been different. The clergy, on the whole, were 'wonderfully pleased' at this declaration, and this was especially true in the diocese of London, where apprehension was, perhaps, the greatest. There followed a sudden outburst of gratitude, such as often accompanies release from tension, and it took the form, on the part of the clergy, of a desire 'to express their Loyalty to his Majesty and thanks for his gracious Assurance in his Address'. Compton felt it unwise to encourage the sending of innumerable effusions to the King, some of which he may have guessed, thus early, might later prove an embarrassment. Rather he himself drew up an Address, and sent a copy of it to his rural deans, 'that the whole diocese might express their unanimous thoughts in the same Words'.[2] It is significant that this Address included the phrase 'our religion established by law dearer to us than our lives'—a form of words which made it, says Burnet, 'very unacceptable'.[3] Nor was James the more pleased when such phraseology found its way into other Addresses.

The King was crowned by the Primate in Westminster Abbey on St. George's Day, 1685, though the new monarch insisted on having the Anglican rites curtailed. Compton attended the Queen throughout the ceremony, escorting her, with the Bishop of Winchester, into the 'theatre'; where, in common with the rest of his brethren, he kissed the King's left cheek as a sign of homage.[4]

This initial popularity of the new monarch was reflected in the elections to Parliament. The House of Commons, when it met on 19 May, was Royalist to the core, and James himself delightedly exclaimed that apart from some forty members, they were all such as he himself would have chosen. It is but fair to Henry Compton, in view of later developments, to notice that

[1] *The Life of Dr. Henry Compton*, pp. 14, 15.
[2] *Ibid.*, p. 14. Also B. M. Cole MSS. lii. 479.
[3] Burnet, *op. cit.*, iii. 7.
[4] Newcombe, *History of the Coronation of James II and Queen Mary*, 1687, p. 97.

he gave the King at this time his valuable support and before the elections wrote to his rural deans as follows:

> You will likewise now have an opportunity to give a real evidence of your profest Fidelity by using your utmost interest among the Gentry and other Freeholders, where you are acquainted, to give their voices for such sober and prudent men as will seek the peace of the Church and the State by promoting the King's and the Kingdom's service. I need not warn you of the great diligence used by the Enemies of both, to make choice of factious and turbulent spirits; and I hope the Truth and Justice of your Cause will make you no less industrious to prevent such wicked and pernicious designs, which bear so fatal an Aspect upon all honest men.[1]

The fears which many of the clergy, and Compton in particular, were thought to have entertained, appeared to some people now to be groundless. Perhaps responsibility was acting as a sobering influence. Loyalist sentiment was also fostered by the rash and irresponsible revolts of Argyle and Monmouth.

Yet though the situation might seem reassuring, and a contemporary could write that the Bishop of London 'seemed to stand pretty fair with the Court', yet Compton in fact had private reasons for not being so sanguine.

A few days after his accession, James had taken the initiative in calling the Archbishop of Canterbury and the Bishop of London to a private audience. A frank discussion of the King's position as a Roman Catholic sovereign in a Protestant country would undoubtedly have been helpful, but the conversation, unfortunately, was disappointing to both parties. Whatever the King offered with one hand, he seemed to take back with the other. With a large-minded generosity, not usual with him, he expressed the hope that their churches might be full, and he urged them to see that their clergy did something about this; but at the same time he said that there must be no preaching against the Roman Catholic religion.[2]

It was the first intimation of the coming storm—a cloud, as yet no bigger than a man's hand, which was later to rain a torrent on the nation.

Though reassuring to the Privy Council, James determined from the outset to leave no ambiguity concerning his own faith.

---

[1] Compton to Strype, 21 Feb., 1685, B.M. Cole MSS., lii. p. 479.
[2] L. Von Ranke, *History of England*, Oxford, 1875, iv. p. 218.

His first step was to have Mass celebrated publicly in defiance of the laws of the land on the second Sunday after his accession, an indiscretion which aroused great anger throughout the country, particularly in London. James's reaction to popular resentment, however, was usually immediate and often violent. He determined to stand his ground, and he again summoned Sancroft and Compton, together with such other bishops as were in town, (10 March) to Whitehall. In unambiguous language the King told them what his policy was to be. 'I will keep my word', he promised, 'and will undertake nothing against the religion established by law, assuming that you do your duty towards me; if you fail therein, you must not expect that I shall protect you. I shall readily find the means of attaining my ends without your help.'[1]

Sancroft and Compton could not fail to notice 'the vivacity of his expression', the threats that he used, and his regarding the whole matter as involving his personal honour. They themselves said little for James was never a man to argue with, and Compton wisely regarded himself as not sufficiently *persona grata* to attempt it. But they both went home full of forebodings for the future, convinced in their own minds that the 'misunderstanding' would increase rather than diminish, and already in a mood to consider 'what steps should be taken to enable them to resist in Parliament'.[2]

It is not our intention, however, to give a detailed account of the course of James's tempestuous reign, except in so far as it is necessary to indicate the part which Compton played in it.

The bloody reprisals which James exacted after Sedgemoor undoubtedly shocked the more sensitive consciences of many even of his own supporters. 'This marble', remarked John Churchill, as he struck the mantel-shelf against which he was leaning, 'is not harder than the King's heart.' It was true. James's policy of promoting Roman Catholics to office in defiance of the law, and his dismissal of Halifax, the Trimmer (21 October, 1685),

---

[1] Lingard, *History of England*, xiv. 10-11 and Note A, p. 289. Also Von Ranke, *op. cit.*, iv. p. 218.

[2] Von Ranke, *op. cit.*, iv. 218. Barrillon (the French Ambassador) suggests (Lingard, *op. cit.*, 289) that there were at the time two parties among the Bishops, one led by Sancroft, more Royalist and less hostile to James's Catholic policy, the other by Compton which was out to suppress both Romanism and Dissent. The diagnosis would seem to be much over-simplified.

because he refused to support any attempt to repeal the Test Act, made clear to all his subjects the King's real intentions. They were made even more apparent when he encouraged the opening of a Jesuit school in the Savoy, and urged on by this Society, proceeded to attempt the Romanisation of England with an energy which alarmed even Innocent XI.

Among the bishops, Compton stood pre-eminent as the determined enemy of Rome, and the head of the Church of England opposition to the king's policy. William Sancroft, though his devotion to the *Ecclesia Anglicana* was deep and sincere, yet lacked that toughness of fibre and militant temperament which earned for his brother of London the title 'The Protestant Bishop'. Compton's efforts to win over the Dissenters during Charles's reign, his unwearied labours on behalf of the French refugees fleeing from their Roman Catholic sovereign, and his anti-papal activities generally, inevitably drew down upon his head the relentless hostility of the imperious monarch who now reigned. Fortunately by means of his series of 'Conferences', to which we have already referred, Compton undoubtedly won the confidence of his own clergy, and their loyalty was to stand him in good stead later on. That the clergy of the metropolis were able to speak their minds freely in their pulpits, and thus openly oppose his Roman Catholic policy, was, of course, a constant irritation to the King. Particularly did the lecturers in the city, who included some of the most famous preachers of the day— Sherlock, Clagett, Fowler, and Horneck—call forth James's anger by their forceful preaching and powerful apologia. With his usual impetuosity, he determined to bring what he regarded as this intolerable situation to an end. Towards the close of 1685 he therefore summoned the Archbishop of Canterbury to an audience and told him bluntly that the Bishop of London must suppress these afternoon lectures, giving as the reason for this peremptory command—it was too naïve even for the guileless Sancroft—'that there might be more time for catechizing'.[1]

This embarrassing message was dutifully passed on by the Archbishop to his brother of London. The Bishop was not, of

---

[1] Bod. Tanner MSS. 31, fo. 268. It is only fair to James to admit that earlier some lecturers had succeeded 'in ousting from many churches the good old custom of catechizing in favour of afternoon sermons'. (See J. H. Overton, *Life in the English Church*, 1660-1714, 1885, p. 190.)

course, taken in by the King's zeal for the catechism; and it did not take him long to make up his mind that he most certainly would not comply with the royal wishes. To make his own position the more clear, he drew up a paper which he gave to Sancroft and which, we may assume, found its way in due course to the royal closet.

These lectures, the Bishop of London explained, were legally established by the Act of Uniformity, and they could not therefore be silenced in this arbitrary manner. Before admission to office, every lecturer had to satisfy the Bishop of the diocese of his conformity with the Church of England, so 'it was not easy for an ill man to come in'. In fact, Compton pointed out, 'there is not one lecturer that I know of now in being who was ever charged for preaching anything in his lecture against the reputation of church and state'. Rather, in the late King's reign, they did 'frankly contribute to the appeasing of them as might be instanced in many particulars'.[1]

Compton realised, of course, as did everybody else, that the King's desire to suppress these lectures arose solely from the anti-Roman Catholic sentiments which many of the lecturers did not hesitate to express. Here the Bishop felt it better to be frank, and he made three comments. First, he promised that if any of them made 'an indecent use of their liberty' he would see that they were 'corrected and reproved according to the measure of the fault'. Secondly (and this must have been most unwelcome to James), 'a modest latitude' he maintained, 'must be allowed on this point whilst we are admitted to assert our own Religion, because many of our Doctrines do necessarily engage us to it'. Thirdly, the suppression of these lectures would not of itself stimulate catechizing, which he had himself constantly done his best to encourage.

He concluded with what may well have been a touch of sarcasm—that he 'did most heartily bless God that has put it into the King's heart to further so good a work amongst us'.[2]

James could not have been pleased with this assertion of episcopal independence.

Nor was Compton's conduct in the House of Lords at this time calculated to mitigate the King's wrath, for he vehemently opposed James's appointing Roman Catholic officers in the army

---

[1] Bod. Tanner MSS. 31, fo. 268.
[2] *Ibid.*

contrary to law. In an intemperate speech to both Houses of
Parliament, in November, informing them of his resolve to do
this, the King had made no effort to conceal his intentions. 'I am
determined not to part with any servants on whose fidelity I
can rely', he said, 'and whose help I might perhaps soon need.'

These were not wise words. They were a deliberate challenge,
and though the Lords first voted formal thanks for this royal
harangue, William Cavendish, Earl of Devonshire, proposed that
a day should be fixed for debating the speech. The Bishop of
London led his brethren, the bishops, in supporting this rather
exceptional procedure. He was no great orator, for his voice
was low and gruff, but he was usually very much to the point.
One who was present on this occasion says that he 'spake long,
calmly, and with great respect and Deference to his Majesty,
yet very full and home'. Ranke writes of this oration that it was
'in a historical point of view, one of the most remarkable speeches
ever made in Parliament'.[1] Certainly it created a great impression
in the country at a time 'when two great powers, usually
opposed to each other, France and Austria, were exerting themselves to the utmost for the promotion of Catholicism'.

In the course of his speech, Compton remarked that it was
clear to the whole nation that the King's appointment of Roman
Catholic officers was but the prelude to their being introduced
into the higher administrative posts. England would then
become a Roman Catholic state. 'The laws of England were like
the dykes of Holland, and universal Catholicism like the ocean—
if the laws were once broken, inundation would follow.' He
concluded with these solemn words: 'I am empowered to speak
the mind of my brethren, and in their opinion, and in my own, the
whole civil and religious constitution of the realm is in danger.'[2]
As he finished, the bench of Bishops stood up to acclaim him.

James soon left no doubt as to what he thought of these
indications of episcopal opposition to his sovereign will. His
reaction was typical of the man. On 2 December it was common
talk that the Bishop of London had been 'removed from his place
as Dean of the Chapels Royal', an office which was given to the
more accommodating Bishop of Durham; and that he was also

[1] *Op. cit.*, iv. 277.
[2] *The Life of Dr. Henry Compton*, p. 16. See also F. C. Turner, *James II*, 1948,
p. 295.

to be replaced as Clerk of the Closet by the Bishop of Rochester.[1] Nor was this all, for two days before Christmas, the King was 'pleased to blot the Bishop of London's name out of the Council Book'—that is, he ceased to be a member of the Privy Council. The reason was obvious to all, though Christopher Musgrave, member of Parliament for Carlisle said it was best known to the King himself, and the wits in the coffee houses facetiously suggested that it was due to the Bishop's travelling into the country on a Sunday morning to marry his nephew the Earl of Northampton to Lady Conway.[2] The fact was, of course, that Compton had become so personally obnoxious to James that the King determined to rid himself of his attendance at Court altogether.

It was now inevitable that during the next few months King and Bishop should be brought increasingly into conflict. Another and equally serious *casus belli*, deliberately chosen by James, soon gave further cause for trouble. The victims this time were the French refugees.

It is, perhaps, understandable that the King's reception of these unfortunate people was as cold as that of many of his subjects was friendly. Particularly was it annoying to his pride that there should be a refugee community in the Savoy established there by his brother, and he endeavoured to offset its influence by founding a Jesuit school in the same neighbourhood which he hoped might serve as an active centre for Roman Catholic propaganda. French Protestants were always anathema to James and this congregation in the Savoy was particularly odious. He now determined that if these refugees would not conform to the Church of Rome at least they should conform in all respects to the Church of England.

As on a former occasion, he summoned the Archbishop of Canterbury, more malleable than Compton, and committed to him the unenviable task of communicating his wishes to the Bishop of London. Once again Compton firmly refused to act in a manner that he regarded as clean contrary to the terms of the original foundation. His brief letter to Sancroft explaining his position was very much to the point. 'It would be an insolent

---

[1] *H.M.C.* Downshire MSS., vol. 1, Parts i and ii, 1924, p. 83.

[2] *Ibid.* App. ii, Report XIV, p. 392 (Portland MSS.). The marriage, as a matter of fact, did not take place, and the result was a duel between the relatives of the contracting parties in Kentish Town fields. See *H.M.C.* Downshire MSS., vol. 1, Parts i and ii, p. 123.

demand in me', he wrote, 'to require more of the French Church in the Savoy, than the late King himself did in the constitution of them, which only requires their Conformity according to the Usage of Guernsey and Jersey, where never surplice or sign of the Cross were ever used or required: and where they have long taken care of their Churches by way of Consistory.'[1]

James's response to opposition, as we have already seen, was usually uncomplicated, and it was not long before he found a further opportunity of manifesting his displeasure. The occasion was as petty as his mind. By long custom, all appointments to naval chaplaincies passed through the hands of the Bishop of London, perhaps because of the ill-defined overseas jurisdiction which had come to be associated with this See. The navy had always been a special interest to James, and it is but fair to admit that his devotion to it was greatly to its advantage. He now instructed the Admiralty, in July 1686, that appointments for the future must pass, not through the hands of the Bishop of London, but through the Archbishop of Canterbury.[2] It was an act of spite typical of the man in some of his moods.

It may well be that it is to this period that the following story belongs, which is recorded by Granger in his *Biographical History of England*. The King was discoursing with the Bishop on some 'tender point', and was 'so little pleased with his answers that he told him he talked more like a Colonel than a Bishop'. Compton replied coldly that 'his Majesty did him honour in taking notice of his having formerly drawn his sword in defence of the constitution, and that he should do the same again if he lived to see it necessary'—words which proved to be prophetic.[3]

All these tokens of the King's acute displeasure were but the prelude to a final offensive, which he was soon to launch against the unfortunate Bishop. One ecclesiastical office alone remained to him, that of Bishop of the diocese of London, and James determined that he should not long exercise even this. His contemporary biographer writes that the position which he held both at home and abroad inevitably made him the 'mark of the Enemy and Hatred of the Romish Party at Court, which had for

---

[1] Compton to Sancroft, 12 May, 1686, Bod. Rawlinson MSS. 983 C., fo. 120.
[2] Bod. Tanner MSS. 30, fo. 87.
[3] Granger, *Biographical History of England*, iv. 283.

some time born a particular Grudge to his Lordship on another Account.'[1]

We have already seen that the King regarded anti-Roman Catholic teaching from Protestant pulpits as a personal insult, and so early in his reign as 15 March 1685, as Supreme Ordinary, he had tried to deal with such affronts in a series of Injunctions issued to the two Archbishops, the sum total of which was 'to forbid Anglican clergy discussing the controverted points of doctrine in the pulpit'. Compton felt deeply, as the months went by and James's policy became more extreme, that he could not let this effort to muzzle the Church of England clergy pass unchallenged—particularly as Roman Catholic propaganda was daily increasing. His regular Conferences with his clergy seemed to provide an opportunity to take public notice of the situation and in 1686 he addressed himself boldly to this subject. He did not mince his words.

Nothing could be more 'pernicious' to Prince or people, he protested, 'than to carry the duty of Submission beyond the Bounds of Reason and due Patience'. True the clergy ought not to bring disputes between Prince and people into the pulpit, but on the other hand, 'if we exalt the King's prerogative above the Law, we do as good tell the people, that notwithstanding their Rights, the King may ravish their wives, spoil their Goods, and cut their throats at Pleasure'.[2]

In unambiguous language he then warned his clergy of the abuse which 'wicked and profane men' would make of the King's 'Notion of having a dispensing Power in himself'; and he concluded his discourse with solemn words, which must have been particularly obnoxious to the King:

We have a Prince of another Religion, who for that Reason cannot choose but be most influenced by our adversaries; and what the Mercies of that Religion are, when exercis'd to the Height, we all very well know. What if we have his Royal Word never so solemnly passed? There is no reason we should expect it to be made good, than we on our part constantly behave ourselves. . . . The least we can expect from one so wedded to that religion is that he should promote it all he could. And therefore should we make

---

[1] *The Life of Dr. Henry Compton*, p. 16. The 'other Account' was his opposing in Parliament the appointment of Roman Catholic officers. See p. 84.

[2] *The Bishop of London's Seventh Letter*, 1690, p. 3.

any default, it is but reasonable for us to expect, that he should endeavour to rid us out of the way.[1]

Nothing could have been more outspoken. It was a declaration of war on the part of the Bishop, and recalls what he said to a friend: 'that 'twas his Duty to discharge his Conscience, to offer the Prince good and impartial Advice, and prevent evil or rectify it.'[2]

Yet though James might issue Injunctions, the feeling among the clergy was so strong that he could not possibly enforce them. Nor could the King rely on the co-operation of the bishops. Even such a Tory as William Sherlock, Dean of St. Paul's, was unable to remain silent in the face of constant Roman Catholic provocation, and as a result he lost his pension. John Sharp, Dean of Norwich and Rector of St. Giles, a fervent and honest high churchman (later Archbishop of York), found himself in an even more serious difficulty. He had received a letter, supposedly from a member of his congregation,[3] asking how the Church of England could really claim to be a true part of the Church of Christ. Such an appeal for guidance, bearing upon the whole theological basis of the *Ecclesia Anglicana*, could not, he thought, be allowed to pass unnoticed. On the Sunday following, therefore, Sharp proceeded to deal with this question, and in the course of his sermon he made some very severe remarks on the claims of the Church of Rome, calling its adherents 'idolaters'.[4]

His discourse aroused great interest and exaggerated reports of what he had said soon reached the ears of the King. Particularly did malicious gossip report that the Vicar had commented with scorn on certain documents in the late King's strong-box which James himself had caused to be published.[5]

In the King's eyes, Sharp's sermon was a deliberate violation of his express command, and he prepared to take action, the more so as it provided a further means of 'getting at' the Bishop of London. On Thursday, 17 June, he accordingly dispatched a letter drawn up at Windsor three days before, to the Bishop at Fulham.

---

[1] *The Bishop of London's Seventh Letter*, 1690, p. 18.
[2] Cockburne, *op. cit.*, p. 24.
[3] More probably, Dr. A. T. Hart suggests (*The Life and Times of John Sharp*, 1949, p. 92) it was 'concocted by a Roman priest with the deliberate design of catching him out in his words'.
[4] *H.M.C. Downshire MSS.*, Vol. 1, Parts i and ii, p. 185.
[5] White Kennett, *A Complete History of England*, 1719, iii, 429-30.

We need little imagination to visualize Compton breaking the seal of this letter with gloomy forebodings. He was not left long in doubt as to the King's latest intentions.

He 'had been informed', and was 'fully satisfied', James wrote, that in spite of his orders the Vicar of St. Giles 'hath in some of his Sermons since preached, presumed to make some unbecoming reflections, endeavouring thereby to beget in the Minds of his Hearers an evil Opinion of Us and Our Government, and to lead them into Disobedience and Rebellion'.

This being so, the Bishop must 'immediately upon Receipt thereof, forthwith suspend him from farther preaching in any Parish Church or Chappel in your Diocese, until he has given us Satisfaction, and our farther Pleasure be known herein; and for your so doing, this shall be your Warrant'.[1]

Compton immediately recognised that he was placed in a most invidious position, and that it was the King's deliberate intention to embarrass him. He was already out of favour at Court; dismissed from the Privy Council, and from his office as Dean of the Chapels Royal. He could not welcome another conflict with James, yet as the recognised leader of the Protestant clergy in London, he could hardly be expected to co-operate in silencing one of his own supporters. To give way timidly and to suspend Sharp would appear an act of shocking weakness, and would certainly undermine his position with his own clergy.

Also the King's directive to the Bishop assumed an attitude to the royal prerogative which Compton had gone out of his way explicitly to condemn. 'The design of the Letter', a contemporary points out, 'was absolutely to forbid preaching against Popery, and the effect of it might be to suspend all the Eminent Preachers in England.'

[1] For the story of these events in detail, we are dependent on an account which Compton himself drew up, and in which he reproduced the relevant documents. This account was published in different pamphlets in substantially the same form. See B.M. Add. MSS., Egerton 2543. Also *A true Narrative of all the Proceedings against the Bishop of London by the Lords Commissioners appointed by his Majesty to inspect Ecclesiastical Affairs*, London, 1689. *An Exact Account of the Whole Proceedings against the Right Reverend Father in God, Henry Lord Bishop of London, before the Lord Chancellor and the other Ecclesiastical Commissioners*, London, 1688. *The Life of Dr. Henry Compton*, pp. 17-39. These four accounts are based on: *A Transcript of sevall transactions relating to the Rt. Reverend Father in God, Henry Lord Bishop of London, taken from the memorials thereof written by himself*, Bod. Tanner MSS. 303, fo. 126 and MSS. 460, fo. 72. I have also consulted A. T. Hart, *Life and Times of John Sharp*.

The Bishop immediately summoned Sharp to meet him at Doctors' Commons and showed him the King's letter. The Vicar of St. Giles was genuinely distressed, for he was at heart a Royalist, and he protested that he had no desire to offend his Majesty, but was willing to give him full satisfaction. Compton thereupon wisely 'desired and advised him to forbear the pulpit till the King's further pleasure be known'.[1] At the same time the Bishop hurriedly consulted his legal advisers and the position which they counselled him to adopt, and which he adhered to throughout his subsequent trial, may be seen in the following letter which he wrote to the Earl of Sunderland.

My Lord,
   I always have and shall count it my Duty to obey the King in whatsoever Commands he lays upon me, that I can perform with a safe Conscience; but in this I humbly conceive I am obliged to proceed according to Law and therefore it is impossible for me to comply; because though his Majesty commands me only to execute his Pleasure, yet in the Capacity I am to do it, I must act as a Judge: and your Lordship knows no Judge condemns any Man before he has Knowledge of the Cause, and has cited the Party. However, I sent to Mr. Dean,[2] and acquainted him with his Majesty's Displeasure, whom I find so ready to give all reasonable Satisfaction that I have thought fit to make him the Bearer of this Answer from him that will never be unfaithful to the King.[3]

The Vicar of St. Giles—he was genuinely upset at having so thoroughly brought upon himself the royal wrath—also drew up 'A humble Petition to the King's most Excellent Majesty'.
   In this document he confessed ingenuously that nothing was so 'afflictive' to him 'as his unhappiness to have incurred your Majesty's Displeasure', for which reason 'he hath forborn all public Exercise of his Function and still continues so to do'. If he had inadvertently offended, then he asked his Majesty's pardon, and promised to be more careful for the future.[4]
   Sharp, at his own request, set out with his petition, and the Bishop of London's letter, to Hampton Court on Saturday, 19 June, confidently expecting that the whole affair would now

---

[1] *Life of John Sharp*, by his son Thomas Sharp, 1825, i. 81.
[2] Sharp was Dean of Norwich.
[3] *The Life of Dr. Henry Compton*, p. 19.
[4] *Ibid.*, p. 21.

blow over. His reception, however, soon showed him that this was not to be the case. He was not admitted to the royal presence, but Sunderland bluntly asked him one question: 'Whether the Bishop had obeyed the order?' The Vicar of St. Giles could only reply 'no', whereupon Sunderland refused to receive his petition. The distressed Sharp hung on at Hampton Court, but in vain. The Council broke up and he returned to London.[1]

But Sharp was reluctant to leave the matter there, and when the Court removed to Windsor, he presented his petition to Lord Middleton. This second move was no more successful, however, because when Lord Middleton brought the matter up at the Cabinet Council 'his Majesty would not suffer it to be read'.[2]

It was obvious that James did not want an accommodation except on the terms of unconditional surrender, for he had already decided on another and more extreme course of action.

To understand the new policy upon which he now determined we must return to the month of April when James had announced, to use a somewhat exaggerated phrase of Macaulay's, that 'he had entrusted the whole government of the Church to seven Commissioners'.[3] The word 'Commission' certainly had a nasty ring. From this Court there was to be no appeal: its members were both prosecuting counsel and jury: they were not required to furnish the accused with a copy of his charge: they were bound by no recognised rules of court procedure.

It is not surprising that when James's design became known, it evoked widespread opposition from both churchmen and lawyers. 'Men of penetration could not conceive that a Protestant Church could long be safe under the administration of a Popish Prince.' Even James hesitated for a while, but this latest opposition goaded him on.

The personnel of this new Court was significant. The chief Commissioner was the Lord Chancellor, the notorious Judge Jeffreys, fresh from his ruthless and bloody Assize, in which he had browbeaten into confession many a poor country yokel who had taken up arms under Monmouth. Perhaps more important in respect of the case he was soon to try, Jeffreys was still smarting under a snub administered to him in the House of Lords by the

---

[1] Sharp, *Life of Archbishop Sharp*, i. 84.   [2] *Ibid.*, i. 85.
[3] Macaulay, *History of England* (Everyman), i. 579.

Bishop of London.[1] Associated with Jeffreys were three ecclesiastics and three laymen. First was Sancroft, Archbishop of Canterbury, but his conscientious regard for the law of the land would not allow him to serve, though his natural timidity and personal loyalty to James induced him to decline on the grounds of failing health. Then came Nathaniel Crewe, Bishop of Durham, a servile flatterer of the King, who had followed Compton in the office of Dean of the Chapels Royal; and Thomas Sprat, Bishop of Rochester, indolent, kindly and venal, at this time casting covetous eyes on the vacant Archbishopric of York. The three lay Commissioners were the Lord Treasurer Rochester, son of the Earl of Clarendon, who overcame his own scruples in accepting office by persuading himself that he could at least prevent some mischief to the Church, and at the same time keep a salary of £4,000 a year; the Lord President Sunderland, a Roman Catholic; and the Lord Chief Justice Herbert, who had already proved himself a very willing and obedient tool in the King's hands.

On Tuesday, 3 August, the Commissioners met and opened their Commission. Their first act was immediately to send a citation to the Bishop of London, summoning him to appear before them on Monday, 9 August, to answer such matters as 'on his Majesty's behalf shall and there be objected against him'.[2] News of this imperious summons soon leaked out. There was great gossip in the coffee houses: news-letters throughout England and to Ireland contained much speculation: diarists such as Nathaniel Luttrell were full of alarm for the future.

On Monday, 9 August, the Bishop of London, under no illusions, doubtless, as to the severity of his ordeal, duly appeared before the Commissioners at Whitehall. The Lord Chancellor opened the proceedings by bluntly remarking that the Bishop was aware of the King's Injunctions to the Archbishops, against which Sharp had undoubtedly offended : and that he also knew that the Commissioners were empowered to take cognisance of all ecclesiastical offences. The question that the Bishop must answer therefore was a very simple one: why had he not suspended

---

[1] *The Harleian Miscellany*, ed. William Oldys, London, 1809, p. 594, writes that Compton 'distinguished himself in the House of Lords by a severe rebuff to the insolence of Jeffreys'.

[2] *An Exact Account*, p. 11.

Dr. Sharp for preaching sedition against the Government when the King had expressly commanded him to do so?

Compton, speaking with dignity and restraint, answered that the question was, perhaps, not quite so simple as this. In what he had done, he had followed the best legal advice, and if his counsel had misled him, he hoped that he might be excused—a plea which we are not surprised drew forth from Jeffreys the obvious rejoinder: *Ignorantia juris non excusat.*

The Bishop then asked for a copy of the Commission, and of the charge against him. Both were reasonable requests in a court of law, but the Lord Chancellor, who dominated the proceedings, peremptorily refused. The Commissioners, he said angrily, were 'quite satisfied upon what account they met'—and anyhow the Bishop might obtain a copy of the Commission at any coffee house.[1] Compton again protested that he had been quite unable to procure a copy, and that as a peer and a bishop occupying a public station, and before a Court from which there was no appeal, it was necessary for him to read the terms of the Commission under which the Court met. The Commissioners then withdrew for a quarter of an hour, and on re-assembling the President reaffirmed that the Bishop could not have a copy of the Commission, nor of the charge against him, which simply was: 'Why did he not obey the King and suspend Dr. Sharp?'

Seeing that it was quite useless to press these two requests, Compton now asked that at least he might be allowed reasonable time to prepare his defence, particularly since it was August, and most lawyers were out of town. 'You can get counsel', interjected Jeffreys rudely and with heavy humour, 'unless you can be satisfied with none but those that be abroad.' Finally the Lord Chancellor agreed to an adjournment for a bare week, since 'the King's affairs will not suffer long time'.[2]

The Bishop of London's behaviour had been dignified throughout, and as he withdrew, he expressed the hope that there 'would be some consideration shown of his Family's and his own Sufferings and constant Loyalty'.

On Monday, 16 August, the Bishop again appeared before the Commission, bringing with him his brother Sir Francis Compton, his nephew the Earl of Northampton, his brother-in-law, Sir John Nicholas, 'and several other Persons of Quality'.[3]

[1] *An Exact Account*, p. 11.   [2] *Ibid.*, p. 13.   [3] *A True Narrative*, p. 4.

The Bishop immediately acquainted the Commissioners that in spite of the assurance that he would find a copy of the Commission at any coffee house, he had in fact been quite unable to procure one till yesterday: and had therefore had no time to see whether it could have reference to him as a peer, or could be made to extend to the particular charge brought against him. Thus he definitely needed more time to prepare his defence. 'Well put, well put, my Lord speaks nothing but truth', shouted Sir Thomas Clarges from the back of the Council Chamber.[1]

Jeffreys began the proceedings with one of his very rare apologies. 'When I had said that Copies of the Commission were in every Coffee House', he explained rather sheepishly, 'I did not mean by that that your Lordship frequented such Places but that the Commission was common [talk] in the Town.'[2] As to the objections against their jurisdiction, however, the Commissioners could not even consider them, for 'they were well assured of the legality of it, otherwise they would not be such fools as to sit here'.

After further discussion, it was at length agreed that Compton should have a fortnight in which to prepare his defence. As the Court filed out, Sir John Lowther, later first Viscount Lonsdale (1655-1700) was heard to remark: 'There are some who have represented me as a Papist, but the contrary shall appear; I will not be ashamed nor afraid to vindicate my Lord Bishop of London's cause before the Commissioners themselves.'[3]

Excitement and interest were now growing, and when Compton appeared before the Commissioners on 31 August, an even greater number of 'Persons of Distinction' attended with him. He had now had time to consult counsel, and with him were Drs. Oldish, Hedges, Newton and Brise, all of whom were men who had risen to eminence in their profession.

The trial (if we can prostitute the word to use it in this context) began with Compton affirming that he had no desire whatever to argue the royal supremacy, or to say anything 'undutiful to the King', yet he had been advised by the civilians whom he had consulted 'that the Proceedings of the Court were directly contrary to the Law of the Land, and his Lawyers were ready to make it good if they might be heard'.[4] Moreover, he must insist that

---

[1] B.M. Egerton MSS. 2543, fo. 257.
[2] H.M.C. Verulam MSS. 1906, p. 90.
[3] *The Life of Dr. Henry Compton*, p. 27.   [4] *Ibid.*

he had 'the right, according to the laws of the Christian Church of all ages, and in particular in the Constitutions of the Church of England, to be tried by his Metropolitan'.[1] Finally, he maintained that the Commissioners could not be competent to try any misdemeanours alleged to have taken place before the Commission was taken out.

These objections were again summarily over-ruled as being directed against the jurisdiction of the Court, and for the same reason the Commissioners refused to accept the written plea which the Bishop had brought with him.[2] In this document the Bishop specified the statutes under which the setting up of a Court of Ecclesiastical Commission was declared utterly illegal.

As Compton had begun by questioning the jurisdiction of the Court, it might have been expected that he would refuse to plead when the objection was thus over-ruled. In fact this is what Sancroft thought he should have done, for to plead subsequently was a tacit recognition of the Court's legality.[3]

As this question of jurisdiction had been disposed of, at least to the satisfaction of the Lord Chancellor, the Court now asked the Bishop to give his answer to the only question which really mattered—why had he not suspended Dr. Sharp pursuant to the King's command? The Bishop's reply to this specific charge was then read by Mr. Bridgeman, and it followed the general lines of his earlier letter to the Earl of Sunderland. Immediately upon receiving the King's letter, he said, he took legal advice and was informed that since it was addressed to him as Bishop of London, he must act as a judge, and in this capacity he could not suspend any of his clergy 'before such a clergyman was called on, or admitted to make his defence'. He had represented this to the Lord President in order that he might receive further instructions from His Majesty but had heard no more. In the meantime he had advised Dr. Sharp 'to forbear preaching till he had applied himself to the King'; and he then awaited 'his Majesty's further Orders to proceed against him judicially in case he should not at that time give His Majesty the satisfaction required'.[4]

To this written statement the Bishop added verbally that if the word 'suspend' be interpreted in its strict judicial sense, it

---

[1] We may be sure that Sancroft would not have welcomed such a procedure.
[2] The written plea was later printed.
[3] D'Oyly, *Life of Sancroft*, 1821, i. 232. [4] *An Exact Account*, p. 26.

must entail a citation followed by a legal process, and even at the command of the King this procedure could not be dispensed with. If on the other hand 'to suspend' merely meant to silence, then he had in reality obeyed the royal wishes.

The Bishop of London's counsel then proceeded to enlarge upon his verbal statement with a wealth of precedent and common practice, into the intricacies of which, however, we will not follow them. They maintained that Compton had most certainly obeyed the King in so far as he could legally do so: that no matter how much the Bishop might be anxious to please his Majesty he could not suspend any of his clergy *ab officio* without acting in the capacity of a judge. 'I affirm', said Dr. Hedges, 'if a Prince or a Pope command that which is not lawful, it is the duty of a judge *rescribere*, which is all that he can do.'[1]

This, of course, was the crux of the whole matter. 'As in nature', added Dr. Newton, 'no Man can be required to do that which is impossible, so no man can be obliged to do an unlawful act. This Rule obliges all Men in the World, in all Places, and at all Times.'[2] Even the word of the King could not make an unlawful act lawful.

At the end of the hearing, Compton asked for a copy of the minutes of the proceedings. 'I know no minutes they keep', said Jeffreys, and the request was refused. The Bishop was then commanded to appear again before the Commissioners on Monday, 6 September, when the verdict was to be given.

There seems, according to Burnet, to have been some difference of opinion among the Commissioners when they came to deliberate. Jeffreys and the Bishop of Durham, the former the most forthright the latter the most servile, of James's supporters, were for suspension during the King's pleasure. The Bishop of Rochester and the Lord Chief Justice mustered their courage and were for acquittal.[3] The Earl of Rochester also at first favoured a verdict of 'not guilty', but when he learnt that the price of such a betrayal of the King's interests was likely to mean his having to part with the white staff, his passion for office overcame his scruples.[4]

On Monday, 6 September, after being kept waiting some two

---

[1] *An Exact Account*, p. 26.   [2] *Ibid.*
[3] *A Letter from the Bishop of Rochester*, 1688, p. 12.
[4] Burnet, *op. cit.*, iii. 111.

hours, the Bishop heard Mr. Bridgeman pronounce the sentence of the Court as follows:

Whereas Henry, Lord Bishop of London, has been convened before us, for his Disobedience, and other his Contempts mentioned in the Proceedings of this Cause; and the said Bishop having fully been heard thereupon, we have thought fit upon mature Consideration of the Matter to proceed to this our definitive Sentence, declaring, decreeing, and pronouncing, That the said Henry, Lord Bishop of London, shall for his said Disobedience and Contempt, be suspended during His Majesty's pleasure: And accordingly we do by these presents suspend him the said Lord Bishop of London; peremptorily admonishing and requiring him thereby to abstain from the Function and Execution of his Episcopal Office; and from All Episcopal and other Ecclesiastical Jurisdiction, during the said Suspension, upon pain of Deprivation and Removal from his Bishopric. Given under our Hand and Seal the 6th day of September, 1686.[1]

The Order was not signed by the Commissioners, probably because of their disagreement, though it appeared under the joint authority of their seal.

The Bishop again showed great dignity, for having been refused permission to speak before the passing of the sentence, he silently withdrew, wisely regarding it as 'folly to speak afterwards'.[2]

A few days later a warrant was issued to the Dean and Chapter of St. Paul's Cathedral 'to cause the said Sentence to be affixed on the Door of the Chapter House, and on the Place now called the South Door of the said Church; to the end that Public Notice may be taken of the said Suspension'.[3]

On 20 September, the Dean and Chapter met to certify under their seal that the sentence had been exhibited for 'a competent space of time'. On the same day they made two solemn protestations, first, that what they had done pursuant to the Order of the Ecclesiastical Commissioners was 'an Act merely Ministerial'; and second, 'that in case the Episcopal See of London be now void by the Suspension of the Lord Bishop, which, from good advice

---

[1] *An Exact Account*, p. 29.   [2] *Ibid.*
[3] B.M. Add. MSS. 15, fo. 551. The copy of the sentence (with three small pin holes in it) which was fastened to the door at St. Paul's is still in the Cathedral Library.

they are informed is not, Or when the same shall so certified to be void, They are and shall be ready and willing to nominate 2 or 3 of the Major Canons of the said Cathedral Church . . . and to send the names of such persons to his Grace, the Lord Archbishop of Cant[erbury] to the end his Grace may choose and constitute an Official of London to exercise all manner of Episcopal Jurisdiction during the said Vacancy.'[1]

But not all James's servants were so accommodating as some of the Commissioners or even as the Dean and Chapter of St. Paul's. Mr. Franklyn, the King's Proctor, resigned his office rather than involve himself in the promulgation of a sentence of which he so heartily disapproved.[2]

There was no appeal from the Court of Ecclesiastical Commission so that unless Compton were to defy the King there was nothing more that he could do.

Comment on the case is, perhaps, superfluous. Even if it be allowed (which no reasonable person can easily allow) that the King in 1686 as 'Supreme Governor of the Church of England' was bound in the discharge of this supremacy by no canons or statutes, but that his sovereign will could express itself solely according to his own royal pleasure—even if we allow this fantastic hypothesis it can still hardly be denied that the suspension of Compton was an act of tyranny largely motivated by personal animosity. The Bishop had in fact gone as far as was reasonable in obeying the King and had silenced Sharp for the time being.

James himself in his 'Memoirs' admits that the prosecution was generally thought a 'harsh proceeding', but his defence of his own conduct is not very convincing. It was clear, he says, that the Bishop 'was not sincere and hearty in the matter'. Either he questioned his authority to command, or had deliberately disobeyed him. In fact, James pleaded, it was a sign of his own royal moderation that he had been content with a suspension, and had not insisted on deprivation.[3] Others, however, ascribed this 'clemency' to different motives, for had James gone so far as this, the Bishop would certainly have sought redress at Common Law, and the Lord Chief Justice had privately warned the King that the Bishop's freehold would be protected.

[1] Bod. Tanner MSS. 460, fo. 172.
[2] B.M. Add. MSS. 15, fo. 551.
[3] J. S. Clarke, *The Life of James II*, 1816, ii. 91.

Henry Compton as a young man,
from a portrait at Compton Wynyates

Nor is *A Vindication of the Proceedings of His Majesty's Ecclesiastical Commissioners*, which was not published till 1688, any more convincing. As to the jurisdiction of the Commissioners, the writer maintained that II Car. 16 did not in fact abolish all Courts of Commission but only those exercising a particular authority. A judicial process, he wrote, was not necessary 'when the Delinquent is fallen under the sentence *a jure* . . . and therefor the Ordinary, Chancellor, or Archdeacon whose work it is to declare such as are *ipso facto* Excommunicated or Suspended to be so, do not then act as judges, but as Parties engaged in the Defence of Ecclesiastical Laws.'[1]

Precisely what this means we must leave to the reader.[2]

Such an extreme assertion of the royal authority could not be allowed to pass unchallenged. A reply appeared in *A Letter to the Author of the Vindication* which expressed the constitutional points at issue with admirable clarity. The whole controversy finally depended, the writer said, on whether the King's supremacy was a 'personal supremacy' or one 'defined by law'. Was he *legibus solutus*, so much so that the mere intimation of his will took precedence over canon and statute? Or was he, as King, and Supreme Governor of the Church of England, called upon to exercise an authority in accordance with the known laws of the land?[3]

Between such conflicting views of the royal prerogative there could, in the last resort, be no compromise, and the inevitable conflict between these two patterns of kingship brought William and Mary to Whitehall and removed James to St. Germains.

As to the Commissioners, Sprat later found it necessary to justify his part in the proceedings. He did not know the terms of the Commission, he explained, until it was publicly opened in Whitehall, and since it was by then already decided to proceed against the Bishop of London, he felt it a clear duty to sit on the Commission if only to protect the Bishop from his enemies —to prove which he could say that he had voted for his Lordship's acquittal.[4]

---

[1] *A Vindication of the Proceedings of His Majestie's Ecclesiastical Commissioners against the Bishop of London, and the Fellows of Magdalen College*, London, 1688, p. 30.

[2] The reader will find an attempted explanation in T. Sharp, *Life of Archbishop Sharp*, i. 78, 79.

[3] *A Letter to the Author of the 'Vindication'*, by Philominus Anglicus.

[4] *A Letter from the Bishop of Rochester, etc.*, 1688, p. 4.

So far as Compton was concerned, his suspension increased rather than diminished his influence in London, for he was now looked upon as a martyr to the Protestant and constitutional cause. Burnet writes that 'the bishop was more considered than ever and more considerable in his character abroad.'[1] The Princess of Orange, at The Hague, took up the cudgels on behalf of her old preceptor, and interceded for him with the King, only to be sharply reprimanded for her pains. She also wrote to the Bishop expressing her sympathy, and assuring him of 'the great share they both of them took in the trouble that had befallen him'.

John Evelyn duly noted that the whole affair was thought 'an extraordinary way of proceeding' and was 'universally resented'.[2]

To Crewe and Sprat, in co-operation with White, Bishop of Peterborough,[3] there was entrusted the unenviable duty of administering the See of London as Commissioners of the diocese during Compton's suspension.[4] Their task was by no means easy. The clergy were still devoted to their own Bishop, and it was his 'secret intimations' which guided their policy. Sprat, after the Revolution, was emphatic that he and the Bishop of Peterborough (he did not say the same of the Bishop of Durham) entered upon their unwelcome task with Compton's good will, and that they 'acted nothing in it without the greatest respect to his interest'. 'They maintained the Bishop's Officers in their full Rights and Privileges', and when James's sustained animosity would have removed the Lord Mayor's Chapel altogether from the jurisdiction of the Bishop of the diocese, they withstood their royal master to the face. 'We never invaded any of my Lord Bishop's Preferments that fell void in that Interest', he writes. 'We disposed of none but according to his own Directions. We used his Clergy with the same affectionate Care and brotherly Love as he himself had done: who was on that Account as dear to them, as any Bishop in Christendom was to his Diocese.'[5]

This removal from public affairs must have been particularly irksome to one of the Bishop's active temperament, and in March, 1687, he petitioned the King to restore him to the

---

[1] Burnet, *op. cit.*, iii. p. 112.   [2] Evelyn, *op. cit.*, ii. 257.

[3] The request of the Dean and Chapter of St. Paul's seems to have been ignored. See pp. 97, 98.

[4] Luttrell, *A Brief Historical Relation*, i. 388.

[5] *The Bishop of Rochester's Second Letter to the Right Honourable the Earl of Dorset and Middlesex*, 1689, p. 13.

exercise of his episcopal authority.[1] The matter was referred to the Commissioners. According to Sprat the request would have been granted had the Bishop been willing to make a formal submission to the King—but he resolutely refused to purchase his restoration on these terms.[2]

His retirement to Fulham did not, of course, entirely cut him off from ecclesiastical affairs (as we have seen), nor did his devotion to botany which led him at this time to stock his gardens at Fulham 'with new Varieties of Domestic and Exotic Plants' occupy all his energies.[3] Part of his retirement he seems to have spent at Castle Ashby in Northamptonshire, where he found congenial occupation in giving advice on 'enlarging the garden and filling the loggia in the east front'.[4]

From Fulham and Castle Ashby the Bishop watched the King hurry to his own destruction. Compton's contemporary biographer has suggested that the Bishop was not sorry to escape the duty (he might have refused it) which fell to the lot of the Commissioners, of degrading one of his own clergy, Samuel Johnson, an intrepid republican, who had incurred the King's anger by distributing Protestant pamphlets on Hounslow Heath.

It is unnecessary in a biography of Henry Compton to give at length a list of James's imprudences, particularly since the Bishop was suspended at the time. No one, however, could mistake the significance of the army of 14,000 men which James assembled on Hounslow Heath, nor the fierceness of his attack on the Universities. Cambridge, it is true, escaped more lightly, its Vice-Chancellor alone being dismissed, but against Oxford, the traditional home of loyalty and non-resistance, the King visited his particular displeasure. The Master of University College, who declared himself a convert to the King's faith, was authorised to retain his post in defiance of the law. Massey, another Roman Catholic, was presented by the Crown to the Deanery of Christ Church, and Farmer, a fellow-religionist of uncertain morals, was forced into the Presidency of Magdalen, most wealthy of Oxford Colleges.

On 5 December, 1687, perhaps with some relish, the King removed the Bishop of London's nephew, George, Earl of

[1] Luttrell, *op. cit.*, i. 388. See also Burnet, *op. cit.*, iii. 112.
[2] *A Letter from the Bishop of Rochester*, p. 12.
[3] *The Life of Dr. Henry Compton*, p. 42.   [4] Compton, *op. cit.*, p. 139.

Northampton, from the Lord Lieutenancy of Warwickshire, 'for refusing to carry out his instructions for enforceing the repeal of the laws against the Catholics'.[1]

James next proceeded to dismiss his two kinsmen, Edward, Earl of Clarendon, Lord Lieutenant of Ireland, and Lawrence, Earl of Rochester, the Lord Treasurer, in each case because they would not adopt his religion. A Roman Catholic, Lord Belasyse, became First Lord of The Treasury, and another of the same faith, Lord Arundell, Lord Privy Seal.

Compton's opposition to the royal policy, now that he was suspended from office, was of necessity unofficial, but it was none the less real. As one of the Governors of the Charterhouse, a position he still held, the Bishop was able to thwart the King's efforts to force upon the foundation a member of the Roman Catholic Church.

We must be careful not to judge an incident of this kind by the liberal standards of the nineteenth century. It is a complete anachronism to regard James as the enlightened champion of toleration in a very intolerant world. The real conflict was not between persecution sponsored by zealous Whigs and liberty championed by an enlightened monarch; but between respect for law, broadening out into liberty, and an arbitrary despotism, obedient to nothing but the royal will. When James issued his Declaration of Indulgence it says much for the perspicacity of the more enlightened Dissenters, who would for the moment have benefited, that they were able to make just this distinction.

James, in the last year of his reign, made little effort to disguise the fact that despotism was his ultimate goal, but he was to discover that the way of the despot in England (fortunately) is hard. Parliament stood four square in his path, and he found it impossible in practice to secure control over it no matter how much he might try to manipulate the elections in the boroughs. Early in 1688, however, he committed the cardinal error of his tragic reign.

On 27 April, 1688, the King announced a fresh Declaration of Indulgence, by which the penal laws against Nonconformists and Roman Catholics were alike dispensed with, and every Act which imposed a religious test as a qualification for office in Church and State was abrogated.

[1] *Universal Magazine*, June 1740.

This deliberate throwing down of the gauntlet united Churchman and Dissenter, Cavalier and Republican, and the outcome of it was to bring over from The Hague the son-in-law and daughter of James—to whose policy at this time, and Compton's share in it, we must now turn.

CHAPTER SEVEN

THE COURT AT THE HAGUE

THE Earl of Danby's greatest triumph was his persuading Charles II to consent to the marriage of Mary, daughter of James by his first wife Anne Hyde, to William, Prince of Orange. For William it was to prove, in a crisis, the strongest card in his hand in the game of power-politics against the ambitions of the King of France. Louis XIV received the news of the wedding 'as he would have done the loss of an army'.[1]

William of Orange, though diseased in body, for he was the victim of a constant asthma which racked his frame with a terrible cough (particularly in the mists of Kensington), yet possessed a spirit which was absolutely indomitable. His sad, pale countenance, with the long aquiline nose and aloof mien, suggests immediately the man of destiny. So he conceived himself. The Prince had learnt his statesmanship from De Witt, and his secretiveness from the loneliness of his early years. The ambition of his life, to which he felt himself called, was to preserve inviolate the religion and independence of his own country against the nationalist aggression of France. The task was not easy, for Louis XIV presided over a nation whose power was pre-eminent in a Europe in which Spain was on the decline, Austria wasted by her struggles with the Turks, Germany suffering from the devastating effects of the Thirty Years War, and Sweden exhausted. Thus William realised that he must build up a pattern of collective security—a grand alliance—if the nations of Europe were not to be swallowed up one by one. England, therefore, was important, because on her policy depended the balance of power in Europe. When she was allied with France, as Charles II despite his Parliaments often contrived it, Louis was free to set his armies on the march. When England was allied with Holland, Louis's task became more formidable, and his final chance of success considerably less promising.

The Prince's participation in English politics was determined

[1] Burnet, *op. cit.*, ii. 132.

by this preoccupation, and his usual policy was to support Parliament against the French sympathies of the King. His marriage with Mary was, of course, a great triumph. It meant that one day, provided the militant Whiggery of Shaftesbury did not succeed in placing Monmouth on the throne (and provided that Charles had no legitimate children and James no son) his wife would be Queen of England, and he himself be in a position to influence more directly its foreign policy.

When William, with his bride, sailed for Holland on 28 November, 1677, he also took with him the good wishes of Protestant England. People in this country began to take a greater interest in what was going on at The Hague, and to look to it as safeguarding the hopes of the future. Emissaries went to and fro and William, on his part, followed events over here with an eager concern.

None was more interested in the Court in Holland than the Bishop of London. He had watched Mary and her sister grow up. As Dean of the Chapels Royal he had superintended their education; had appointed their tutors; secured their confirmation against the wishes of their own father; and when the time came for Mary to be given a husband it was he who married her into the House of Orange. Feeling more and more out of sympathy with the Court and its policy as the years of Charles II's reign drew to its close, Compton more and more identified himself with the hopes for the future which rested in Protestant Mary and her Dutch husband. He exchanged many letters with the Princess, and occasionally with the Prince. There was usually some churchman at The Hague sent there by the Bishop who kept him informed of all that was happening, and to whom the Bishop sent letters of so confidential a nature that they were usually destroyed so soon as received. At other times he would send out his own private secretary.[1]

In 1679 Thomas Ken, later the most saintly of the Non-jurors, went out to The Hague, and took the opportunity, very courageously, of remonstrating with William for his cold treatment of his wife. Numerous letters at this time passed between Ken and Compton, most of which show how preoccupied the Bishop was with the Roman Catholic attack on the Church of England, and the consequent need to encourage the Dissenters to conform.[2]

[1] *H.M.C.* App. ii, Report XIV, iii. p. 369.   [2] See p. 73.

Not even such a Protestant stronghold as The Hague was entirely free from Roman Catholic intrigue, but Ken was pleased to be able to report, in September 1680, that a certain Colonel Fitzpatrick had been received into the Church of England, and had proved such a keen convert that 'he has discourst with some of his Romish friends so effectively, that we are in hopes of more converts to our Church and those considerable ones too'.[1] Such news was most welcome to the Bishop, though he reminded Ken in a subsequent letter that in receiving the Colonel into the Church of England he should have insisted on his making an abjuration of Popery.

After Ken's departure, there is a gap in the correspondence between The Hague and Fulham for some years. The extra-ordinary thing, perhaps, is that any of these letters should have survived.[2]

Chaplain to the Princess of Orange from 1681 to 1685 was John Covel, who shared the Bishop of London's enthusiasm for botany. Throughout his stay in Holland, he kept Compton in close touch with what was happening at The Hague, and the Bishop, from his end, regaled him with news for the benefit of the Princess. 'I read the sermon to her the very day it came', he wrote of a discourse the Bishop had sent over, 'and she was extremely well pleased, and satisfied with it: and I was glad of the occasion it gave me more fully to discourse with her Royal Highnesse upon that subject by all which I think I may give your Lordship the assurance of her R[oyal] Highnesse being a very dutifull Daughter (as she may in time be as kind a Mother) of our Church of England; I shall not be wanting to the utmost of my Power to keep her steady, and the work will be much easier, it being (as far as I ever could see) her own proper inclination and opinion.'[3]

Upon Covell's retirement in 1685, the Bishop sent to Holland John Horne, who took with him an episcopal letter of introduction and some books for the Princess. He was very kindly received, he reported to the Bishop, and added: 'My great care now will be to demean myself that you may have no complaints, and in

---

[1] Ken to Compton, 17 Sept., 1680, Bod. Rawlinson MSS. 985 C., fo. 7.
[2] Compton frequently kept the letters he received, some of which are now in the Bodleian Library.
[3] Covel to Compton, 24 Aug., 1685, Bod. Rawlinson MSS. 982 C., fo. 39.

order thereto I humbly crave leave to trouble your Lordship from time to time as anything of difficulty shall occur: that as I have begun, so I may continue to walk by your direction.'[1]

Perhaps it was the Bishop's original intention that Horne should follow Covell as Chaplain to the Princess, but if so he proved himself unacceptable. He did not remain very long in The Hague, for Compton soon secured the position for William Stanley, who in later life became Dean of St. Asaph. This ecclesiastic arrived at The Hague in December 1685, taking with him for the Princess's reading *The Answer to a Papist misrepresented* by William Sherlock, and a small book of his own, *Devotions of the Church of Rome*. Almost his first care was to send a letter to the Bishop, thanking him for the 'trust' that he had 'reposed' in him. 'By the blessing of God', he wrote, 'I will endeavour to make good the character which your Lordship is pleased to give of me. I confess I have found a kinder reception than I expected: and all things as agreeable as I could desire. Her Highness is doubtless one of the best tempered persons in the world and everyone must needs be happy in serving her. . . . On Christmas Day, which was last Tuesday, we had a very full Sacram[ent] & her Royal Highness with all manageable Devotion at it. . . . If your Lordship have any advice or directions to give me or commands to lay upon me, I shall always conscientiously study & follow them.'[2]

The Princess certainly seems to have won golden opinions from all those who knew her. 'Last Friday', Stanley wrote again later, 'we kept her Royal Highness's birthday; God send us a joyful keeping of very many of them, and make her every day more and more a blessing to our Church and Nation. The Princess is extremely constant and regular in her public devotions.'[3]

Compton was always avid for news no matter from what quarter, and he was particularly interested in anything which concerned the doings of the Prince of Orange upon whom so much depended. Here Stanley was on the whole reassuring. True the Prince was not particularly interested in establishing a Protestant library at The Hague, a scheme which was very dear to the heart of the Bishop; but despite this shortcoming Stanley

---

[1] Horne to Compton, 27 Nov., 1685, Bod. Rawlinson MSS. 982 C., fo. 39.

[2] Stanley to Compton, 22 Dec., 1685/1 Jan., 1686, Bod. Rawlinson MSS. 983 C., fo. 106.

[3] *Ibid.*, 1 Jan., 1686, *ibid.*, fo. 99.

could say that he found him 'an extraordinarily good tempered person, & for ought that I can perceive well effected to our Church'. Monsieur Menard, he added, 'hath preached in a Church in the Town whither the Prince and others go constantly, & the Princess & her Family come to our Chappel in the house'.[1]

This reference to Monsieur Menard, a French refugee minister, caused Compton some uneasiness, and he immediately communicated his fears by means of a personal messenger to the Princess. The Bishop was particularly anxious that William should from time to time join with his wife in public worship. Fortunately Stanley's next letter was reassuring. 'That which I spoke to her R[oyal] H[ighness] concerning Mr. Menard', he reported, 'hath had some effect. . . . The Prince comes to prayers on Sunday afternoons with us & is very grave & regular at our Church services, but never comes at other times for indeed he hunts & is abroad all day besides. But he professes an admiration v[ery] often for our Church. I have discoursed with Mr. Menard— He professeth a mighty zeal & value for our Church & hopes to live 2 years in England in communion with us. He comes to prayers sometimes.'[2]

It seems as if Compton was already envisaging a time when the Prince's religious allegiance, and particularly his attitude towards the Church of England, would be a matter of great political moment.

News of the Bishop of London's growing estrangement from the Court was soon common talk at The Hague. 'Her R[oyal] Highness as well as myself', Stanley wrote, 'would desire to enquire more particularly into your Lordship's case at the Court of England if it might be without offence; indeed she hath asked me often concerning it; & I have told her what I have heard from England but that may be rather a conjecture than truth. If your Lordship convey it safely to me, I believe it would oblige her much. I hope your Lordship hath still access to the Princess of Denmark[3] & make use of it to good purpose.'[4]

Reports of the Bishop's appearance before the Ecclesiastical Commission also were not long in reaching Holland. The anxiety

<hr>

[1] Stanley to Compton, 1 Jan., 1686, Bod. Rawlinson MSS. 983 C., fo. 99.
[2] *Ibid.*, 15/25 Mar., 1686, *ibid.*, fo. 104.
[3] Mary's sister Anne, later Queen.
[4] Stanley to Compton, 15/25 Mar., 1686, Bod. Rawlinson MSS. 983 C., fo. 104.

which was felt by the Princess for her old preceptor can be seen in the following extract from a letter written to Compton by Stanley on 16 August.

Your nephew Mr. Nicholas coming to you, I could not but send this to acquaint your Lordship with the state of things here, because I can do it with more freedom, than I durst do it by Common Post. We are all in such pains here because we know this is the day assigned to your Lordship to give in your Answer to the Commissioners. I can assure your Lordship that even your Clergy cannot have a greater concern for your Lordship than all have here & I pray God but a good Issue of all things for the good of the Church & your Lordship so true a patron of it. Though I know her R[oyal] Highness writes to your Lordship by Mr. Nicholas, yet I cannot but acquaint your Lordship with somewhat which perhaps she would not tell you of. It is that She, seeing things coming thus to extremity against your Lordship, hath this day written to the King in your behalf, making as far as she can your cause her own. And she discoursed with me about it, arguing thus, that things being gone so far, by such an address she could do your Lordship no harm, but it was possible she might do some good.[1]

Concern for the Bishop was not Stanley's only anxiety. Present at the Court at The Hague, by invitation of Prince William, was that dynamic and not unlovable Scotsman, Gilbert Burnet, who seemed destined to evoke either extreme affection or deep hostility in all those who were brought into relationship with him. Sometimes his broadmindedness alienated even his friends, as it did when he disapproved of the indiscriminate persecution of Roman Catholics after the so-called Popish Plot. His arrival at The Hague, where he became in fact William's secretary, not only made Stanley uneasy; it also aroused the fierce indignation of James II. For once the King and the Bishop of London were of a common mind. 'I am loth to trouble your Lordship with anything more', Stanley wrote to Compton, 'only I cannot but take notice that Dr. Burnet will stay here & is perpetually desiring to talk with the Princess in private & too often gets the liberty.' Dr. Burnet was everything at The Hague, largely because of his 'intolerable impudence and pressing importunity'. Last Sacrament Day he 'served the sacrament both to the Prince and the Princess; and walked about in a Cloak like

[1] Stanley to Compton, 16/26 Aug., 1686, Bod. Rawlinson MSS. 983 C., fo. 107.

one of their[1] ministers'. It might help to mend matters, Stanley suggested, if the Bishop were to write to the Princess, and more particularly to the Prince.[2]

The Bishop's reply to this letter (and several others which he wrote to Stanley) unfortunately miscarried. There seems to have been a great deal of tampering with the post to Holland so that the only safe way of carrying on a correspondence was by private messenger. Stanley informed Compton later:

> I received your letter by the French minister, together with the enclosed for her Royal Highness. I immediately gave her Highness the Letter, and am commanded to return the enclosed from her Highness in answer to it. In your Lordship's letter to me, you seem to have written severall letters to me, whereas I can truly affirm that I have not received any Letter from your Lordship since the night before Mr. Nicholas went from us, which was last 26 August. Her Royal Highness doth tell me that some flowers, I suppose Aurriculas, came to her, but I never knew of them till now. And therefore if your Lordship hath written anything to me with them or without them, it is miscarried. . . . I am glad to see that her R[oyal] Highness doth not yet go to hear Dr. Burnet notwithstanding that I hear it is reported in England that she doth. I wholly abstain from him.[3]

In taking this attitude to Burnet, Stanley had the full support of the Bishop of London and in fact was acting under his definite instructions. The doings of this energetic Scotsman formed the burden of Stanley's letters to the Bishop and of the Bishop's letters to Stanley during 1687. 'I am very glad', the Chaplain reported on 18 February, 'that I have carried myself so much a stranger to Dr. Burnet who so constantly and imprudently haunts everybody here . . . for I find it that the King's envoy here hath told publicly that he hath desired their Highnesses to forbid him their presence.'[4]

This intervention by the King's envoy, the Marquis d'Abbeville, a worthless sycophant if we can believe Macaulay, was successful in March in securing the official dismissal of Burnet from the Court, for William dared not, at this stage in his fortunes, risk an open breach with his father-in-law. It was a

---

[1] i.e., Dutch.
[2] Stanley to Compton, 16 Aug., 1686, Bod. Rawlinson MSS. 983 C.
[3] *Ibid.* 21/31 Dec., *ibid.*, fo. 103.
[4] Same to same, 18 Feb., 1687, *ibid.*, fo. 109.

banishment, however, which was formal rather than real. Though for the next eighteen months Burnet was officially denied access to the court, he was in fact still consulted by the Prince, and was kept busy writing pamphlets on his behalf.

Burnet seems early to have recognised that behind Stanley's sustained coldness there was the hostility of the Bishop of London, and as a result he himself sent a protest to Fulham, which drew forth two letters from the Bishop to Stanley written on 5 January, and 24 February. In his reply to these epistles Stanley again assured Compton that he had completely 'abstained' from Burnet's company, as much from his own inclinations as 'in obedience to your Lordship's Letter'.[1]

It is clear, as we have suggested before, that for once the Bishop of London and the King of England saw eye to eye, but it was not easy to convince the King's envoy that this was the case. When Stanley told the Marquis d'Abbeville that he had kept clear of Burnet in accordance with Compton's 'express direction and order',

he seemed surprised at it (so Stanley reported to the Bishop), and asked me seriously whether your Lordship had ever written to me not to countenance Dr. B[urnet]. I assured him you had—He told me he was glad of it, and that he would acquaint the King with it in your Lordship's behalf, & desired me to show him your Lordship's letter to that purpose if I could. I have not promised him but I have your Lordship's first letter to me concerning Dr. B[urnet] that might be safely shown to him, if it was worth the while. I have here enclosed a transcript of it that your Lordship may see it is perfectly safe, & unexceptionable, if the M[arquess] should desire to see it at my return; And indeed it is the only letter that I have kept of your Lordship's & it was by a great chance that I kept this.[2]

But neither the King's nor the Bishop's hostility could unsettle Burnet in the Prince's esteem.

Another preoccupation in Compton's correspondence with Stanley was of a more personal nature. The Bishop was very anxious to secure a position in the Court at the Hague for his nephew Nicholas, but despite all his efforts it became evident that this young man would have to wait his turn.

Stanley's letters, with their reports on the doings of the Prince and Princess, their references to extremist busy-bodies such

[1] Stanley to Compton, 21/31 Mar., 1687, Bod. Rawlinson MSS. 983 C., fo. 110.   [2] *Ibid.*

as Sir Rowland Gwyn, their tittle-tattle as to Papist spies who came to hear him preach, and their tirades against Burnet, give a vivid picture of life at The Hague. The fact that many of Compton's letters never reached their destination shows that James was suspicious of William and of the English colony around him. In one of his last extant letters Stanley informed the Bishop that 'the Princess is pleased often to send for me to inform her of the affairs of England, as to its constitution & govern[men]t, both in church & state which is very fit for her to know & which is but little known here.'[1] Mary's loyalty was soon put to the test for the King sent her a long epistle, hoping thereby to unsettle her devotion to the Church of England. The protestant schooling which she had received from Compton now stood her in good stead, and she sent back a reasoned reply of her own composition—a fact which she herself later communicated to the Bishop. If we may believe Thomas Tenison, then Vicar of St. Martin's, her counterblast was well done.[2]

In such an uncertain political world, William's obvious policy (and he was temperamentally suited to it) was to wait upon events and not to allow himself to embark upon hasty and ill-considered schemes, suggested by the unwise counsels of discontented people who had fled to The Hague. He had already seen Argyle and Monmouth rush to their doom. The succession, in the event of James not producing a male heir, would devolve upon his wife and he was content to wait.

The most shrewd observers in England were at one with him in supporting such a policy of splendid inactivity. In December 1686, for example, Lord Halifax, the Trimmer, wrote confidentially to William advising him to say little and to be patient.[3]

Such advice, however, did not prevent the Prince from keeping up a secret correspondence with influential people in England; nor did it prevent them—Clarendon, Rochester, Nottingham, Fitzpatrick, Devonshire and Bedford—from sending letters over to The Hague. Churchill assured the Prince that he himself and Princess Anne (she was already under the domination of the redoubtable Sarah) would remain Protestants whatever happened. In May 1687, the restless and ambitious Danby proposed that

---

[1] Stanley to Compton, 31 Mar., 1687, Bod. Rawlinson MSS. 983 C., fo. 110.
[2] E. Carpenter, *The Life and Times of Thomas Tenison*, p. 83.
[3] Dalrymple, *Memoirs of Great Britain and Ireland*, 1790, ii. 56.

the Prince should meet a group of English Protestants so that plans for the preservation of their religion might be decided upon: and in September he followed this up by asking for a personal interview. 'I made some attempts last summer', he informed William, 'and some private ones in this to have seen if I could have gained leave to go into Holland with the same indifferency that is permitted to many others: but I still found designs were laid to do me more prejudice by that journey than I could have done service to your Highness.'[1]

William, fortunately, did not depend for information solely on the emigré colony which had collected around him, nor on the letters that came to him from London. From time to time he sent trusted envoys over to England to feel the pulse of the nation and to report on events. Such a visitor was Dykvelt who made the journey in 1687. Trained in the school of De Witt, this statesman had thrown in his lot with William after the fall of that great minister. He was eminently suited to the task which the Prince now entrusted to him, for he possessed the arts and easy manner of the diplomatist, together with a quite exceptional knowledge of English affairs. Though he came over officially accredited by the States General, it was generally suspected that his real mission was to the opposition. Certainly his presence whipped James into a fury. Dykvelt, so James complained bitterly to William, 'had not taken the right measures of affairs here, by giving so much credit to some that do not wish me and the monarchy well'.[2] The King could not conceal his distrust of the Prince's intentions even from the Prince's servant. 'My nephew's duty', he protested to Dykvelt, 'is to strengthen my hands. But he has always taken a pleasure in crossing me.'

Among the people with whom the Dutch envoy especially made contact was the Bishop of London, who was still suffering under the frustrations of his suspension. What passed between them we are left to conjecture, but we may be fairly safe in assuming that the Bishop assured Dykvelt of the firm determination of the clergy to preserve their Protestant liberties. Compton also gave him a brief note to take back to his master, which had of course to be in general terms, but which, in the light of subsequent events, has great significance. 'I was very glad to receive

[1] Dalrymple, *Memoirs of Great Britain and Ireland*, 1790, ii. 56.
[2] *Ibid.*

so good assurance of your welfare', he wrote, 'as Monsieur Dickvelt brought over. It is not only for your near relation to the Crown, that you are so much prayed for here, but for your usefulness to it. For if the King should have any trouble come upon him, which God forbid, we do not know any sure friend he has to rely upon abroad, besides yourself, whom God therefore long preserve a blessing to the King and the Kingdom.'[1]

Dykvelt's mission was followed by another undertaken this time by Count Zulestein, a straightforward and gallant soldier, who was a cousin-german to William. He also made approaches to the leaders of the opposition, and took back with him much confidential information as well as letters to William from many influential Englishmen. Among these was one from Compton written on 5 September, 1687, most of which we quote:

> Your remembrance of me by Mons. Zulestein has obliged me to acknowledge that great honour by this means; and though I have nothing of moment proper to communicate by writing, nevertheless it is of moment for me not to lie under the imputation of ingratitude, lest I should justly lose so great a satisfaction, as sometimes to be owned amongst your most humble servants. If you shall find by the account Mons. Zulestein gives you, that I have communicated to him nothing worthy that confidence you were pleased to recommend, I beseech you not to believe that it has proceeded from any reservedness, where I had so strong an assurance from yourself, but that I had no more to say; for since my misfortune of lying under his Majesty's displeasure, I frequently retire into the country out of reach of great news. . . . We have daily reports how busy the priests are amongst the conventicles, but we hope a few discoveries will make that party wiser. The clergy continue very firm to their principles, very watchful over their flocks, and very dutiful to the King, and next to my allegiance I can confidently aver, there is no duty which I shall not cheerfully pay to your service and pray God for your prosperity all the days of my life.[2]

James was not, of course, entirely unaware that there was a good deal of going and coming between the court at The Hague and the opposition party in England, though it is unlikely that he realised the full extent of it. It was impossible, in such a situa-

---

[1] Dalrymple, *Memoirs of Great Britain and Ireland*, 1790, ii. 73.
[2] *Ibid.*, ii. 85.

tion, for the relations between him and William to be friendly, and they were now made worse by a bitter quarrel between them over the six British regiments in the pay of the United Provinces. James insisted that these soldiers should be put under the command of Roman Catholic officers. William was equally insistent that they should not—and as he paid the piper it was not unreasonable that he should expect to call the tune.

It was against the background of these worsening relations between Whitehall and The Hague that the Bishop of London sent the following letter to the Prince on 27 October, 1687.

The terms by which you were pleased to express yourself in reference to the Church of England were every way so obliging and satisfactory that I look upon myself as bound in duty to acknowledge the deep sense I and every true member of the same Church ought to have of so great a blessing. And though you are at present[1] at a distance from us, and not so well able to partake of the fruits of so good intentions, yet when we shall have served this king with all fidelity, so long as it shall please God to continue him amongst us; as none that you know will question the sincerity of your performance, so I make no doubt, but you will soon find the benefit of having taken up so wise resolutions. For Sir, you that see all the great motions of the world; and can so well judge of them, know there is no reliance upon anything that is not steady in principles, and profess not the common good before private interest. I pray God to continue to be gracious to you, and to direct and prosper all your counsels, and to crown the endeavours of your life with the consummation of all happiness.[2]

And so the year 1688 came, a year fateful not only for the fortunes of James and William, but also for England and Europe: a year which is still remembered by most Englishmen as a time of deliverance.

[1] The phrase 'at present' in the light of future events seems fraught with significance.
[2] Dalrymple, *op. cit.*, ii. 87.

CHAPTER EIGHT

A SOLDIER BISHOP

WE have taken the story of events in England up to the announcement by the King of his Declaration of Indulgence on 27 April, 1688.

The news was received by the London clergy in a mood of sullen resentment. James's next decision that it should be read in all the London Churches on two successive Sundays, 20 and 27 May, and in the country on 3 and 10 June turned this resentment into active opposition. By this injunction the King was endeavouring to make every clergyman *particeps criminis* and this was more than ordinary flesh and blood could stand. True the clergy had obeyed two similar requests from Charles as Ordinary (though even then Compton and Sancroft had advised the King against this procedure)[1] but he had wisely refrained from saddling the bishops with the task of distributing and enforcing the reading of the Indulgence.

A meeting of the London clergy at which they decided to petition the bishops to act in the matter took place in the Temple on 11 May. Their Lordships, with the exception of Chester and St. David's, were entirely at one with their clergy in opposing this latest manifestation of the King's will, and they met together at Lambeth. Compton, though he was still under suspension and therefore could not officially associate himself with any approach to the King, was yet present, taking part in the deliberations and approving the decision taken.[2] After a long discussion it was agreed that the bishops should move by way of a personal appeal to James. Sancroft then drew up a very moderate petition in which he humbly explained the 'great averseness' of the bishops to publishing the Indulgence, since the royal dispensing power had been declared illegal by Parliament.

Immediately after their meeting, the bishops, with the excep-

---

[1] *H.M.C.* App. vii, Report XIV, p. 258 (Ormonde MSS. N.S., vol. iv).

[2] He gave his 'approbo' on 23 May to 'The Petition of some of the Bishops to his Majesty against distributing the "Declaration of Liberty of Conscience' ": but he did not sign the actual petition to the King. See *The Correspondence of Henry Hyde*, p. 478.

tion of Sancroft who had been forbidden the Court, and of course Compton, waited on James at Whitehall. The King was 'abroad' when they first arrived, but on his return they were immediately admitted to his presence. With great humility, Lloyd, Bishop of St. Asaph, presented the petition in the name of his brethren. The King immediately recognised the Archbishop's handwriting, and then proceeded to read the document with increasing fury. 'It is a standard of rebellion', he shouted angrily, and after venting his displeasure upon Turner of Ely in particular, he dismissed them abruptly, reiterating that he expected to be obeyed. 'God hath given me this dispensing power, and I will maintain it', he declared firmly.

The bishops returned by water to Lambeth only to find to their great consternation, that the petition they had presented to the King was already on sale in the streets of London. Who was responsible for this gross breach of faith? We may dismiss Sancroft immediately, for his conscience most certainly would not have allowed him to do it, beside which he declared later that he knew of only one copy, and that was the one he himself had written for the King. There is, however, another, in Lloyd's handwriting, in the Tanner MSS. in the Bodleian Library at Oxford, but though the Bishop of St. Asaph might have desired such publicity, he could hardly have had time to execute such a plan, for he went immediately from the bishops' meeting to Whitehall. The facts seem to point to Henry Compton. He was present with the bishops, and would have had no difficulty in making a secret copy and securing its immediate publication (perhaps in co-operation with Henry Sydney), while the bishops were at the Palace. Also such a deed fits in with Compton's hasty temperament, his occasional irresponsibility, his anxiety to be 'up and doing', and his great hatred for James.[1]

Certainly it was not a wise thing to do, for it could not but reflect on the bishops. It is equally possible that it was Compton, again, who wrote the letter which was sent off next day to every clergyman in England, advising against reading the declaration.

[1] This is the view taken by Dr. Hart in his *William Lloyd*, 1952, p. 100. Dean Luckock, however (*The Bishops in the Tower*, 1887, p. 153), suggests that Sunderland was the culprit. He did it, Luckock supposes, to widen the breach between the King and the Bishops because, though one of James's ministers, he was secretly in the service of William of Orange.

Compton had time on his hands, and doubtless felt the frustration of his suspension which prevented him being numbered with the 'Seven'.

There then followed those great scenes in English history which the colourful pen of Macaulay has made live again. Sunday, 20 May, was awaited by Londoners with growing excitement, and by the Court with increasing concern. Only in four London parish churches, and the great Abbey of St. Peter, Westminster, was the hated Declaration read: and in these it was mumbled before congregations in process of leaving as soon as the first words were uttered.

James had made a serious miscalculation, for the country clergy would undoubtedly follow the lead of their brethren in London. Most men, and certainly his brother, would have seen the red light, recognised the danger, and then retreated with whatever dignity such a situation allowed them to muster. But the King was thoroughly convinced that it was compromise which had led his father to the scaffold. He even thought of issuing a second Declaration and this was actually sent to the printers, though almost at once withdrawn. Lord Sunderland wisely suggested that the offenders should be left to their own consciences, but James determined that the rebellious bishops should be brought before some more tangible tribunal. Even the notorious Jeffreys shrank from using the Court of High Commission for this purpose since the country had not forgotten the case of Compton. Instead, as he must suggest something, he advised a prosecution of the bishops, in the Court of King's Bench, for publishing a seditious libel, though this, of course, had one serious drawback—trial by jury.

On the evening of 8 June, the seven bishops were accordingly summoned before the King in Council. Compton (perhaps regretful that he was not one of them) had meanwhile been active behind the scenes on the bishops' behalf. He waited on them constantly, and on the day of their appearance hurriedly sent the following letter to the Archbishop: 'I was yesterday in town but had not the time to wait upon you. I thought it therefore my duty to give you the best intelligence I could meet with which was this. They were resolved before the time of your appearing to make all the Clarks of the Council justices of the Peace.

He that discovered this seemed likewise to hint it was done to capacitate them to take your several recognisances. What use this may be I know not but I thought it my duty to impart so much.'[1]

When the bishops duly came to the Council, the Lord Chancellor made a determined effort to browbeat them into submission and self-incrimination, but he found that these determined ecclesiastics were not such tractable material as the illiterate peasants captured after Sedgemoor. The bishops, though they were without counsel, had yet been carefully primed when to keep silent. Finding all intimidation vain, Jeffreys at length bluntly stated that a criminal information would be exhibited against them in the Court of King's Bench, and he then called upon them to enter into recognisances. The 'Seven', however, had already been privately advised not to do this and they steadily refused, protesting that they were peers of the realm. It was for thus standing on their rights that they were immediately to suffer. A barge was forthwith manned, and under a heavy guard, but supported by the sympathetic acclamations of the people of London, the bishops were rowed down the Thames and lodged in the Tower. James took the precaution of doubling the guard at this ancient fortress. He was not made any easier in his mind when he learnt later that the bishops had not long been in captivity before they were waited upon by a delegation of ten Nonconformists.

The Bishop of London felt keenly the imprisonment of his brethren, and came closer in heart to the Archbishop of Canterbury at this time than at any other period in his life. The short and simple letter which he sent to the tired Sancroft on the first day of his confinement expresses a genuine warmth of feeling springing naturally from a real concern. We will allow the letter to speak for itself.

This comes to bring that service to you, which by the help of God shall be never wanting. I am sorry with all my heart, that his Majestie has no more confidence in his best friends. I pray God give you your health during your continuance in this place, which will, I hope, be but for a very short time. How long I shall be from you, I cannot tell, but you may be assured that my heart shall be ever with you. And whilst I am at liberty, I beseech

[1] Compton to Sancroft, 8 June, 1688, Bod. Tanner MSS. 28, fo. 61.

you not to spare me in any thing I am able to performe. It is not now a time of ceremony. And therefore I should hate myself, if I had the least regret in undergoing any duty, whereby I might most express myself, etc.[1]

Excitement, meanwhile, was growing and the nerves of most Londoners were on edge, when, on 10 June, a month before the event was expected, the Queen gave birth to a son, who in Macaulay's unforgettable phrase was destined to 'seventy-seven years of exile and wandering, of vain projects, of honours more galling than insults and hopes such as make the heart grow sick'. The fact that the delivery was premature, that the Princess Anne was at Bath, and that no responsible and trusted Protestants (such as the Hydes) were present—an omission due to the King's stupidity—led to a general, though groundless, suspicion that James had practised a foul deceit. The way was being prepared for the later fiction of the warming-pan.[2]

Meanwhile the Bishop of London continued to visit his brethren regularly in the Tower. He was in fact their liaison with the outside world, and he went to great pains to secure three noblemen who were prepared to stand bail for each bishop when he appeared in Westminster Hall.[3] Compton also advised them to obtain the services of Sir John Holt as counsel—in some ways a surprising choice. 'I know he has a hearty desire as well as skill to serve you', he wrote to Sancroft on 12 June. 'If you have any commands for me', he added, 'I beseech you to send them by the bearer.'[4]

William, of course, was being kept in close touch with all that was happening in England, though he seems to have heard of the birth of the young Prince without suspecting that many were frankly incredulous. So much was the Prince behindhand with the news in this respect that he even sent Count Zulestein over in person to convey his congratulations to the King—an action which he later came to regret.

So far as the seven bishops were concerned, William could hardly write to them direct, but he did express his own concern to Compton and received from the Bishop the assurance that

[1] Compton to Sancroft, 9 June, 1688, Bod. Tanner MSS. 28, fo. 70.
[2] Even Sunderland tried to persuade the King to use the opportunity of the Prince's birth to issue a general pardon in which might be included the bishops.
[3] This did not in fact prove necessary, Bod. Tanner MSS. 28, fo. 76.
[4] Compton to Sancroft, 12 June, 1688, *ibid.* fo. 77.

such interest 'had its just effect upon them: for they are highly sensible of the great advantage both they and the Church have by the firmness of so powerful a friend'.[1]

The birth of the Prince proved to be the decisive factor in determining the opposition to take an extreme course. While the bishops were in the Tower awaiting their appearance at King's Bench, clandestine meetings took place in the house of the Earl of Shrewsbury,[2] and a highly secret letter in code, written by Sydney, in which the signatories were all represented by a number, was sent over to The Hague on 18 June. This epistle showed clearly that a group of noblemen were no longer prepared to suffer passively while the power of the Crown increased, and constitutional liberties were whittled away. In view of the importance of this letter, and its significance in relation to the Bishop of London, we propose to quote the following paragraph in full:

'This I suppose will be safely delivered, but yet I shall not say much; in a few days you will receive another, wherein you will know the minds of your friends. I believe you expected it before now but it could not be ready; this is only in the name of your principal friends which are 23. [Nottingham], 25. [Shrewsbury], 27. [Danby] 31. [Compton] 33. [Sydney][3] to desire you to defer making your complement till you have the letter I mention; what they are likely to advise in the next you may easily guess, and prepare yourself accordingly.'[4]

William's position, however, was by no means easy. He had learnt the lesson of Argyle and Monmouth, neither of whom was a foreigner. He knew perfectly well that to land in England, leading a contingent of Dutch troops, and fighting a series of battles would arouse the national hostility to the foreigner which might well prove James's greatest asset. His success must depend on the support he could secure from the English themselves, particularly on the loyalty of the noblemen, and the unwillingness of the mass of the people to fight for the King. Fortunately James had played into his hands by his last wanton attack on

---

[1] Dalrymple, *op. cit.*, ii. 105.

[2] Ranke (*History*, iv. 399) writes that the plotters often met in the garden at Fulham, but I have been unable to find any primary authority for this assertion.

[3] Sydney had earlier sent to William a list of ten 'conspirators' all of whom were to be designated by a number. 'This I desire you to keep by you', he wrote. Dalrymple, *op. cit.*, ii. 105.   [4] *Ibid.*

the bishops which inflamed national sentiment as never before in his reign.

On Friday, 15 June, the bishops appeared before the Court of King's Bench, when they protested that they had been unlawfully committed. This objection was unreasonably over-ruled. They then pleaded 'Not Guilty' and were committed for trial on 29 June, until which time they were allowed to be at large on their own recognisances, since the King was anxious that the strength of feeling behind the bishops, clearly manifested in the willingness of so many noblemen to stand bail according to the arrangement which Compton had made, should not be revealed to the public.

At last the day of the great trial arrived. Westminster Hall and its approaches were crowded. The jury were sworn in, one of them, Michael Arnold, brewer to the King, expressing his personal dilemma as follows: 'Whatever I do I am sure to be half ruined. If I say "Not Guilty", I shall brew no more for the King; and if I say "Guilty", I shall brew no more for anybody else.'

The trial opened with a discussion of legal technicalities, namely, whether it could be proved that the petition to the King had either been written or published in Middlesex. It seemed possible that the prosecution might break down at the outset on this point, but the intervention of Lord Sunderland, brought into the Court in a sedan chair, and greeted by a shout of 'Popish Dog', turned the tide against the bishops. Counsel then directed themselves to the more fundamental issues, namely, whether the petition was in law a seditious libel. Compton, who was almost certainly present at the trial, may well have questioned, at this stage of the proceedings, the wisdom of his having the petition printed. It was the young Somers, however, who in a few telling phrases, destroyed the case for the Crown. The paper was not false, he tersely said, as a perusal of the parliamentary journals would make plain: it was not malicious for the bishops had been forced by the King to act in this way; and it was not seditious because it was merely a private petition.

Night came before the jury retired, when the bishops' solicitor wisely guarded the door of their chamber. At last the obstinate brewer gave way—he had much to lose—and they were all agreed on their verdict. At ten o'clock Sir Roger Langley uttered the words 'Not Guilty'. A great shout was immediately raised 'that one would have thought the Hall had cracked'.

It was taken up outside, and reverberated even in the Palace of Whitehall.

On the very day of the acquittal, while the bonfires in London were still burning, Admiral of the Fleet Arthur Herbert stole out of the city in the guise of a common seaman. He embarked for Holland bearing a letter which was destined to change the course of English history, and by so doing that of the Continent. It was signed in cypher by Shrewsbury, Devonshire, Danby, Lumley, Russell, Compton and Sydney, and was in the latter's handwriting. It was the all-important message to which reference had been made in the former epistle of 18 June.

This momentous letter, which the disguised Admiral took over with him, began as follows:

We have great satisfaction to find by 35 [Russell] and since by Mons. Zulestein that your Highness is ready and willing to give such assistance as they have related to us. We have great reason to believe we shall be every day in a worse condition than we are, and less able to defend ourselves, and therefore we do earnestly wish we might be so happy as to find a remedy before it is too late for us to contribute to our own deliverance. . . . We who subscribe this will not fail to attend your Highness upon your landing, and to do all that lies in our power to prepare others to be in as much readiness as such an action is capable of, where there is so much danger in communicating an affair of this nature, till it be near the time of its being made public.[1]

The letter then went on to urge the Prince to let them know definitely whether he saw 'fit to adventure upon the attempt': and if so, 'at what time preparations can be so managed as not to give them warning here, both to make them increase their force, and to secure those they suspect would join with you.'[2] It is significant that the invitation was signed by two tory leaders, four whigs and one bishop.

The Rubicon had been crossed and no one was more eager to make the passage than Henry Compton. Had things gone wrong, and the letter been discovered, none of the signatories could have made any effective defence against the charge of treason.

At the end of July, the Bishop of London wrote a personal letter to William, which in view of his having signed the former document assumes an added significance. 'I dare likewise to take

[1] Quoted in Dalrymple, *op. cit.*, ii. 107.　　　　[2] *Ibid.*, ii. 107.

upon me to assure you', he said, 'that both they that suffered[1] and the rest who concurred with them, are so well satisfied of the justice of their cause, that they will lay down their lives before they will the least depart from it. I should say something of myself, but I had so lately an opportunity of making my mind known to you that it can be to no purpose to say more now to you, than that I am under all the obligations in the world of approving myself, Sir, your Highness's most devoted and faithful servant.'[2]

William began his preparations for coming over to England with a rapidity and secrecy which his uncommunicative nature made easy. English noblemen began to cross surreptitiously over to The Hague—Shrewsbury, the high-church Macclesfield, Peterborough and Russell. Lord Sunderland, though he stayed in England, added to his perfidy by betraying James in the most base manner to William.

The Prince of Orange now drew up a Declaration, or rather one was drawn up for him by the Grand Pensionary Fagel which was later revised and shortened by the indefatigable Burnet. This document declared in straightforward language that the fundamental laws of England had been broken, and its liberties invaded; the government of the Church unconstitutionally committed into the hands of a group of Commissioners; the franchises of the boroughs invaded, and Roman Catholics illegally admitted to office. In response, therefore, to the requests of many lords spiritual and temporal, the Prince of Orange had decided to cross over to England with no thought of conquest, but only to secure a free and lawful Parliament which would sit in judgment on these things. The seventh article of this declaration gave Henry Compton the honour of a special mention as follows: 'The said Commissioners have suspended the Bishop of London, only because he refused to obey an Order that was sent to him to suspend a worthy divine, without so much as citing him before him to make his own Defence.'[3]

It was impossible for James any longer to be unaware of his danger. Rumours of what was happening reached him at Whitehall, and finally a dispatch from D'Abbeville, his envoy at The Hague, confirmed his worst fears. It is said that when James read it he turned unnaturally pale and remained silent. At last, at

---

[1] I.e. the seven bishops.   [2] Dalrymple, *op. cit.*, ii. 107.
[3] *The Life of Dr. Henry Compton*, p. 43.

the eleventh hour, even this obstinate and perverse monarch, who
had so often refused counsel even from the Pope, decided on a
policy of appeasement. Each day the *Gazette* began to give
expression to a newly-found royal clemency. On 28 September,
he summoned the Bishops of London, Ely, Bath and Wells,
and Peterborough to an audience,[1] but the Bishop of London
could not be found, it being rumoured that he had gone north
'to his sisters'.[2] The King then gave notice of his intention to
restore Compton to his episcopal function,[3] and on 30 September
the Ecclesiastical Commissioners accordingly removed his
suspension.[4] Compton, however, in the unsettled state of the
nation, 'took no steps to resume his duties or to thank the King
for his restoration'.[5]

In these circumstances, the Bishops in London (Compton was
not one of them) were encouraged to request an audience with
the King which he graciously granted on 3 October. Admitted to
the royal presence the aged and unhappy Sancroft addressed his
sovereign in humble and earnest tones. He implored him to follow
up his recent good resolutions by going even further. Would he
not, once and for all, abolish the Court of Ecclesiastical Commission, place the government in the hands of those legally
qualified to exercise it, restore their charters to the towns, replace
the Fellows of Magdalen College, and appoint an Archbishop to
York? And also, added the aged Primate respectfully, before
whom there now hovered a vision of better things, if the King
desired to be restored to the affections of his people, he would do
well to reconsider the points of difference between the Church
of England and the Church of Rome, which if he did, might
persuade him to return to the Church of his father and grandfather.[6]

While these events were taking place in London, a series of
conferences among opposition leaders was being held secretly in
the north. Danby, accompanied by Lord Dunblane and Charles
Bertie, had journeyed to Ritson Hall near Knaresborough, the
family seat of the Goodrickes, 'where Sir Henry was then amusing his leisure and providing for possible eventualities by turning

---

[1] *The Correspondence of Henry Hyde*, 1828, p. 188.
[2] See p. 126.   [3] Luttrell, *A Brief Historical Relation*, i. 464.
[4] *The Bishop of London's Register*, St. Paul's Cathedral.
[5] Macpherson, *Original Papers*, ii. 62.
[6] Clarke, *The Life of James the Second*, p. 188.

his garden into a small fortress'.[1] In this secluded spot, far from prying eyes, the 'great design' was discussed, and many Yorkshire gentry, who could be trusted, introduced to it. It is possible that Compton made the long journey from London to be present, though if this were so,[2] he was certainly back in town by the end of October. But present or absent, we may assume that he was not unaware of these deliberations.

William's preparations were all this time proceeding apace and were now almost complete. On 16 October he bade a touching farewell to the States General of Holland, and on the 19th he put to sea in a frigate called the *Brill*. Two days later, however, the fleet was back in port, having been scattered by wind and tempest. But William remained calm and undismayed, and on 1 November he was at sea again.

Towards the end of October, copies of the Prince's Declaration began to circulate surreptitiously in London. One agent was arrested and a packet containing a number of them was taken to James. He destroyed all but one which, as he read, filled him with alarm and despondency. What perhaps distracted him most was the statement that William had been invited to England by a number of lords spiritual and temporal. He immediately summoned Halifax, Clarendon and Nottingham to the Palace but all denied any knowledge of such an invitation.

But there was one spiritual lord mentioned in the declaration against whom James knew that he had particularly visited his anger; whom he had always cordially disliked; whom he had contrived to disappoint of the Archbishopric and illegally to suspend from his office. The King's thoughts turned inevitably to the Bishop of London and he summoned him to a private audience on Wednesday, 31 October, by a messenger sent to Fulham. The Bishop, however, was in the country, and did not return until it was too late to obey the royal commands that day. Believing (erroneously) that all the bishops had been likewise

---

[1] A. Browning, *Thomas, Earl of Danby*, i. 390.

[2] Amongst the manuscripts of the Earl of Cowper (*H.M.C.* App. iii, Report XII, p. 179) there is a letter from George London to Thomas Coke, dated 18 Aug., but most unfortunately without any year given. He states that he had been with the Bishop of London, who intended to go north to Derbyshire and to visit the gardens of Lords Chesterfield and Ferrers, and the Duke of Devonshire. These names (see pp. 137 and 367) certainly seem significant, and suggest that the year is 1688.

summoned, he wrote immediately to the Archbishop of Canterbury begging to know 'only by word of mouth, what the matter is, that I may attend accordingly'.[1]

On the next day, Thursday, 1 November, the deferred interview took place, and we can well imagine that it was with some trepidation that the Bishop entered the royal presence. The King (as was his custom) soon got down to business. He had the copy of William's Declaration in his hand, and he read the short passage which referred to the invitation of the lords spiritual and temporal. With typical bluntness he asked the Bishop whether there was any truth in it.

Compton's position was not enviable. He was in fact the only ecclesiastic who had signed the invitation to William. To admit that he had done so would not only bring punishment on himself: it might well incriminate others, some of whom were guiltless, as well as help the King in his defence measures. The Bishop at least preferred the lie inferential to the lie direct. 'I am confident', he replied, 'that the rest of the Bishops would as readily answer in the negative as myself.' The King, obviously relieved, replied graciously: 'I believe you are all innocent', and then added that he wished them to make a public announcement of their abhorrence of the project.

Compton had long ceased to regard a royal wish as a command that he must obey, and he quite reasonably asked that he might see the Declaration. This the King refused, and the Bishop then protested that time must be given for the bishops to consider the matter. 'Every one', said James as he dismissed Compton, 'is to answer for himself. But I will send for my Lord of Canterbury who shall call you together.'[2]

On Friday, 2 November, Compton with the Archbishop and those bishops who were in London again waited upon the King in response to a royal summons. James briefly acquainted them with the circulation of the Prince's Declaration, and commanded Lord Preston to read it. He then asked the bishops, one by one, whether they had in fact joined in any such request to William. They all replied that they had not, Compton merely remarking that he had already given his answer the day before. The King then repeated his royal pleasure that the bishops should publish a

---

[1] Compton to Sancroft, 31 Oct., 1688, Bod. Tanner MSS. 28, fo. 215.
[2] Macpherson, *op. cit.*, i. 277.

denial of the charge made against them. Such an avowal would be much to his service, he said.

Sancroft pleaded that he must have time to consult all his fellow bishops, but the King insisted that the matter was urgent, and that there was no time to summon the bishops who were out of London. Their Lordships then withdrew, the Archbishop merely saying that he would call together as many of his brethren as he could.[1]

There can be no doubt that these proceedings were very distressing to the Archbishop of Canterbury. No man was more convinced in his Protestantism, but none had a deeper sense of his duty to the throne or more respect for the sacred nature of the oaths he had taken to the King. The very thought of sending a petition to the Prince of Orange was abhorrent to him. Whatever might be his private opinion, however—it seems that in this respect he would have been willing to meet James's wishes—he found that his brethren, under Compton's leadership, were not prepared to give way. They would issue no public disclaimer. It is not surprising that the Bishop of London should be foremost in urging such a refusal, and it was he who drew up a document: 'Reasons why the Bishops refused to vindicate themselves in a public manner', which set out at length the case for declining.[2]

These 'Reasons' were in themselves both cogent and ingenious. 'A general clause in a declaration not avowed or published', Compton maintained, 'was not a sufficient ground for a man or a number of men to vindicate themselves as if they were concerned in it.' Suppose the King should make it punishable to read the Declaration, what then? As the Bishops had at 'all times adhered to their duty and allegiance', so they were 'less willing to do anything now, which might distinguish them as men marked with a particular character of suspicion, since they thought their loyalty less blemished by not being called in question, than it would be by the clearest vindication, that can be made upon it upon this occasion.' There were other difficulties also. A public statement in the name of the bishops in or near London might suggest either that the others did not support it, or that those

---

[1] Compton drew up an account of both interviews for Sancroft's benefit. See Bod. Tanner MSS. 28, fo. 227.

[2] *Ibid.* 27, 229. The document is headed, in Sancroft's handwriting, *Some Reasons agst giving any Paper of Abhorrence.* The rest is in Compton's hand.

who had signed had more cause to vindicate themselves. Moreover, since in the Prince's Declaration reference was made to lords temporal as well as spiritual, why should the latter alone be called upon to publish a disclaimer?

Such powerful arguments (though Compton was not, perhaps, the man to put them forward) convinced the bishops, when they met at Lambeth on 5 November,[1] that it would not be prudent to comply with the King's wishes. The decision was almost certainly distressing to the Archbishop, for two days previously he had drawn up his own vindication as follows: 'Whereas there hath been of late a general apprehension that his Highness the Prince of Orange hath an intention to invade the Kingdom in a hostile manner . . . for my own discharge [I], profess and declare that I never gave him any such invitation by word, writing, or otherwise. Nor do I know, nor can believe, that any of my reverend brethren, the bishops, have in any such way invited him.'[2]

Mention of William of Orange recalls us to the fortunes of that fleet of six hundred ships, which under the welcome impetus of a Protestant wind, was heading towards England. This same breeze which blew William's armament to her shores kept James's fleet safely locked up in the Thames. The King confidently expected that the Prince would try to land in Yorkshire, and he made his defence plans on this assumption. But William, after encouraging this delusion, suddenly swung his fleet into the Channel. On 5 November, a day already famous (or infamous) in English history, the Prince stepped ashore at Torbay, and immediately began his march to London. The response from the west was not at first very heartening, and even Calvinistic William began to have misgivings. For a week no great landowner threw in his lot with him: but with Plymouth seized in his rear, his forces began to grow stronger, and it was a great encouragement when John Lord Lovelace joined his standard.

James was now forced to recognise that the situation was very serious indeed. 'All trade and commerce is now very dead', Luttrell noted in his diary, 'hardly any money stirring, they that

---

[1] *The Correspondence of Henry Hyde*, p. 493.

[2] Macpherson, *op. cit.*, i. 279. It is almost certain that Sancroft did not present this document to the King; but it undoubtedly suggests that he had misgivings about the attitude of his brethren.

have it not caring to part with it.'[1] On 6 November, still un-
certain exactly where William had landed, the King summoned
Sancroft, Compton, White of Peterborough, and Sprat of
Rochester, to a secret conference in his closet.[2]

The Archbishop bore himself at this most trying interview
with dignity and courage, conscientiously interpreting the sense
of his brethren. The King asked for the public disclaimer which
he was to bring him. Sancroft replied that the bishops were not
concerned to clear their fame to the world. But James—he was
obviously distressed and overwrought—could not leave the
subject and he repeated that he was expecting the bishops to
express publicly their abhorrence of the Prince's invasion. The
bishops again insisted that though they would assist him as
Christian ministers, and as members of the Upper House, they
yet could not oblige the King in this matter for reasons which
they had already stated. 'I have done', James replied at last rather
pathetically, 'I will urge you no further. Since you will not help
me, I must trust myself and my own arms'.[3]

The news of William's landing, and of his advance through
Devonshire, was not long in reaching London. For James it meant
a last-minute readjustment of his defence plans. The King was
already in a highly nervous condition, and Sancroft headed a
delegation of lords spiritual and temporal who united in urging
him to call a free and legal parliament, and to start negotiations
with William. James was not pleased, and he addressed himself to the bishops in particular with great bitterness. 'I could not
prevail on you the other day to declare against the invasion;
but you are ready enough to declare against me. Then you would
not meddle with politics. You have no scruples against meddling
now. You have excited this rebellious temper among your flocks,
and now you foment it. You would be better employed in
teaching them how to obey than in teaching me how to govern.'

In the capital a state of apprehension kept everyone on edge.
One thing, however, was quite certain. James could not stay idly

---

[1] Luttrell, *op. cit.*, i. 476.

[2] The Bishop of Rochester in his account does not mention Compton as
present, but he is almost certainly in error. See *The Correspondence of Henry
Hyde*, p. 497. Also the Bishop of Peterborough in a letter to the Bishop of St.
Asaph on 7 Nov. (Clarendon, *Correspondence*, ii. 502), says that the King accused
Compton and Sancroft of 'changing their minds'.

[3] Clarendon, *ibid.*

in London, and on 19 November he arrived in Salisbury where the headquarters of his army were stationed. His only chance of success lay in securing a quick victory over William's forces, which was the reason why the Prince and the Duke of Schomberg, an old campaigner, were determined to avoid battle. Already some sixty men of rank had joined William, and the spirit of his army was high. At this crisis in his destiny, it is but fair to James to admit that he did not know upon whom to rely. As the two armies drew nearer to each other, John Churchill discovered that his protestant conscience would not allow him to serve a Roman Catholic sovereign: and Prince George of Denmark (husband of Anne), who had irritated James by remarking 'Est-il possible' as the news of fresh desertions came in, himself silently withdrew to the Prince after an embarrassing supper with James at Andover. Cornet Hatton Compton, a kinsman of the Bishop of London, with two or three subalterns and some two hundred men, also went over to William; and it was said that the Bishop's brother, Sir Francis, would have followed suit, but for the fear that his Major would place him under arrest. 'One can well imagine the perplexity he was in', writes a descendant, the present Earl of Northampton, 'between his duty as a soldier and his sympathy with the cause of William, the latter of which was no doubt influenced and intensified by the uncompromising attitude of his favourite brother Bishop Henry'.[1]

In these unnerving circumstances, having suffered earlier a prolonged attack of nose bleeding, the King decided to return to London. It was the beginning of the end.

James arrived in town on the evening of 26 November, where he was immediately met with the unsettling news—more bitter than any he had received hitherto—that his own daughter, the Princess Anne, had fled. 'God help me, my own children have forsaken me', he cried. To tell the story of her flight, in which the Bishop of London was intimately involved, we must retrace our steps.

The advance of the Prince of Orange from the west was the signal for risings throughout England. The city of York, whither the Earl of Danby had proceeded, declared for the Prince. At Derby, the Earl of Devonshire mustered the great lords of the midland and eastern counties.

---

[1] William Bingham Compton, *op. cit.*, p. 121.

In London, the news of these events, and in particular the defection of Churchill and Prince George of Denmark, filled Anne with alarm. She had already written to William (her brother-in-law) the week before, approving his enterprise, and she was now entirely under the domination of that remarkable woman, Sarah Churchill. On Saturday, 25 November, a courier rushed to the Princess announcing that the King was returning to London. Anne was thrown into a state of panic more, perhaps, on account of her beloved Mrs. Freeman than for herself and she declared that rather than see her father she would jump out of the window. Escape to William was impossible, for the King's forces lay in between—but the road to the north was still open.

It was at this juncture that the Princess's old tutor, the Bishop of London, came to the rescue. Though most of his fellow conspirators had either gone over to Holland, or had fled from London, Henry Compton was still in the city. He was always prone to sudden enthusiasms, and was a born romantic. He also was as anxious as Anne not to be in London when James returned. Nor could he forget that he had solemnly promised to join William when he arrived in England. The Bishop therefore determined to cast caution to the winds, and to appear openly as the Prince's supporter. He was at the time in semi-hiding in Suffolk Street, and according to the story which the Duchess of Marlborough put on record many years afterward,[1] he communicated to her at the Cockpit where he might be found 'if her Royal Highness should have occasion for a friend'. The Princess, when she heard of the offer, immediately sent Sarah to the Bishop, who told him that her mistress was determined to leave the Court and to put herself under his care. Some of the ardour of youth and the passion of the gallant seem to have returned to the middle-aged Bishop. He promised to consult his friends in the city, and to be in the neighbourhood of the Cockpit at midnight in a hackney coach 'in order to convey the Princess to some place where she might be private and safe'. The Bishop proceeded to confide the scheme to his nephew the Earl of Dorset—some twenty years earlier the biggest rake in town—who eagerly agreed to share in it.

It was essential, of course, that the news of the escapade should not leak out, and the Princess accordingly retired to bed at her

[1] *An Account of the Conduct of the Duchess of Marlborough*, pp. 16-18.

usual hour. Soon after midnight, however, in company with the redoubtable Sarah, and Lady Fitzharding, and one servant, she silently stole from her bedroom in to the Cockpit down a back stairway.[1] Waiting for them was a hackney coach, guarded by the Bishop and the Earl of Dorset. The Princess and her attendants walked to the coach. It drew off and they soon found themselves in the Bishop of London's house in Aldersgate Street.[2]

Anne left behind her a letter for the Queen in which she explained how that torn between her loyalty to her husband and to her father she had decided to remove herself until she heard 'the happy news of a reconcilement'.[3]

The Princess had escaped not an hour too soon, as Compton later related to Danby with some relish.[4] When Prince George left the King at Andover, James had immediately dispatched orders to London that guards be posted outside Anne's lodgings, though she was not to be told of it. So at 3 o'clock in the morning, these security measures were taken, but with the result, so the Bishop of London commented, that 'this order concealed her till ten o'clock which was great advantage to us'. When the flight was discovered, the Queen screamed out 'as if she had been mad'.

The following morning the party left London by the dangerous wilds of Epping Forest, till they came to Loughton, where they refreshed themselves at the house of Mr. John Worth, a blustering county justice. They then proceeded to the Earl of Dorset's mansion at Copt Hall, and made a short stay, Lady Dorset 'furnishing them with everything'. Here the Earl left them. Then on they went through the quiet countryside of Hertfordshire to Hitchin, where they took some refreshment at an inn, and according to local gossip 'sat in a cart saying that but for their flight it [i.e. to sit in a hangman's cart] might have been their lot'.[5] At Castle Ashby, which they reached on 28 November, the Earl of Northampton attended them, and recruited a body of horse to serve as a protection for the Princess.[6]

---

[1] This stairway is said to have been especially constructed some six weeks before.
[2] The doings of this night may be read in *H.M.C.* App. v, Report XI, p. 214 (Samuel Pepy's account): Clarendon, *Correspondence and Diary*, ii. 207.
[3] Curtis Brown, *The Letters of Queen Anne*, p. 44.
[4] Compton to Danby, 2 Dec., 1688, *H.M.C.* App. ix, Report II, p. 461.
[5] *Memoirs of Thomas Earl of Ailesbury written by himself*, p. 191.
[6] William Bingham Compton, *op. cit.*, p. 145.

Feeling now more secure, the party proceeded leisurely to Market Harborough, in which old market town Anne disclosed her identity. Here they were joined by a large number of gentry, led by Lord Cullen and Sir Charles Shuckburgh. And so they proceeded to Leicester where the mayor and aldermen honoured them 'with two noble banquets' and showed them 'all demonstrations of respect and joy'. The Princess warmed to this hospitable reception, being 'wonderful pleasant and cheerful', while Compton thanked the civic fathers for their entertainment, adding that 'he was forced to lay aside the Bible at present, but hoped very suddenly to take it into his hands again'.[1] On 21 December, they left Leicester, marching into Nottingham in the afternoon of the following day.

The Bishop certainly seems to have entered into this quixotic adventure with real spirit and martial enthusiasm. Perhaps, as he 'preceded the Princess's carriage in a buff coat and jack boots, with a sword at his side, and pistols in his holsters',[2] he remembered, across the years, those far off days in the Life Guards.

The Bishop's first task in Nottingham was to write a soldierly letter to the Prince of Orange. It is worth quoting: 'We are just arrived here, and found the gentlemen here much disposed to go in with you. Her Highness has a desire to go with them that she may be under your protection. That you may therefore contrive how to secure her passage to you, it is fit you should know the condition of our troops here; they are very raw and defective of good officers. We shall march a thousand and increase every day very much, but still we are very weak in discipline. I beseech you therefore, Sir, to advise best of this matter what forces will be necessary for you to send and wherever I shall meet them and when.'[3]

This report was confirmed in a similar epistle sent to the Prince by the Earl of Devonshire.[4]

It had been Compton's original intention to join Danby at York, but he now saw that such a meeting would neither commend itself to William, nor would it restore Anne to her husband. Yet he promptly sent off an express to the Earl giving

---

[1] Hatton, *Correspondence*, ii. 118.
[2] Macaulay, *History of England*, ii. 103.
[3] Dalrymple, *op. cit.*, ii. 250.
[4] *H.M.C.* App. ix, Report XIV, p. 453 (Lindsey MSS.).

him the news of his arrival in Nottingham. It was doubtless with a feeling of pride, not unmixed with satisfaction, that he began his letter with these words: 'My Lord, I have this afternoon got the Princess safe hither, where we intend to stay three or four days till we hear from the Prince.' After recounting, in brief, some of the details of the journey, he concluded: 'We want your advice extremely here and some of your horse if you can spare them.'[1]

The news which this letter brought was of great interest to Danby, though it placed him in a difficult position. The Earl was anxious to play the role of mediator between James and the Prince of Orange, and for this reason wished for a stalemate between the contending parties rather than the victory of either side. To this end he recognised at once the power and prestige which would result from his having the Princess under his protection. Thus he replied immediately congratulating the Bishop on the 'good news' that his letter contained, and confessing his willingness 'to lay all other considerations aside for the safety of the Princess'.

Yet, on the other hand, Danby's immediate objective was to secure Hull, for which the prospects were fair.[2] Would it not, therefore, be better, he enquired, for Anne to come to York, particularly as the Castle at Scarborough was now safely held, which meant that, if the need arose, she could escape by sea?[3]

In a more private letter to the Bishop, Danby wrote:

I should have been extreme glad to have waited immediately upon the Princess (who I am overjoyed is brought safe out of their hands by your Lordship's prudent conduct); but it is impossible for me to leave this place till all move. I heartily wish her Highness amongst us here, both for her security and the great addition it would give to our interest in these parts, which would be no less than the securing the whole north; but I doubt not but your Lordship's conduct and counsells will advise her what is best. Your Lordship knows me so well that I hope you will give her Highness an assurance of my readiness to pay her the uttermost of my service.[4]

---

[1] *H.M.C.* App. ix, Report II, p. 461.

[2] As a matter of fact, Hull had declared for a free Parliament before this letter reached Compton.

[3] Danby to Compton and Devonshire, 4 Dec., 1688, B.M. Leeds Papers, Packet 13*b*.

[4] Danby to Compton, 4 Dec., 1688, *ibid.*

Compton realised that he could do nothing until he heard from the Prince, and he replied to Danby on 5 December in a letter which we cannot forbear quoting in full:

My Lord,
　　I am heartily glad to hear you are in so good a posture, and wish myself with you for many reasons. We are here a considerable body of men, and they are daily coming in from all parts. But we want officers extremely, which you may easily believe when I make so great a part of the council of war. We have sent an express to the Prince, so that we can take no resolutions till we hear from him. However, the Princess is extremely sensible of the readiness of your parts to give her assistance. We shall certainly take our resolutions one way or another before Saturday. I do not find here any preparation to give an account wherefore we are met, or what resolution to take in reference to the prudential part of being in a posture to convince the world that we have a share in standing by and seeing the nation have right.[1]

Meanwhile Compton, who was the titular leader of the party which had gathered around Anne at Nottingham, was not finding it easy to keep the peace. Disagreements broke out between those who regarded themselves as definitely in revolt against James, and those who thought of themselves simply as protecting the Princess. In the last category was such a prominent nobleman as Lord Chesterfield, who had brought with him a hundred horse, but who absolutely refused, even at the personal request of Anne, to join her council. 'I replied', the noble lord wrote later, 'that I was come a purpose (if there were occasion) to defend her person with my life against any that would dare to attack her; but as to my being of her council, I did beg her pardon for desiring to be excused, because I had the honour to be a privy councillor to the King her father; and therefore I would not be of any council for regulating troops that I perceived were intended to serve against him.'[2]

There were also many disputes over precedence among both nobles and gentlemen, and the uncertainty as to what the next step was to be did not help matters: but on 8 December, the Prince's instructions to the Bishop arrived, in which William made it clear that he was determined to prevent the Princess

[1] Compton to Danby, 5 Dec., 1688, M.B. Leeds Papers, Packet 13*b*.
[2] *Letters of Philip, Second Earl of Chesterfield*, 1829, p. 49.

putting herself under the protection of the ambitious Earl of Danby. After expressing his pleasure at the news of the 'happy arrival' at Nottingham, the Prince said: 'I believe that you cannot do better than come immediately to Oxford. I march tomorrow to Hungerford, then to Newbury, and on to cross the Thames where it is most convenient. . . . I cannot express to you the impatience that I have to see you.'[1]

Such explicit instructions must be obeyed, and Compton had no option but to let Danby know the latest development, which he did in two letters written on 8 December. In the one he confessed that had he not heard from the Prince before Monday he 'had certainly carried the Princess to York', but that now he had 'received orders from the Prince to come to Oxford' In the other he wrote: 'The enclosed[3] will give you the reason why it is impossible for us now to meet. I am sorry with it for all my heart because I could have unburdened myself to you. But this is now no help, we must be gone early tomorrow morning. The Prince wants horse, and therefore would be glad if you would send any that you have to spare. I once more pray God send us a happy meeting and am most heartily, My Lord etc.'[4]

Thus the journey to Oxford commenced on 9 December, and as a consequence, so comments his biographer, there 'was destroyed completely Danby's vision of himself as a northern general, holding the balance in her name[5] between James and William'.[6] Compton, certainly, had no desire to co-operate in playing such a dangerous game.

The march to Oxford produced no military incidents, but it was far from a happy progress. The contingent now included fifteen noblemen, among whom were Devonshire, Northampton, Chesterfield, Manchester, Grey, Carteret, and Cullen, besides a few hundred gentlemen. In such company, the Bishop of London would have been wise to relinquish his military command altogether, but he seems to have stuck to it with some tenacity. Was not the whole enterprise due to his initiative?

When the party reached Leicester, they were joined by the militia of the surrounding counties, and on the following day

[1] *H.M.C.* App. ix, Report II, p. 460b.
[2] Compton to Danby, 8 Dec., 1688, B.M. Leeds Papers, Packet 13b.
[3] I.e. the letter from William.
[4] Compton to Danby, 8 Dec., 1688, B.M. Add. MSS. 2803, fo. 373.
[5] I.e. Anne's.   [6] Andrew Browning, *Thomas, Earl of Danby*, i. 407.

Compton on his own initiative summoned both nobles and gentlemen to meet together in Anne's presence—much to the annoyance of Lord Chesterfield who felt that as a member of the King's Council he should have been taken into the Bishop's confidence. At this meeting Compton read a paper inviting all present to enter into an association to take reprisals on the Roman Catholic population if the Prince of Orange should be killed—a proposal which hardly became his episcopal character.[1] Chesterfield refused point blank to comply, and his lead was followed by Lords Scarsdale, Ferrers, and Cullen, together with a hundred gentlemen. The Princess was said to be 'extremely angry'.[2]

So this, not wholly united, party continued its journey through Coventry, Warwick (where Chesterfield departed), Banbury and on to Oxford, where Anne had the great joy of being re-united to her husband on 15 December. Much had happened since they had last met. Over twenty years later, Thomas Hearne preserved a vivid recollection of Captain Compton, clad in a blue [3] cloak and brandishing a drawn sword, riding through the streets of the city at the head of his troops, with his cornet, Sir Justinian Isham, bearing a standard on which was written in golden letters: 'Nolumus Leges Angliae Mutari.'[4] Behind the Bishop were the Princess, and the Earl of Northampton, the latter leading five hundred horse, probably drawn from the Warwickshire militia.[5]

It was a long time before Henry Compton was allowed to forget this escapade. Macaulay writes that the Bishop accepted the captaincy 'with an alacrity which gave great scandal to right thinking Churchmen and did not much raise his character in the opinion of the Whigs'. John Kettlewell, who had dedicated his *Measures of Christian Obedience* to the Bishop in 1681, promptly removed his name from the next edition, 'judging this strange appearance of my Lord of London, not to be so very conformable to that of a Christian Bishop, or to those measures of Christian loyalty which were laid down by him in that excellent Discourse'.[6] To 'rescue' Anne was one thing: it was another matter to appear in arms.

[1] See p. 141.   [2] *Letters of Philip, Second Earl of Chesterfield*, 49.
[3] Other authorities say it was purple! Macaulay speaks of it as 'buff'.
[4] T. Hearne, *Remarks and Collections*, 1886, p. 304.
[5] *H.M.C.* App. vii, Report XII, p. 229 (Fleming MSS.).
[6] Hickes, *Memoirs of the Life of Mr. John Kettlewell*, 1718, p. 52.

The fact was, of course, that though the conception of the soldier-bishop might have been familiar in the days of the knights templar (or even to Bishop Leslie in Ireland, who between the two opposing armies prayed that 'God would stand neuter in this cause that his strong right hand might gain the victory'), in the England of the late seventeenth century it was not so easily understood. Even a friend of the Bishop's wrote after his death: 'He rescued our present Sovereign; he hid her (as it were) till Popish Tyranny was overpast. For this too, how invidiously, nay how contradictorily, has he been treated? He has been envied and arraigned for the self same thing; as if he had done both too much and too little.'[1]

The remainder of James's short stay in London was one of fitful hope and bitter despair. He had now thoroughly lost his nerve, just when he most needed it, and he consequently set his mind only on escape. Thus he was not in earnest when talking of calling a 'free parliament', nor sincere when thinking of negotiating with William. His first concern was to dispatch his wife and baby to France, and on 11 December he himself left London, throwing the great seal into the Thames near Lambeth. Release, however, was not yet. He was intercepted at Sheerness and brought back to London on 16 December, the day after Compton and Anne marched through Oxford. But on a rainy morning a day later, he left the city, in which he had reigned so short a time, by a barge at Whitehall stairs. He was never to return. On Christmas Day, in company with the Duke of Berwick, he stepped ashore at Ambleteuse on the soil of France.

It was not only the fall of a monarch, and the collapse of a royal house—it was the end of an age.

[1] T. Gooch, *op. cit.*, p. 11.

CHAPTER NINE

THE POLITICAL SETTLEMENT

THE Bishop of London may well have entertained a feeling of satisfaction as he returned to London in December 1688. He had played a dangerous game. He had openly defied James, shocked his ecclesiastical brethren by appearing in arms, and risked life and fortune on that foreign prince who had espoused the cause of English liberty. Yet he had won through. The cause with which he had so dangerously associated himself had triumphed. James was in France, William at Whitehall. 'The bloodless Revolution' had been brought about with a rapidity and thoroughness which took both Protestant and Roman Catholic by surprise. Tory and whig, churchman and dissenter had been brought together in common opposition to a ruthless despot who threatened the freedom of all. But now the cause of the oppression was removed. At first a suppliant at the Court of Versailles, James was soon regally established at St. Germains. What now?

As always happens after successful revolutions, the unity which had been forged in adversity began to show signs of weakening after its immediate object had been achieved. There were many and urgent problems waiting to be settled which submitted it, unfortunately, to exceptional strain. What was the new legal settlement to be? What status was William to occupy in it? Was the throne vacant, and if so, in whom did sovereignty now reside?

Some of the tories, and a few bishops, were certainly alarmed at the startling change in the state of national affairs. They had never for a moment envisaged a situation in which their own sovereign would be domiciled in a foreign land, and a foreign prince established at home.

Henry Compton, however, suffered from no moral scruples, as his public behaviour made apparent. Certainly he lost little time in paying his respects to the Prince, for whereas on 15 December he was in Oxford, on 21 December he was at Whitehall at the head of his clergy, presenting a congratulatory address to William. Nor was he accompanied only by his fellow clergy of the Church of England, for, finding a number of dissenters equally anxious to greet their new Prince, he boldly presented them also.

The address which the Bishop of London drew up for the occasion was typically forthright. The clergy came, he said, 'to pay him their humble Duties and grateful Respects for his very great and most hazardous Undertaking, for their Deliverance and the Preservation of the Protestant Religion, with the ancient Laws and Liberties of the Nation'.[1]

William in his reply graciously thanked them for their attendance, assuring them 'that the great End of his difficult and chargeable Expedition was to preserve and secure the Protestant Religion (his own Religion and their Religion)[2] for which purpose he should not think anything (no not life itself) too dear to Hazard'. 'I have always had a great Esteem for the Clergy of London', he concluded, 'and a value for the service they have done Religion, and will take care they shall live at Ease, and ever give Testimonies to my Affection for the Church of England, depend upon it.'[3]

One who was present on this occasion says that the Prince spoke very earnestly,[4] as he might well do, for such an early approach to him was politically of great value. When the brief ceremony was completed, the Bishop conducted his clergy into the presence of his old pupil, Princess Mary, whose fortunes he had followed with a truly parental eye. She had now been in London just a week, and Compton addressed to her a few simple words of welcome, to which she replied with equal simplicity that 'she desired nothing more than the prayers of the clergy for her'.[5]

These early signs of the Bishop of London's satisfaction at the course which events had taken stand in marked contrast to the hesitations and scruples which some of his brethren, the bishops, began to display. On the way from Torbay to London, while in Exeter, some of William's most earnest supporters persuaded Burnet to draw up an 'Association'—we saw Compton trying to

[1] *The Life of Dr. Henry Compton*, p. 45. Also White Kennett, *Complete History*, i. p. 521.

[2] This was very cleverly expressed for William, of course, was a Calvinist.

[3] White Kennett, *op. cit.*, i. 522.

[4] *The Autobiography of Symon Patrick*, 1839, p. 143.　　[5] *Ibid.*

commend it at Leicester—which had as its main object the defence of the Prince's person. The rumour now began to circulate in London that employment in the Government would be restricted to those who were prepared to sign this document. Of the bishops, so Sir Philip Musgrave, a life-long Royalist, reported to that extreme high churchman, Lord Dartmouth, only the Bishop of London was prepared to comply.[1]

William's cause had certainly prospered, and he was now anxious to identify himself with that Church which had played so large a part, although at times passively, in the success of his undertaking. He therefore signified to the Bishop of London his desire to receive the Sacrament of Holy Communion according to the rites of the Church of England. The Prince had been in England on at least three former occasions, but it is unlikely that he had 'communicated' before in this country. Compton welcomed this assertion of Protestant 'solidarity', and himself celebrated the Holy Communion in the Chapel of St. James on the last day of what had been an eventful year.

The Bishop of London's own enthusiasm, coupled with his temperamental impetuosity, made him eager to speed up the pace of events, and early in January 1689, he instructed his clergy to omit the prayer for the Prince of Wales in the public liturgy and in the prayers before the sermon—an order which most of the clergy were glad to obey, having already gone so far as to pray simply for the King and the Royal family, without the mention of any name. Sir Thomas Clarges, however, was not the only contemporary who made an indignant protest, reminding one of Compton's clergy, Thomas Tenison, at St. Martin's, that such changes could be authorised only by Act of Parliament.[2]

It now became increasingly obvious that there were great differences of opinion as to what ought to be done, not simply between whig and tory, churchman and dissenter, but within the ranks of the whigs and tories themselves. No one had foreseen the situation in which the country now found itself; no one ever can foresee the precise course of a revolution.

At one extreme were the rigid tories who wished to recall James unconditionally. Such men deplored what had happened, and lamented the sins of their countrymen in having set forth their

---

[1] *H.M.C.* App. i, Report XV, p. 143 (Dartmouth MSS., vol. 3).
[2] E. Carpenter, *The Life and Times of Thomas Tenison*, p. 92.

hand against the Lord's anointed: but these, for the time being, constituted such a small minority as to be almost negligible. At the other extreme were the militant and doctrinaire whigs who rejoiced that the throne was vacant, not through the flight of James, but because (so they maintained) James had violated the contract between King and people upon which the continuance of all government finally depends. These men, on terms, were prepared immediately to offer the throne to William.

Between such extremes, there was a great and bewildering variety of opinion. William Sancroft, for example, who took the opportunity of calling together all those who had been associated with him in the famous trial, was the leader of those tories who were prepared to accept, as a fact of bitter experience, that James was unfit to discharge the duties of his high office, but who still thought that his status as King was sacrosanct, and that their oaths to him were inviolable. They were prepared to allow William to take over administrative responsibility under some such title as *custos regni* or Regent, while James remained titularly king.

The Earl of Danby, the leader of the moderate tories (and Compton's former ally), who it was whispered had made up his mind to be 'the great man in the Government',[1] came forward with a compromise which was certainly ingenious, and which he claimed was more in harmony with legal precedent and with the known laws of the land. James II, he said, had in fact abdicated, as was clear from his flight and removal to France. But the throne could not be vacant, for it descended inevitably from the monarch to his heir, who in the present circumstances (in view of the widespread suspicion attaching to the birth of the 'pretended Prince of Wales') could only be Princess Mary, eldest daughter of James, and wife of William of Orange. She was *de jure* already Queen, and it was merely a matter of form, necessary to make the matter clear, for the Houses of Parliament to declare her to be such.

This very attractive, but perilous, *via media* was thought by many contemporaries to have the advantage of enabling a large number of tories and high churchmen to save face, while at the same time in fact declaring for William. Compton was prepared to give it his support.[2] Indeed Clarendon reports that when in an

---

[1] *H.M.C.* App. i, Report XV, p. 143 (Dartmouth MSS., vol. 3.)
[2] A. Browning, *op. cit.*, i. 428.

assembly of peers, which met at the time of James's flight, Lord Paget proposed the immediate proclamation of Mary as Queen, Compton joined Lord North in seconding this motion, which did not, however, secure much support.[1]

On 22 January 1689, the House of Commons—it was not legally such, of course—met to make its momentous decision. After prolonged and sometimes heated discussion, a mediating formula was hammered out which tried to conciliate varying points of view. It declared that 'King James the Second, having endeavoured to subvert the constitution of the Kingdom by breaking the original contract between King and people, and by the advice of the Jesuits and other wicked persons having violated the fundamental laws, and having withdrawn himself out of the kingdom, had abdicated the government, and that the throne had thereby become vacant'.

It was now (29 January) a matter of getting this omnibus resolution through the Upper Chamber, and here difficulties began to show themselves. The tory Lords Rochester and Nottingham were for a Regency, Halifax and Danby against it. The Archbishop of Canterbury did not attend—this was an act of weakness—though the bishops generally were known to be behind Rochester and Nottingham. It was no surprise, therefore, that the Archbishop of York, with eleven of his brethren, voted for a resolution in favour of a Regency. Only two bishops, Compton and Trelawney, voted against it—so strong was 'the horror of a Deposing Power'[2]—but their vote proved decisive, for the motion was lost by a narrow margin of 51 to 49.[3] But this negative decision still left the problem of what was to be done unresolved, and the resolution of the Lower House was now debated clause by clause. Was the throne vacant? Halifax said 'yes', Danby 'no', and this was characteristic of the stalemate throughout. A parley then took place in the Earl of Devonshire's house, but no solution seemed in sight.

In the midst of this uncertainty a Day of Thanksgiving was held on 31 January, and a religious service, drawn up by the two tory bishops Ken and Sprat, was held in St. Margaret's Church,

---

[1] Clarendon, *Correspondence*, ii. 235.
[2] White Kennett, *op. cit.*, i. 510.
[3] Burnet, *op. cit.*, iii. 377 n. Also *H.M.C.* App. ii, Report XIV, p. 425 (Portland MSS.).

Westminster, at which the preacher, however, was Gilbert Burnet, most militant of whigs. As darkness fell that night, the much tried citizens of London gave vent to their feelings in a blaze of bonfires and fireworks.

Still the constitutional deadlock remained. The Upper House returned to its deliberations, and decided at last, following the lead of Danby (by 55 votes to 41) that the throne was not vacant.

This cleavage between the two Houses seemed to offer little hope of an immediate solution. But there was one man, and one man only, who could at least simplify some of the complications. William had so far said very little, preferring, wisely, to let the nation make its own decision. He now revealed something of what was going on in his own uncommunicative mind. If they wanted a Regency, he said in effect, they could have one, but they must not look to him to occupy the office, nor could he, despite his great affection for his wife, consent to be her 'gentleman usher'. This forthright and candid declaration brought the Upper House down to earth, and immediately introduced a sense of reality into deliberations which had hitherto smacked a little too much of a Union debate at a University. The two Houses met together in a free conference. The changed atmosphere was seen when all but three lords agreed that James had abdicated, and by a vote of 62 against 47 the throne was declared vacant. It was now almost a formality to declare William and Mary King and Queen, with the administration of government in the hands of the Prince. On Wednesday, 13 February, the Crown was formally offered to them, and accepted.

The ceremony, as befitted its solemn and historic character, was a brilliant one. The clerk to the House of Lords read the Declaration of Rights, which had been drawn up by Somers. Halifax, in the name of all the estates of the realm, requested the Prince and Princess to accept the throne, and William, on behalf of his wife and himself, replied: 'We thankfully accept what you have offered us.' They then moved in procession to the great gate at Whitehall, and after the trumpets and the battle drums had burst forth and died away, and Garter King at Arms had proclaimed the Prince and Princess of Orange King and Queen of England, they adjourned to the Chapel Royal, where the Bishop of London preached the sermon.[1] What he said has unfortunately not come

[1] Luttrell, *op. cit.*, i. 503.

down to us, though one of the congregation has recorded his text: 'Neither circumcision availeth anything, nor uncircumcision, but a new creature.'[1] The choice of the preacher was both fit and proper, for no man had worked harder for this moment, or could direct the thanksgiving of the nation to Almighty God with more heartfelt sincerity.

In fact, Henry Compton's part in moulding the shape of events had been by no means unimportant. He 'was not only most instrumental in the Revolution', a contemporary writes, 'but the most Zealous in Promoting the Peace and Settlement of it'.[2] The conscientious scruples which made Sancroft and a number of bishops feel it impossible to go back on their oaths inevitably led to the Bishop of London becoming the leader of those clergy who were enthusiastically behind the Revolution. For his part, he had neither misgivings nor regrets. *Pars magna fui* he might well have said without exaggeration.

Amongst the first acts of the new King, on 14 February, was the establishment of his Privy Council. It came as no surprise that Compton was made a member and also was given the post of Groom of the Stole.[3] Danby was appointed Lord President. On 20 February, the London clergy in a great body, headed by their Bishop, went solemnly in procession to Whitehall, where they offered their own congratulations on William's and Mary's accession to the throne. The King received them in a most friendly spirit for he well knew the value of such ecclesiastical support, the loss of which had contributed to James's losing his crown.[4]

While these events were going on, Sancroft was more or less in voluntary confinement at Lambeth. It is a great pity that he absented himself from the Convention Parliament, for no conscientious scruples ought to have prevented him from speaking in favour of his own plan for a Regency (in fact his scruples ought to have encouraged him to do this), though such efforts would almost certainly have been unsuccessful.[5] Also as Archbishop of

---

[1] *H.M.C.* App. iv, Report XIV, p. 217 (Kenyon MSS.).

[2] White Kennett, *op. cit.*, iii. 521.

[3] Luttrell, *op. cit.*, i. 502.   [4] *Ibid.*, p. 504.

[5] It is, perhaps, only fair to the Archbishop to add that he is reported to have 'sent the Bishop of London to the Prince, assuring his Highness that it was only his indisposition that kept him from the Convention, and that he did and would in all things concur with what his brethren the Bishops acted'. See *H.M.C.* App. ii, Report XIV, p. 422 (Portland MSS.).

Canterbury, the nation had a right to expect public guidance from him at a time of crisis. His misgivings were, of course, understandable. He had taken solemn oaths of allegiance to James, and so long as the exiled monarch lived he felt he could not go back on them. That James was unfit to rule, that he must never again be entrusted with the administration of government, and therefore that someone must act in his stead—all this he was prepared to allow. But James's status as King by divine right, and the strict male descent in his family, these must remain inviolate and were beyond the jurisdiction of any earthly tribunal.

That the good old Archbishop should overcome his scruples so far as to advocate an expedient which left James an empty title devoid of any effective power shows both the sensitivity of his nature and the unpractical cast of his mind. It tended to reduce politics to the level of mere verbal quibbles. Of course the problem was a very difficult one for men who had, in season and out of season, extolled the sacrosanct character of the monarchy, and maintained that it was answerable to God alone. To remain loyal to this preposterous doctrine, the more scrupulous of the clergy were now to suffer, and the fact that the number included such men as William Sancroft and Thomas Ken is a testimony to their disinterestedness.

So far as Compton was concerned, it is but fair to say that he had certainly neither preached nor practised the duty of non-resistance during the reign of James II. Quite the reverse. In most explicit terms he had maintained that a limit must be set to arbitrary government, and that the royal authority must be exercised in harmony with the known laws of the land, if any man's property were to be secure. It may be that the Revolution had not in every jot and tittle worked out in the precise way the Bishop wished—no revolution ever does fulfil its leaders' hopes. Even that strict whig Thomas Tenison later admitted to the Earl of Clarendon that 'there had been irregularities in our settlement; that it was to be wished things had been otherwise; but we were now to make the best of it, and to join in support of this government for fear of worse'.[1]

Compton's own views may be seen in two letters which he wrote at this time.

[1] Clarendon, *Diary*, ii. 300.

The first was to an incumbent in Essex, who did not find it easy to accommodate his conscience to the change of ruler. He may be taken as typical of not a few country incumbents. The present case of the Church of England, the Bishop pointed out to him, differed altogether from the situation in which the early Christians found themselves, when 'all the Laws of the several Nations were against them; so that they could pretend to no civil right'. In such a case, he agreed, there could be no remedy but 'prayers and tears when the Magistrate presses beyond Conscience'. But though an analogy could not properly be drawn with the early Church, yet the Fathers had left one important lesson behind them—'whatever Revolutions happened in the Roman Empire, they still paid their Obedience, and offered up their Prayers for those that were in Possession of the Government.'[1] Hobbes could not have urged more forcibly the duty of obedience to a *de facto* government; and the following passage from the Bishop's letter is an admirable summary of the contemporary whig point of view: 'Our Religion, Liberty and Property are secured by the Civil Constitution and Fundamental Laws of the Kingdom. There is a mutual Obligation between the King and the People, the one to protect, the other to obey. Both protection and obedience are prescribed by, and confined to, the Laws as Fortescue, Bracton, and all the best Lawyers have taught us.' To such sentiments William Coke, surely, would have said 'Amen'.

Yet there was one question which the Bishop realised that the incumbent in Essex might well ask him, namely 'who is to decide Civil Rights, when Disputes arise between King and People, and who is then to judge of these Laws?' Here Compton once again was content to fall back on a purely practical answer. 'No doubt', he replied, 'the Body of the Nation assembled in the best manner the present Exigencies of Affairs permit.'[2]

The letter concluded, maybe a little brutally, with the Bishop confessing that he just could not understand those who, though abandoning any real allegiance to James, were yet prepared to cling 'to the thankless Adherence only to a bare Title'.

The second letter was addressed to his own rural deans. In this epistle he urged them 'to take all opportunities at this

[1] *A Letter concerning Allegiance*, 1710, p. 4.
[2] *Ibid.*, 1710, p. 5.

time to lay before the People the great Blessings we enjoy by this wonderful Revolution, which has procured to us so full a Deliverance from Popery and arbitrary Power, that during our Captivity, we would have purchased it with the Hazard of our Lives, and the Expense of our Fortunes'.[1]

It will be immediately seen that Compton's attitude was that of the practical man of affairs, far removed from the hesitations of such as Sancroft who were more easily influenced by theological principle.

But if the Archbishop refused to co-operate in getting things done, and chose to remain inactive at Lambeth, then it was obvious that things would have to be done without him. So far all that was publicly known of his private thoughts was that he resolutely declined to be a party to the 'Revolution Settlement'. It was imperative, however, that the King and Queen be crowned; and new Bishops appointed. The Bishopric of Salisbury, for example, was vacant by the death of Dr. Seth Ward. No man had more claims on the good-will of William than the garrulous but kind-hearted Scotsman, Gilbert Burnet, and it was fitting that he should be the first person to owe his promotion to the good-will of the new King. The choice did not prove to be a popular one amongst the rank and file of the clergy (Compton was never one of his admirers) for he was regarded as an unorthodox, latitudinarian churchman, too kindly disposed to the Dissenters.

Yet the question of more immediate interest concerned the attitude of the Archbishop. What would he do about Burnet's elevation to the episcopate? At first he intimated that he could not obey the wishes of the Sovereign; that it was impossible for him to have anything to do with the consecration of a bishop against his conscience. Had he persisted in this attitude Parliament would have been forced to intervene, and a painful controversy must have followed. As it was, the Archbishop's conscience allowed him to adopt a compromise which seems in some respects curious. He could not take part in the proceedings himself, that was clear; but he was prepared (reluctantly, it is true) to issue a commission by which the Bishop of London, together with the Bishops of Winchester, Llandaff, St. Asaph and Carlisle, were to act in his name. Thus was Gilbert Burnet consecrated Bishop in the chapel of Fulham Palace on 31 March 1689.

[1] Compton to Strype, Jan. 1689, B.M. Cole Add. MSS. lii. 480.

Compton's relations with Sancroft during these months of uncertainty could not have been easy, particularly as the Bishop was taking over more and more of the Archbishop's responsibilities. As the Coronation drew near, and the ordering of the ceremony was left to the Bishop of London, so it was necessary for him to procure from Sancroft the books and papers relating to former occasions. A personal interview would probably have been painful to both parties, so Compton wisely requested that the relevant documents might be sent to him at Fulham.[1]

While preparations for the Coronation were thus proceeding, the Convention had converted itself into a Parliament, and the statute which effected this included a clause that no person should sit in either House after 1 March 1689, unless he took the oaths to William and Mary. There was a great deal of speculation as to who would, and who would not, comply. Some extreme tories, who had never disguised the fact that they were adherents of the exiled monarch, confidently predicted that the 'non-jurors' would be so considerable as to make effective government impossible. Particularly was the attitude of the bishops a matter of serious concern to the supporters of William. But there were powerful motives of self interest—apart from principle—encouraging conformity. It was a condition of office.

The Bishop of London was eager to show his loyalty at the first opportunity. On 2 March, with three bishops and seventy-three temporal peers, he took the oaths—and within a week a hundred more had done so. The number included many who must have sworn with mental reservations; Thomas Watson, Bishop of St. David's, for example, and Lords Aylesbury and Dartmouth. In the Lower House no fewer than four hundred members were sworn in on 2 March.

The day of the Coronation drew on apace. It was clear that Sancroft had definitely decided to take no part in it, so that in drawing up an 'Act for the Establishing of the Coronation Oath', Parliament made provision for the ceremony to be conducted either by the Archbishop of Canterbury or the Bishop of London. The latter was no liturgical scholar, but he was concerned that William and Mary's crowning should not be of so attenuated a nature as to encourage any distinction between a king *de facto* and a king *de jure*.

[1] Compton to Sancroft (undated), Bod. Tanner MSS. 28, fo. 8.

Of his ordering of the service Dr. Jocelyn Perkins writes:

A practical man of affairs, he was far less fitted for the task than Sancroft. None the less his work, which may be styled the seventh recension of the Order of Coronation, though by no means devoid of blemishes (it had to be carried out in four weeks) was infinitely more satisfactory than that of Sancroft and entitles him to credit which he has not always received. The Eucharist was at once restored, and Compton went right back to the oldest precedent of all, that of Archbishop Egbert, by inserting the Coronation Service in the middle of it, an arrangement analogous to the consecration of a Bishop. He also followed Egbert's precedent by placing the ceremony of the Crowning last of all instead of the Investiture with the sceptre, thus producing an effective climax. A prayer for the consecration of the Oil expressed in extremely definite language was inserted, presumably in place of the consecration earlier in the day in St. Edward's Chapel. Last of all, with a stroke of genius, which interpreted to perfection the whole outlook of our race, he introduced the Presenting of the Bible to the Sovereign 'the most valuable thing that this world affords' the moment after he has received the Crown.'[1]

On the other hand, it must be admitted that Compton perpetuated not a few of Sancroft's errors and added some more of his own ; so much so, that that great liturgical scholar, H. A. Wilson has stated that 'the general result of Compton's revision was that nothing remained in its place without change ; and . . . very little of it left at all'.[2]

But the opinion of the liturgical scholar is not the last word, and as Dr. Perkins has suggested, it was a stroke of practical genius to introduce the gift of the Bible, and to make the crowning the grand climax. It is significant that the William and Mary recension has since undergone little change.

On 11 April, with all the traditional ceremony, and with a revised coronation oath, the King and Queen were crowned in Westminster Abbey, a few hours after the news reached London that James had landed in Ireland. It was Henry Compton who performed the ceremony. On one side of the Bishop was Lloyd of St. Asaph carrying the paten, and on the other Sprat of Rochester, also Dean of Westminster, with the chalice. But as a class, the bishops were conspicuous by their absence. For

[1] J. Perkins, *The Crowning of the Sovereign*, 1937, pp. 89-90.
[2] Quoted in *ibid.*

the first time, the Commons were seated behind the altar above the Confessor's Chapel. Also in attendance and near the Bishop, was his nephew, the Earl of Northampton, who carried the King's cross and sceptre.

Compton delighted to tell in later years—for the scene lived long in his memory—of a 'small accident' which caused some embarrassment during the ceremony. They had reached that point in the Coronation service when the King and Queen made their first offering, a roll of silk and thirty pieces of gold. But nothing happened. The Lord Treasurer of the Household and the Lord Chamberlain stared blankly at each other. It was obvious that someone had blundered, but William, never really at home in this kind of ceremonial, did not prove very helpful. Finally the Earl of Danby came to the rescue, took out his purse, and extracting the required sovereigns, passed them on to their Majesties.[1]

No more appropriate preacher could have been selected than the Bishop of Salisbury, who chose a text which echoed the hopes of many of the congregation. 'The God of Israel said, He that ruleth over men must be just, ruling in the fear of God. And he shall be as the light of the morning when the sun riseth, even a morning without clouds: as the tender grass springing out of the earth, by clear shining after rain.'

[1] *The Life of Dr. Henry Compton*, p. 49.

CHAPTER TEN

PERSONAL DISAPPOINTMENT

THE political revolution was in a sense over. William and Mary were crowned; the Convention was converted into a legal Parliament; oaths of loyalty to the new sovereign had been laid down as a condition of its membership. It is now time that we look at the religious settlement, which was in painful process of being worked out.

Some of the bishops and a number of the clergy were known to be unable conscientiously to take the oaths to William and Mary. What was to happen to them? For the time being they themselves took their cue from Sancroft, who had pursued a policy of masterly inactivity, although he did go so far (as we have seen) to issue a Commission empowering others to act in his name. To retain his seat in the Upper House he must now take the oaths to William and Mary; but, more important, what of his office as Archbishop, and the position of his other brethren, the bishops and clergy who thought like him?

Yet these were not the only religious problems which awaited settlement. What of the Dissenters who had, for the most part, stood four square with the Church of England in opposing the policy of James, even declining to accept liberation under the Declaration of Indulgence? Were they now to be rewarded by a repeal of the Clarendon Code, thereby being made capable of civil employment without the expedient of Occasional Conformity? Before the Revolution, even Sancroft had urged upon the bishops in his own province the need for encouraging friendly relations with the Nonconformists, in order to secure unity of action against a common attack. In fact, a tentative scheme for comprehension had been drawn up, and the Archbishop, together with his brother of York, and such representative clergy as Tenison and Simon Patrick, embarked upon a review of the liturgy with the intention of making the Book of Common Prayer more acceptable to the Dissenters.[1]

---

[1] The proposals which they drew up have never come to light. Some of them may have been incorporated into the proposals of 1689. See pp. 161, 167.

William, although a sincere Calvinist, was yet no religious bigot. Nice distinctions of theology seemed to him unimportant when compared with the freedom of Holland and the liberties of Europe. Moreover, he could abstract himself from the passions of the day in a way which most Englishmen found impossible. In his declaration from The Hague on 10 October, 1688, he had declared himself in favour 'of such laws as might establish a good agreement between the Church of England and all Protestant Dissenters, and cover all those who live peaceably under the government from all persecution on account of their religion'. So far as William was concerned, he was even prepared to be conciliatory to Jacobite as well as Dissenter, and he hoped that he might play off the one against the other. Addressing both Houses of Parliament on 1 March, 1689, he said: 'I know you are sensible there is a necessity of some law to settle the oaths to be taken by all Persons to be admitted to such Places. I recommend it to your Care to make a speedy provision for it; as I doubt not you will be sufficiently against the Papists, so I hope you will leave room for admission of all protestants that are willing and able to serve.'[1]

What William and the whigs wanted was a Toleration Act which would give freedom of worship to the Dissenters; and a Comprehension Act which would so adapt the English liturgy as to encourage the more reasonable of them to re-enter the Church of England. A Toleration Act was in fact passed in 1689, which allowed liberty of worship to those who would accept thirty-five-and-a-half out of the Thirty-nine Articles; but the Comprehension Bill, though it was 'the fruit of much thought among Anglicans of all shades of opinion',[2] did not succeed in passing through the House of Commons which, instead, petitioned William to summon Convocation.

The Bishop of London was whole-hearted in his support of both of these Acts, even trying to commend them in a tactless letter to Sancroft, which Macaulay has rightly called a 'very curious composition'. 'We are now entering upon the Bill of Comprehension', Compton wrote, 'which will be followed by the Bill of Toleration.   These are two great Works in which the being of our Church is concerned, and I hope you will send to

[1] Cobbett, *Parliamentary History*, v. 183.
[2] Hart, *William Lloyd*, p. 134.

the house for copies. For tho' we are under a conquest God has given us favour in the eyes of our Rulers: and we may keep up the Church if we will.'[1]

The reference to a 'conquest' does not seem a very happy one. It may represent a rather clumsy way of trying to conciliate Sancroft, or conversely, an extreme and provocative expression of whig opinion; but whichever way we interpret it, it is utterly at variance with the Bishop's public utterances, all of which regard the Revolution as a peaceful deliverance. Some of William's supporters, it is true, did at first claim that the Prince had effected a conquest (Gilbert Burnet, for example), but this was condemned as 'odious' by both Houses of Parliament.[2]

William was undoubtedly disappointed at his failure to get a Comprehension Bill through Parliament, and he was probably equally disconcerted when he found both Houses unwilling to adopt a conciliatory policy towards the Jacobites. The Lords decided (as we have already seen) that all who held civil office should take the oaths of allegiance to William and Mary, though in respect of ecclesiastical preferment they softened the severity of this requirement by laying it down that 'every divine who already held a benefice might continue to hold it without swearing unless the Government should see reason to call on him specially for an assurance of his loyalty'. Such a sensible mediating clause showed real statesmanship, but it was to prove too liberal for the Lower House.[3] The debate in the Lords (the King was present) was certainly interesting. Lord Wharton, who could recall many years of change and upheaval, remarked rather contemptuously: 'I am a very old man and have taken a multitude of oaths in my time; and I hope God will forgive me if I have not kept them all, for truly they are more than I can hope to remember.' The Earl of Macclesfield, who was an old Cavalier and had come over with William from Holland, declared that he was of the same opinion, though he had not always taken the same oaths as Lord Wharton. In his judgment all that such oaths did was to provoke people to declare against the Government.

The Bishop of London spoke at some length in this debate, and it is to his credit that he championed the liberal point of view,

---

[1] Bod. Tanner MSS. 27, fo. 41. It should be noticed that the Comprehension Bill was based on Sancroft's own proposals of 1688.

[2] Kennett, *op. cit.*, iii. 650.   [3] See next page.

though he unfortunately did so in such a way as to make himself a little ridiculous. It was obviously within the power of the King, Compton asserted, to tender these oaths for the quiet of the Government, yet for himself he was against multiplying such tests. So far as the bench of bishops was concerned 'forcing these oaths will rather disturb men's passions and make men's minds more uneasy'—an admission which may be regarded as particularly magnanimous in view of the speaker's ambitions. Perhaps it would have been better if the Bishop had finished his speech at this point, but he went on to add, amidst a roar of laughter, 'that there was not nor could be made an oath to the present Government that he could not take'.[1]

The House of Commons, however, would not hear of any special treatment for the clergy and bishops, and insisted that all those who held any office, ecclesiastical or civil, must be placed on exactly the same footing. This meant that all were required to take the oaths by 1 August, 1689, six months' grace being allowed for second thoughts. The Lords (it was not the only time that they took a more liberal view than *vox populi*) at first determined to resist this amendment, and there was another spate of conferences between the two Houses. But the Commons would not budge, and the Lords were reluctantly forced to give way.

The result of these debates, and in particular the failure of the Comprehension Bill, showed William and his ecclesiastical advisers that it was not possible to use Parliament at this juncture to make the Church of England more acceptable to the Dissenters, and that the only course to adopt, following the advice of Tillotson, was to encourage Convocation to take the initiative in this matter.   In the meantime it was hoped that passions in Parliament would cool. The result was the setting up, by the Crown, of an Ecclesiastical Commission consisting of a number of prominent churchmen, whose task was to recommend such 'concessions' to Convocation as would 'make for the union of Protestants'.

This move by William evoked a great deal of opposition from those tories who were suspicious of its design. The word 'commission' certainly had a nasty ring, and some protested against its exclusively clerical membership. It was hoped, however, that

[1] Burnet, *op. cit.*, iv. 80. Also Cobbett, *op. cit.*, v. 230-1.

this way of procedure would avoid the errors of the Savoy Conference in 1661, when the opportunities for debate then afforded to the Dissenters encouraged them to make what many members of the Church of England regarded as extravagant demands. In 1689 the proposed changes were to be decided upon by the *Ecclesia Anglicana* itself, and the Dissenters were to be presented with a *fait accompli*.

The Bishop of London was, of course, an almost automatic choice on this Commission, and he found himself in company with eight bishops (nine if we include Simon Patrick, Bishop-elect of Chichester) four deans (among them Tillotson, Stillingfleet and Sharp) and such leading clergy as Tenison, Beveridge, Scott, Fowler, Jane and Grove.

The Commission opened its sessions on 10 October, 1689, in the Jerusalem Chamber in Westminster Abbey at 10 o'clock in the morning, but it was soon apparent that some of the Commissioners were unwilling or reluctant to serve. The Archbishop of York, the Bishops of Carlisle and Exeter, and Drs. Montague, Beaumont and Batteley appeared neither at the first meeting nor subsequently. Thus only twenty-four Commissioners were present at the first session (when a discussion of the Apocrypha took place) and at the second session on 16 October dissension began. Thomas Sprat, Bishop of Rochester, immediately arose and questioned the authority of the Commission 'whether they did not fall under the statute of *praemunire* in meeting according to it'. For himself, he explained, he could not feel secure, particularly in view of his own experience on a Commission [1] in King James's reign, unless he were reassured by the opinion of twelve judges. Moreover, since this Commission was 'to prevent Convocation it could not be taken well by them to be called together to confirm that which they had no hand in'. Dr. Jane, Regius Professor of Divinity at Oxford and a protégé of the Bishop of London, embarrassed his master by taking his cue from Dr. Sprat, declaring that the Bishop of Rochester had convinced him of the doubtful status of their proceedings.[2]

---

[1] I.e. that which suspended Compton.

[2] *Parliamentary Papers* 1850, vol. 50, 'Copy of the Alterations in the Book of Common Prayer prepared by the Royal Commission for the Review of the Liturgy, 1689', p. 96.

Such a challenge to the legality of the Commission could hardly be ignored if it were to continue its sessions, and Compton felt it necessary (particularly in view of his former chaplain's misgivings, and the reference to the Commission in King James's reign under which he himself had suffered) to make his own position clear. He had no scruples about it whatsoever, he said. The setting up of the present Commission had been approved by the Upper House of Parliament, and if the attitude of the Commissioners should frustrate its purpose, then 'the work would be taken out of [their] hands and done without the clergy'. The deliberations of the Commissioners, moreover, would in no sense invade the rights of Convocation but simply shorten its labours: Convocation remained perfectly free to accept or reject the proposals placed before it.[1]

What Compton said succinctly—he was usually brief and to the point—was repeated by Simon Patrick, fresh to his episcopal honours, at greater length. It seemed at one time that this second session was to end in general disorder. Dr. Jane—always a difficult man—rose in great indignation to leave, after the Bishop of St. Asaph had tactlessly moved that 'those who were not satisfied about the Commission might withdraw and not be spies on the rest'.[2] Perhaps it was the Bishop of London who persuaded him to remain. Finally, however, the Commissioners agreed to get down to business, and after the session Compton dined with the Bishops of Worcester and Chichester, and Drs. Aldrich and Williams, being joined by Tenison and Grove.

During the next month there were eighteen sessions of the Commission, and Compton was the only member present on all occasions, possibly because he presided. There was, of course, a great deal of talk, and the airing of different points of view on such controversial subjects as baptismal grace, episcopal ordination, and the 'controverted ceremonies'. The cleavage between high and low church, orthodox and latitudinarian, was unfortunately only too apparent throughout—that is between those who were concerned with the 'catholic witness' of the Church of England, and those whose main preoccupation was to do something practical for the Dissenters; though even here Stillingfleet was

---

[1] *Parliamentary Papers* 1850, vol. 50, 'Copy of the Alterations in the Book of Common Prayer prepared by the Royal Commission for the Review of the Liturgy, 1689', p. 96. [2] *Ibid.*, p. 103.

careful to point out that 'they sat there to make such alterations as were fit, which would be fit to make were there no Dissenters and which would be for the improvement of the services'.[1]

Compton was never much at home in theological debate of a too technical nature (neither his studies nor his interests inclined him that way) and from the reports of the discussions which have been preserved, he does not seem to have taken a very prominent part in the deliberations. He was essentially a practical man, and for reasons which will shortly appear he was not too happy on the Commission. He was all in favour of the compromise for which Stillingfleet, Tillotson, Burnet and Tenison were working, and which Aldrich, Jane and the high churchmen generally were equally anxious to frustrate. But an unfortunate personal cleavage between Compton and one prominent member of the Commission complicated the theological issue, and was not helpful to the general purpose for which the Commissioners had assembled.

The main practical questions confronting the Commission *vis à vis* the Dissenters concerned the famous 'controverted ceremonies' which prevented many of them from joining in communion with the Church of England.[2] There was also the vexed question of 'orders'. Both subjects bristled with difficulties, and tempers rose as a consequence, Dr. Aldrich walking out of the Jerusalem Chamber to return no more. It was eventually decided to leave optional the sign of the cross in baptism, and the posture (whether kneeling) in which to receive the Holy Communion. We may be confident that the Bishop of London was in favour of this gesture to conciliate the Dissenters.

But the other matter, the attitude to be taken towards Nonconformist ordinations, was even more difficult. Were they 'valid', or must such ministers be episcopally ordained before they could be allowed to officiate in the Church of England— and if their orders were accepted as valid, what about those of the reformed churches abroad and the Roman Catholics?

Jane and the high churchmen were solid for re-ordination of all Nonconformists without any exceptions or reservations:

[1] *Parliamentary Papers* 1850, vol. 50, 'Copy of the Alterations in the Book of Common Prayer prepared by the Royal Commission for the Review of the Liturgy, 1689', p. 96.

[2] They were: the sign of the Cross in baptism; whether to receive the Holy Communion kneeling; and the use of the surplice.

ubi episcopus ibi ecclesia was their yardstick. Tenison and the liberal churchmen, on the other hand, were prepared to waive this requirement in particular cases. Unfortunately no detailed report of the discussion on this subject survives, though it is certain that Compton supported the liberal point of view, for he himself replied to the high churchmen who argued that if they accepted the orders of the Nonconformists then they must certainly do the same for those of the Roman Catholic Church. We did not question the validity of Roman Orders, the Bishop argued, but only 'the sufficiency of the Evidence for them', particularly since we had no communion with that Church and knew only too well 'the Cheats which she puts upon us'.[1] Dr. Beveridge, the life-long champion of high Anglicanism, replied indignantly that neither had we any communion with the Dissenters or the reformed churches of the Continent; only to be firmly rebuked by Compton who reasserted that we did enter into communion with them, and that they were willing to give all reasonable satisfaction in respect of their orders.[2]

After prolonged debate and much loss of temper, the Commission finally agreed to recommend the hypothetical re-ordination of Dissenters and foreign Protestants, but where Roman Catholics were concerned simply to re-ordain.

On the whole, however, the Commissioners, despite their disagreements and differences in ecclesiastical loyalty, managed to work together with a conscientious regard for what they felt to be right. True Stillingfleet had to admonish one theologian 'Doctor, Doctor, charity is better than rubrics', and tempers often rose; but we may accept as essentially true the judgment made by Tillotson's biographer: 'Matters were well considered and fairly and calmly debated: and all was digested into an entire conviction of anything that seemed liable to any just objections.'[3]

It remained to see what reception the recommendations of the Commissioners would receive from Convocation when it met, but already, unfortunately, the passions of churchmen had been inflamed, and a theological climate created which was to prove unfavourable to sober discussion. This may be seen in a contemporary pamphlet *A Letter to a Friend, containing some Queries about the new Commission* which attacked most of its members for

---

[1] *Parliamentary Papers* 1850, vol. 50, 'Copy of Alterations', p. 102.
[2] *Ibid.*   [3] Birch, *Life of Tillotson*, p. 190.

having 'Tenderness and Moderation to part with everything but their Church Preferments', while at the same time demanding 'Latitude to conform to a Church *de facto* which had Power on its side'.

The reaction which invariably follows revolution was beginning to manifest itself in 1689 in a fervent attachment to the Church of England, and a disinclination, now that the immediate danger was past, to do anything for the Dissenters. Much depended, of course, on the character of the Convocation, particularly of the Lower House, where former experience suggested that feeling against the Nonconformists would be most bitter, and support for the privileges of the Church of England most vocal. It was particularly important that those who stood for moderate reform—that is those who were willing to make changes in the Book of Common Prayer to conciliate the Dissenters—should show a united front. But this was not to be, for a division of a most unhappy kind had already been introduced into the ranks of the reformers—and it involved Compton, Bishop of London.

No one, we repeat, can question the Bishop's anxiety at this time to effect a 'comprehension', a fact so undoubted that it proved an embarrassment to his high-church biographer over twenty years later, who felt it necessary to excuse his being so 'zealous' on its behalf.[1] Yet it was the Bishop of London who helped to make the scheme miscarry in Convocation. The circumstances were as follows.

Death had caused many vacancies on the episcopal bench, and as a result Burnet (as we have already seen) was made Bishop of Salisbury, Stillingfleet Bishop of Worcester, Simon Patrick Bishop of Chichester, and Ironside Bishop of Bristol. These were all consecrated by Compton in the Chapel of Fulham Palace.

It might have been expected that the divines elevated in this way would have included John Tillotson. He was known to be intimate with William and Mary, to be a man of liberal views, and generally popular by reason of his attractive personality. Moreover, he was a great friend of Burnet who had the ear of the King and Queen. Yet his name did not appear in the list of the newly-appointed bishops.

[1] T. Gooch, *A Sermon, etc.,* 1713, p. 17.

There were other bishoprics, however, which would need to be filled if certain ecclesiastics persisted in their refusal to take the oaths. Might it not be that this was the reason for Tillotson's omission from the first list of bishops?—at least this was how people began to gossip among themselves. Was it not certain, for example, that Sancroft would decline the oaths, and that the King must be already considering his successor? Was not Tillotson just the man whom William's statesmanship and Mary's piety would wish to see at Lambeth?

Those who were thinking in this way would have been even more confident had they known that when Tillotson on kissing hands at his appointment to the Deanery of St. Paul's—to which he was appointed from the Deanery of Canterbury—thanked the King 'for setting him at ease for the rest of his life', William had replied 'No such thing, Doctor, I assure you', and then went on to intimate that St. Paul's was but a stepping stone to Canterbury. The Dean was not only surprised but disturbed at the news. *Nolo episcopari* is so often the conventional protest of the ambitious cleric that it is seldom taken seriously, but we may credit Tillotson by believing that in him it was sincere and from the heart. His sensitive nature shrank from an office of this kind as may be seen in his frank letters to Lady Russell. To the King he ingenuously protested his unfitness and urged the claims of another —not Henry Compton, but a friend, Stillingfleet, Bishop of Worcester.

Rumours of what was in the King's mind soon travelled up the river to Fulham, where they rankled in an all too human heart, and had their indirect effect on the scheme for a comprehension. To co-operate enthusiastically with Tillotson at this juncture, to sink personal jealousy for a common cause, this the Bishop just could not do. Their personal relationship began to deteriorate immediately into an open rupture with the most unfortunate consequences. Even before he left the Deanery of Canterbury for St. Paul's, Tillotson had reason to suspect that the Bishop was uneasy. In August 1689, the Dean was appointed by the Chapter of the Cathedral to exercise the archi-episcopal jurisdiction in the province of Canterbury during the suspension of Sancroft. It was the normal procedure during a legal vacancy at Lambeth, but in the present situation it undoubtedly irritated Compton, upon whom many of the Archbishop's responsibilities were now devolving. In his distress he proceeded to approach Stillingfleet, suggesting that the present occasion did not constitute a regular vacancy, and that therefore the customary precedents did not apply. The reply to his inquiry left no doubt as to the Bishop of Worcester's views. There could be no question whatever, Stillingfleet wrote, but that the present suspension of Sancroft did constitute a legal vacancy according to the canons, and that during such a suspension the right of jurisdiction devolved upon the Dean and Chapter of Canterbury.[1]

Compton wisely decided to let the matter rest. It may be, of course, that there was a genuine doubt in the Bishop's mind as to where jurisdiction in fact lay ; but it is, unfortunately, more in keeping with the Bishop's attitude at this time to suspect that he was moved by a feeling of personal irritation against Tillotson.

The Bishop of London was not alone in beginning to develop a sense of grievance. There are always disappointed people after a Revolution, usually among those who think they have deserved most. Particularly were there two brothers, both noblemen, whose sister was the Queen's mother, who felt that their nearness to the throne, and their unique services at the Revolution merited special consideration. We refer to Lords Clarendon and Rochester.[2]

The second Earl of Clarendon's behaviour during the reign of James II and throughout the first few years of William and Mary, constitutes a problem for the psychologically-minded historian, and it is perhaps unfair to simplify it, as does Macaulay, by assuming that he was motivated solely by self-interest. Personal ties, political principles, and a desire to further his own ambitions—these were not easily reconciled to serve a consistent policy, and it seems that he followed now one, now the other. His own scheme for a regency having been unsuccessful, he never took the oaths to William and Mary. At first he was in favour of the attempt at comprehension, but later, in April, he expressed surprise to the Vicar of St. Martin-in-the-Fields that anyone could possibly support it.[3]

His brother, the Earl of Rochester, was in an equally discontented mood. He again had advocated the setting up of a regency, and had placed himself at the head of the church tories.

---

[1] Stillingfleet, *Miscellaneous Discourses*, 1735, p. 234.
[2] Birch, *Life of Tillotson*, p. 199.   [3] Clarendon, *Diary*, ii. 275.

True, unlike his brother, he took the oaths to the Government, but maybe a natural desire to retain his pension proved a powerful inducement to do this.

The two disgruntled brothers now repaired to Oxford, where they found equally discontented high churchmen waiting to receive them, namely, Dr. Aldrich, Dean of Christ Church, and Dr. Jane, Regius Professor of Divinity. The result of these clandestine meetings was soon to be seen in the Convocation that followed. More important from the standpoint of this biography is the fact that Compton was almost certainly privy to these deliberations, and that the disappointments of all concerned met in a common hostility to Tillotson. The result was the decision to put Jane forward as Prolocutor of the Lower House of Convocation.

All eyes now turned to this clerical assembly which met on 21 November, 1689, not in St. Paul's—it was still in process of being re-built, though its lofty dome had already been raised— but in the Henry VII Chapel in Westminster Abbey. The Bishop of London, in the absence of Sancroft, was elected President of the Upper House.[1] It was a colourful scene. On the right and left of Compton were seated those bishops of the Province of Canterbury who had taken the oaths, all of them arrayed in gorgeous raiments of scarlet and minever. Below them were assembled the presbyters, among whom was Tillotson, so soon to occupy the position of primate. What thoughts were in the mind of the Bishop of London as he surveyed the scene? Perhaps he reflected how passing might be the position of honour which he now occupied.

If the scheme for a comprehension were to go through, it was imperative that the right kind of person should be elected as Prolocutor in order to guide the deliberations of the Lower House. Tillotson, by temperament, and also because of his position on the Commission, seemed to many of his friends the obvious person. But when the time came for the election, the results of the Oxford conversations were soon apparent. A great deal of lobbying had obviously been done on behalf of Dr. Jane, the Bishop of London's former chaplain. This irresponsible high churchman, it will be remembered, had nearly walked out of the meetings of the Ecclesiastical Commission in disgust. Rochester

[1] Luttrell, *A Brief Historical Relation*, i. 607.

and Clarendon were behind his nomination, and Compton seems to have intrigued for him. Tillotson, recalling these days in a letter to Lady Russell written in October 1690—and we must remember how cautious he was in his judgments and free from petty personal spite—asserted quite definitely that 'the Bishop of London was at the bottom of that storm which was raised in Convocation last year', and that it was all 'on my account . . . out of a jealousy that I might be a hindrance to him in attaining what he desires, and what, I call God to witness, I would not have.'[1]

When the election for Prolocutor came before the Lower House the names of Tillotson and Jane were proposed. Tillotson was known to have the support of William and Mary, but it availed nothing. Jane was successful by a majority of over two to one. It was a defeat for the cause of comprehension, and a bad augury for what was to follow. Also events in Scotland, where the Episcopalians were being 'rabbled' out of their livings by the Presbyterians, played into the hands of the high churchmen and did not create a background favourable to calm discussion.

It is difficult not to pass judgment on Compton for what must appear his irresponsibility at this time. He had long been distinguished as a strong supporter of doing something for the Dissenters, and at the meetings of the Commission he had given comprehension his blessing. Even in Convocation in his speech to the Lower House (see later) he supported it. Yet he must have known that whatever slender chance there might be of the Lower House accepting the proposals of the Commission depended on the election of a Prolocutor who was favourable to them. Tillotson filled the bill admirably: Jane did not. It was all too often the weakness of Compton that personal considerations swayed his judgment, and gave to his actions a bewildering inconsistency.

On 25 November, Dr. Jane, the Prolocutor, was presented to the Bishop of London, the President, and according to the usual custom made a short oration in Latin. Dr. Jane left no doubts as to his own attitude. The Church of England, he said provocatively, was unique in its excellency, and unsurpassed by any other Church in Christendom: it stood in no need of improvement. His concluding words *Nolumus leges Angliae mutari* must have reminded

[1] Birch, *op. cit.*, p. 241.

some of the clergy of a banner, borne in front of a bishop, now in their midst, through the streets of Oxford.[1]

The Bishop of London, in reply, made it equally clear that he for his part, was still officially behind the scheme for comprehension, though he weakened the effectiveness of his support by a flattering reference to the Prolocutor as a man of 'modesty and learning'. 'They ought', he said, 'to endeavour to come to a temper in those Things that were not essential in Religion, thereby to open a Door of Salvation to abundance of straying Christians. It must needs be their Duty to shew the same Indulgence and Charity to the Dissenters under King William, which some of the Bishops and Clergy had promised to them in their address to King James.' He ended his speech with words taken from the address of Joseph to his brethren—thereby, comments his contemporary biographer, exhorting the clergy to 'Unanimity and Concord'.[2]

Never was exhortation more necessary or less heeded, though for a brief time comparative peace prevailed. Compton was informed of a defect in the Commission for want of the Great Seal, under which the Convocation sat, and this had first to be put right. The new Commission was brought in person to the assembled clergy by the Earl of Nottingham, who also bore with him a letter from the King, reiterating that he had brought them together, not simply because it was customary for them to meet with Parliament, but also 'out of a pious zeal to do everything that might lead to the establishment of the Church of England, which was so eminent a part of the Reformation'.

The Earl of Nottingham, not content with having delivered the King's letter (it was he who had introduced the Comprehension Bill into the House of Lords), took it upon himself to address a few words to the clergy, in which he urged soberness and moderation. An advocate less calculated to soothe ruffled tempers it would be impossible to imagine.

Such a message from the King demanded some acknowledgment, and this provided the opportunity for the battle to begin. The Upper House proposed an address of thanks expressing gratitude to William for having called them together 'to endeavour the reconciling of the Dissenters'. The Lower House,

---

[1] *The Life of Dr. Henry Compton*, p. 52 ; Birch, *op. cit.*, p. 202.
[2] *Ibid.* p. 53; also Birch, *op. cit.*, p. 202.

perhaps naturally, refused to thank the King for committing them to a project which the majority disapproved, and was determined to do its best to prevent. Instead they drew up an address expressing appreciation to the King for his Protestant zeal, at the same time promising to consider 'with all Calmness and Impartiality' whatever should be offered to them. It was this amended version which the Bishop of London presented to the King on his throne in the Banqueting House, William concealing his undoubted disappointment in a 'gracious reply'.

'This', comments a writer sadly in 1713, 'was the first unhappy Foundation of the Differences of the Convocation, that more or less have kept up in this Nation ever since, which has proved a stumbling block to many pious Souls.'[1]

The time had now come for Convocation to deal with the recommendations of the Ecclesiastical Commission, but the Lower House had no real intention of doing so. Rather it began to concern itself with the plight of the Nonjurors—could they not be made capable of sitting in Convocation even though they were deprived of their ecclesiastical office under statute? More important to the clergy of the Lower House than the conciliation of Dissenters was the future of these deprived clergymen. Next it turned its attention, with some asperity, to certain books 'of dangerous Consequence to the Christian Religion and the Church of England'. The Lower House became more and more interested, and its members more and more excited. Calmness and impartiality of discussion, essential to a fair hearing for the re-commendations of the Commission, was wisely seen by the supporters of comprehension, and by the Bishop of London, to be impossible in such an assembly in such a mood. It would be worse than useless to introduce the proposals, and would in fact serve only to incite the clergy still further. William realised that he must accept the situation, and Convocation was prorogued on 25 June and soon after dissolved with Parliament.

Thus no judgment was ever passed by Convocation on the proposals of the Commissioners, and they were quietly shelved once and for all. Many of those who at the time had been most anxious for a comprehension later rejoiced that the particular changes in respect of the Prayer Book had miscarried. Gilbert Burnet discerned the hand of Providence in the rejection, and

[1] *The Life of Dr. Henry Compton*, p. 54.

felt later that even if passed the proposals would not have achieved
their object so far as the Dissenters were concerned. Even that
liberal-minded man Thomas Tenison, who became Archbishop
of Canterbury in 1694, never tried to re-open the question, but
preferred to keep silence, refusing to publish the report of the
Commission, because, as he said, 'if they came to be public they
would give no satisfaction to either side, but rather be a handle for
mutual reproaches for one side would upbraid their brethren
for having given up so much; while the other would justify their
non-conformity, because those concessions were too little, nor
yet passed into a law'.[1]

Those who had striven in vain for a comprehension now
turned their energies to preserve for the Dissenters at least the
right of Occasional Conformity, which became the object of tory
attack for the next twenty years.[2] What Henry Compton thought
at the time of the failure of the Commissioners' proposals we do
not know. In public, at least, he had been one of their warmest
supporters, and had spoken on their behalf in Parliament, on the
Commission, and at the Convocation. Yet by his hostility to
Tillotson he had contributed to the ruin of their slender chances of
success and in this respect had played a double game. Already
his anger at the proposed elevation of the Dean of St. Paul's had
cooled somewhat his enthusiasm for the Dissenters, and was to
help in making him part company with the whigs.

If the outcome of this Convocation was disappointing to
some of the Dissenters, for most of them it was more than
compensated for by the solid benefits of the Toleration Act of
1689, to which we have already referred. So important a change
did this piece of legislation bring about in their whole status
that Compton devoted his eighth 'Conference' (which extended
from the end of 1689 to the summer of 1691) to a consideration
of how his clergy 'ought to behave themselves under a toleration'.[3] His intention was to encourage his brethren to recognise
frankly the new situation, but he was forced to admit later that in
this he had been much misunderstood. Many 'unadvised and false
Representations' had been brought against him, he complained,
'as if he designed to disturb and interrupt that Repose which the

---

[1] Birch, *op. cit.*, p. 190.   [2] See p. 192.
[3] *The Bishop of London's Eighth Letter to his Clergy upon a Conference how they
ought to behave themselves under a toleration*, 1692.

Laws had given to the Dissenters. Whereas God is my Witness, I had no such thoughts but as much to the contrary as possible.'[1]

The Bishop's main contention at the Conference was that if both the Church of England clergy and the Dissenters respected each other's legal position under the Act, then it would 'render Charity triumphant over Division . . . and make us one Spirit tho' of different Minds'. Yet in practice, the Bishop said, the Toleration Act was greatly abused, for many took advantage of it, on the pretext of being at a meeting house, to go to a tavern, to 'loiter in the fields', or even to do business. Here the clergy must stimulate the civil authorities to enforce the Elizabethan statute which laid down a shilling fine for such absenteeism. They must work with the Dissenters to this end, remembering that such a common activity could have the added advantage of encouraging 'familiar and friendly conversation'.

It is sad to think that Compton's attitude to Dissenters should have become so much less tolerant in the reign of Anne.[2]

But we must now return to the year 1689, when the passing of the months brought nearer the time when the Archbishopric must be filled. It was an embarrassing and anxious period for the bench of bishops. Sancroft was in a mood to be easily offended, and Compton was not always tactful. Little matters, insignificant in themselves, could easily lead to friction. A typical instance may be quoted from a dispute over the presentation to a living. The curacy of Maidstone became vacant, due to the incumbent refusing to take the oaths. The Bishop of London, thinking that Sancroft would do nothing about a successor, set about securing the appointment for a nominee of his own. Sancroft immediately took offence, and the Bishop felt it necessary to write him a rather stilted letter of explanation. He was 'unhappy not to be better known to his Grace', he said, and equally surprised 'to receive a reprimand'. He had certainly recommended a fit person to Maidstone, but he would go no further in the matter without his Grace's approval.[3]

At another time Sancroft, prompted by Lloyd, was under the impression that Compton, in co-operation with Danby, Nottingham and the Bishop of St. Asaph, had 'violently pressed the

---

[1] *The Bishop of London's Eighth Letter to his Clergy upon a Conference how they ought to behave themselves under a toleration,* 1692. p. 3.   [2] See p. 192.
[3] Compton to Sancroft, 22 Sept., 1689, Bod. Tanner MSS. 28, fo. 82.

filling up the vacant Bishoprics and other livings'. The facts, however, seem to point the other way, and to suggest that when Compton realised that Tillotson would almost certainly be made Archbishop, he did his best, at the eleventh hour, to persuade Sancroft to come to terms with the Government. Certainly on 31 December, 1689, taking with him the Bishop of St. Asaph, he waited upon Sancroft—the Bishops of Norwich and Ely were with the Archbishop—'pressing to know' what he could do to prevent their being deprived. The period of grace would soon be over, Compton reminded the Archbishop. Could they take ' no steps towards the Government?' But it was too late, for Sancroft had made up his mind once and for all. 'They could do nothing', he replied firmly. 'If the King thought it fit for his own sake, that they should not be deprived he must make it his business; they could not vary from what they had done: and besides they were not now altogether, and therefore could make no other answer.'[1]

The period of grace expired in February 1690, but it was not till April of the next year that Sancroft was formally deposed. In this latter month the Bishop of London again called on the former Archbishop at Lambeth and they spent some two hours together in the company of White, the nonjuring Bishop of Peterborough. 'O quantum Mutatus ab illo Hectore; so kind and debonaire, and so obliging, that it would have pleased you to observe it', so Sancroft later commented to a friend. The conversation this time seems to have been the possibility of Sancroft making a declaration with the object of retaining his revenues.[2]

It was now obvious to everybody that further discussion with William Sancroft was useless. Also it was known, though only to a small circle (Macaulay unkindly suggests that it must have been a large circle since Burnet was privy to it), that William and Mary definitely intended Tillotson to be his successor. In October 1690, the Dean had been summoned to the royal presence, and

---

[1] *The Correspondence of Henry Hyde,* 1828, p. 299.

[2] G. D'Oyly, *The Life of William Sancroft,* 1821, ii. 11. We may add that though Compton was opposed to the principles of the Nonjurors yet his warm heart went out to them in their later hardships. It was largely through his personal intervention that Frampton, the deprived Bishop of Gloucester, was allowed to retain the living of Standish. See S. Evans, *Life of Bishop Frampton,* 1876, p. 190. See also Frampton to Compton, 9 July, 1690, Bod. Rawlinson MSS. 985 C, fo. 19.

(to quote his own words to Lady Russell) the King 'then renewed his former gracious offer in so pressing a manner, and with so much kindness that I hardly knew how to resist it'. Tillotson's sensitive nature undoubtedly dreaded the repercussions of his appointment—the disgust of the Nonjurors, and more especially the resentment of the Bishop of London, whose jealousy he had already experienced in Convocation. 'I told his Majesty', he wrote to the same lady, 'that I was still afraid his kindness to me would be greatly to his prejudice especially if he carried it so far as he was pleased to speak of . . . for I plainly saw they could not bear it: and that the effects of envy and ill will towards me would terminate upon him.'[1]   But William was not the kind of man to submit to pressure of this kind. With the wisdom of the experienced diplomatist, he replied that 'if the thing were once done, and he saw no remedy, they would give over, or think of making the best of it'.[2] What particularly carried weight with Tillotson was the King's intimation 'that if he Refused he would not fill up any of the Bishoprics during the lives of any of the present Bishops'.[3]

Fear of Compton's malice was not the only factor which made the Dean of St. Paul's hesitate. He particularly disliked the thought of 'outing' the old Archbishop, or as he himself expressed it, of being 'a wedge to drive out Sancroft'. In fact he was reported to have told the King that he 'would with great[er] chearfulness have received his commands to have gone to the Indies than to Canterbury'.[4]

Yet if those in the inner circles knew what awaited Tillotson, those not so intimate in the counsels of William confidently expected that Compton would move to Canterbury as a matter of course. In August 1690, for example, a news letter reported that the Bishop of London was going to Lambeth, Worcester to London, St. Asaph to Worcester, Bangor to St. Asaph, and the ambitious Dr. Jane to Gloucester.[5] Even as late as the end of March 1691 it was still common talk 'that the Bishop of London will be made Archbishop of Canterbury'.[6]

[1] Birch, *Life of Tillotson*, p. 241.   [2] *Ibid.*
[3] Sayre to Charlett, 30 Apr., 1689, Bod. Ballard MSS. 45, fo. 67a.
[4] *Ibid.* This was in April 1689.
[5] *H.M.C.* App. vii, Report XII, p. 287 (Fleming MSS.).
[6] *Ibid.*

It is doubtful whether Compton took much comfort from such uninformed gossip, or was in any way encouraged by the reflection that there had been no married Archbishop since Parker, and that he, unlike Tillotson, was a bachelor. Yet hope, probably, lingered on. When William departed, in January 1691, for the congress at The Hague, no nominations having yet been made to the vacant sees, the Bishop of London accompanied the King at his own expense, and on his own initiative,[1] 'the only one of his Dignity and Order that attended him thither'. He returned home in the middle of March. Perhaps it was a last and desperate effort to commend himself to William, but if so, it was already too late, and his presence may well have been an embarrassment to the King. The latter had firmly made up his mind, and he did not wait long in making his decision public after his return home.

The blow when it finally fell, on the evening of 23 April, was a bitter one to the emotional Henry Compton. Doubtless the kindhearted Sancroft was moved to pity when he wrote the following words to Lloyd: 'Yester night the Bishop of London, knowing nothing of these promotions, was ready to enter the Council Chamber, when a friend pulled him by the sleeve, and shewed him the whole scheme; whereupon he retreated.'[2] There is something pathetically final in these last three words. Not only had he been overlooked for Canterbury, but all the promotions arising out of the nonjuring schism had been decided upon without any consultation with him whatsoever.[3]

For a second time, one of his own clergy, not in episcopal orders, and again from the Deanery of St. Pauls, had been preferred before him, this second time in even more aggravating circumstances. In 1678 he had been frustrated by James, then Duke of York, an avowed enemy: in 1689 he was disappointed by a supposed friend.

Compton had undoubtedly rendered unparalleled services to the cause of the Revolution. When others held back, he had risked life and fortune, and was the only ecclesiastic to sign the

---

[1] The Miscellaneous Works of Bishop Atterbury, iv, 454.

[2] Sancroft to Lloyd, 24 April, 1691, *Dr. William's Collection of Original Letters*.

[3] Compton must also have been sorely irritated by the rumour that he was to be consoled for his loss of the Archbishopric with the hand of Danby's daughter, Lady Plymouth, in marriage. *H.M.C.* Portland MSS., iii. 467, Portledge Papers, p. 110.

invitation to William. He had in fact perjured himself on the Prince's behalf, and shocked his brethren by appearing in arms. For over a year he had been acting for the Archbishop on state occasions, had crowned William and Mary, and presided at Convocation. As a bishop in his own diocese he had proved himself energetic and efficient, popular with his clergy and easy in his relations with the Dissenters. He had been personally responsible for the religious instruction of both Mary and Anne and had married both of them to foreign princes. The case for his appointment to Lambeth seemed overwhelming.

Why then was he passed over? That it was a deliberate snub and that it so appeared to contemporaries is certain, since they could not fail to recognise his unique claims. Even his contemporary biographer sheds no light on it. He writes:

> The See of Canterbury had been vacant above two years, and but a very little Prospect that the good old Archbishop Sancroft would ever comply with the Times. Wherefore the King before he went over into Holland to make the campaign of 1691, resolved to fill it up.[1] The Nobility of the Bishop of London's Birth, the Nature of his Education, Singleness of Life, the Generosity of his Temper, Greatness of his Sufferings, Contempt of Riches, and the Conspicuity [*sic*] of his Services both before and after the Revolution, to say nothing of his unvariable Steadfastness to the Interest of the Church and State, recommended him in the general Opinion of the World to the Dignity of Metropolitan: If we believe common Fame, it was what he himself expected. But the Royal favour inclined another way, and Dr. John Tillotson, then Clerk of the Closet to his Majesty and Dean of St. Paul's, was preferred to that See.[2]

It is significant, perhaps, that family papers at Castle Ashby are no more revealing, nor are there any family traditions which throw more light on this vexed problem. The sixth Marquess of Northampton, in his privately circulated *History of the Comptons* writes: 'It is difficult to say what was the reason for his not getting the Primacy. It was said that his preaching was without much learning. . . . The real reason is probably deeper; in spite of his popularity at Court, he seems to have made many enemies by his high handedness.'[3]

[1] William did not make any public announcement until his return from the Hague.
[2] *The Life of Dr. Henry Compton*, pp. 58-9.
[3] William Bingham Compton, *op. cit.*

Despite such 'popularity at Court', one thing seems quite certain, namely, that Mary, a woman of genuine piety, and sincerely interested in the welfare of the Church, who knew the Bishop of London intimately, did not want him as Archbishop: and that Tillotson, when he himself was seeking to withdraw from the Primacy, suggested not Compton, the obvious choice, but Stillingfleet. Gilbert Burnet, who had the ear both of the King and the Queen, supported the nomination of Tillotson, and though he recognised the Bishop of London's Protestant zeal, yet regarded him, perhaps unfairly, as 'weak and wilful'.

Was it therefore some defect of character, some temperamental irresponsibility, which made William and Mary emphatic that they did not want Compton at Lambeth? Though both monarchs had benefited from the Bishop's duplicity to James at the Revolution, it may be that they were in a measure shocked at such conduct in a churchman and felt that they could not really trust him. Perhaps, also, the prescient William recognised that such an appointment would exacerbate the feelings of the Nonjurors; perhaps he himself preferred someone to whom he did not owe so much.

The immediate effect upon Compton of his being passed over was extreme and he made little effort to conceal his disappointment. When Tillotson was consecrated on Whitsunday, 1691, in the Church of St. Mary-le-Bow, he preferred to stay away, and his place was taken by Mew, Bishop of Winchester, who was assisted by Burnet, Stillingfleet and Hough. Most of the nobility, including Compton's old friend Danby, were present, and it was one of the most splendid gatherings since the Coronation. Nor did the Bishop attend at Tillotson's admission to the Privy Council.[1]

This private sulk went on for some time. When James Blair came over from Virginia to promote the founding of the College, later known as William and Mary College, he found the Bishop of London ill, resentful, and unwilling to go to Court or to make any approach to the King. Blair's letter to Governor Nicholson, written at the end of the year, is a sad commentary on the state of affairs at Fulham. 'I found myself obliged', he writes, 'to take new measures from what I had proposed to myself. The Bishop of London was at this time under a great cloud, and mighty

[1] Carte MSS. 79, fos. 350, 358.

unwilling to meddle in any court business, for notwithstanding his great merit from the present government, he had been passed by in all the late promotions, and the two archbishoprics had been bestowed on two of his own clergy, viz. Dr. Tillotson and Dr. Sharp, so that notwithstanding the Bishop of London's great kindness to Virginia, yet I found he was not at this time in so fit circumstances as to manage a business at Court, as was expected.'[1]

We hope that even the most severe of moralists will not be over-anxious to cast the first stone. Of course Compton ought to have risen above such a display of bad temper—but the disappointment was extreme.

[1] Pennington, *Commissary Blair*, p. 8.

CHAPTER ELEVEN

A TORY BISHOP

IN the State Papers Domestic belonging to King William's Chest in the Record Office, there is a document bearing the date 1690 which has on it a list of well known public characters with a description of their political loyalty. The Bishop of London is included and it is recorded of him that he 'has influence over most of the Whig party'.[1]

It is the purpose of the following chapter to indicate how this came to be less true as the years went on, and in fact that it was not entirely accurate even when it was written.

When William ascended the throne in 1689, he did not wish to be regarded simply as the King of the whigs. Though he could not but recognise that it was in the main through their powerful support that he had triumphed, yet he had no desire to ally himself exclusively with one party lest he should find himself too dependent upon it. Danby, for example, was most certainly not a whig, and yet he had played an important part in bringing William over to England. It was only the fear of Jacobitism, and the acute personal rivalries between the whigs and tories, which prevented William choosing his ministers where he would, and convinced him that he was safer with the former. Burnet admits quite frankly that in the winter of 1689 'the Whigs began to lose much of the King's good opinion, by . . . the coldness that appeared in everything that related to the public, as well as to the King in his own particulars'.[2] This 'coldness' was especially apparent in their reluctance to settle upon the new monarch the reversion of the Crown for life 'lest he would grow arbitrary in his government . . . and strain for a high stretch of prerogative'.[3]

The King's undoubted annoyance, and his determination to assert his independence, provided the tories with a great opportunity to push their own claims, particularly when the whigs introduced the unpopular Corporation Bill into Parliament and William used the occasion to prorogue Parliament.

---

[1] *S.P.D.* King William's Chest, Record Office, 8, no. 25.
[2] Burnet, *op. cit.*, iv. 60. [3] *Ibid.*, iv. 61.

The Bishop of London, while these events were taking place, found himself in a difficulty. His relations with Danby, and his family connections, inclined him to the tories: his extreme hatred of Rome and his hostility to James's policy of absolutism had made him increasingly identify himself with the whigs. But after the Revolution, the political situation began to change as the dangers of the former reign receded. True Compton was eager for comprehension but this was more a 'hangover' from the past than a present conviction: and even before his disappointment over the Archbishopric soured him, his sympathies with the whigs cooled. What he wished, perhaps, was to be a King's man if William would but make this possible.

At the new elections which followed William's prorogation, the tories were returned, and they determined to change the lieutenancy of London, since under a commission which the King had issued soon after his accession, they had been totally excluded. It was to the Bishop of London that William now turned 'to prepare a list of those who were known to be Churchmen, but of the more moderate [sort] . . . so the two parties in the city might be kept in a balance'.[1]

Henry Compton immediately took counsel with his old patron Danby, and the result was far from a 'balance', for the Bishop put forward a list which, according to Burnet, contained 'the most violent Tories in the city, who had been engaged in some of the worst things that passed in the end of King Charles's reign'. Certainly the publication of the names aroused a storm, and a Committee of the Council was appointed to go into the matter though the members were 'so named that they approved it'. The whole incident, Burnet reports, was 'a great grief to the Whigs'.[2]

Yet such conduct—and it is important to say this—did not necessarily strike Compton as odd, for the distinction between the parties was not as yet hard-and-fast, and William himself did not want it to become so. What Tillotson's appointment did, however, was to convince Compton that he was not to be numbered among those whom the King took into his confidence. The result was that he withdrew himself from the life of the Court and passed through an unhappy and unsettled phase. In 1692 the gossips reported that the Earl of Rochester and the Bishop of

[1] Burnet, *op. cit.*, iv. 72. [2] *Ibid.*

London were 'forbidden coming to the Princesse [Anne] till further order':[1] and a little later the same gossips whispered that 'the Prince and Princess of Denmark went to St. Albans and dined with the Earl of Marlborough and the Countess, and Bishop of London'.[2]

Such a dinner party may not seem important but it becomes so when we remember that at this time Anne was on very bad terms both with the King and Queen, and was being used as a tool by some of the more factious tories. Mary and Anne, while separated, seem to have lived on most affectionate terms, but when they came to see much of each other their relations were not so happy. Mary was too talkative, and Anne too silent. There were also financial grievances, for William had granted away James II's private estates, with the result that a motion was brought into the House to increase Anne's civil list pension to £30,000. To William it seemed obvious that Anne was being unscrupulously employed to make a separate interest against him, and the complete ascendancy which Sarah Churchill was known to exercise over her made the situation more sinister. William retaliated by witholding the Order of the Garter from Sarah's husband, and Anne's relations with Whitehall became so strained that in December 1691 she was said to have regretted the failure of her father's naval expedition. John Churchill was dismissed from the Court for suspected Jacobitism, and when the King and Queen insisted that Anne should dismiss the masterful Sarah, she absolutely refused to part with her. 'Mrs. Freeman' and 'Mrs. Morley' consequently retired together to the Duke of Somerset's residence at Sion House.

Such was the background in which the dinner party met at St. Alban's in the summer heat of 1692. No one has recorded what the Prince and Princess of Denmark, John and Sarah Churchill, and the Bishop of London said to each other, but we may hazard a shrewd guess. Of one thing also we may be fairly certain. Had a particular matter of ecclesiastical preferment turned out differently for the Bishop, he would not have been present. As it was, the dinner party probably added to William's embarrassments.

Nor were Compton's relations with the Court made any easier by the fact that in this same month (July) he was contesting

[1] Luttrell, *op. cit.*, ii. 522.   [2] *Ibid.*, ii. 592.

the presentation of St. James's, Piccadilly, against the Queen—
a small thing, maybe, but not without significance—and that
later in October 'a *quare impedit* was taken out against the Bishop
of London for inducting Dr. Lancaster into St. Martin's, the
Queen claiming the next right of presentation'.[1]

Some irresponsible people at this time went so far as to suggest
that the Bishop was wavering in his loyalty to the throne.
His biographer writes: 'It is possible there may be some weak
or prejudiced Persons, who may imagine the Bishop of London to
have inclinations to favour that cause [i.e. James] which evidently
must be the cause of Popery, to which certainly no English
Clergyman or any other was more averse.'[2] That James did not
regard Compton as a possible convert to the Court at St. Germains
may be seen from the fact that when he issued his Declaration
from France on 20 April, 1692, inviting all his loyal subjects to
join him, 'his lordship [of London] was so far from countenancing
any such Design that he was one of those excepted by Name in
that Declaration'.[3] James could neither forget nor forgive.

On 22 November, 1694, Archbishop Tillotson died at the
age of sixty-four. Did Henry Compton anticipate that this third
and unexpected vacancy would at last translate him to Lambeth?
Dr. Birch, the biographer of the late Archbishop, writes that he
did, but it must seem extremely unlikely that he who had been
twice rejected should have been encouraged to regard his chances
in 1694 as a real possibility. His attitude to Tillotson in Convocation, his consorting with Anne and the Churchills, must
surely have convinced him that if William would not have him
in 1690, when his services at the Revolution were so recent, then
he would not have him some four years later. This is certainly the
view taken by his early biographer who writes: 'I do not
remember there were any Expectations that his Lordship on the
death of Archbishop Tillotson, which happen'd before the end of

---

[1] Luttrell, *A Brief Historical Relation*, ii. 582. See also *S.P.D.* Will. and Mary,
23 July, 1692, 4, no. 65 and 6 Oct., 4, no. 72. Compton was unsuccessful in
respect of St. Martin's, but secured his will in Feb. 1694, when he appointed
Dr. Lancaster to succeed Dr. Goudge, the Queen's choice. (*S.P.D.* 8 Feb., 1694,
Will. & Mary, E.B. 2, p. 306. Also Luttrell, *op. cit.*, iii. 394.)

The presentation to St. James's Westminster, continued to be disputed and
it was not till Jan. 1695, that the House of Lords decided in favour of the Crown's
nominee, Dr. Wake, against Dr. Birch, the nominee of the Bishop. *S.P.D.*
Will. & Mary, 15 Nov., 1694, E.B. 4, p. 10. Also Luttrell, *op. cit.*, iii. 426.

[2] *The Life of Dr. Henry Compton*, p. 59.   [3] *Ibid.*

13

the year 1694, should be translated to the See of Canterbury.'[1] Mary was known to favour Stillingfleet, but he was 'too old to rise',[2] and Tillotson himself had recommended as his successor Tenison, Bishop of Lincoln. The latter's election to Canterbury was confirmed on 16 January, 1695, in St. Mary-le-Bow Church, and on this occasion the Bishop of London was present, a fact which suggests that he was now beyond disappointment.

But before this ceremony took place, the new Archbishop had performed a very sad duty, namely, to preach in Westminster Abbey the funeral sermon of Queen Mary, who died just after Christmas at the early age of thirty-two.

We may well believe, so warm was his heart, that her death came as 'an unexpressible Grief to the good Bishop of London'[3] and that it gave him much to think over. They had known each other for a long time, and he had had a great deal to do with her in her early and formative years. Yet somehow Mary does not seem to have liked him, and the Bishop established better relations with her sister. It was as much Mary's doing, as her husband's, that Compton was passed over for the Archbishopric.

William's distress at the loss of his wife was undoubtedly genuine, for her constant loyalty had at last succeeded in winning even his sluggish affections. Compton took the opportunity on 10 January, 1695, to wait on the King in person and present an address of condolence. William, much moved, replied 'that the Church of England had lost their best friend, yet he was resolved to stand by it during his life'.[4]

The practical outcome of the King's grief was an intention to encourage a 'pious and laborious Clergy',[5] and to this end he decided to set up a small Commission 'to recommend fit persons to all ecclesiastical preferment . . . and to seek out the best and worthiest men they could find that such only might be promoted'.[6] We are not concerned here with the history of this Commission, but with calling attention to one significant

---

[1] *The Life of Dr. Henry Compton*, p. 60.

[2] The story is that Stillingfleet, remaining seated, greeted Tenison with these words when they first met after the latter's appointment to Canterbury.

[3] *The Life of Dr. Henry Compton*, p. 60.

[4] Luttrell, *op. cit.*, iii. 425.

[5] Foxcroft, *A Supplement to Burnet's History of My Own Time*, p. 406.

[6] When Stillingfleet died in 1699 he was succeeded by John Moore, Bishop of Norwich.

omission in its personnel. Archbishop Tenison, a good whig, was an obvious choice, as also was Sharp his brother of York, though he was more of a tory. Gilbert Burnet, a personal friend of William, and most forceful of whigs, could hardly be excluded, and there were two others—Edward Stillingfleet, Bishop of Worcester, a good legalist, and William Lloyd of Lichfield and Coventry, one of the seven bishops. Henry Compton was not included, and once again it could hardly have appeared as other than a deliberate snub. It meant that his influence on preferment in the Church (except that in his own gift) was negligible. He was not in a position to approach William direct; nor were any of the Commissioners, with the possible exception of Sharp, likely to seek his advice. It could have given him little satisfaction to recall that earlier in the reign on 6 November, 1690, William had placed him on a Commission to deal with ecclesiastical affairs in Ireland, a Commission which in fact first met in his lodgings in Whitehall, and there wisely decided 'to send home the clergy in Ireland who were here [i.e. in England] to their respective curacies, if they lay in such places as were under his Majesty's protection'. But this Commission, according to Simon Patrick, seems to have petered out.[1]

Thus Compton's position of isolation continued throughout William's reign, and this is seen in the insignificant nature of his extant correspondence, together with the paucity of material about him. It is, perhaps, to his credit, that when the country became alarmed at the discovery of a plot to assassinate the King, the Bishop of London was foremost in joining an 'Association for the Defence of the King's person and Government', and urged his clergy to do the same.[2] When three nonjuring divines gave absolution on the scaffold to two Jacobites, Sir William Perkins and Sir John Friend, 'without a previous Confession made and Abhorrence expressed by the Prisoners of the horrid Crimes for which they died', he again joined his episcopal brethren in publicly condemning them.[3]

On 2 December, 1697, a Day of Thanksgiving was observed throughout the country for the successful prosecution of the foreign war. It was ushered in with the ringing of bells, and came

[1] Simon Patrick, *Autobiography*, p. 159. Also *S.P.D.* Will. & Mary, 6 Nov., 1690, H.O. Minute Book 1, p. 65.
[2] *Life of Dr. Henry Compton*, p. 61. [3] *Ibid.*

to an end, in London, with a magnificent display of fireworks which cost no less than £10,000. Earlier in the day, the Lord Mayor of London, 'with several companies of the livery men of the City', went in procession to St. Paul's, where the Bishop of London preached. The King was not present, he being at Whitehall, where his favourite, Gilbert Burnet, preached an 'eloquent sermon'. For this reason, so Luttrell reported, the Bishop of London's discourse 'will not be printed'.[1] They never were!

Opposition to the whigs, however, and to many friends with whom he had previously stood shoulder to shoulder, now became almost the Bishop's rule, though there was no question of any association with the 'King over the water'. Three examples of this seeking new company, not necessarily important in themselves, may be mentioned.[2]

The first comes from the year 1698, and concerns Sir Charles Duncombe, who when he died in 1711 was reckoned the richest commoner in England. After the Revolution, he dabbled in politics, became a member of Parliament, and opposed the establishment of the Bank of England. In 1698 an angry House of Commons expelled him and lodged him in the Tower on the grounds that he had falsely endorsed a number of Exchequer bills. His friends in the Lords rallied to his cause, and by one vote (it later raised a constitutional issue) 'rejected the bill against Mr. Duncombe[3] and discharged him from the Tower'.[4] The voting in the House of Lords on this occasion was particularly interesting. The whig Archbishop of Canterbury and seven whig bishops were solid in support of the accused, as were John Sheffield, Duke of Normanby (the patron of Dryden and the friend of Pope), Sydney Godolphin, and John Churchill, later created (in 1702) Duke of Marlborough. Against him were Lord Rochester, the Earl of Peterborough, John Sharp, Archbishop of York, Thomas Sprat, Bishop of Rochester, Sir Jonathan Trelawney, Bishop of Exeter (he had supported Anne against

---

[1] Luttrell, *op. cit.*, iii. 313. Also *S.P.D.* Will. III, 8, no. 113.

[2] In 1695 the Rev. W. Hayley, writing to Sir William Trumbull from All Souls' College, protested that the report that he (Sir William) was 'whiggish' would be controverted by the fact that he had the support of Compton and the Bishop of Rochester. See *H. M.C. Downshire MSS.*, vol. 1, Parts i and ii. p. 561.

[3] He was not knighted till 1699.

[4] Luttrell, *op. cit.*, iii. 356. Also Record Office *S.P.D.* 32, Will. III, 10, fo. 4.

William), Edward Fowler, Bishop of Gloucester (who 'wheeled about with the Tories'), Thomas Watson, Bishop of St. David's (almost a Jacobite) and Henry Compton. The voting list does not represent a clear cut division between whig and tory, but it does indicate the kind of company which the Bishop of London was now cultivating.

Mention of Thomas Watson (1637-1717), Bishop of St. David's, furnishes another pointer as to where Compton's political affinities were now leading him. This extraordinary ecclesiastic, son of a seaman, owed his elevation to the episcopate to his friendship with James II. After the Revolution he disappointed his whig enemies (they were many) by taking the oaths to William and Mary, but his real allegiance was known to be to the 'King over the water'. His violent toryism, and his consequent harassing of his whig clergy (some of whom, it must be admitted, were very lax in discharging their clerical duties) led to charges of extortion, simony and *crimen falsi* being brought against him. On 24 July, 1694, Archbishop Tillotson appointed a commission to visit his diocese, suspending the Bishop while investigations were proceeding. From this date there began a legal struggle between Watson and two Archbishops of Canterbury which did not end till the Bishop's deprivation by Archbishop Tenison was endorsed by the House of Lords on 25 January, 1705. There can be little doubt that the sentence would have been less extreme had the Bishop of St. David's not been so violent a tory. It is significant, therefore, that when Thomas Tenison passed sentence of deprivation *ab officio et beneficio* on 3 August, 1699, for simony which he claimed to be 'fully proved', Henry Compton alone of the bishops —the others were Worcester, Salisbury, and Lichfield—dissented.[1]

Our third example concerns John, Lord Somers (1651-1716), sometime Lord Chancellor, than whom there had been no more consistent supporter of the Revolution or more zealous defender of English liberty. Towards the end of William's reign, however, many attacks were made against him by tory opponents in the House of Lords, first in connection with his support of the expedition of the notorious Captain Kidd, and secondly on the grounds of his accepting grants of Crown property. William stood by him as long as he could, but Somers's position became more and more

[1] Luttrell, *op. cit.*, iv. 544.

difficult. In 1701 matters came to a head when he was impeached
by the Commons for the part he had played in the negotiations
relating to the Partition Treaty of 1698. The Bill passed through
the Commons, but was finally rejected by the Lords. A consistent
opponent of Somers in the Upper House was the Bishop of
London. He was one of thirty who protested against there being
a snap debate in the Lords before the Commons were 'ready to
make good their Impeachment', and he entered his reasons for so
doing in the Journal of the House.[1] When the Lord Keeper
finally put the question 'That the Lord Somers be acquitted of the
Articles against him exhibited by the House of Commons',
the Bishop of London voted with the minority against him.[2]

William's reign was now nearing its close: but before the
Princess Anne ascended the throne, she was to suffer a sad blow
in the death of her son, the Duke of Gloucester—the only one of
her children who had shown any hope of survival. The funeral in
Westminster Abbey at nine o'clock in the evening of 10 August,
1700, which the Bishop of London, as befitted his relations with
the Princess, attended, was a solemn and pathetic ceremony. The
guards, consisting of four hundred men, made a lane from the
House of Lords to the east door of the Abbey to keep off the mob
and every other man had a flambeau in his hand which lit up the
sombre spectacle in the gathering darkness.[3]

On 9 March, 1702, William III died in Kensington palace.
The Bishop of London was not present at the death bed—he
would probably not have been welcome—and it was left to good
Archbishop Tenison to minister to the dying King with his usual
devotion. Anne was now Queen.

The late King's main concern had been the successful prosecution of the war in Europe, and this, in spite of himself, had
meant in practice that he was forced to rely on the whigs. The
Revolution was too recent, the menace of resurgent Jacobitism
too real, and suspicion of the loyalty of many tories only too well
founded, for William to place his confidence elsewhere. Compton
had deliberately chosen, after his personal disappointment, to
be among those who were not trusted.

The accession of the new Queen brought a new situation.
In her first Parliament she declared 'her heart to be entirely

---

[1] *The Life of Dr. Henry Compton*, p. 63.   [2] *Ibid.*
[3] Luttrell, *op. cit.*, iv. 675.

English', and not long afterwards, in questionable taste, she intimated that she was 'resolved not to follow the example of her predecessor in making use of a few of her subjects to oppress the rest. She would be Queen of all her subjects and [would] have all the parties and distinctions of former reigns ended and buried in hers'.[1]

These were brave words but in practice affairs did not quite work out like this. The Queen's main loyalty—and it is not to her discredit—was to the Church of England, and she was genuinely distressed when she thought it 'in danger'. As to her public policy, she affirmed that 'her own principles must always keep her entirely firm to the interests and religion of the Church of England, and would incline her to countenance those who had the truest zeal to support it'. As part of this loyalty to the Church, she had been taught to distrust the whigs, and she had responded readily to this tuition. It may be that it was one way of overcoming a slight feeling of guilt for her own attitude at the Revolution. Thus in practice Anne identified herself with the tories, and it was only the exigencies of the foreign war which in the middle years of her reign forced her to turn to the whigs. When the military crisis was over she was free again to turn to the tories.

So far as Compton was concerned, the accession of the new Queen seemed to promise the end of his sojourn in the wilderness. He had special claims upon her favour—a long relationship going back to her youth, unique and unorthodox services to her at the Revolution, and the rediscovery of the toryism of his family after his disappointment over the Archbishopric. The Archbishop of Canterbury, and the Bishop of Salisbury, foremost of all ecclesiastical whigs, were soon given evident signs of the royal displeasure. 'Upon the accession of a new sovereign to the Throne', writes a contemporary, 'it was but natural to see new Faces at Court, and several of the Old ones dismissed from it.'[2]

If the Queen turned away from Tenison and Burnet, she as certainly turned towards Sharp, Archbishop of York, who fittingly preached the coronation sermon, and to her old tutor Henry Compton, Bishop of London. The latter's biographer

---

[1] Sir J. Leveson Gower to Lord Rutland, *H.M.C.* Rutland MSS. II, 173.
[2] *Memoirs of the Life and Times of Dr. Thomas Tenison*, 1715, p. 101.

writes: 'His Lordship as he ever had a very large share in the Esteem and Favour of this Princess, who knew his heart as well as her own to be entirely English, and that no consideration whatsoever should ever be able to divert him from the true Interest of the Church and the Crown, he was not only continued a Member of her Majesty's most honourable Privy Council, but was frequently consulted in Private, especially about the Affairs of the Church.'[1] Another friend states that 'his Access became easier at Court and he had a greater Power and Interest'.[2]

It may be said of the Bishop's relations with the new Queen that they were consistently cordial, though in some respects he does not seem to have enjoyed her complete confidence. For example, when one of her subjects presumed to write her 'Life', she got into touch with Compton who promised that this work should not be published. Yet the Queen remained uneasy, and felt it necessary to write to Mr. Secretary Harley as follows: 'I dare not trust the Bishop in this matter, and therefore desire you would give yourself the trouble to enquire after this book, and take care it may not be printed, for it would vex me very much to have such a ridiculous thing as this appear in the world.'[3]

One of the first things that the Bishop did was to persuade the Queen—we suspect that she did not need much persuading—not to renew the Commission for Ecclesiastical Affairs which had endeavoured, though without over much success, to control ecclesiastical appointments right up to the end of William's reign. It had, on the whole, been consistently used to prefer whigs, and Compton (as we have seen) was not even a member. The Bishop (doubtless seconded by Sharp) now suggested that the Queen should keep preferment in her own hands, so far as political events made this possible.[4] Thus throughout her reign he was able to exert a measure of influence such as he had not wielded since the accession of James. Compton himself told Thomas Gooch that he 'gave her Majesty such reasonable (and to her own pious Inclinations such agreeable) Advice, upon the Vacancy of two Dioceses, as occasioned their being well filled, when 'twas little expected'.[5]

---

[1] *The Life of Dr. Henry Compton*, p. 64.
[2] Gooch, *A Sermon, etc.*, p. 13.
[3] *H.M.C.* Marquess of Bath MSS. i. 97.   [4] Gooch, *op. cit.*, p. 12.
[5] *Ibid.*, p. 12.

Signs of royal favour were not long in coming Compton's way. On 2 November, 1702, Anne made him Lord High Almoner in place of the Bishop of Worcester, an office which established him in a peculiarly personal relationship with the Sovereign, for which very reason Compton had been deprived of the equally personal office of Dean of the Chapels Royal in the reign of James II. It may well have seemed to the aging Bishop an act of tardy justice thus to be reinstated by the last of the Stuarts. On 14 January, 1703, Gilbert Burnet was informed that his lodgings in Whitehall were to be made over to the Bishop of London.[1]

The tension between whig and tory, which divided both Parliament and Church, found expression during Anne's reign in the disputes which disgraced Convocation, and which eventually led to its suppression, in 1717, for over a century. Constitutionally the status of Convocation had been irrevocably changed when, by a private agreement between Archbishop Sheldon and Lord Chancellor Clarendon, in 1664, the clergy gave up their right to separate taxation in their own assembly. Henceforth, the Crown had no financial interest in summoning Convocation, so that if for any reason the King found it undesirable for Convocation to meet, he could dispense with its services without hardship—and this is precisely what happened. William, after the disputes over comprehension, preferred a Convocation which did not deliberate because of the fierce dissensions within that body itself, dissensions which were the inevitable reflection of the conflicting principles of the day. The Upper House, especially after the nonjuring purge, was on the whole latitudinarian in theology, and anxious for an accommodation with the Dissenters. The Lower House, in the main, was orthodox, High Church, and concerned to champion the rights of the *Ecclesia Anglicana.* The whig Archbishop Tenison took his stand on the undoubted historic fact that Convocation was one constitutional assembly meeting in two houses, and that he was its President: Francis Atterbury, the dynamic leader of the tory clergy, maintained, on the other hand, with the support of a bogus scholarship, that the Lower House had independent rights under its Prolocutor, and that the Crown was obliged to summon Convocation with Parliament under the *praemunientes* clause.

[1] Luttrell, *op. cit.*, v. 257.

What is particularly important, so far as this biography is concerned, is that Atterbury was the protégé of Henry Compton. This vigorous churchman was ordained *circa* 1687, and his oratory, together with his forceful personality, soon gained him a great reputation in London as a preacher. Compton was not long in discovering his ability. In 1691 the lectureship of St. Bride's became vacant, and there were many candidates for this attractive post. The Bishop of London, however, appointed Atterbury 'over their heads', thus earning the gratitude of the Parish Vestry, who in October ordered 'that the Bishop of London should have thanks returned to him for recommending and licensing Mr. Atterbury as lecturer'.[1] Atterbury now had a London pulpit from which he could propagate his High Church Anglicanism, and the Bishop continued to show him favour. He was soon made a chaplain to William and Mary (the King was concerned to win over the tories) and in 1693 a preacher at Bridewell.

Atterbury's efforts to secure the summoning of Convocation had the active support of Compton, and this episcopal backing proved invaluable. The Archbishop and the rest of the whig bishops preferred a non-sitting assembly, and John Moore, Bishop of Norwich, writing to Tenison at this time, expressed the hope that if Convocation were to meet, then it would not be granted a licence to do business.[2] But the demand for Convocation increased in volume, and in 1700 William's ministry accepted office only on condition that it be allowed to meet concurrently with the newly-elected Parliament.[3] The King bowed before the storm, and he agreed that Convocation should be allowed to do business—and so began that ecclesiastical strife which persisted throughout the reign of his successor.

Now was the great opportunity for Atterbury's constitutional thesis to be put into practice, and for the writ *praemunientes* to be executed by the bishops upon their clergy. He and the Bishop of London accordingly consorted much together, for Atterbury believed that if Compton would but give a lead, then the Bishops of Exeter and Rochester (Trelawney and Sprat) would summon up their courage and follow suit. A letter of Atterbury's

[1] J. Nichols, *The Miscellaneous Works of Bishop Atterbury*, iii. 32.
[2] Lathbury, *A History of the Convocation*, 1842, p. 346.
[3] E. Carpenter, *The Life and Times of Thomas Tenison*, p. 251.

to Bishop Trelawney, on 2 January, 1702, makes the position clear:

> There is another thing which I will presume to mention to your Lordship, in relation to your parliament writ. It is of the utmost importance to the Rights of the Church and towards the success of the cause, that that writ should be executed upon the inferior clergy, as before the Restoration it was constantly done and particularly in your Lordship's See; the records of which happen to be more particular and full to the purpose than those of any other Cathedral in England. The Bishop of London, I believe, will execute it in his diocese. I have talked with the Bishop of Rochester upon it, and he says if your Lordship and the Bishop of London do it, he will do it also.[1]

Neither Sprat nor Trelawney need have entertained any anxieties as to Compton's intentions. He peremptorily stopped in his diocese the execution of the Archbishop's mandate for the summoning of Convocation, and dispatched him a letter in which he asked the Archbishop whether 'since the inferior clergy are called to Parliament by the clause *praemunientes*, and since that clause has all along from the beginning of the Reformation till lately been regularly executed (as appears in the records cited in the late Rights, Powers, etc., of a Convocation, p. 615) his Grace will not think it proper to give directions to his lordship to intimate to all the Bishops of the Province, when he sends his Grace's provincial mandate to them, that they should execute, not that only, but the parliament writ also, as heretofore they were accustomed'.[2]

While writing in these terms to the Archbishop, Compton at the same time assured Atterbury that 'whatever answer the Archbishop returns', he intended 'to execute the *Praemunientes* and to transmit the Parliament writ, together with the Convocation writ, to the clergy of his diocese'.[3] The Bishop of London's firmness certainly kept his brethren firm, though the whig Archbishop would naturally not comply with his wishes. Thomas Sprat promised, on his part, 'that if the Bishop of London did it, he too would', and on 14 January, 1701, he wrote triumphantly to Trelawney: 'My Lord and I have summoned the clergy by a parliament writ, according to the clause *Praemunientes*, as well as by the Convocation writ. We doubt not but your Lordship will do the like'.[4]

[1] J. Nichols, *op. cit.*, iii. 11.   [2] *Ibid.*, iii. 13.   [3] *Ibid.*   [4] *Ibid.*

It was hardly to be expected that a Convocation ushered in amid so much controversy, and known in advance to be divided within itself, would find its deliberations very peaceful. The consistent policy of the Archbishop of Canterbury was to assert his undoubted constitutional position as President of the whole Convocation, and thereby to insist that it was one assembly meeting in two houses. The policy of Atterbury, Compton and the tories generally was to exalt the rights of the Prolucutor as head of the Lower House, and to set up thereby an 'independent interest'.

The history of this Convocation lies outside the scope of this work, though we may perhaps note that in 1711 Francis Atterbury signalised his triumph by securing his election as Prolocutor in opposition to White Kennett, the leader of the Bishop's party in the Lower House. Old Archbishop Tenison was now more or less isolated at Lambeth, and this encouraged Atterbury (the tories had come into power) to secure a change in the licence by which 'the Archbishop was not, as was usual on former occasions, nominated President, neither was he consulted previous to its being issued'. Compton's name appeared in his stead, and Sharp was consulted by the ministry concerning the business to be laid before the Convocation, though it did not concern his Province.[1]

Not only did Compton take an active part in securing the summoning of Convocation in England, but he was also equally active in procuring its revival in Ireland, where it had not met since 1666. Parliament, of course, had frequently assembled in that country, and the clergy maintained that they should legally have been summoned to meet at the same time, a fact which led to a protest from the Irish bishops in the House of Lords against what they regarded as the virtual liquidation of their own constitutional Assembly. Complaints against this suppression were frequent and vociferous, and on 5 October, 1697, William King, at the time Bishop of Derry and the real leader of the agitation in Ireland, wrote to the Bishop of Waterford: 'I own a Convocation necessary and I had hot disputes about it in England; but all assemblies that have been long chained up prove unruly when first let loose; and I am afraid this would prove in our present juncture a reason of abrogating them altogether.'[2]

---

[1] *The Life of Dr. Henry Compton*, p. 82.
[2] Mant, *History of the Church of Ireland*, 1840, ii. 96.

It was obvious that for many reasons the Government, as in England, preferred a Convocation which did not meet for business, and the situation in Ireland was made more complicated by the rivalry between William King, translated to Dublin in 1703, and Narcissus Marsh translated from Dublin to Armagh earlier in the same year. Marsh suspected that King was championing this demand for a Convocation in order to set up the Archbishopric of Dublin as supreme over that of Armagh. Nor were the personal relationships between these two men made easier by the financial complications which arose out of Marsh's move. In June 1703, he was corresponding with Compton concerning arrears of rent in Dublin which he had not yet received, and he complained that he had been unable to save out of the revenues of that See since he had 'expended all [he] could spare for erecting a public library'.[1] He also expressed to Compton (and to Archbishop Tenison) his anxiety at the prospect of a Convocation. If the Queen should grant a licence, then he urged that there should be no innovations in it, but that it should be directed to him (i.e. Marsh) as 'Primate of all Ireland'.[2]

The Queen and the tories—they both alleged that they championed the rights of the Church—were definitely on the side of summoning Convocation, and amongst the latter were, of course, Compton and Atterbury. Writing to Bishop Trelawney, Atterbury admitted that he had been 'twice or thrice with the Bishop of London in this affair'. Compton also did his best to encourage William King, Archbishop of Dublin, 'the person that transacts all in Ireland', 'to insist to the utmost with the Ministry here for a Convocation'. 'If you lose your Convocation', he wrote to him, 'we shall not long keep ours in England. . . . I know not which way the wind sets, but in what corner so ever it is, or hath been for some time, I am sure it hath blown no good to the Church in either of the three Kingdoms.'[3]

William King, thus encouraged by one who had the ear of the Queen, kept up the pressure, and later came over to England where he found the tories active in his support. Finally all difficulties were overcome and Convocation was summoned to

[1] Marsh to Compton, 7 June, 1703, B.M. Add. MSS. 29, 584, fo. 103.
[2] *Ibid.*, 16 Jan., 1704/5, Bod. Rawlinson MSS. 983 C., fo. 159.
[3] Nichols, *The Miscellaneous Works of Bishop Atterbury*, iii. p. 111.

meet for business. Once again, its history lies outside the scope of a biography of Henry Compton, although we may linger over it just long enough to notice the rather gloomy reflections of Narcissus Marsh in a letter to the Archbishop of Tuam, dated 4 July, 1705: "Tis an uncomfortable thing that all assemblies of men can come to some conclusions and agreement save clergymen; that all that have controversies can unite with temper and humanity, only they treat one another with passion and bitterness.'[1]

Ecclesiastical assemblies down to our own day have had an unhappy aptitude for disappointing the hopes of their begetters!

We have already seen that the Bishop of London's whole status was changed by the accession of Anne; that he was now *persona grata* at Court, and, in company with Archbishop Sharp, enjoyed the royal confidence. Thomas Tenison at Lambeth, on the other hand, was only too conscious of his isolation. When, for example, in 1703, the Queen appointed a general Day of Thanksgiving to celebrate the destruction of the French squadron in Vigo, it was the Bishop of London and not the Archbishop of Canterbury who took the lead in drawing up prayers. She herself went in solemn procession to St. Paul's Cathedral,[2] where it seems that Compton's visitation[3] had begun to bear fruit, for a contemporary records that 'everything was managed with the utmost Decency and Order'. The Bishop of London sat on his throne, the Dean and Prebendaries took their places 'within the Rails of the Altar' and the choir was placed in the organ loft. The Bishop himself read the Communion Service—we can see here the influence of the Caroline divines—and Sir Jonathan Trelawney, Bishop of Exeter, preached 'an excellent sermon' on the text 'But as for you, no Man hath been able to stand before you this Day'.[4]

Much less to Compton's credit was his changed attitude to occasional conformity publicly manifested in the debates in Parliament in 1703. The Test Act of 1672, we may recall, made it necessary for any holder of civic or state office to receive the Sacrament once a year according to the rites of the Church of England. William, as we have seen, wished to free the Dissenters

---

[1] Quoted Relton, *History of the Church of England*, p. 205.
[2] Luttrell, *op. cit.*, v. 232.   [3] See pp. 245–249.   [4] Joshua 13: 9.

from the necessity for such an expedient, but he had been unable to secure the passing of a Comprehension Bill, though Compton supported it enthusiastically, even commending it in a letter to Sancroft. Thus were the Dissenters forced to continue the practice of occasional conformity, that is of communicating at their Parish Church once a year, if they wished to qualify for office. It was not, of course, an ideal arrangement. Many came to the Sacrament merely for this purpose, though it is but fair to add that some Dissenters (and this practice continued right into the nineteenth century) felt it a duty to attend their parish church once in the year without any ulterior motive. Whig bishops were in fact anxious that they should do so. Such Dissenters felt that they could not altogether conform to the Church of England: on the other hand, they did not wish altogether to separate. By and large, however, there was a great deal of hypocrisy in occasional conformity, but the responsibility for this must rest largely upon those who imposed such a requirement.

Such a practice, of course, was anathema to tories and High Churchmen. To them it was a clear profanation of the Sacrament, and an invitation to wolves to devour the flock. A common danger had brought Protestant Englishmen together: but those years, in the halcyon days of Anne's patronage, seemed far behind, and High Churchmen were anxious to rid themselves of the last vestiges of an alliance which they had at best regarded as a disagreeable necessity. They determined to prevent the occasional conformity by which the Test Act was made ineffective. In the first session of Anne's first Parliament a Bill to this end passed through the Commons but was thrown out by the Lords. In 1703 it was again introduced in a slightly amended form into the Commons, and successfully negotiated this House, after a debate in which the whig bishops in general, and Archbishop Tenison in particular, came in for a great deal of abuse. It then went up to the House of Lords. Once again the lords spiritual, under the leadership of Tenison and Burnet, closed their ranks, and the Bill was rejected by a majority of twelve. But Compton did not support his brethren, for he voted with the tories.

It is not easy to see how different circumstances could justify this reversal of a former attitude towards Dissenters, nor can we easily accept the embarrassed apologia of his contemporary biographer 'that though it [i.e. occasional conformity] had been [practised] in the former reign, yet those who had the Interest of the Church of England most at Heart, among whom his Lordship was one, saw it then with Grief of Heart, and yet without Prospect of any Remedy'.[1]

The tories and High Churchmen, however, refused to accept this further defeat, in 1703, as final. Another effort was made in the next year to push a similar Bill through Parliament. It did not pass, but in that Indian summer of High Anglicanism, the last years of Anne's reign, an Act against Occasional Conformity secured the approval of both Houses in 1711. 'His Lordship had the Happiness', writes a contemporary High Churchman, 'to live to see it fully accomplished. And 'tis past all manner of doubt that it was a very great Satisfaction to his Mind to find the Church so happily secured by it.'[2]

Fortunately the Act was repealed (together with the monstrous Schism Act of 1714) in 1719, but the Bishop did not have the 'unhappiness' to live to see this return to justice.

From the little that we have said about Convocation, it will be readily understood that Church feeling ran very high during the reign of the last of the Stuarts, and this encouraged the tories, now learning the arts of political strategy, to rally national sentiment around the cry that 'the Church was in danger'. Such a scare was a most valuable party weapon, for it secured the support of a large number of country clergy against the whigs and the foreign war. The whigs were for avoiding excitement and controversy at home, for which reason they consistently opposed the scheme to bring the Electress Sophia (heiress to the throne) over to England. If the Church really were in danger, then the least said about it the better. Their concern was to unite the country behind the military genius of Marlborough, who on the Continent was championing Protestant liberties against the aggression of Louis XIV. We must never forget that the background of these years was a bloody foreign war. August, 1704 saw the great victory of Blenheim, and the next year witnessed the invasion of Brabant. Such tremendous exertions were bound to redound to the credit of the whigs and make the position of the tories difficult. The latter never lost an opportunity of embarrassing their

---

[1] *The Life of Dr. Henry Compton*, p. 67. [2] *Ibid.*

political rivals, and in 1705, combining with the High Churchmen, they introduced a motion into the House of Lords under the specious plea that 'the Church was in danger'.

The debate, as might be expected where the area of discussion was so large and controversial, proved stormy. One whig lord impugned the whole motives of those who had laid the matter before the House and ended his speech with these words: 'Upon her Majesty's happy Succession for some time the Complaint was silent, but when she was pleased to make some alterations in her ministry, it was immediately revived and continued ever since. The Church was in no imminent Danger.'

As his Lordship sat down, Compton walked into the House, and with his accustomed impetuosity, immediately replied. The Church was most certainly in great danger, he protested, for reasons which were not far to seek. 'Prophaneness and Irreligion', he declared, 'is so rife amongst us, and the Licentiousness of the Press so intolerable, from which Books proceed not fit to be read, that a most vile one is lately published by a Clergyman in my own Diocese, which I endeavoured to punish; but he has used such Subterfuges in the Questions of the Law, that I could not come at him.[1] Sermons are preached wherein Rebellion is authorised and Resistance to the Higher Powers encouraged.'

Compton was here referring particularly to a discourse recently delivered by Benjamin Hoadly in St. Lawrence Jewry, in which, so the Bishop complained, the preacher had maintained teaching clean contrary to the doctrine of the Church of England as it was laid down in the first and second parts of the Homily against disobedience and wilful rebellion.[2]

Such forthright toryism was too much for Burnet, who rose to reply to the Bishop. It was Compton's past which made him so vulnerable, and referring to his comments on Hoadly's sermon, the Bishop of Salisbury sarcastically remarked 'that his Lordship was the last man to notice the subject, since, if the doctrine were unsound, he could not understand how his Lordship would be able to justify his appearing in arms at Nottingham'.[3]

---

[1] The reference is to Edmund Hickeringill, see p. 233.
[2] This sermon was taken notice of in Convocation. See Lathbury, *op. cit.* p. 401.
[3] Tindal, *The Continuation of Mr. Rapin's History of England*, 1763, iii. 726.

The Bishop of Salisbury was not the only one who could not understand!

The tories, despite Bishop Compton's support, did not carry their motion. The House by sixty-one votes to thirty decided that the Church was not in danger. With Compton there voted Sharp, Archbishop of York, and George Hooper, Bishop of Bath and Wells.[1]

But the day of the Tories was now at hand, the more surely since Marlborough and his Duchess were losing the favour of the Queen. The very magnitude of the Duke's successes made him less necessary as the French menace wore itself out. The political crisis at home came in 1710, but before it happened the Queen was visited by a personal tragedy. In November 1708, George, Prince of Denmark, died at the age of fifty-five. They were an odd couple. The Prince had little ability, was refused the title of King in 1702, and was bitterly attacked by the whigs for his administration of the Admiralty during the years 1704-8. Yet Queen and Prince were genuinely attached to each other, and Anne, to whom the passing of the years brought one tragedy after another, was overwhelmed with grief. In her anguish she turned to the preceptor of her youth, and his warm heart did not fail her. Writing from Fulham on 8 November, Ralph Bridges, the Bishop's Chaplain, informed Sir William Trumbull that 'the Bishop is a pure good man and takes a world of care of the Queen on this mournful occasion. He visits her every day'.[2] On the Sunday following the Prince's death, Atterbury preached before the Queen.

In 1708, the Queen had still six years to live, but the turning point of her reign came in 1710. On 5 November, 1709, Dr. Henry Sacheverell preached what proved to be a notorious sermon in St. Paul's Cathedral before the Lord Mayor. From a letter of the Bishop's Chaplain it seems that Compton was responsible for his occupying the pulpit on this occasion.[3]

Sacheverell's preaching had no great learning to support it. He was a tory of the most extreme kind, whose thinking was dominated by two strong prejudices. One was a most violent and almost pathological dislike of the whigs, whom he regarded as scarce fit to live: the other was a deep

---

[1] *The Life of Dr. Henry Compton*, p. 69.
[2] *H.M.C.* Downshire MSS. vol. 1, Parts i and ii, p. 863.   [3] *Ibid.*

and passionate attachment to the principle of 'non-resistance'. His November the fifth sermon consisted of variations around these twin themes. Gilbert Burnet was the natural target for his rather clumsy wit, and the preacher made much of the fact that whereas the whigs 'formerly laboured to bring the Church into the Conventicle, now they labour to bring the Conventicle into the Church, which will prove its inevitable ruin'. The sermon, according to the usual custom of those days when such productions were 'hot news', was published in due course. It was immediately seized upon by the House of Commons, who declared it to be a seditious libel and called for the preacher's impeachment.

The whigs had played into the tories' hands. The martyr is often thrice blessed, and Sacheverell was from henceforth a 'made man'. The feeling of London was solid behind him, and enthusiastic crowds guarded his lodgings. Forty-thousand copies of his sermon were sold in a matter of days. Even Queen Anne's coach was surrounded by an excited mob who cried that 'they hoped her Majesty was for Dr. Sacheverell'.

The preacher had no more enthusiastic or energetic supporter than the Bishop of London. In fact, when we remember that he was now seventy-seven years of age, his energy was remarkable. 'His Lordship, as well as may other excellent Churchmen and good Patriots, rightly judging that the Doctor's cause was that of the Church of England stickled [sic] with all their might on his behalf.'[1] On the other hand, the Bishop of London's nephew, Spencer Compton, Earl of Wilmington, a zealous whig, was one of the Committee appointed to draw up the articles of impeachment.

We are not concerned in this biography, however, with the general course of Dr. Sacheverell's trial, which lasted from 27 February, 1710 to 20 March, and ended in a three-years suspension from office. During these weeks, Compton was most assiduous in his attendance at the Upper House. The tories fought every inch of the way, and after the Earl of Nottingham had secured the passing of a declaration that in proceeding against Dr. Sacheverell they must abide by the known usage of Parliament, the Bishop was one of those who tried to secure an adjournment. The manoeuvre was unsuccessful, but Compton with

[1] *The Life of Dr. Henry Compton,* p. 76.

forty-eight others, entered a protest. Thus the debate continued, and when the House resolved that 'upon Impeachments for high Crimes and Misdemeanours, by writing or speaking, the particular words supposed to be Criminal were not necessarily to be expressly specified',[1] the Bishop of London, in company with the Archbishop of York, the Bishops of Rochester, and Bath and Wells, dissented. Eventually the House went on to discuss whether the Commons had made good their first article of impeachment. In the course of this debate, both Burnet and Talbot, Bishop of Oxford, spoke strongly against the doctrine of passive obedience, while Hooper and Compton came dangerously near to asserting it, though contemporaries were forced to admit that the Bishop of London did not maintain it in such a crude manner 'as the Dr. Sacheverell had managed it'.[2] When the question was put, the Lords agreed that the Commons had made good their case. Compton once again voted in the minority and was one of those who entered a protest 'because by the Laws of the Land, the Laws of Parliament, and the inherent Rights of Peerage, every Peer was to judge for himself both of the Fact as well as of the Law'.[3]

This vote did not end the lengthy and rather cumbrous procedure, which the friends of Sacheverell managed to make more lengthy at each stage. It was now necessary to debate the general question whether the Doctor was in fact guilty of 'the High Crimes and Misdemeanours charged upon him by the Impeachment of the House of Commons'. Here he was finally condemned by a majority of seventeen votes. Compton voted with the minority and was one of thirty-four Peers who protested against the verdict, and against the sentence of three-years suspension.[4]

Commenting on these proceedings in Parliament, the tory Thomas Hearne (who never liked Compton) writes: 'The clergy may thank themselves for these sad troubles occasioned by their Defection in giving up the Doctrine of Non-Resistance and Passive Obedience in the late Revolution, and tho' now they insist upon it, yet 't is only a Reproach to them, and they are only laughed at for it.'[5]

---

[1] *Journals of the House of Commons*, xvi. 241.
[2] Thomas Hearne, *Remarks and Collections*, ed. Doble, 1889, ii. 362.
[3] *The Life of Dr. Henry Compton*, p. 78.
[4] *Ibid.*   [5] *Op. cit.*, ii. 362.

The sentence was as severe as Parliament dared make it, but it was clear to everybody that it was a nominal victory only and as bitter as defeat. The trial proved to be, if not a crime, most certainly a blunder. It provided an opportunity for tory sentiment to rally around the throne and the Church, and the final outcome of this resurgence was the fall of the whig ministry in 1710. Thus Harley was made Chancellor of the Exchequer, and Henry St. John, Secretary of State. At long last, the Queen felt that she could breathe freely, since her beloved Church was no longer in danger. She had escaped from her whig imprisonment. The *vox populi* asserted itself in a sudden welter of emotion, and numerous loyal addresses were presented at Whitehall. The Bishop of London's age did not, for a moment, make him lag behind his countrymen in zeal. On 22 August, 1710, he led his clergy in person and presented an address to the Queen, congratulating her on the change of ministry. It is significant, however (according to one authority), that nearly half of the beneficed clergy of London could not in this associate themselves with their Bishop, and even some of those who did so had 'reservations'.

They were pleased, so ran the Address, to make this 'dutiful Application' to her Majesty, particularly 'since the acknowledgment of her Hereditary Title, and Irresistable Authority was openly and boldly represented as a plain Declaration in favour of the Pretender.' For their part, they were 'steadfastly purposed to pay all Duty, and Allegiance to her Majesty, their rightful and lawful Sovereign, whose Title to the Crown by Descent had been affirmed and recognised by all her Liege People in full Parliament.' They knew of no other person who had any 'Claims to their Obedience', and they acknowledged the illustrious House of Hanover as having 'the only Right of ascending the Throne and indisputable Title to their Allegiance'.[1]

A careful reading of this Address shows that its sentiments were, perhaps, not so extreme as a cursory glance might suggest. In many respects it was artfully, and we cannot but suspect, deliberately ambiguous. Well may we sympathise with the author of a contemporary pamphlet who confessed that he had read the Address with 'Care, Eagerness, and Expectation',

[1] The Address is reproduced almost in full in *The Life of Dr. Henry Compton*, pp. 79-81. It does not seem to have been published at the time.

particularly in respect of the 'controverted Points of Hereditary Power and Non-Resistance', but found the 'words so artfully chosen [that he] immediately fell upon this Reflection: To what a Pass have so many of the Protestant Clergy reduc'd themselves? Either they really believe a Doctrine which they have not Courage or Honesty enough to own and assert plainly, or they make a Shew or Pretence of asserting what they do not really believe.'

Behind the phraseology of the Address, so this pamphleteer maintained, there lay a very real dilemma, and it was from this that the ambiguity sprang. What did its author mean by the phrase 'Hereditary Title'? Did he understand a 'Right by Birth, antecedent to, and independent of, the Laws of the Land', or a 'Title to the Crown as the Laws and Constitution of the Kingdom have given to the Heirs of such a Family, Qualified according to those Laws, and deriving under them'? If he meant the former, then it was clear that Anne had no such right: if the latter, then why all this tirade against the whigs? The same ambiguity attached to the phrase 'Irresistible Authority'. Was this meant to imply that no one could legally resist her Majesty's legal authority, a fact which was obvious; or that the power of the Crown was 'irresistible and *legibus solutus*', a contention which many would strongly oppose?[1]

Most whig contemporaries saw in the Address an avowal of unrestrained toryism, sponsored by the one man whose past ought to have persuaded him not to make it. Even from distant Ireland, Edward Pearson reported overhearing a conversation in a coffee house in which the Address of the Bishop of London was 'much reflected upon'.[2]

We must not, perhaps, be over-anxious to sit in judgment on the Bishop, but it is difficult not to offer some comments of a critical nature as to his attitude to *l'affaire Sacheverell*. We must make full allowance for a change of political atmosphere across the years. There was a vast difference between the religious situation under James II, a fervent Roman Catholic with undoubted absolutist ambitions, and that which prevailed under Queen Anne, whose unfaltering devotion to the Church of England was the controlling loyalty of her life. Yet we cannot

[1] *Some Short Remarks upon the late Address of the Bishop of London*, 1711, p. 13.
[2] *H.M.C.* App. ii, Report XIV, 21 (Portland MSS. vol. v).

ignore the fact that certain principles were involved. Compton's attitude in Parliament, and his sponsoring of an Address of this kind, made it difficult for ordinary people to see how such a course of action could be reconciled with the policy which he had followed earlier at the Revolution. No one could have been more definite at that time that in the last resort an absolutist monarch, no matter how good might be his claim by hereditary right, must be got rid of. Resistance to him became not only permissible but a solemn duty.

Compton himself would have said, of course, that the situation had entirely changed: that Anne could be trusted in a way that James could not, and that as a bishop sworn to defend the Church, he could no longer regard the throne as other than its protector. When he had been eager to made an accommodation with the Dissenters, that was because the safety of the Church of England was bound up with such an alliance. Now it was no longer necessary, and it was better to forget the past. A drowning man will clutch at a serpent, but when he is brought safe to shore he will not necessarily make a pet of it.

Such an apologia might be made, but it leaves a nasty taste in the mouth. Also, despite the changed situation in Anne's reign, Compton could not but be conscious of the real danger of Jacobitism. In fact there had been an abortive rebellion not long previously, and the Bishop knew only too well that many noblemen had compromised themselves, and that even Anne was, in her heart, more sympathetic to claims from St. Germains than from Hanover—and St. Germains meant a Roman Catholic sovereign. It was only a combination of exceptional circumstances which led to the peaceful accession of George I. If the Old Pretender had ascended the throne in 1714, the passive obedience which Compton preached up in Parliament might well have left the country helpless in the face of new attacks on its liberty. If resistance to a tyrannical monarch is legitimate in principle, then it can never be right, even with the best of monarchs on the throne, to preach non-resistance. Though the Bishop's address to Anne does support the Hanoverian Succession, yet if the Jacobites had been able to present England with a *fait accompli* the whole tenor of its teaching could have been used to justify a change of government. Formal consistency is not necessarily always a political virtue, and at this time political parties were not rigidly defined. But there were broad principles dividing, shall we say, Atterbury from Burnet, and it is therefore difficult to see Compton's changed political outlook as the legitimate transition from one point of view to another.

We are not surprised that the Bishop was subjected to a number of caustic criticisms by whig contemporaries. One attack in a *Letter concerning Allegiance*[1] took a form which must have been particularly painful to him, for its author published both a private letter sent by Compton to a clergyman in Essex soon after the Revolution urging him to take the oaths, and a damaging extract from *The Bishop's Seventh Letter to his Clergy* in 1686. 'Was there ever a more open avowal of the Lawfulness of Resistance to a King of England not governing by Law', the writer asked; and need those clergy who had refused to subscribe the Address be ashamed because 'they are unwilling to seem to favour those Doctrines and Terms which alone carry forward the Interest of the Popish Line here at home?'[2]

The *Letter concerning Allegiance* was not long in appearing in the bookshops, and it quickly went through four editions.

Another attack appeared a little later in *Some Short Remarks upon the late Address of the Bishop of London and the Clergy to the Queen in a Letter to Dr. Sm-l-ge.*[3]

Here the writer sarcastically observed that the author of the 'Address' seemed more concerned with making the position of the whigs difficult than with maintaining the Protestant Succession. As for the Bishop of London, he was free to interpret the ambiguous phrases only one way. By 'hereditary' he must understand 'legal' and by 'irresistible' that which 'in some Cases may be resisted', since 'his letters, his Conferences, and above all his seasonable and glorious Resistance at the Revolution demonstrate this to have been his Opinion at above Fifty Years of Age; and it cannot with Charity be supposed that he has embraced new Opinions after that Age: or that he now either thinks or acts inconsistently with what he did about twenty years ago'.[4]

The Bishop, perhaps wisely, did not attempt any reply, nor did any of his tory friends undertake it for him. Doubtless

---

[1] *A Letter concerning Allegiance, written by the Lord Bishop of L——n to a Clergyman in Essex presently after the Revolution, Never before published,* 1714.
[2] *Ibid.,* p. 16. [3] *Some Short Remarks, etc.,* p. 13. [4] *Ibid.*

even they thought there was not much to be said. In fact the Bishop never did publicly attempt any explanation for his change of front, either by justifying his late attitude on the grounds that he was really consistent but times had changed; or by owning that he was misled in the principles which he had professed at the Revolution.

There remains one further question concerning the Address. The Bishop presented it and subscribed to it, but did he write it? The probable answer is no. On a former occasion[1] rather than allow separate individual addresses to be sent up to the throne, he had sponsored an official one for the diocese. It seems likely that the Address in 1710 was written by Dr. George Smalridge, though whether as one alleged it was 'drawn up and fixed before the Bishop had the small honour paid him of being led into the design,' we cannot tell.

Dr. Smalridge was a great personal friend of Atterbury, and was for many years deputy to the Bishop of London's protégé, Dr. Jane, in the Regius Professorship of Divinity at Oxford. He was well known in London for his preaching, being lecturer at St. Peter-le-Poor, Broad Street. It is just possible that he drew up an Address for his own use and adapted it later for official purposes: or more likely that Compton asked him to undertake the writing of it. Whatever the truth, the ambiguities in expression, and the reference to the Hanoverian Succession, were probably included to save the Bishop embarrassment. Though on the surface a thoroughly tory document, and as such in harmony with the Bishop's present views, yet it could be interpreted in such a way as not to disown his former opinions.

What is most significant is that, whoever wrote it, the Bishop was willing to sponsor it and to present it to the Queen. It was the last act of his life which was to bring him prominently before the public.

The pathetic fact about the Bishop's closing years is that he actively encouraged just those elements in the nation which would have by-passed the Act of Succession in the interests of the Pretender, had they been given half a chance. Had the 'King over the water' come to the throne it is just conceivable

[1] See p. 79.

that the solid benefits of the Revolution Settlement, for which Compton had laboured so hard, would have had to be fought for again.

As it happened, Compton was already over a year in his grave when the last Stuart Sovereign died on 1 August, 1714. 'Sleep', wrote her physician, Dr. Arbuthnot, 'was never more welcome to a weary traveller than death was to her.'[1]

1 Quoted in H. Paul, *Queen Anne*, p. 124.

PART II
A DIOCESAN BISHOP

CHAPTER TWELVE

A FATHER IN GOD

WHEN Henry Compton was appointed Bishop of London in December 1675, he entered upon an office which he was destined to hold, except for the two years of his suspension, till his death on 7 July, 1713.

It cannot be fairly claimed that there was much in his ecclesiastical career previous to his going to Fulham which suggested that he would make a conscientious Father in God. He had shown little personal interest in the spiritual needs of his parishioners in the various livings which he had held, and in no one instance had he seen fit to discharge a resident ministry. But the unexpected does sometimes happen, and there can be no doubt that during the thirty-eight years that he presided over the See of London, and in spite of his erratic intrusion into affairs of state, Henry Compton showed himself a truly zealous and painstaking bishop, beloved by his own clergy. In fact it is not in matters of ecclesiastical politics that he is seen at his best, but rather in the day-to-day discharge of his diocesan duties.

His predecessor, Humphrey Henchman (1592-1675), whom Charles II always remembered with gratitude for aiding his escape after the Battle of Worcester, was seventy-one years of age when appointed to London, so that he could hardly be expected to display great energy in what was admittedly a most difficult office. There had been a great deal of unsettlement of late years and London had, perhaps, suffered in this respect more than any other city. The fact that it was the seat of government made it particularly responsive to political change, while the traditions of the Commonwealth lingered long in a vigorous non-conformity. Hence ecclesiastical life was often troubled and disturbed. Henry Compton determined, not only to put the London clergy in the forefront of the religious struggle against Rome—a policy in which he may be said to have succeeded—but also to create a more orderly and effective parochial life in his large diocese. To do this, since he was a practical man, he realised that he must himself be active, must get to know his clergy, and see that the existing machinery of the Church operated. In this respect he may again claim to have been largely successful.

We have already seen that Compton introduced a novel feature into the life of the diocese by his Conferences at St. Paul's, to which he summoned the clergy of the cities of London and Westminster, a feature which had its counterpart in the country parishes in meetings summoned by the rural deans. The Bishop himself presided at the central gatherings and introduced the discussion. Later he summarised the results of the Conference in a printed letter which he sent to all the clergy of the diocese. A single Conference might stretch over a period of years and consist of a number of meetings. In all, there appear to have been twelve Conferences, the last taking place in the years 1701-2-3.[1] It was inevitable that during the reigns of Charles and James most of them should have been devoted to the theological questions in debate between the Roman Catholics and the Church of England, but this was not always so, and it became less true after the Revolution. Frequently the Bishop turned his attention to the problems which the clergy met in their parishes,

[1] The following is a list of the Conferences with the subjects discussed:

1678   Conference on Baptism, Lord's Supper, Catechizing—summarised in Letter I, 25 Apr., 1679.

1679   Conference on Half Communion, Prayers in an Unknown Tongue, Prayers to the Saints—Letter II, 6 July, 1680.

1680   Conference on Confirmation, Visitation of the Sick—Letter III.

1682   Conference upon Canons 38 and 54—Letter IV, 6 Apr., 1683.

1683   Conference on Canon 118—Letter V, 19 Mar., 1683.

1684   Conference on Canons of 1603—Letter VI, 18 Apr., 1685.

1686   Conference upon King's Letter of 1685—Letter VII, 10 Dec., 1686.

1689-91   Conference on how to behave under a Toleration—Letter VIII, 29 Mar., 1692.

1695   Conference upon Injunctions 5 and 10 in the King's Letter, 15 Feb., 1695—Letter IX, 1699.

1697   Conference upon the King's directions to the Archbishops and Bishops for preserving unity in the Church, 3 Feb., 1696—Letter X.

1699-1700   Conference upon the King's Proclamation for preventing immorality and profaneness—Letter XI.

1701-2-3   Conference on whether Set Forms be necessary—Letter XII.

The first six Letters which Compton wrote were published in a collected edition, *Episcopalia, or Letters of the Bishop of London to the Clergy of his Dioces*, in 1686, apparently without his consent, and in order to prejudice him in the eyes of the Government. (Wood, *Ath. Ox.*, p. 969.) This collection was reprinted as late as 1842 with a memoir by S. W. Cornish. In addition to this collected edition, Letters 7, 9 and 11 were published separately. Letter VIII was either never published, or if it was, no trace of it now survives.

and to the pastoral side of their ministry. Perhaps we may illustrate.

The idea of the Conferences seems to have been born in January, 1678, out of pressing parochial needs, when the Bishop of London called his clergy to meet him at St. Paul's, and particularly recommended four things. (1) That they made a rota of preachers for Wednesdays and Fridays during Lent, in the Churches of St. Bride's in the west, and St. Christopher's in the east. (2) That they would think of some way to suppress private christening, except in case of necessity. (3) That they would 'restore catechizing in all their Churches in the afternoon.' (4) 'That they would meet him in that place once a month to consult about the state of their parish and parishioners.'[1]

The second injunction concerning 'private christenings at home' undoubtedly called attention to a very real abuse. The clergy must stop this practice, Compton insisted, and if people refused to bring their babies to church, then the clergy must refuse to register them.[2] The Bishop's constant vigilance in this matter seems to have borne fruit, for the custom almost disappeared in the diocese during his episcopate.

As to catechizing, the Bishop never ceased to recommend it during his many years at Fulham. Certainly there was a great need for such systematic teaching at a time when Londoners had suffered so much from change and upheaval. 'In full assurance of your complying', he told his clergy, 'I shall only recommend one method to you, that whatever part of the Catechism you expound one day, you should make those you catechize give you an account next day of its meaning; so that you may be assured of the understanding and improvement each person receives from that Instruction.'[3] In a Conference with his clergy soon after the Revolution, Compton was still emphasising the same need for frequent catechizing in order that children might be taught the first principles of their religion, and also trained in obedience to their parents and 'superiors'.

The last injunction suggesting a regular monthly meeting may appear to have been aiming a little too high; yet it was out of this first successful coming together that the regular Conferences developed, since the Bishop found that his clergy appreciated the

[1] *The Diary of Edward Lake*, p. 21.
[2] S. W. Cornish (ed.), *Episcopalia*, p. 3.   [3] *Ibid.*, p. 11.

opportunity of meeting each other. Hence, later in 1678, three such gatherings took place, when the subjects for discussion were Holy Baptism, Half Communion, and the need for catechizing.

In 1680 there were two Conferences both of which were concerned with matters of parochial interest, namely, confirmation, visitation of the sick, and the conduct of services. It was Compton's constant ambition to help his clergy in the day-to-day discharge of their duties, and here his practical common-sense stood him in good stead. He realised that the backbone of the Church of England was its parochial ministry, and that upon the clergy finally depended the spiritual health of the nation. The clergy must get to know their people, he constantly repeats, and must adapt their teaching to the needs of their flocks. As to regular visiting of the sick, he admonished, 'we ought to take our Blessed Saviour's example, who did not stay till he was called, neither remained in Heaven until the world should become worthy to receive Him. . . . Therefore nothing less than an absolute impossibility should discourage us from performing this duty, for which sometimes prayers only are required, sometimes the communion, sometimes absolution.'[1]

The Bishop well realised the importance of the worthy performance of public worship, and it was a subject to which he turned in his eleventh Conference upon the King's proclamation for preventing immorality and profaneness. Here he particularly advised 'a hearty and serious pronunciation of the Divine Service', and strongly deprecated 'long and expatiating prayers before the sermon lest either we should be thought to esteem the public offices deficient or give occasion to others to be of that opinion'.[2]

The question of extempore or set forms of prayer was one of the questions in debate between the Church of England and the Nonconformists. So important did the Bishop consider the subject that he devoted to it his twelfth Conference, and later gave his own thoughts on the matter in a letter to his clergy. 'It seems to me', he wrote, 'a very bold and rash undertaking for any Man to come into a Congregation, and in their name offer up to God prayers they were never acquainted with before, so that a Man is under a Surprise what Faculty first to Employ.'[3] Set

---

[1] Cornish, *op. cit.*, p. 31.　　　　　[2] *Ibid.*, p. 45.
[3] *The Bishop of London's Twelfth Conference*, 1707, p. 3.

My Lord

This comes to bring that service to you,
which by ye help of God shall be never wanting. I am sorry with all my heart, that his
Maj:tie has no more confidence in his best friends.
I pray God give you your health during your
continuance in this place, which will, I hope, be
but for a very short time. How long I shall
be from you, I cannot tell: but you may be
assured my heart shall be ever wth you. And
whilst I am at liberty, I beseech you not
to spare me in any thing, I am able to performe. It is not now a time of ceremony. And therefore I should hate my self, if I had ye least
regret in undergoing any duty, whereby I
might most express my self my Lord
                                    Your Grace's most faith-
                        full & obedient servt. H. London

A letter from Henry Compton to William Sancroft
during the latter's imprisonment in the Tower of London,
from the Tanner MSS in the Bodleian Library

forms of prayer, had certain obvious advantages, for their language was 'well weighed that nothing be uttered unbecoming an address to the Divine Majesty'.[1] Moreover, they expressed needs which were common to all men, avoided being 'tedious and perfunctory', and enabled a congregation to prepare their minds 'in advance'.

Compton never tired of extolling the virtues of the Book of Common Prayer, and at this same Conference he went through the offices of Morning and Evening Prayer, and stressed the need for the due observance of Saints' Days. The Church of England liturgy, he said, was 'well adapted neither to offend the Apprehension of any particular Person, nor want scope enough to admit any reasonable Sense that . . . anyone, in his own case, would suggest'. He particularly advised his clergy to read a little book written by a layman, one Seymour, *Advice to the Readers of the Common-Prayer*.[2]

Preaching was then, as now, an important part of any clergyman's ministry. Here Compton had many wise and practical things to say, particularly at his eleventh Conference, when he had especially in mind 'those [clergy] who have left the Universities before they had time to inform themselves of a competent system of Divinity'. Such pastors, he said, must 'weigh well what they are going to do, for it is not little Harangues sprinkled with Philosophy that will do the Business they come about'.[3] In their sermons, they must endeavour to instruct their people 'on the whole mind of God so far as relates to things necessary for salvation'. In doing this they must make themselves understood. 'They ought', he counsels, 'to suit the harangue to their Auditors, to express themselves in as plain familiar Terms as possible and use Expressions for edification of the Mind and not to tickle the Ear.' Therefore they should 'observe what sort of people they have to deal with', whether they were 'babes in Christ' needing milk, or more 'advanced in godliness requiring doctrines that lead to higher experience'.[4] As to apologetics, since miracles had ceased, it was imperative that the preacher should give solid reasons to support the Christian claim, reasons which would be the more powerful

---

[1] *The Bishop of London's Twelth Conference*, 1707, p. 4.
[2] Cornish, *op. cit.*, p. 45.
[3] *The Bishop of London's Eleventh Conference*, p. 21.   [4] *Ibid.*, p. 23.

15

if they were of a practical nature, since 'true Philosophy will take place but with a few'.[1] He suggested that at some time during Advent, the clergy should preach against drunkenness, during Lent against blasphemy and profaneness, and from Easter to Whitsunday on the neglect of the Lord's Day.

Perhaps, at this point, we may turn, for a moment, to a meeting of clergy at Brangham under Dr. Goodman, the rural dean, on 26 September, 1679. The preacher at this Conference was George Hickes, later the nonjuring bishop, and in the general discussion which followed the sermon the clergy turned their thoughts to the best way of discharging their ministerial duties.[2] The report sent to the Bishop is significant for it shows what was in the minds of the ordinary parish priests, who, it is obvious, were preoccupied with what we should now call 'getting across to the people'. Many of them seem to have felt that there was a lack of that 'plain and practical preaching' which had most effect on the consciences of the 'common people'. This was one of the causes, they suggested, why some of their flocks went to the Conventicles. Extempore preaching, so felt the majority, was on the whole most effective. 'We should endeavour', so the rural dean interpreted their thoughts to the Bishop, 'to make use of as much action in our preaching as would consist with gravity, because by such things the generality of people were taken.' As to their general demeanour in the parish, 'gravity of conversation, as opposed to jesting, drolling, and talkativeness was much commended, especially in the presence of the common People'. Frequent visitation of the sick, they agreed, 'afforded the best opportunities (when people were most serious and least proud, passionate and pharisaical) of conveying wholesome principles unto them'. Particularly important was it 'for the interest and reputation of the whole body [that] the Clergy be in true love and correspondence with each other'. In this respect they were of opinion that meetings of the kind to which they had been summoned were 'highly convenient', and they expressed the hope that such gatherings might continue and that other dioceses would 'imitate the method'.

Not all the brethren, however, seem to have echoed the last sentiments for Dr. Goodman found it necessary to write to the

---

[1] *The Bishop of London's Eleventh Conference*, p. 23.
[2] Goodman to Compton, 26 Sept., 1679, Bod. Rawlinson MSS. 983 C, fo. 38.

Bishop as follows: 'Some of our younger clergy, and to whom these meetings would be especially useful, have this last time and some former times, been negligent to attend upon them. I have therefore sent them word that if they persevere in that neglect, I will return their names to your Lordship, which intimation, I hope, will prove sufficient.'[1]

The health and spiritual vitality of the Church must largely depend on the quality of the parish clergy and the ideal that they set themselves. Life for them was not easy, particularly in view of the undoubted moral decline which followed the strictness of the Commonwealth. Certainly the Bishop never lost an opportunity of reminding them of the high calling to which they had dedicated themselves. They must proclaim the Gospel message in season and out of season; hence the need, he said, for themselves to know its message.[2] They were as 'watchmen' who must take 'constant heed' of their flocks, admonishing the disorderly, informing on those who neglected their Sunday worship, recalling heretics as those 'under gross mistakes'. Such constant vigilance, he admitted, might make them unpopular, but they must recognise that they were not private people but 'public ministers',[3] 'stewards', whose primary duty was to deal as 'physicians' with 'spiritual ills'. 'Is it not Wisdom to consult Men in their respective Professions as occasion requires?' he asked, 'and not to go to a Carpenter to fit us with Clothes, or to a Taylor to build a House.' Thus the clergy must be able to make a spiritual diagnosis and prescribe the cure. 'We ought to have proper remedies ready for every moment of our lives', he told his clergy. The remedy was 'the whole mind of Christ'.[4]

If the clergy were to discharge such a noble conception of their office, then their own lives must be beyond reproach. Here Compton overwhelmed them with good advice, both at the Conferences, and in the printed letters which summarised the proceedings. Ministers of the Gospel were like soldiers on active service (it was his favourite simile). They must be highly trained and submit to discipline. They must avoid things which others might see fit to indulge. Cards, dice and gaming—these

[1] Goodman to Compton, 24 May, 1679, Bod. Rawlinson MSS. 983C, fo. 22.
[2] *The Bishop of London's Eleventh Conference*, p. 21.
[3] *Ibid.*, p. 25.   [4] *Ibid.*, p. 32.

'at best were an idle amusement', and it was wiser to refrain, 'for liberty, especially in things of this kind, is like an edged tool, which if not skilfully managed cuts the fingers if not the throat of him that uses it'.[1] As to public houses the clergy must not frequent them, though the Bishop allows that they 'are necessary for Travellers and Way Faring People and convenient many times for meeting upon common Business'.[2]

One of the obvious ways, of course, of improving the moral tone of the clergy was to be more strict in accepting candidates for ordination. During the brief period when Compton took over many of the duties of the Archbishop of Canterbury, he secured a letter from the King to 'be communicated' to the bishops of both provinces (February 1690) urging that they 'apply themselves to the duties of their episcopal function, be very careful in ordaining fit persons to the ministry, and keep a strict watch over the clergy of their dioceses'.[3]

This letter, we may pause long enough to notice, reads typically of the practical Bishop, and we may infer that he had a large hand in drawing it up. For example, it exhorted the bishops to 'confer often with [their] clergy', and to see that they were 'performing the public offices of worship gravely and devoutly, preaching the word of God plainly and practically, without running into needless controversies, and administering of the holy sacraments frequently, with that reverence which is due to the institutions of Christ; and catechizing the youth, visiting the sick and distressed, and doing all such things in their stations as may tend to promote the honour of God, together with peace and charity among all their neighbours; themselves giving a good example to their flock by walking before them in all holy conversation and godliness'.[4]

It was to the subject of ordination that the Bishop addressed himself in his Conference held in the years 1695 and 1696, when he asked his brethren to consider the Injunctions which William III had issued in February 1695, at the prompting of Archbishop Tenison. It was the purpose of these Injunctions to see that the canons were enforced which regulated ordination,

---

[1] *The Bishop of London's Ninth Conference*, p. 16.   [2] *Ibid.*, p. 17.
[3] S.P.D., Will. & Mary, 13 Feb., 1690, 53, p. 235; Luttrell, *A Brief Historical Relation*, ii. 15. This letter is reproduced in Wilkins' *Concilia Magnae Britanniae*, iv. 641.   [4] Wilkins, *op. cit.*, iv. 622.

that pluralities be kept within the bounds of the law, that marriage be solemnised only after banns or a proper licence, and that the bishops superintend the lives of their clergy. There had been so much religious upheaval during the last fifty years that lawlessness had crept into the church. Canons were ignored; statutes not enforced. Compton was at one with Archbishop Tenison in his determination to restore law and order, and to promote efficiency among the clergy. Nothing was, therefore, more important than to see that those who offered themselves for ordination were of the right kind, and this meant taking letters dimissory seriously. 'We are apt to be of too easy a disposition in this case', the Bishop warned his clergy, 'and either out of an unwillingness to disoblige a Friend, or a desire to please him . . . to flatter ourselves with a general Presumption that all is well and so yield to a blind Compliance . . . but the ill Consequences are such as to admit of no Excuse. For the Fitness of the Person to be admitted as to his Morals depends for the most part so entirely upon the Integrity of the Testimonial, that a Failure on this side renders the Certifier partaker of another Man's sins, by loading the Ordinance of God with a heavy and so a mischievous scandal.'[1]

The Bishop spoke from experience for he himself was seldom able to say 'no'. One contemporary writes that 'he found it hard to resist an importunate man',[2] while another affirms that he was 'not nicely cautious . . . and trusted too much to the Recommendation of others'.[3] On the other hand, a friend who had opportunities of observing his administration at close quarters states: 'All the regular Process enjoined by the Canons was duly observed. Timely notice required, just Testimonials of their Sobriety of Life, Attainments in Study, and Orthodoxy in believing: and these [were] followed with a strict Examination into their Learning and Faith by his Reverend Archdeacons and Chaplains and by himself also in every Ordination.'[4]

But mere exhortation to his clergy at these Conferences was not enough, though it did enable the brethren to know what was in the mind of their Bishop and what he expected of them. His concern doubtless inspired others. What mattered more was

---

[1] *The Bishop of London's Ninth Conference*, p. 9.
[2] Gooch, *A Sermon, etc.*, p. 19.
[3] Cockburne, *The Blessedness of Christians*, p. 23.
[4] Whitfield, *A Sermon on the Death of the late Lord Bishop of London*, p. 16.

how far the Bishop in his day-to-day administration of the diocese was able and willing to make his policy effective. Conferences were no alternative to the regular and constitutional means of enforcing discipline, and it is to this practical aspect of the Bishop's work that we now turn.

First to hand were the Bishop's own visitational powers which he determined to make a reality. By the Canons of 1603 every bishop was required to hold a triennial visitation of his diocese and to confirm at the same time: but this represented an ideal which not many diocesans managed to achieve. Compton, however, visited his diocese assidously in person throughout his whole episcopate, going from archdeaconry to archdeaconry. There is evidence that the Bishop visited in August 1677,[1] July 1685,[2] September 1690,[3] 1693-4,[4] 1700,[5] and 1706;[6] and he was actually engaged on a visitation when he died in July 1713.[7]

Unfortunately we have no full details of these visitations, and the fact that they took place is only a deduction, though a certain one, from some casual reference. Yet there still exist the returns for the parochial visitation of the Archdeaconry of Middlesex, which the Bishop undertook in July 1685; the Charge which the Bishop gave his clergy in 1693-4; and the Articles which he exhibited at his diocesan visitation in 1706. From this material there is no reason to doubt the truth of what Thomas Gooch said of Compton after his death: 'He knew the ill Consequences that arise to Religion and the Church, by the Non-Residence of Ministers; and therefore much less would he, who in the ancient Style was the Eye of the Diocese, set such a fatal and dangerous example. He resided not only always in the diocese but (I may truly affirm) in every Part on't. He visited Parish by Parish, to shew that his Clergy should do so, and from House to House.'[8]

The procedure of these episcopal visitations is well known, but may be summarised here in brief. The Bishop sent out 'Articles of Visitation and Enquiry' to the ministers, church-wardens, and sidesmen of every parish he was to visit, advising

---

[1] Bod. Tanner MSS. 40, fo. 100.
[2] Bod. Rawlinson MSS. 983, fo. 91.
[3] *Ibid.* 984 C, fo. 82b.
[4] *The Bishop of London's Charge to the Clergy of his Diocese at his Visitation begun Anno 1693*, 1696.
[5] Luttrell, *op. cit.*, iv. 652.   [6] Bod. Rawlinson MSS. 984 C, fo. 117.
[7] Gooch, *op. cit.*, p. 13.   [8] *Ibid.*

them also at the same time of his intention to confirm. The incumbents and churchwardens then presented their returns at a central church in the archdeaconry. The tendency was for most bishops to delegate the day-to-day visitation to their officers, and to confine themselves to confirming and to giving the clergy a charge which was later published. This was most certainly not the practice of Compton. Not only did he conduct his visitations personally, but he also went from parish to parish making his own enquiries.

Perhaps it will help if we see to what matters the Bishop directed his attention during his visitation in 1706, the Articles of which can be taken as typical. They may be briefly summarised under seven subject headings: (1) 'Churches and Chapels with the Ornaments and Furniture thereto belonging.' (2) The churchyard, houses, glebe, and tithes. Here the Bishop pointedly asked: 'Is the Dwelling House, and all the Out-houses of your Parson, Vicar and Curate kept in good and sufficient Repair; and does he from time to time, and as there is Occasion, take care to repair what is amiss?'[1] (3) Ministers. Here he asked: 'Does your Minister diligently instruct the Youth of your Parish in the Church Catechism? And does he endeavour to reclaim all Profane Persons, Papists and Sectaries; and press the great Duties of true Faith, Piety, Justice, Temperance, Charity, Allegiance and Conformity? And is he diligent in visiting the Sick, and satisfying the Doubts of troubled Consciences? Lastly is he Peaceable, Sober, and exemplary in his Conversation, and grave in his Demeanour, Company, Hair and Apparel?' Also does he officiate on the Lord's Day, and at the Litany on Wednesday and Friday? (4) Parishioners. The questions here go into considerable detail. 'Are there any Jews, Heretics, Papists, or Schismatics, and are they studious to prevent the Orthodox, or insolent towards them for doing their Duty? Do any upon that Pretence [i.e. that they go to a Conventicle] wholly abstain on Sundays from coming to any Public place where there are Prayers or Sermons, but spend their time in Ale Houses or Household Affairs?' (5) Parish clerk and sexton. (6) Schoolmasters, physicians, and midwives. Here the Bishop asked whether any of the above practised without the permission or licence of the ordinary. (7) Ecclesiastical officers and illegal fees.

[1] *Articles of Visitation and Enquiry etc.*, London, 1706.

These questions give a picture of the way in which the life of the church was integrated with the life of the nation, and they also suggest that there had been a great deal of unsettlement of late years.

Yet it was not enough to issue Articles of Enquiry: many a lax bishop did that. What mattered was the thoroughness of the visitation, and the steps taken to redress what was found amiss. We are fortunate in still possessing the details of Compton's parochial visitation of the Archdeaconry of Middlesex in 1685.[1] Between 20 July and 8 October, he himself visited seventy parishes, in each one of which he conducted a very careful and detailed examination of the church and the parsonage house, in company with the vicar and churchwardens. On an average he inspected some four parishes a day. In three only was he unable to gain entry into the church, or conduct his visitation. At St. Mary-le-Bow (22 July) the churchwardens appeared but 'had no Keys of the Church, so that my Lord was denied entrance': at Hampstead (27 July), and Knightsbridge Chapel (29 July) nobody appeared at all.

The thoroughness with which the Bishop went about his business may be seen in such a typical entry as that relating to Tottenham Parish Church which he visited on 20 July: 'A third lock to be put on the Chest and the Register Books to be kept in it. A new Bible & new Common Prayers, Books of Articles, Canons, and Booke to register Strange Preachers to be bought. The covering of the Steeple to be repaired, the Communion Table to be railed in.'

Some churches, but on the whole not many, sadly needed repair. At Edmonton, the Bishop ordered that 'the ceiling of the north aisle be attended to, the buttress to the north side of the church be mended . . . and the soil to be removed out of the Churchyard'. The Earl of Salisbury was instructed to repair the chancel at South Mimms, and the churchwardens were required to restore the steeple at Littleton. The vicarage of the delightful parish of Laleham on the Thames was found to be in a very dilapidated condition and the Bishop insisted that repairs be set in hand.

Inside the churches, Compton paid special attention to the communion vessels. In each case he drew up a detailed inventory

[1] Bod. Rawlinson MSS. 983, fo. 91. See also 'Liber Visitationis parochialis Comitatus Middlesexiae', fol. 138 in St. Paul's Cathedral Library.

and at Paddington, for example, he found it necessary to order that 'a silver Paten and flagon be bought'. Enfield Parish Church was told to purchase a new communion table and to rail it in. Similar orders were given to the churchwardens of Hatford Bow, in which case the Bishop particularly enjoined that the communion table be placed under the east window. The ministers of Stepney, Shadwell and Sudbury were informed that they must use a surplice while officiating in church.

It would be tedious, perhaps, to list in detail the Bishop's orders, though in their cumulative effect they show the great care which he took over his visitations. A few more examples, therefore, must suffice. He insisted that the rails around a tomb in the churchyard of St. Paul's, Shadwell, should be removed: that Highgate Chapel set up the King's Arms: that Hammersmith purchase a new surplice, a communion cloth, and a cushion for the pulpit: that Chelsea invest in a Book of Homilies and the Thirty-nine Articles: that Shepperton erect a sounding board over the pulpit: that St. Clement's Dane hang up a Table of Affinity in the porch: and that Stanmore Magna be required to fix three locks on the parish chest, provide a proper book for the clerk's accounts, and a register for strange preachers. Only at St. Martin-in-the-Fields, where conscientious Thomas Tenison was vicar, did the Bishop of London feel it unnecessary to give any orders at all.

Although Compton usually found something amiss, this visitation does not suggest that churches by and large were in a bad condition, certainly not so neglected as they became a hundred years later.

It is a pity that we have no details of the Bishop's other visitations, but there is no need to assume that they were any less thorough. There is still extant, however, the returns of a visitation held, under the instructions of the Bishop, by William Beveridge, Archdeacon of Colchester.[1] As might be expected, the churches in this out-lying part of the diocese were in a more dilapidated condition than those nearer London. The church of Coggeshall, for example, was in a particularly bad way. It needed, so the Archdeacon reported, a new carpet, a linen table cloth, a Book of Homilies and Canons, and a Table of Affinity—while the floor of the church was in a very shaky condition. His orders were therefore very much to the point. 'The rubbish on the outside of

[1] Bod. Rawlinson MSS. 983 C, fo. 69.

the Church and Chancel must be taken away. The windows about the Church want mending. There want some poles and Rails about the fence of the Churchyard. There are six bells of which the tenor is crackt.' Nor was the religious state of the parish thought to be too happy, for Beveridge ordered the church-wardens 'to give notice to the people to send their children to Church to be catechized', though it is but fair to add that this last injunction was found to be necessary in many parishes in the archdeaconry. The chancel of Southbright church was par-ticularly noted as being in a bad state; and the minister of Bracon Marsh was required to set the communion table against the wall of the east end of the chancel, to white-wash the walls of the church, and to rough-cast the steeple. In a great number of parishes orders were given to 'new paint' the King's Arms, to provide cloths and napkins for the communion table, sounding boards for the pulpit—and at Aberton to make an allowance for the clerk.

Such visitations undoubtedly stimulated local interest in the parishes, and we are fortunate in being able to add to these returns from the proceedings of the Bishop's Court under his Chancellor Dr. Henry Newton, though we must be careful not to see the diocese through the eyes of a legal official.[1] Happy is the parish which has no legal history, and most parishes in Compton's day were fortunately in this position. It is clear, however, from the records of the Court, that the Bishop's own energy inspired his legal officials to be business-like and efficient. The extant documents mostly concern mere routine activities—licences for vaults, applications for pews, the registering of fees, and litigation over wills. But perhaps of most interest are those which relate to church restoration schemes which were set in hand during Compton's episcopate. The Bishop himself always took a great interest in such undertakings, and often insisted on making a personal visit to the site, before his Chancellor granted a licence for building operations to commence. Once again we quote a few typical examples, beginning with the Church of St. Andrew's, Undershaft, since this provides an excellent illustration of the 'correct' procedure in such cases.

[1] There are some bundles of manuscripts in the Lord Mayor's Vestry at St. Paul's Cathedral containing a number of letters and documents which passed through the hands of Dr. Newton, the Bishop's Chancellor.

Here the church was certainly in a bad condition, and the parishioners at their vestry meeting in 1704 decided to inform the Bishop of its plight. His Lordship promptly issued a commission to 'Edward Strong, Junior, mason, Richard Jennings, carpenter, and John Smallwood, joiner' ('very judicious and skilful workmen and Artificers') who visited the church and sent in a report to the Chancellor of the diocese, dated 23 June, 1704. Their survey was interesting, and shows amongst other things the damage which resulted from the custom of burying under the floor of the church. The pews, plating, flooring, altar rails and pulpit were so 'decayed' that in their opinion, it would be cheaper to instal new. In addition, the whole church needed to be 'whitened', the iron work scraped and painted. The cost of these extensive repairs was estimated at £1,151.

The Chancellor, armed with this report, himself visited the church on 27 June, and then drew up an order requiring the vestry to fix a rate. By this means £840 was raised and the work set in hand.[1]

Another church which gave cause for serious anxiety was that of Ridgewell in Essex, and in this case the Bishop visited the parish in person. He found the fabric, to quote his own words, 'much dilapidated and ruinous.' There was 'a breach in the Aisle'; the walls needed 'whitening'; the communion table was rickety; and there was no gallery. The Bishop gave orders that these matters should be attended to, but he later realised that the cost was beyond the limited means of the parishioners. He therefore issued a licence which permitted the churchwardens to pull down a 'ruinous old chapel' situated on the north side of the chancel and to use the materials.

On another occasion, the Bishop travelled to Colchester to the Parish of St. Michael's, where the presentments of the churchwardens were read over to him while he made a tour of the 'several buildings'. He then gave orders on the spot that 'the shed ag[ain]st the East Window of the North Aisle be let down that a clear light of three feet be left at the upper part thereof': that 'the Door leading on the leads over the said north aisle be fastened and nailed up so as not to be used': and that 'the pulpit and desk be moved to the first pillar on the south aisle'.[2]

[1] Bundle 4, St. Paul's Cathedral [2] *Ibid.*

The church of Eastwick in 1704 was severely damaged by a 'dreadful storm of wind', and in March of the same year the parishioners petitioned that they might take down one of the aisles in the church in order to repair the rest of the building.[1] Such, unfortunately, was no exceptional request; though a contrary petition was received from the 'Vicar, several inhabitants and Churchwardens of Kensington', where the church was not large enough to contain the congregation. In this instance they secured a licence to take down 'the north aisle and Chancel', and to 'erect and build another' on a much grander scale.[2]

It was finance which proved the great obstacle to many restoration schemes, and this was met in a variety of ways, not all of them particularly happy. In many cases the money obtained from the imposition of a parish rate was not adequate. Sometimes permission was then given to pull down an aisle, to sell a 'crakt bell', or to dispose of land. In the case of those churches damaged in the Great Fire, the Bishop was often asked to make an application for a grant from public funds.[3]

We are not surprised that records of the Bishop's Court reveal that there were parishioners who were not happy about their parson and were anxious to get rid of him. Mr. John Huskinson, Vicar of Steple-in-Gengy in Essex, certainly did not command the respect of his flock. In his case, the churchwardens deposed in 1696 that he never preached regularly, that he was 'of very loose conversation', was 'frequently in drink', and was often 'absolutely unfit to officiate'. To fill up the cup of his misdeeds, on the Sunday after Christmas Day he entered the church, attempted to pull the surplice off the officiating minister, and finally walked out with the Prayer Book under his arm in spite of the protests of the village constable who was a member of the congregation.[4]

Similarly unfortunate in their minister were the congregation of Knightsbridge Chapel, where Mr. Sheales seems to have done his best to convert this place of worship into a rough-house. Unwilling himself to do duty, he was equally unwilling that anyone else should do it for him. He obstructed the ministration of Holy Communion, struck Anna Busby during divine service, and as a crowning gesture shot the preacher 'and

---

[1] Bundle 4, St. Paul's Cathedral.   [2] *Ibid.*
[3] *Ibid.*   [4] Bundle 2, *ibid.*

cared not though he should be hanged at the said Chapel for the Crime'.[1]

The parishioners of Basildon laid a deposition against their minister before the Bishop, complaining bitterly that he would neither repair the chancel, nor preach. 'Your petitioners have no Body to visit their sick or bury their dead', they wrote sadly.[2]

But it was not always the parishioners who disliked their parson: sometimes it was the parson who disliked his parishioners. Dr. Woodroffe, Rector of St. Bartholomew's in the City, entered a protest on 8 December, 1701, against one of his church-wardens, Licourt by name. So far from setting an example, this officer, so the Rector maintained, neglected divine service; disposed of the communion monies in a manner contrary to the canons; on one occasion tied up the bells; and on another—it was a public fast day—he forcibly took the key from the clerk, and locked up the Church. The Bishop conducted a personal visitation, and peremptorily ordered that this state of affairs be brought to an end.[3]

Perhaps the most amusing parochial *contretemps* took place at Hillingdon in Middlesex where Lady Carteret, certainly 'a great lady', had a country house. As became her rank, she enjoyed the luxury of a private pew in the Chancel of the parish church, where, however, she strongly objected to keeping close company, during divine service, with some of the more rustic villagers. While on a visit to her Ladyship, the Bishop was escorted round the church, and rashly promised that something should be done. It was left to the Vicar to carry his diocesan's assurance into effect, but he found his task by no means easy. The head singer, in the name of all his companions, refused to leave the chancel 'to sit in an Ally', and others, equally privileged, claimed an 'ancient Right'—a right which some parishioners were prepared, if need be, to defend at law. Lady Carteret in a fit of pique refused to attend the Church until her grievance was attended to and reminded the Bishop of London of his promise. Greatly disturbed, the Vicar wrote to Dr. Newton, the Chancellor, begging that whatever orders his Lordship chose to give, might not be directed to him as incumbent, since he had no wish 'to be further concerned in this Business'.[4]

---

[1] Bundle 2, St. Paul's Cathedral.   [2] Bundle 3, *ibid.*
[3] Bundle 4, *ibid.*   [4] *Ibid.*

The visitational returns and the records of the Bishop's Court enable us to gain a rough picture of the condition of many churches during the episcopate of Henry Compton. On the whole it is not such a gloomy one as we are sometimes led to believe. It shows that the revival under Laud had not been altogether barren of results, and that most of the churches had not yet fallen into the sad condition so common during the years 1750-1850. True, something needed to be done in most, but such work was not usually very extensive. The Bishop of London was himself a practical man, and most of his orders were designed to see that the church was kept decently and in order, and that discipline was enforced. We may say, with some degree of confidence, that these visitations, carried out at regular intervals during his episcopate of thirty-eight years, had their beneficial effects upon church life in his diocese. Also they gave Compton the opportunity of addressing his clergy in, perhaps, a more formal manner than was customary at his Conferences. The Bishop did not bother to secure the publication of these charges with the exception of that given in 1694. This address, from which we have already quoted, was a forthright appeal to his clergy to be law-abiding members of the Church of England, accepting gladly such discipline 'so far in use as the necessity of Decency and Order required, in the Judgement of those who have the Rule over the Church'.

If such visitations were to have their full effect, however, it was imperative that the Bishop should secure the whole-hearted co-operation of his archdeacons and rural deans. The Bishop determined that this latter office, in particular, should not be just a polite sinecure, but an effective means of implementing his policy of reform. We have already seen how he used these officers to summon the Conferences in the countryside, and also required them to send in a report of their proceedings, with a list of absentees. Early in his episcopate he drew up a paper *Instructions for Rural Deans*,[1] which left no doubt as to what the Bishop expected from them. We cannot do better than quote his own words:

> You are diligently to enquire and give true information to the Right Reverend Father in God Henry, Lord Bishop of London or his Chancellor, of the names of all such persons, Clergy or lay, within Your Precincts as are openly or publicly noted and defamed, or vehemently suspected of any such crimes or offences as is to be

[1] Bod. Rawlinson MSS. 984 C, fo. 123.

punished or reformed by the authority of the Ecclesiastical Court. You are likewise to make a return to the said Bishop of London or his Chancellor into the Registry of the Consistory Court of all the Clergy who die within the Deanery. . . . Ye are likewise as occasion shall require to inspect the Churches, Chancells, Chapels and Houses belonging to the Parsons and Vicars within your District, and to give Information of their Decays and Dilapidations to the Ordinary. You are likewise to call the Clergy together when the Ordinary shall appoint and take Care of dispersing such Orders as shall be communicated to you and make Returns accordingly. You are likewise to take care that the Persons presented to the Bishop to be confirmed by him should be fit and duly qualified for the Bishop's Confirmation by a strict examination and causing them solemnly to renew the Vow which was made in their Name at their Baptism.[1]

The Bishop's own energy undoubtedly went a long way in securing the co-operation of the rural deans, and as they were his own appointment, he was able to choose the right men for this responsible office. The few letters which remain between the Bishop and Dr. Warley, rural dean of Witham, show how Compton kept in constant touch with this deanery, and we can safely assume that what was true of this part of his diocese was equally true of another. We quote a few instances of his care. In April 1707, when Dr. Warley was starting his visitation, the Bishop urged him to 'examine' certain matters 'very carefully', and to let the Bishop's mind concerning them be known. 'I will suffer none to be Curate to more than one place', he declared though he was prepared to allow such a clergyman to decide for himself which curacy to retain.[2] Secondly, the rural dean was to enquire into the 'disorders' which were alleged against an incumbent, one Chambers, so that the Bishop might proceed against him, if necessary, in his own Court. A month later, probably while Dr. Warley was busy with his visitation, Compton was again corresponding with him, this time concerning the parish church at Frinton, in respect of which the Bishop had already ordered a commission to be sent down to the rural dean. The Church was obviously in a shocking condition, and the purpose of the commission was to determine, by making a survey of the fabric, 'whether if the Body of the Church should be taken down, the

[1] Bod. Rawlinson MSS. 984 C. fo. 123.
[2] Compton to Warley, 17 Apr. 1707, B.M. Add. MSS. 27,797, fo. 55.

Chancel may not serve for both Uses'. The rural dean was instructed to take some 'honest workmen' with him that they might 'draw up a just Estimate of the Charges of what you shall decide'.[1]

Nor was it only the archdeacons and the rural deans whom the Bishop wished to keep vigilant and active: he was equally concerned that the churchwardens should discharge the duties laid upon them. Thus on 16 March, 1683, he sent a letter to all incumbents in the diocese, complaining that the churchwardens generally had been 'very remiss in making due Presentments; particularly did this apply to such as absent themselves from the Holy Sacrament of the Lord's Supper'. The clergy must therefore insist that their wardens present to the archdeacon, at his next visitation, the names of all those in their parish, above sixteen years of age, who had not communicated at Easter. The Bishop ordered that his letter be read in Church on the following Sunday.[2]

Such episcopal admonition was not without effect, for in the parish registers of Hillingdon it is recorded that on Easter Day and Low Sunday '300 Persons received the Communion, alarmed to their duty by an order from Henry Lord Bishop of London'.[3]

Compton was encouraged to send a similar letter on 14 February in the following year, this time adding that the wardens were to present 'all Masters and Mistresses of Families, together with all School Masters and School Mistresses that send not their Children and Aprentices to be catechized according to the Canon; since the Neglect of this seems to have been the Occasion in a great Measure, of all other profane Omissions in religious Worship'.[4] A like admonition went out again next year, the Bishop adding this time that the parochial clergy must set their hand 'to the truth of what they [i.e. the churchwardens] present'.[5] In a letter sent to his clergy in 1684, Compton told them they must insist that the old wardens make their presentments before the new ones be sworn in.[6] The same year, upon enquiry, he found that in several parishes the Proclamations and Acts of Parliament which were appointed to be read in church were in fact ignored, because 'being loose papers and changed from one churchwarden to another', they were often lost. The practical

---

[1] Compton to Warley, 13 May, 1707, B.M. Add. MSS. 27,997, fo. 58.
[2] *Circular Letter to the Clergy of his diocese of London*, 1682-3.
[3] J. S. Burn, *The History of Parish Registers in England*, ed. J. R. Smith, 1862, p. 186.   [4] Bod. Tanner MSS. 34, fo. 265.
[5] *Ibid.*, fo. 245.   [6] Cornish, *Episcopalia*, p. 60.

bishop got in touch with the King's printer and persuaded him 'to print them all together'.[1]

The churchwardens, however, were not uniformly co-operative (to have been so would have often made them unpopular in the parish) and the Bishop did not always find them helpful even, for example, in his attempts to buy up the advowsons of poor livings in Essex. Particularly was this the case in a cure of souls on which Compton had spent a sum of £1,200. Here the Bishop was forced to call in Dr. Warley in order to persuade the churchwardens to repair the church and churchyard —otherwise, the Bishop threatened, 'I shall reserve the revenue for some other use and take the Church and Churchyard into my own hands to dispose of where it may seem more acceptable'.[2] The matter seems finally to have been settled amicably, for the Bishop turned his attention to the 'glass paint' and the furniture in the Church. 'I do verily believe you will find', he wrote, 'that if you turn the coat of arms the other way, all will stand right.'[3]

The tasks of the rural dean were certainly manifold, varying from dealing with recalcitrant churchwardens to advising their clergy, in the name of the Bishop, whom to support at an election. In November 1701, when the country was in the throes of a crucial contest, Compton wrote a letter to Strype, rural dean of Barking, requiring him to inform his clergy that 'as matters stand in Essex, in my judgment, we shall be greatly wanting to ourselves and our common-good, if we do not take the best interest we can, and be vigorous ourselves for the choice of Sir Charles Barrington and Mr. Bullock'. 'It will be for the reputation of the Church, and for its service', he added, 'if we are unanimous'.[4]

These are small matters, of course, but they illustrate excellently the Bishop's preoccupation with the day-to-day life of the diocese, and how wide were his interests.

One of the great problems facing the Church during Compton's episcopate—it has never really been without it—was the poverty of a large number of the clergy, particularly in country parishes. 'If I be asked, why then have ye such scandalous

---

[1] *H.M.C.* Downshire MSS, vol. i, parts i and ii, p. 27.
[2] Compton to Warley, 3 May, 1708, B.M. Add. MSS. 27,997, fo. 65.
[3] Same to same, 25 May, *ibid.*, fo. 75.
[4] Compton to Strype, 20 Nov., 1701, B.M. Cole MSS. vol. lii, p. 485.

Priests', the Bishop once wrote, 'I answer with another Question, why then have ye such scandalous Maintenance in many Places'.[1]

The matter had received the attention of Parliament when in 1677 an Act was passed 'For the Augmentation of poor Livings', but Archbishop Sancroft was forced to admit, some three years later in a letter to Compton, that it had not been implemented. On the contrary, endowments were 'by degrees daily more and more diminished & the little that is left . . . swallowed up and lost'.[2]

Such financial embarrassment had unfortunate results quite apart from the frustrations it created in many of the clergy themselves. In 1677, the Bishop's chaplain received a letter from a resident of Marks Tey in Essex complaining of a sermon preached by a Nonconformist in the parish church. The facts were that the endowment of the living was so small that the parish was without an incumbent, and on Sunday the pulpit was free to whatever Dissenter cared to occupy it. Doubtless a Nonconformist goose was regarded as better than no goose at all, but to loyal churchmen it seemed a scandal. 'We hope when his Lordship shall be acquainted herewith', a parishioner complained to Fulham, 'he will take some course to deprive these men of that liberty they take to preach in a parish church.'[3] Preaching of course, was often the Nonconformist's *forte*, and the writer went on to say that not only did this particular Dissenter fill the parish Church of Marks Tey, but he also succeeding in emptying that in the neighbouring village.

Henry Compton was well aware of the situation and he certainly did what he could through his own private means, and also by encouraging others, to make better provision for the clergy. 'He bought in many Advowsons', Thomas Gooch said of him, 'from those struggling hands, which are apt to ensnare and wound Men's Consciences. He gave great sums for the rebuilding of Churches, and greater still (for this he knew was the best placed Bounty) for the buying in Impropriations and settling them upon poor Vicars.'[4]

In 1676 Compton was given an exceptional opportunity of

---

[1] *The Bishop of London's Seventh Letter*, p. 15.
[2] Sancroft to Compton, 2 Feb., 1680, Bod. Tanner MSS. 282, fo. 76.
[3] Poole to Jane, 6 July, 1677, Bod. Tanner MSS., Rawlinson MSS. 984 C, fo. 12.   [4] Gooch, *op. cit.*, p. 16.

helping several poor parishes in the county of Essex. This arose
from the will of Dr. William Clerke, Dean of Winchester, who
bequeathed a number of legacies from an estate in Tillingham,
for the augmentation of ten poor livings, of which four were
specified by name—Buckingham, St. Alban's, Maldon, and Stony
Stratford. It was made a condition of receiving a grant (a sum of
£30 a year), that the parish should co-operate to the extent of
finding a like amount. Dr. Clerke entrusted the Bishop of London
with the carrying out of his will, a most tedious undertaking,
since it led to difficulties with the Dean and Chapter of St. Paul's
who had an interest in the estate at Tillingham, and also involved
him in a vast correspondence over many years.[1] Nor were the
parishes always willing to do their part, and often the Bishop had
to press them to co-operate if they wished to benefit. The Parish
of Buckingham, for example, proved particularly dilatory, and
Compton tried to encourage the Vicar by telling him what other
parishes had managed to do—but all to no purpose. 'I have done
my best endeavours', the Vicar wrote despairingly in December
1687, 'to persuade my parishioners to a complyance with your
Lordship, but cannot prevail with them to come to any resolution
of doing what is required of them. My Lord, Buckingham is a
very poor town, they want a good town stock and a good town
trade whereby they might be in a better capacity than now they
are of promoting this good and charitable work of raising a
contribution to answer Dr. Clerke's charity.' Yet the Vicar was
anxious not to let his flock down in the eyes of the Bishop, and
he added: 'However, my Lord, I have this to say for the Parish
of Buckingham, that they are a loyal people and very conformable to the C[hurch] of E[ngland].'[2]

As late as 1695, the parish of Dedham was still struggling
to raise its quota, and when Compton was in Colchester (probably
on a visitation) he took the opportunity of discussing the matter
with William Burkett, its Vicar, who as a result agreed to make
a personal contribution if the parish would find the rest.[3] Fortunately he was able later to assure the Bishop that it had consented
and in fact had raised more than the amount required.[4]

[1] Sherlock to Compton, 4 June, 1695, Bod. Rawlinson MSS. 984 C, fo. 94.
[2] Pashler to Compton, 20 Dec., 1687, *ibid.* 983 C, fo. 120.
[3] Burkett to Compton, 5 July, 1695, Rawlinson MSS. 983 C, fo. 143.
[4] Same to same, 10 Dec., 1695, *ibid.*, fo. 145.

The terms of the bequest were certainly a stimulus to local effort. They encouraged Colchester, for example, to raise a sum of £550 by 1683, a fact which the Vicar reported to the Bishop with pride. The bequest also enabled Compton, in certain cases, to insist on much needed reform. Such was the case with Stony Stratford where the Bishop absolutely refused to settle £30 a year on the parish so long as the existing curate, named Chelsey, who was said to be a drunkard and to have referred to Bishop Barlow as 'an old doting fool', was in charge.[1]

In other instances Compton tried to persuade the patrons to do something about their livings, particularly when they were in his own diocese. We may take as a typical example the parish of Hatfield Broad Oak in Essex which was in the gift of Trinity College, Cambridge. Here the Bishop managed to induce the Master to increase the stipend of the incumbent by £10 per annum.[2]

Another living in which the Bishop showed a personal interest was that of Pleshey in the same county. The Church here was 'of considerable antiquity and hath several of the Royal Family interred there', and in 1707 Compton managed, through the co-operation of the local gentry, to secure a thorough restoration of the fabric. Unfortunately there was no income for a minister, and in 1712 the Bishop wrote to the Earl of Oxford asking that the Queen herself might do something to help, in view of the royal associations of the church.[3]

It may be said of Compton that in his relations with individual clergy he was uniformly helpful and sympathetic: certainly he preferred to secure discipline through persuasion, though he could be severe at times. John Cockburne, preaching the Bishop's funeral sermon, remarked that he had 'often heard him regret those Defects of our Discipline which bound up the Hands of the Bishops, and rendered the censuring of heretics slow and difficult. But to compensate this in some measure, he showed all the Marks of his private Displeasure to such as were tainted with these Errors, and he avoided all Fellowship with them.'[4] This may have been true of his later years when he undoubtedly

---

[1] Barlow to Compton, 3 July, 1690, Rawlinson MSS. 983 C,, fo. 129.
[2] Bod. Rawlinson MSS. 984 C, fo. 75.
[3] *H.M.C.* App. ii, Report XIV, p. 223 (Portland MSS. Vol. V).
[4] Cockburne, *The Blessedness of Christians etc.*, p. 20.

became less liberal, as, for example, in his relations with William Whiston, but by and large he was no bigot. When persuasion failed, however, he did not hesitate to resort to the law.

What he wished sincerely was to encourage his clergy to be resident, hard working and loyal to the *ethos* of the Church of England. Such an ambition demanded constant vigilance and to promote it he was always open to suggestion. Even Burnet comments on his essential humility, which may be illustrated from a small incident. Sometime after the Revolution, he was in conversation with a Nonjuror, who being understandably in somewhat frustrated mood, complained that the rubrics, homilies, and canons of the Church of England were almost entirely ignored. The Bishop listened patiently and then asked him to be more precise, assuring him that he would welcome any suggestions, and be 'more obliged to him than to any man in England'. The result was a long letter in which the writer endeavoured to particularise. Among the Cathedrals, he alleged, only at Christ Church, Oxford, was there a weekly Communion: in parish churches the rubric which required the tolling of the bell for evensong was not observed: parishioners were not exhorted to communicate three times a year: notorious evil livers were not rejected from the Sacrament: the clergy did not preach four times a year on the King's supremacy: and children were not regularly catechized. 'From all which', this Nonjuror wrote, 'I make this one conclusion. There is not any one Rubric in all the Common Prayer Book that pertains to the wholesome discipline of the Church, but which is wholly or at least partly neglected.'[1]

There was some truth behind such exaggeration, and there were occasions when Compton was forced to exercise discipline. On the whole, however, the diocese of London was probably in a much more healthy state than most others, and in fact tended to attract the more alive parsons, often to the detriment of the countryside. Thus a country clergyman wrote in 1692: 'I have heard some wise Men affirm, who understand the present posture of things in the City of London that there are a considerable number of Men there, who are Curates or Lecturers or Readers, or at least Candidates for such Places, that have Cures

[1] Bod. Rawlinson MSS. 983 C, fo. 46.

in the Country which they leave, and some of these Cures not well provided for.'[1]

Compton's attitude to pluralism was that of most reformers of his day. He was forced to recognise the necessity for some measure of it owing to the shortage of clergy and the poorness of so many cures, but he tried to see that licences were granted not 'for the advantage of the person but the place'.[2] On one occasion he persuaded Sancroft to refrain from issuing a dispensation to an incumbent named Wright who wished to add Whitechapel to the cure he already possessed.

Compton's episcopal register, unfortunately, is not very helpful here, but it does show him enforcing residence on the incumbents of Hadley and Rayleigh. It contains a list of the Bishop's collations and institutions *in camera sua apud Whitehall*, and also an inventory of parochial fees fixed at annual vestry meetings.

But though the register does not tell us very much (*The Act Books* seem to have disappeared altogether) it yet suggests, together with the records of the Bishop's Court from which we have already quoted, that the day-to-day administration of the diocese was systematic and efficient. There were times when the Bishop had no compunction about taking severe action. We quote a case which comes to mind.

The Vicar of Chelmsford, when visiting the town gaol, came across a certain John Thomas, who claimed to be, and in fact was, a clergyman. The career of this ne'er-do-well is not without interest. Some six years after he left Oxford, he was ordained by Guy Carleton, Bishop of Bristol, and served as a curate at Stalbridge near Shaftesbury. His Vicar, perhaps wisely, 'cast him off', with the result that he came to London where Compton, always on the look out for naval chaplains, sent him to the port at Sheerness. He was no more successful there. however, and left to become usher in the free school at Duncannon in Ireland, where the same thing happened again. He returned to London, and then begged his way by road to Chelmsford. On a Sunday evening in August 1683, he got himself very drunk, and on being refused admittance to another ale house, proceeded to break the windows. He became abusive, 'was prodigiously wicked in cursing and swearing and bawdy talking', with the result that

---

[1] *A Second Letter to a Bishop from a Minister of his Diocese*, 1692, p. 24.
[2] Compton to Sancroft, 9 Mar., 1681, Bod. Tanner MSS. 37, fo. 264.

the local constable 'carried' him before the justice of the peace who promptly committed him to the common gaol. In this sad plight he was visited by the Vicar of Chelmsford, who reported the whole matter to Compton. 'He is in a shameful habit', he wrote, 'a Gown without a sleeve, a cassock ragged and torn, hardly a shoe to his feet, not a penny in his purse. He sent for me and while discoursing [with] him I had this narrative from himself; he has his orders with him. I saw them, they are all the worldly goods he hath. He deserves to be degraded, and if his orders be taken from him to be sent as a common Seaman.'[1]

The Bishop of London promptly sent the letter on to the Archbishop, suggesting that if he 'could be degraded, it would be a very just example and useful'. 'If your Grace can do nothing with him', he added, 'I will have his Orders taken from him, his ragged habit taken off his back, and him whipt from constable to constable, till he comes to his last abode. I humbly beg your pardon for this interruption and this venom.'[2]

Sometimes Compton's vigilance could be almost excessive. In 1703 a number of high spirited young noblemen 'committed some faults' in St. James's Church, Piccadilly, exaggerated reports of which reached the Bishop. Compton immediately started a prosecution, but later knowledge convinced him that the 'faults' were 'not so enormous as they were first represented to be'. The culprits tendered an abject apology to the Bishop, and made a handsome donation to the poor of the parish. Compton accordingly stopped the prosecution, and a paper detailing what had happened was read out in the Church.[3]

Perhaps the most difficult man with whom Compton had to deal was Edmund Hickeringill, the notorious and eccentric Vicar of All Saints Church in Colchester, who earlier in life had been a Baptist, Quaker, free-thinker, and soldier of fortune. In Colchester he made his presence felt in a variety of ways. He was said to have conspired to oust Sir John Shaw from the office of recorder: to have concealed the last will and testament of one of his parishioners: and to have sold the church bells to the neighbouring parish of Wix. These and other rumours led to twenty-four charges of barratry being brought against him at the

---

[1] Bod. Tanner MSS. 34, fo. 122.
[2] Compton to *Sancroft*, 22 Aug., 1683, Bod. Tanner MSS. 34, fo. 123.
[3] Nichols, *The Miscellaneous Works of Bishop Atterbury*, iv. 357, 363.

Chelmsford Assizes in March 1681, when the prosecution was conducted by Sir George Jeffreys, soon to become more notorious than the defendant. There was an entertaining passage of arms between the two (Hickeringill conducted his own defence) and great was the excitement when the jury brought in a verdict of 'not guilty'.

Extraordinary stories about Hickeringill, particularly as to the way in which he conducted the affairs of his Church, continued to go the rounds in Chelmsford. He was said regularly to solemnize marriages without requiring either banns or licence. For this offence the Bishop of London, in June 1681, brought him before Sir Robert Wiseman in the Court of Arches of the Province of Canterbury. His conduct in court was certainly unusual. He refused to remove his hat, and insisted on speaking in Greek. Nor when he at last condescended to use his native tongue was his language very complimentary. 'Vipers had poison in them, but their flesh was an extraordinary medicine. Even the vilest or worst of God's creatures had something good in it, saving that Court which never did any good or ever would', he shouted.[1] As to his diocesan, he treated him with equal contempt, both before the court and in two scurrilous pamphlets which he produced at the time.

'A Bishop? Sayest? Thou lyest, Him Cornet call
Of the Black Regiment that Gaols us all.'[2]

It came as no surprise when the sentence of the court was three years suspension from office.

Compton would have been wise, perhaps, to have let matters rest at this point, but he was soon goaded into anger by a report from a clergyman in Colchester, the Reverend Samuel Harris (not a very pleasant character), who alleged that at the vestry meeting of St. Botolph's Church on 4 April, 1681, Hickeringill had stood up and said: 'The Bishop of London is a bold, daring and impudent man for sending some heads of divinity to all his clergy in these parts which are contrary to law. His lordship is very ignorant and I can prove his Lordship to be concerned in the damnable plot'—a reference to the Popish 'plot' against the King's life.

[1] *Scandalum Magnatum*, p. 68.
[2] E. Hickeringill, *The Black Nonconformist*, 1709, p. 174.

The Bishop took legal advice and decided to sue Hickeringill for *scandalum magnatum* under a statute of Richard II which made it a heinous offence to defame a prelate or a duke. The trial came off at the Chelmsford Assizes on 8 March before Sir Francis Pemberton, the Lord Chief Justice, when the Bishop of London was represented by Sir George Jeffreys, who had old scores to settle. On this occasion, however, though Hickeringill declared that he had never spoken better in his life, Sir George triumphed, and Compton was awarded £2,000 damages.

The sentence was a crushing financial blow to the Vicar of All Saints, and despite several approaches from Hickeringill, the Bishop of London made it clear that he would not remit the fine except at the price of unconditional surrender. In this resolve he remained adamant, and finally in the Court of the Arches, on 27 June, 1684, before Sir Richard Lloyd, Fellow of All Souls, the proud Hickeringill signed a complete and abject apology, admitting his 'hienous Crimes and Offences', acknowledging that he had behaved in a way 'scandalous to his sacred function as a Priest', and had 'demeaned himself before the Court with great impudence'.[1]

Restored to his parish, Hickeringill showed little signs of genuine repentance. In 1701 he was again in trouble and was fined £4,000 for altering the rate books of the parish of Wix which were brought before him as a commissioner of taxes; and in November 1705, the Bishop of London again brought him before his Court for the indecency of a published work *Survey of the Earth*. His few remaining years, till his death in 1708, were spent in editing his works, lest posterity should neglect his genius.

We can hardly blame Compton for bringing Hickeringill to the Court of the Arches for persisting in marrying people without banns or licence; in fact, it was his duty to do so as diocesan. But we may well question the wisdom of his proceeding against him for *scandalum magnatum*. True Hickeringill had gone out of his way to be offensive, but no one really took him very seriously. Restraint, however, was not one of Compton's most marked characteristics.

Mention of the abuse of clandestine marriages may serve to remind us that it was one of Compton's constant preoccupations

---

[1] *The Most Humble Confession and Recantation of Edmund Hickeringill*, London, 1687.

to see that all marriages within his diocese were solemnized only
after due publication of banns or upon a regular licence granted
by an ecclesiastical court. Such a policy had behind it the
support of the Government, for three Acts of Parliament were
passed in William's reign which visited punishments both ecclesiastical and civil upon contracting parties and clergymen who
took part in such irregular unions.

Unfortunately at the time of the passing of these Acts a
Commission had been issued to a certain Dr. Payne which had as
its ostensible purpose the correcting of abuses, but which in fact
made it possible for the legislation to be by-passed. The Bishop
of London could not ignore this threat to his jurisdiction, and
he drew up a very vigorous protest which he sent to the Lords
Justices on 29 July, 1695. What happened in practice, Compton
pointed out, was that Dr. Payne took advantage of the late Act
which insisted on licences to grant them himself. 'May it please
your Excellencys', the Bishop concluded, 'to cause the said
Commission to be revoked, as not being, or having been, of any
use to the Public, as was pretended at the granting of it, but
has proved in effect the contrary.'[1] To support his case, the Bishop
also drew up a paper, *Some Reasons for suspending Dr. Pain's
Patent*, in which he set out his arguments at length. His chief
complaint was that the Commission in asserting a matrimonial
jurisdiction over certain parishes within twenty miles of London
had the effect of encouraging 'ill disposed vicars' to defy their
Bishop. It set up Dr. Payne as their visitor, and already this had
had disastrous results. Nor was this gentleman beyond granting
blank licences.[2]

Fortunately for the Bishop of London, the Archbishop of
Canterbury was equally opposed to the Commission, and on July
30 his Grace appeared in person before the Lords Justices and took
the opportunity of reading a letter from Compton. The Lords
Justices saw the force of the Bishop of London's arguments, and
they recommended that the Commission be revoked 'as rather
authorizing abuses than reforming them'. This was finally done
on 10 September.[3]

Yet the abuse of clandestine marriage continued to defy

[1] B.M. Add. MSS. 28, 879, fo. 68.
[2] Bod. Rawlinson MSS. 983 C, fo. 7.
[3] *S.P.D.* 26 July, 1695, Will. III, E.B. 274, p. 58.

episcopal vigilance and had to await the Hardwicke Marriage Act of 1753 for its final suppression.

Yet it was not only marriage which sometimes constituted a problem, for many were the practical questions on which the clergy asked the advice of their bishop. Such was the case with William Alchorne, Vicar of High Ongar, who sought the approval of Compton in the following rather exceptional circumstances.

A young servant in his parish spent the evening drinking with his cronies, was finally taken to bed drunk, and died before the morning. What about the burial? The father visited the Vicar in great distress and complained bitterly that his son 'was abused by the company and forced to drink': but no evidence to support this contention was forthcoming at the inquest, when the jury brought in a verdict that the young man was 'accessory to his own death'. The coroner, on being questioned by Alchorne, gave it as his opinion that such a finding did not deprive of Christian burial since there was no suggestion that the deceased 'intended' to destroy himself. But the Vicar felt that he could not conscientiously use the words that God 'of his great mercy had taken unto Himself the soul of our dear brother here departed'; and since he felt it necessary to deter others from a 'like wickedness' he decided that the body must be interred at night without the office of burial. 'I humbly beg your Lordship's pardon', Alchorne wrote to the Bishop, 'but I did what I thought was best in so rare and unusual a Case.'[1]

Across the letter, the Bishop has written in his own hand: 'It was well done.'

We have often had occasion to notice the legacy of the Commonwealth in a certain lawlessness, and a reluctance in many parishes to conform to the more disciplined pattern of the Church of England. In March 1710, the 'door keepers of Hammersmith' refused altogether to accept the minister whom the Bishop nominated to preach in their chapel. Compton determined not to be defied openly in this way, and upon his complaint to the House of Lords, these refractory parishioners (or some of them) were ordered into custody.[2] Doubtless these people were half Dissenters and preferred to manage their own affairs.

---

[1] Alchorne to Compton, 17 Nov., 1682, Bod. Rawlinson MSS. 985 C, fo 14.
[2] Luttrell, *op. cit.*, v. 562.

Many incumbents, for precisely the same reason, found it most difficult to exercise their lawful authority, or to see that things were carried on decently and in order. Very often the Bishop's post bag contained evidence of deliberate lawlessness. We quote a typical letter from David Jenner, Vicar of Great Warley: 'The King's Arms are wanting in our Parish Church and the Commonwealth's are visible on the walls. I have used all possible arguments to have the King's Arms set up and the Commonwealth's chopped out, but some dissenting and schismatical men in the parish oppose both and are very vexatious to me. I have told the Churchwardens and constables I would complain to you about it.'[1]

Mention of 'schismatical men' reminds us that during the first part of Henry Compton's episcopate the sects were particularly active in the city of London. In 1677 the Bishop instituted a survey, being anxious to find out the precise strength of the Fifth Monarchy Meetings in London and Southwark. In the latter he found there were ten such gatherings, many of them representing groups of 200 and over. Some of the particulars about them are interesting. We read of Mr. Eager, an Anabaptist, who teaches 200 'soules' in his own house; of a 'dangerous meeting' in Winchester Park; of Jasper Batte, John Norton and Stephen Draper, 'dangerous persons' who conduct a Quaker meeting; of Mr. Turner, a haberdasher, who had gathered round him no less than 300 people.[2]

In London itself, there were six meetings of which the Bishop was able to discover particulars. The places where they assembled —Glovers Lane, Beech Lane, Cripplegate, Bell Lane—illustrate how London in those days grouped itself around the city: and the occupations of the leaders show how often the backbone of independency was the small tradesman.

When the Bishop's list was as complete as he could make it, he sent it off to the Earl of Danby, for such meetings were often regarded as centres of political disaffection.

As part of his jurisdiction as Bishop of London, Compton was responsible for supplying chaplains to the navy, and with these he tried to keep up a regular correspondence. The effectiveness of a naval chaplain when afloat depended not only on his

---

[1] *S.P.D.*, Car. II, 19 Aug., 1681, 416, no. 123.
[2] B.M. Add. MSS. 28,093, fo. 212.

own character and ability but also on the attitude of his captain. In 1698, for example, the Bishop received a pathetic letter from John Swanne, complaining bitterly of his senior officer, whom he described as a 'drunkard and profane swearer'. Because his sermons had proved unacceptable, he had been promptly confined to his cabin.[1] John Hog, chaplain on board the *Mermaid*, received the pay of, and was treated like, a common sailor.[2] Certainly life at sea in those days was what we should now call 'tough'.

The fault was not always on the side of the captain, for often naval chaplains were the kind of men who could not settle down in parochial life, though it was not possible to get enough even of these. Compton was constantly on the look-out for likely recruits, particularly when some conscientious captains themselves took the initiative in approaching him for chaplains. Thus Richard Kirby of H.M.S. *Southampton* wrote from Plymouth asking that the bearer of the letter, John Adgcomb, might be appointed chaplain to his ship,[3] while Samuel Meade, commander of H.M.S. *Brigantine* made a similar request for one John Davis.[4] Such petitions make it evident that there were captains who were anxious that the chaplain should play his full part in the life of the ship. Such was undoubtedly the case with Sir George Rooke (1650-1709) now remembered for his seizure of Gibraltar, though owing in some measure to party prejudice he was relieved of his command in 1704 when he returned home. Rooke was appointed commander-in-chief of the Mediterranean fleet in 1695, and it was at the end of this year that Compton wrote to John Hext, chaplain on board the flagship, asking what conditions were like afloat. Hext replied from Cadiz Bay that the city was as dirty as could be, and that 600 men from the fleet had already died since they arrived there. Sir George, he was happy to say, had prayers on board ship twice a day, but more chaplains, he pleaded, were desperately needed.[5]

The need had long been recognized, and in 1697 an Order in Council allowed those serving at sea (or in the Plantations) to retain their fellowships or benefices in England. Compton, in

[1] Bod. Rawlinson MSS. 983 C. fo. 147.
[2] Rose to Compton, 28 May, 1709, *Ibid.* 985 C, fo. 90.
[3] Kirby to Compton, ? 1694, *Ibid.* 984 C, fo. 88.
[4] Meade to Compton, 17 Feb., 1705-6, *Ibid.* 984 C, fo. 113.
[5] Hext to Compton, 13 Jan. 1695-6, *Ibid.*. 984 C, fo. 113.

his anxiety to provide chaplains, does not always seem to have been sufficiently discriminating in his choice of fit and proper persons. Certainly John Thomas, whom we have already had occasion to notice, was hardly the right type, and even Compton's biographer writes:

A new War breaking out against France and Spain, in the Possession of the Duke of Anjou, in the first year of her Majesty's Reign: It made an addition to the Burden already laid upon the good Bishop's Shoulders, it being his business to provide and recommend Chaplains for the Service. I have heard some People, who, I believe, were not really Enemies to his Lordship, blame his conduct about ordaining and sending some Persons into the Service, who were not fully qualified either as to Learning or Morals for so sacred a Function. That some of them might be so in such a Number is not improbable; there was a Judas even amongst the twelve . . . [But] some I have known myself who have applied to his Lordship for Ordination, and notwithstanding they brought sufficient Testimonials with them, he has for some time put them off, and persuaded them to betake themselves to some other Employments, which he took them to be much better qualifyed for.[1]

The story of Compton's administration of the See of London for over thirty-eight years is one of steady application to duty, of hard work, and sustained enthusiasm. He left behind him a more devoted clergy whom he inspired with his own zeal. Such was reflected in 'monthly sacraments in all our churches';[2] constant catechizing; a stricter observance of Good Friday; the abandonment of the 'ill custom of Baptyzing Children in private houses'; and the frequent confirmations which the Bishop held in St. Paul's Cathedral and throughout his diocese.

[1] *The Life of Dr. Henry Compton*, pp. 64-5.
[2] I.e. in the City of London.

CHAPTER THIRTEEN

VISITOR OF ST. PAUL'S CATHEDRAL

A S Bishop of London, Compton was Visitor of St. Paul's Cathedral, and it is to the discharge of this responsibility that we now turn.

It was perhaps inevitable that the Cathedral should have suffered during the period of the Commonwealth, for London was the centre and stronghold of the Parliamentary party. The Dean and Chapter were accordingly 'dispersed', so that at the Restoration, when John Barwick, who had shown remarkable courage during the Civil War, was appointed Dean,[1] he had to set about reorganising the Anglican life of the Cathedral almost *de novo*. It was first necessary 'to restore the Celebration of Divine Service by the Sacred Music of the Choir', since there was only one regularly admitted minor canon, and it was doubtful if even he, 'who had taken upon him to sustain the whole College in his own person and to lay hold upon the property', was in priest's orders. What is certain is that for a large number of years he had never been known to perform divine service in the Cathedral.[2]

Such was the state into which the Cathedral had been allowed to fall during the period of the Commonwealth. Barwick, however, applied himself conscientiously to his difficult task, and he was particularly anxious to secure a regular and more frequent celebration of Holy Communion. Unfortunately he was handicapped by bad health and he died on 22 October, 1664. His successor was not long in office before the Cathedral suffered another and overwhelming disaster.

On Sunday, 2 September, 1666, Samuel Pepys was awakened by his maid Jane at 3 o'clock in the morning with the alarming intelligence that there was 'a great fire in the City'. He was soon back in bed, however, little suspecting what was to follow: but on 7 September, after a nerve-wracking week, he wrote: 'Up by five o'clock; and blessed be God! find all well; and by water

---

[1] Actually the first Dean after the Restoration was Matthew Nicholas but he lived only a month after his appointment.

[2] Sparrow Simpson, *Registrum Statutorum*, 1873, p. li.

to Paul's Wharf. Walked thence and saw all the town burned, and a miserable sight of Paul's Church, with all the roofs fallen, and the body of the choir fallen into St. Faith's.'[1] The old Gothic Cathedral was in fact damaged beyond hope of repair, and in the great conflagration some eighty-nine parish churches went up in flames. Questions of reform had now to give way to rebuilding, though the Dean and Chapter did manage to fix up the western part of the Cathedral for services—it had suffered least and the Renaissance façade by Inigo Jones was almost intact.

The rebuilding of St. Paul's proved to be what Dr. Trevelyan has called a 'vast common effort', and the business of raising the necessary money went on for a number of years. Many and various were the schemes which the commissioners for rebuilding—of which body Compton became a member on his translation to London—adopted. They managed to persuade Parliament to put a tax on all coal entering the Port of London and to allocate it for this purpose. The vast building scheme undoubtedly inspired the imagination of Compton, and he was himself active in raising money in various ways. In August 1676, for example, he wrote from 'the office of the works in St. Paul's, to Gilbert Sheldon who, as a former dean, was equally enthusiastic, asking him in the name of all the Commissioners to write to the Bishops suggesting that 'commutations of penance might be sent through him.'[2]

More interesting, perhaps, are the directions which Compton himself sent to his brethren the bishops in July 1678, which show clearly the difficulties in the way of collecting money in some parts of the country. It is obvious that some people had mixed feelings as to the colossal expense which the rebuilding involved. Let the clergy, Compton writes, encourage their flocks to see the new Cathedral as an expression of gratitude for the return of peace, and as a unique opportunity of building 'for the glory and splendour of God's worship in so advantageous a situation'. Such a fine and majestic building would be an abiding 'honour to the nation'. Also, the Bishop rather artfully suggests, let the clergy constantly remind their congregations that the enterprise was a 'magnificent charity', since it was a means of feeding many poor people by giving them honest work to do.[3]

---

[1] *The Diary of Samuel Pepys*, ed. G. G. Smith, 1925, p. 417.
[2] Compton to Sheldon, 31 Aug., 1676, Bod. Tanner MSS. 40, fo. 16.
[3] *Ibid.*, 145, fo. 231.

Nor was this last statement entirely without foundation, for the demands upon Portland stone which Wren's masterpiece entailed gave new life to the isle and its inhabitants. Quarries were opened, piers and roads built.

The Bishop was nothing if not practical and his letter concluded by instructing the clergy to get a subscription book, and to read his brief in the Church, enlarging upon it themselves where necessary. Afterwards, in company with the church-wardens, they must visit every house in the parish.

On the whole the various appeals were not unsuccessful and the task of rebuilding went on.

By 1683 a great deal of Wren's work at the east end was complete, and Compton felt that the way was now clear for this part of the new Cathedral to be used for public worship. He therefore suggested to the Dean and Chapter that a move be made from the west to the east end. The Bishop's approach seems to have been made in a rather informal manner through one of the Prebendaries who referred the matter to a colleague one George Stradling.

Compton also expressed the hope that the Sacrament might be celebrated weekly, and the sermon 'removed' out of the body of the Church into the choir.[1]

This desire to replace the old 'sacrament Sunday' by regular weekly communion was part of a movement common among reforming churchmen at the time. Simon Patrick, who held the Deanery of Peterborough *in commendam* with his stall at Westminster Abbey, was very active in this respect in his own cathedral, and in fact preached three sermons on it. But he was unable to persuade the Dean of Westminster to follow his good example.

Prebendary Stradling (to whom we return) decided to talk the matter over with Archbishop Sancroft, under whom he had served for many years at St. Paul's, and who obviously still kept in close touch with the life of the Cathedral. Sancroft agreed as to the advisability of a weekly communion, but as to a general move to the east end, and the transference of the nave sermon into the choir, he thought (so Stradling reported to Compton) that nothing should be done, 'at least for the present'. It seems strange that a Prebendary of St. Paul's should have gone to the

[1] Stradling to Compton, 23 Feb., 1683, Bod. Tanner MSS. 34, fo. 273.

Archbishop for a definite ruling—he writes in a letter to the Bishop that Sancroft 'has not given any order at all and therefore I conceive does not expect anything should be done'—for Compton as Bishop of London was undoubtedly Visitor of the Cathedral. Perhaps it was a legacy from the time when the Archbishop as well as Bishop exercised visitatorial powers.

With building operations nearing completion, Compton continued to press for the Cathedral to be tidied up, and for public worship to be conducted 'decently and in order'. He at length decided to act in the matter. The Dean was William Sherlock (1641?-1707) a skilful controversialist who had for a short time been a Nonjuror, until, according to his own account, he was converted by Sancroft's publication of Overall's Convocation Book. He is remembered to posterity—when he is remembered— by his *Treatise on Death*, which is still worth reading. On 16 July, 1696, Compton served a notice on the Dean and Chapter summoning them to appear before him at a visitation to be held on 7 September.[1] The intention was to correct those abuses which had crept into the life of the Cathedral during the unsettled period of the last fifty years. All letters of orders were to be shown to the Bishop together with licences for pluralities.

The notice of the Bishop's intention caused great consternation at the Cathedral. It was some fifty-seven years since William Laud had visited the Dean and Chapter, and then they had tried to resist it. In a humble petition to the Crown they then protested that 'it doth not appear by any Records belonging to his Grace or the Church that the Dean and Chapter have ever been visited by any Metropolitical Power notwithstanding the rest of the Diocese hath been so visited'.[2]

When we remember the relationship between Laud and the King, it is not surprising that this protest met with a cool reception. Charles replied that he was 'resolved for the settlement of peace and good order in the Church that no place should be exempt from Archiepiscopal Visitation. And least of all the Church of St. Paul in regard that it appears by their own Suggestions that the rest of the Diocese hath been visited and *de jure*

---

[1] *Bishop Compton's Register*, St. Paul's, 94b. Also B.M. Add. MSS. 34,268, fo. 20.
[2] *Ibid.*, fo. 18.

ordinario it is known that the Archbishop or Bishop ought to begin with his Visitation at the Cathedral. . . . And therefore His Majestie requires Submission of the Dean and Chapter to the Visitation of the Present Archbishop of Canterbury and his Successors.'[1]

Thus Laud visited in May 1639, and did what he could, in his own forthright way, to correct abuses. He was particularly distressed at the condition of the crypt and ordered that it should be 'rescued from further prophaneness'. He further required that surplices, hoods, and square caps should be worn in the Cathedral; and that so soon as the leases fell in the houses of the Dean and Chapter should be made available for the pre-bendaries and minor canons.

There had been no visitation when Compton became Bishop of London since this time, and doubtless the lapse of years, together with the protest against Laud's assertion of his right, had encouraged a tradition of independence. Compton's citation, therefore, came as a great blow to the Dean and Chapter, and they met to discuss it. Since they could hardly deny his jurisdiction absolutely, they reluctantly agreed to ask him to come, not officially as Visitor, but informally—in fact, they said, they had long thought of doing this. The Dean's nervous and somewhat naïve letter to the Bishop, with its implied threat, shows plainly the apprehension of the Chapter.

'After mature consideration of the whole matter', the Dean wrote to the Bishop, they were of opinion that 'the excellent ends your Lordship intends in this Visitation may more effectually be attained by your Lordship's presence and advice in Chapter.' They had always intended to consult him in this way before the Choir was opened, but they must point out to his Lordship that 'though we are resolved, as far as it is possible to avoid all occasions of difference, yet we are afraid that the very nature of a visitation will unavoidably raise some disputes, which by a long disuse of visitations had been happily quieted'.[2]

Such a way of proceeding, Compton was convinced, would not 'effectually answer his expectations', and he persisted in visiting officially. Hence at 10 o'clock, on 7 September, 1696, the Bishop arrived at the 'south gate' of the Cathedral, and was dutifully received by the Dean, by Dr. Stanley (Archdeacon

[1] B. M. Add. MSS. 34,268, fo. 18. [2] *Ibid.*

of London) and the rest of the prebendaries and minor canons. The Bishop then retired *ad cameram* and put on his episcopal habit. This done, he went into the Cathedral and was busy there for the next three hours. It was on an occasion like this that his practical wisdom stood him in good stead. He first examined the letters of orders of the Cathedral clergy and commanded peremptorily that those who had not exhibited them should do so by 6 October. He then explained why a visitation was necessary, and 'told the Dean that they should bring in all their Orders for the Disposition of the Quire and other parts of the Church'. The Dean then interposed by asking the Bishop to put down in writing what he expected the Chapter to do in this matter. Finally Compton prorogued the visitation till 6 October.

The visitation proved to be a very long-drawn-out affair, for the Dean and Chapter were not very co-operative, and skilfully employed delaying tactics. As late as October 1698, the Bishop was still visiting the Cathedral, a fact which drew forth from the Dean and Chapter a formal protest which Sherlock read to their Visitor in the presence of his brethren. In this document he protested solemnly on behalf of the Dean and Chapter against the constant prorogations to which they had been subjected, and which he alleged were 'prejudicial to the laws and jurisdiction of the Dean and Chapter and contrary to the oaths, statutes and laudable customs of the Church'.[1]

The atmosphere in which Compton carried out his inquiries was not, therefore, very congenial, and the Bishop experienced great difficulty in finding out the exact position in respect of the prebends' houses. Nor were the minor canons any more co-operative, and in May 1698, the Bishop ordered 'that such of the Minor Canons as have not exhibited a terrier belonging to their stalls . . . do exhibit and bring [them] into his Lordship's Office by the first of July next'.[2]

The question of the cathedral statutes also proved thorny. The Bishop asked the Dean bluntly whether he had them in a book, and if so, would he exhibit them. The Dean replied with equal bluntness that 'they had no such book', which drew forth from the Bishop the express command that such a volume must be provided and presented to him the next time he came to the Cathedral.[3]

[1] B.M. Add. MSS. 34,268, fo. 25.   [2] *Ibid.*, fo. 27.   [3] *Ibid.*

Compton was nothing if not persistent, and his patient firmness finally won the day, for he was able to give to the Dean and Chapter new statutes, which, with the slight emendations made in them by Bishop Gibson in 1725, laid down the pattern of worship in the Cathedral for the next hundred years. Certainly the need for an episcopal visitation may be seen, not only from the reluctance of the Cathedral clergy to exhibit their licences, terriers and leases, but also from the orders which the Bishop felt it necessary to issue, particularly in respect of divine service.

Before we give a summary of the Bishop's statutes, it may be as well to notice that while the Visitation was still going on the Choir of the new Cathedral was opened, the day chosen being one of particular significance. On 2 December, 1697, thanksgiving services were held all over England for the Peace of Ryswick, and this occasion seemed an opportunity to show off Christopher Wren's masterpiece, now nearing completion. The Lord Mayor and Aldermen gave colour to the proceedings by turning up in force in their 'formalities', accompanied by 'several companies of livery men of the city'. The Bishop of London preached the sermon, but what he said has not come down to us, for the sermon was not printed, because (so a contemporary writes) the King was not present.

The Bishop's statutes, therefore, came at the right time, for a new chapter in the life of the Cathedral was being opened. We propose, therefore, to give a brief summary of them.

Morning and evening prayer were to be said throughout the year, in the summer at 6 a.m. (in the winter at 7 a.m.), and at 6 p.m.[1] This responsibility fell in turn to the minor canons, the Sub-Dean, however, who was one of their number, being exempted. Mattins was also to be sung in the choir at 10 a.m. (on Sundays at 9 a.m.), and evensong at 3 p.m. The first lesson, at these latter services, was to be read by a vicar choral and the litany, when used, was to be sung by two minor canons. The cardinals had the embarrassing responsibility of recording the attendance of the clergy and vicars choral, those being deemed absent who entered the choir without their surplices or in the morning after the venite, and in the afternoon after the first psalm. Nor was this the cardinals' only responsibility.

[1] According to James Paterson *Pietas Londinensis, or the Present Ecclesiastical State of London*, 1714 p. 222, said mattins and evensong took place in 'the Chapel'.

They were to see that there was no irreverence among the singers, and that they all stood and knelt as the rubrics required. They were also to catechize the choristers. The venite and psalms, we may notice, were ordered to be sung antiphonally, ' et harmonica'. The Sub-Dean was to make out the 'bills' (i.e. the musical lists) and to direct who sang the anthems, though here he must seek the approval of the Dean. The Sub-Dean was certainly a significant person for when the Dean or the residentiary canon was absent, he was to officiate at the Holy Table.

The system, in respect of fines, which the Bishop laid down, was certainly designed *pour encourager les autres*. The fine for absence was twopence, and at the end of each quarter the monies thus collected were to be distributed amongst the brethren in proportion to their attendance.

The Bishop then turned his attention to the important matter of preaching, and his regulations here remained in force throughout the nineteenth century. All canons, major and minor, before the sermon were to read the prayer enjoined in canon 55. Any prebendary not preaching on his appointed day, and not finding a substitute, was to be fined 20s. which sum was to be given to his deputy. Normally if a prebendary could not fulfil his turn, he must give notice to the Dean three weeks beforehand, failure to do which incurred a fine of 40s. The Dean and the residentiaries must see that sermons were preached on Feast Days and such Fasts as were appointed by public authority.

Concerning Holy Communion, Compton required that there should be a celebration every Sunday and Feast Day 'at which all in Holy Orders were to communicate, unless hindered by some lawful cause to be approved by the Dean and Chapter'. The Bishop if present was to act as celebrant, and if not, the Dean or Sub-Dean. The *Trisagion* and *Gloria in Excelsis* were to be chanted by the choir; and the gospeller and epistoler were to collect the alms.[1]

Compton may well have felt that his visitation, despite all the difficulties which he encountered, was well worth while. He had certainly started the new Cathedral off on the right lines,

[1] See W. Sparrow Simpson, *op. cit.*, pp. li-liv. These 'Injunctions' are written down in the second part of Bishop Compton's Register: and there is also an undated transcript Bod. Rawlinson MSS. 372 C, fos. 5-10. The most accurate copy of the Bishop's Injunctions was that drawn up by the Bishop's Chaplain Hall, Vicar of Acton, *The Statutes of the Cathedral Church of St. Paul.*

and when his successor visited it in 1725 he needed only to make slight alterations in the times of the services and in the amount of the fines. The general pattern as Compton laid it down remained unaltered. Certainly it proved in the interests of the Cathedral that the Bishop of London insisted upon exercising his visitatorial rights.

CHAPTER FOURTEEN

THE PLANTATIONS OF AMERICA

IT is, perhaps, strange, that some of Henry Compton's most conscientious work should have been done in a country which he was never destined to visit (though he often wished to do so)[1] and which was separated from him by some 3,000 miles of dangerous ocean. As Bishop of London he inherited a loosely defined jurisdiction over the American Colonies—the Plantations —the origin of which has proved a real problem to subsequent historians. Thomas Sherlock (1678-1761), himself Bishop of London, writing in the middle years of the eighteenth century, and anxious to show how precarious this legal jurisdiction really was, maintained that it had arisen quite fortuitously because at the time of the founding of Virginia the Bishop of London 'was a great promoter of the Plantations . . . and had collected and paid in £1,000 towards a College in Virginia. The Company, therefore, as was natural, applied to him, a member of their own Society, for his Help and Assistance to provide Ministers, and this is the first instance we meet with the of Bishop of London's concern in the ecclesiastical Affairs of the Plantations.'[2]

Modern historians, however, have suggested that more probably 'the proper place to look for the origin of the precedent—for it had a basis no more definite or authoritative—on which the Bishop of London's jurisdiction rested, is in the Stuart policy, instigated by Laud, of seeking to extend the Church of England Establishment to every part of the world where the English government had a footing'.[3]

Thus the customary jurisdiction which Compton inherited when he became Bishop of London in 1675 had a very slender legal foundation, though he accepted the great burden which this spiritual care of the Plantations laid upon him with energy,

[1] Gooch, op. cit., p. 13.

[2] Sherlock, To the King in Council. Some Considerations humbly offered by Thomas Bishop of London, relating to ecclesiastical Government in his Majesty's Dominions in America. See appendix to Porteus, A Review of the Life and Character of Archbishop Secker, 1733, p. 105.

[3] A. L. Cross, The Anglican Episcopate and the American Colonies, 1902, p. 12.

enthusiasm and disinterested zeal. It will be the purpose of this chapter to show that he never spared himself in his efforts to promote the welfare of his fellow countrymen during the thirty-eight years of his episcopate. We shall see him drawing up numerous reports, writing innumerable letters, interviewing governors, attending many meetings—all with the settled purpose of strengthening the establishment of the Church of England in that vast territory.

Nor were the white settlers the only objects of his care. He never forgot that there were native Indians, and African negroes, all ignorant of the faith.

The spirit which Compton brought to bear upon his great task found expression in a letter to an anonymous correspondent early in 1676. 'As to the care of your Churches', he wrote, 'with the rest of your Plantations which lies upon me as your diocesan, so to discharge that trust, I shall omit no occasion of promoting their good and interest.'[1] He may be said to have lived up to this high ideal.

The news that the Bishop of London was anxious to exercise an effective ecclesiastical jurisdiction over the American Colonies came as a great encouragement to loyal members of the Church of England in the Plantations particularly since they felt the need for episcopal guidance, and often suffered from a sense of isolation. This must not be taken to mean, however, that the settlers as a class were prepared to welcome the assertion of a spiritual oversight from London. It will be necessary, therefore, to say a few words about the religious situation in the Plantations, in order that we may rightly assess the difficulty which confronted the Bishop as he took over his duties.

The colonisation of America was piecemeal and spasmodic, which meant that each state had its own history, and therefore presented its own problems. Virginia, for example, became a Crown colony as early as 1624, and its population in 1671 had risen to 40,000 which included some 2,000 negro slaves, and 6,000 English convicts and redemptioners. Here the Church of England was in a more favourable position than elsewhere. It was legally established and there were over forty parishes. Maryland, on the other hand, was settled by Roman Catholic gentry under a grant to the second Lord Baltimore in 1632, and it received its

[1] Cross, *The Anglican Episcopate and the American Colonies*, p. 12.

name from Henrietta Maria, the French wife of Charles I. In 1649, the year when the King suffered both for his duplicity and convictions, Maryland was made a 'land of sanctuary', where all religious denominations were to be tolerated, a fact which led to the inflow of a large number of Puritans from Virginia. Conditions in the West Indies, where the Church as a whole was more firmly rooted than on the mainland, were again quite different.

It will be necessary to return to the different problems in the various colonies; we have quoted the cases of Virginia and Maryland, at the outset, only to illustrate that one of the great complications which faced Compton in any attempt to secure effective ecclesiastical oversight was the need to treat each state separately, and to deal with their governors one by one. But this was never easy, for not only were there frequent changes in personnel, but as a class they tended to be suspicious of a rival jurisdiction. Also there were great differences, made more acute by varying traditions of settlement, between a crown and a proprietary colony. No over-all policy was therefore possible.

The colonists, by and large, were not very tractable material, since they were mixed in origin and outlook. Many of them had fled from England to avoid either religious or political persecution. Their own country had been too 'strait' for them, and they preferred liberty even though it entailed exile. Others were recruited from the ranks of the adventurers, and these were often turbulent and unruly. The planters, moreover, whose tyranny over native Indians and imported Africans was notorious, did not welcome a religion, in no matter how diluted a form, which inevitably had the result of causing unrest amongst the slave population.

Nor was the political and religious situation in America the only obstacle in the way of Compton's exercising a real authority. The Bishop was constantly brought up against the physical fact that the Plantations were some 3,000 miles distant—a sea journey of three months. The reply to a letter sent from Fulham in January would not reach England until July, probably later—and yet in the meantime the problem which initially caused the correspondence might well be getting worse. The erring minister knew that he could prolong his case almost indefinitely, and such ministers were, unfortunately, not uncommon.

In fairness it must be admitted that the lot of the Church of

England clergyman in America was not enviable. He was all too often conscious of the hostility of the settlers; he was oppressed with a feeling of isolation; and forced to live from hand to mouth. Even as late as the episcopate of Bishop Robinson, a missionary in Maryland confessed sadly that he had not a friend in the province except the governor. He was fortunate, for others had not always this support.

In such conditions it was hard for a man to keep his own self-respect, particularly as the Church of England clergy were themselves such a mixed bag—missionary idealists, adventurers, French refugees, displaced Scottish Episcopalians, and the generally disillusioned. Yet despite this wide field of recruitment, their numbers were all too few. In 1679 (four years after Compton became Bishop of London) there were only four Church of England clergy in North America outside Virginia and Maryland. In Virginia there were forty-four parishes with twenty clergy, and in Maryland twenty-six parishes with thirteen. Conditions, on the whole, were somewhat better in the West Indies. As early as 1661 an Act had been passed in Barbados 'for the encouragement of all faithful ministers in their Pastoral Charge within the Island', but unfortunately the tyranny of the vestries resulted in there being only five clergymen on the island in 1680.[1] Things were about the same in Jamaica.

From this summary introduction, it is clear that there was much to be done by any bishop who was really concerned that the *Ecclesia Anglicana* should make a more valuable contribution to the spiritual life of the Plantations.

The first question which Compton had to ask himself was of great practical importance. If he were to exercise a jurisdiction which might well prove unpopular, what was its legal basis and precisely how far did it extend? To secure the answer, he applied to the Lords of Trade and Plantations who, realising the importance of the enquiry, passed the following minute at a meeting on 21 January, 1676: 'that enquiries be made concerning the authority of the Bishop of London over foreign plantations, for which the Charters of Virginia and New England are referred to, most probably about 1629 when Bishop Laud was in chief authority'.[2]

---

[1] C. F. Pascoe, *Two Hundred Years of the S.P.G.*, 1901, p. 512.
[2] Sainsbury, *Calendar of State Papers, Colonial Series, America and West Indies*, 1675-6, 1893, no. 789, p. 338.

The search was accordingly undertaken but revealed little other than that in 1633 the Merchant Adventurers in the churches in foreign parts 'in all things concerning their Church Government . . . should be under the jurisdiction of the Lord Bishop of London as their Diocesan'.

Such a slender support for his jurisdiction Compton rightly regarded as inadequate to bear the strain to which he knew he would subject it. Effective oversight, in face of opposition, demanded a secure legal basis, not one so ill-defined or tucked away in the minute books of forgotten meetings of the Council. It must be definite in character and of such a nature that governors, clergy and settlers could not legally dispute it. The Bishop therefore persuaded the Committee to insert the following order in the instructions to all colonial governors: 'That God be duly served, and Holy Days and the Sacrament administered according to the rules of the Church of England . . . our will and pleasure is that no minister be preferred by you to any ecclesiastical Benefice in that our Colony without a Certificate from the Bishop of London of his being conformable to the Doctrine of the Church of England.'[1] This clause was first inserted in the instruction of Culpeper, Governor of Virginia.

The authority thus granted to Compton may not appear large nor was it all that he could have wished, since it was personal to the governor, and had to be renewed with each new appointment, but at least it was definite. Henceforth it became the Bishop's settled policy to insist on his jurisdiction and to see that each governor recognised it.

It was under such an authority (with behind it the tradition of a customary jurisdiction) that Compton and Robinson (and Gibson for the first years of his episcopate) asserted their claims as diocesan. We must not, however, rule out the probability that Compton, in addition, secured an Order in Council which placed the ecclesiastical jurisdiction of the American colonies permanently in himself as Bishop of London. True no such minute exists in the council books today, but Compton certainly seems to refer indirectly to its passing,[2] and there is a significant blank

[1] *New York Documents*, viii. 362.
[2] See Compton to Lord Howard, Governor of Virginia, Fulham MSS. Virginia Box, quoted Cross, *The Anglican Episcopate and the American Colonies*, p. 31. '. . . I do most heartily thank your Lordship for the great care you have

page in the minute book about this time, suggesting an insertion which was never made.[1]

That the Bishop was regarded as legally possessing a continuing jurisdiction is further indicated by the fact that when he was deprived of his office by the Ecclesiastical Commission, his colonial authority was delegated to the three ecclesiastics who took over his jurisdiction.[2]

As well as placing his jurisdiction on a firm legal basis, Henry Compton was also anxious to find out exactly what the religious situation in the Plantations was, so that he could decide his policy accordingly. That all was not well was common knowledge, and many were the letters from America which confirmed this. Such a memorandum as that sent over by John Yeo, on 2 August, 1676, under the title *Deplorable Condition of Maryland for want of an established Church* may be taken as typical. It was Compton's intention to find out exactly what was wrong.

Thus he studied carefully the literature that flowed in to Fulham, a great deal of it the result of his own enquiries, with the result that by July 1677 he was in a position to present to the Lords of Trade and Plantations a *Memorial of Abuses which are crept into the Churches of the Plantations*.[3] These 'abuses', some nine in number, give a vivid impression of what could all too easily happen in a country where spiritual supervision was ineffective

---

taken in setting the Church under your government. There is a constant Order in Council remaining with Mr. Blaithwaite that no man shall continue in any Parish without Orders; nor any to be received without a Licence under the hand of the Bishop of London for the time being, and that the Minister shall always be one of the Vestry. This order was made four or five years since, and I can make no doubt among others you have it in your instructions. The King has likewise made one lately that except Licences for Marriage, Probate of Wills, and disposing of the Parishes, all other Ecclesiastical Jurisdiction shall be in the Bishop of London.' It is also important to notice that in *An Account of the present State of the Government of Virginia*, drawn up by Henry Hartwell, James Blair, and E. Chilton (*c*. 1696) we read: 'King Charles II gave the B. of L. jurisdiction over all the Churches in the English Plantations, except as to three things, viz. marriage licences, probate of wills, and inductions of ministers which are reserved to the several Governors.' J. W Fortescue, *Calendar of State Papers, Colonial Series, America and West Indies*, 1904, p. 664.

[1] Cross, *The Anglican Episcopate etc.*, pp. 31–33, argues the pros and cons.

[2] On the accession of William and Mary, Compton resumed his jurisdiction and when the Committee of Lords and Plantations was reconstituted on 16 Feb. 1689, the Bishop was the only ecclesiastic among its twelve members.

[3] Sainsbury and Fortescue, *Calendar of State Papers, Colonial Series, America and West Indies*. 1677–80, 1896, no. 337, p. 117.

and in some parts non-existent. In Virginia, it was said, the 'profane custom of burying in their gardens, orchards and other places still continues'.

We quote the first 'abuse' in the Bishop's own words: ' That the King's Right of Patronage and presenting to all Benefices and Cures of Souls which happen to be void in any of the Plantations is not duly asserted and practised by the several Governors in so much that some Parishes are kept vacant where a lawful minister may be had, and some persons are commissionated to exercise the ministerial function without Orders both in Virginia, Barbados and other places.'[1]

The other 'abuses' may be briefly summarised—that the profits of vacant benefices were misused; that ministers were frequently non-resident and held more than one cure of souls; that very little provision was made for their accommodation except in Virginia; that the maintenance of ministers was both inadequate and precarious, and that in Maryland there was none at all; that the vestries 'pretended an Authority to be entrusted with the sole management of church affairs, to exercise an arbitrary power over the Ministers themselves'; that the marriage laws were not enforced in Virginia.

This list of 'abuses' is significant. It shows the difficulty of introducing into a distant country the pattern which had worked itself out historically in another: it suggests a determination to assert, rather than to submit to, control.

The Lords of Trade and Plantations—of which body Compton was made a member soon after his translation to London—took the Bishop's *Memorial* into their consideration, and agreed that something should be done to remedy this grievous state of affairs. Hence under the date 10 November, the Committee's Journal records that 'in relation to the law for the maintenance of the ministry, all the particulars in the Bishop of London's Memorandum their Lordships think very necessary to be observed and are of opinion they ought to make part of the Governor's instructions'.[2]

The assertion of independence by the vestries, to which the Bishop called attention, long remained a serious problem. On

[1] Sainsbury and Fortescue, *Calendar of State Papers, Colonial Series, America and West Indies,* 1677-80, 1896, no. 337, p. 177.
[2] *Ibid.,* no. 475, p. 176.

14 January, 1680, Compton again took the initiative and as a result of his motion (in the Committee) concerning 'The State of the Church in His Majesty's Plantations', the King issued an Order in Council enjoining that the Lords of Trade and Plantations 'signify His Majesty's pleasure unto His respective Governors in America, that every Minister within their government be one of the Vestry in his respective parish, and that no vestry be held without him except in case of sickness, or that after notice of a vestry summoned, he absent himself'.[1]

It was undoubtedly a great encouragement to the Bishop that the Lords of Trade and Plantations were willing to support him in his policy of reform. His membership of this body was in fact a powerful asset, for it meant that he could give advice—which advice was usually taken—on any matters which affected the Church in the Plantations. Particularly he could see that no proposed legislation invaded the rights of the Church or his own jurisdiction.

Meanwhile the Bishop patiently continued to collect information.

In July 1677, Lord Baltimore, the Roman Catholic Governor of Maryland, and the son of a more distinguished father, presented in person a paper to the Lords of Trade and Plantations setting forth the state of affairs in his province. It may help us to understand the situation, if we remember that the first Lord Baltimore was granted a Charter in 1632 which conveyed to him as 'absolute lord and proprietor' almost unlimited territorial and governmental rights in Maryland. In the *Memorial* which the second Lord Baltimore now presented to the Lords of Trade and Plantations, he reminded them that for the encouragement of settlers a law had been passed giving toleration to all who believed in Jesus Christ, and guaranteeing that none should be molested on account of his religion. This law, he pointed out, had been generally respected and had worked very successfully.[2]

The significance of these remarks was obvious. Lord Baltimore was in fact saying that he did not wish a supremacy vested in any one denomination. There were four ministers of the Church of England in Maryland, he reported, each with his own plantation.

---

[1] Sainsbury and Fortescue, *Calendar of State Papers, Colonial Series, America and West Indies*, 1677-80, 1896, no. 1264, p. 469.

[2] *Ibid.*, no. 348, p. 121.

There were also adequate churches and meeting-houses, all kept in good order, for the use of Presbyterians, Independents, Roman Catholics, Anabaptists and Quakers.

This picture of a liberty-loving community dedicated to the principles of John Locke (though Locke would not tolerate atheists and Roman Catholics) was not, unfortunately, the whole story. The Lords of Trade and Plantations also had before them a document sent over by John Yeo to the Archbishop of Canterbury. This presented a picture, not of devotion to the principles of liberty, but of a religious indifferentism which was disastrous to the morale of the people. Many of the inhabitants in Maryland, this correspondent alleged, led openly immoral lives, and profaned the Lord's day.[1]

The Lords of Trade and Plantations, with Compton present throughout, deliberated, and as a result they drew up a paper which they gave to Lord Baltimore in person. In this document,[2] they expressed the hope that 'there are sufficient laws to restrain and punish such evil lives, and oblige men to live at least like Christians though not of the same profession'. They then made a few observations which could not have been welcome to the Roman Catholic Governor, and we may assume that it was the Bishop of London who here took the lead. Their Lordships (so the letter ran), had reason to believe that 'this wicked kind of living proceeds from there being no certain established allowance for the ministers of the Gospel, especially of the Protestant religion according to the Church of England [which was] the cause of a great want of ministers'. They were not unaware of the financial difficulties of the colonists, and the unwisdom of imposing 'unnecessary burdens on the inhabitants'; but they wanted more information from Lord Baltimore as to the precise allowance of the Church of England ministers, the value of the plantations, the number of Protestant families with the size of the congregations, and what they would be willing to settle on a minister.[3]

Two days later Lord Baltimore attended again, and was then promised that when the Lords of Trade and Plantations were convinced that the local congregations had done all that they could for their minister, then help would be forthcoming from England.[4]

---

[1] Sainsbury and Fortescue, *Calendar of State Papers, Colonial Series, America and West Indies*, 1677-80, 1896, no. 349, p. 122.　　[2] *Ibid.*, no. 348, p. 121.
[3] *Ibid.*　　　　　　　　　　　　[4] *Ibid.*, no. 349, p. 122.

The Governor had not long returned to America, however, before he received a letter, of which Compton was a signatory, which complained that from information their Lordships had received it appeared that very few of his Majesty's Protestant subjects were represented on the Council of Maryland. If this were true, then he must remedy it.[1]

Such Protestant pressure from England was not entirely without results upon the political and religious life of Maryland. The Revolution of 1688 gave the Crown the opportunity (in 1691), to overthrow the proprietary government and to set up a royal one, though the proprietor was still allowed to retain his territorial rights. The Church of England was legally established by an Act of 1692, thirty parishes being created, and a toleration granted to Dissenters—but more will be said of Maryland later on.

Meanwhile we return to Compton and his patient finding out of the facts, his encouraging the clergy to write to him, and his keeping the Lords of Trade informed of the religious situation in the Plantations. On 10 November, 1677, the Bishop presented another *Memorandum* to the Committee, this time on Jamaica, which enabled their Lordships to gain an over-all picture of the religious life of the island.[2] There were, he stated, fifteen parishes, but only six churches and three ministers. By an Act of the Assembly, St. Jago was required to contribute £130 per annum towards the support of its minister, Port Royal £200, and every other parish in the island £100.

The Bishop's immediate concern in drawing up the *Memorandum* was to strengthen his own authority, and he proposed that no clergyman be sent over without his licence, that those recommended for such service be not rejected without sufficient cause given, and that once in America they be made members of the vestry.[3]

Once again the Lords of Trade and Plantations supported the Bishop, and an Order in Council ensuring that these proposals be inserted in the Governor's instructions, was passed on 16 November.[4] Thus in 1685, when Sir Philip Howard went out

---

[1] Fortescue, *Calendar of State Papers, Colonial Series, America and West Indies, 1681-1685*, 1898, no. 256, p. 125.

[2] Sainsbury and Fortescue, *1677-1680*, 1896, no. 475, p. 176.

[3] *Ibid.*   [4] *Ibid.*, no. 480, p. 178.

as Governor, his orders included the injunction that he must 'give all countenance and encouragement' to the exercise of the jurisdiction of the Bishop of London.[1]

The Bishop continued to take a lively interest in affairs in Jamaica and he was able to follow the progress of the church there in the letters which he received from both ministers and governors. Sir Thomas Lynch, when Governor, in thanking the Bishop for his concern for their welfare, reported that there were now seven parishes supplied with ministers, but that some parishes had been forced to reduce their allowance. The Church which was being built at Port Royal would be the finest in America, he wrote, and two other churches were also in process of erection. The Governor's comments on the situation generally may be best quoted in his own frank words:

> My duty is to keep you informed of this infant church but this would be better done by a minister or two, were such sober and learned men sent over. A Governor may be over charged with other business, or negligent or irreligious. If some cure or prebendship were set apart it would encourage the needed men to come. You could [then] prevail with their Lordships to establish a permanent system of church government. The want of such a system of civil government has led to seven years of disputes. I believe that in time we may have thrice as many parishes and six times as many people, for this is the most populous and prosperous colony in America except New England.[2]

Compton never found it easy to get an adequate supply of ministers for Jamaica—or elsewhere for that matter. In 1692 the colony was visited by a disastrous earthquake and this did not help recruitment. The appeal to England for more clergymen was constant. In 1703, the Governor, Lieutenant-General Handasyde, wrote to the Bishop: 'I think it is my duty to acquaint you of the great want there is in the island of Divines and if there is not some speedy care taken to supply this defect I'm afraid great inconveniencys may ensue by giving an outlet to prophaneness and immorality.'[3] For himself he added: 'As long as I am in the

---

[1] *New York Documents*, vii. 363.

[2] Fortescue, *Calendar of State Papers, Colonial Series, America and West Indies, 1681–1685*, 1895, no. 757, p. 315.

[3] Porteus, *Ibid.*, 1702–3, 1055, vii.

Government, I shall contribute what lies in my power to make them [i.e. the ministers] easy.'

The co-operation of the Governor, of course, was an indispensable condition of any effective ecclesiastical oversight. If he were a loyal and convinced member of the Church of England, then the Church had the opportunity of making a worthwhile contribution to the life of the colony: if he were obstructive or hostile, then its task became far more difficult. In 1710, for example, the Bishop of London felt it necessary to remonstrate with the Governor of Jamaica for 'having acted contrary to his Commission'.[1]

Our references to Jamaica, however, have led us to anticipate the years, and we must return to the earlier days of Compton's episcopate.

On 28 August, 1680, the Bishop next presented to the Lords of Trade and Plantations a *Memorandum* on the Church in Barbados.[2] The Crown, we must notice, had taken over this Colony after the Restoration, when it abolished proprietary interests in order to confirm the planters in their estates. The population of the island in 1675 was some 20,000 whites and 46,000 blacks.

The Bishop's *Memorandum* illustrates again how difficult it was to secure any settled ecclesiastical discipline. Compton suspected that in spite of the Council's orders ministers were not always made *ex-officio* members of the vestry, and that some of the clergy were not in full orders. Other problems arose out of the bountiful supply of slave labour from which the planters were beginning to amass wealth, and which therefore made them oppose any effective conversion of the slaves, since it might hinder 'their power and disposal of them'. Humane as he was, Henry Compton was no prophetic moralist, and he suggested that these fears be dispelled as groundless. It seemed the practical solution for on the co-operation of the planters depended the possibility of evangelising the slave population.

Sexual relationships, so Compton maintained, were freer in Barbados than elsewhere in America, old restraints often ignored, and incestuous marriages not uncommon. The Bishop therefore ordered that the table of affinity be hung up in every church,

---

[1] Handasyde to Compton, Mar. 1711, Fulham MSS. Jamaica Box, fo. 20.
[2] Sainsbury and Fortescue, *Calendar of State Papers, Colonial Series, America and West Indies*, 1677-1680, 1896, no. 1448, p. 590.

and that a book of canons and homilies be provided. 'They were neither the most virtuous nor sober of people that first planned these colonies; but such as could be got'—so the Bishop sadly reflected on another occasion. Others might have said, from a different point of view, that the tradition of independence was strong.

It is obvious that conditions in a pioneering country like America would not easily accommodate themselves to the traditional English pattern, and the Bishop's most important recommendation in his *Memorandum* was as follows: 'that a Commissary be appointed under the Governor to exercise the ecclesiastical jurisdiction'.[1]

The *Memorandum* makes it clear that Compton's increasing acquaintance with the condition of ecclesiastical affairs in America had now convinced him of certain plain facts.

First, that he must secure the co-operation of the governors and if any of them proved hostile to the Church then he must work for their removal. Secondly (and this will be dealt with at length in another chapter), that more clergy must be encouraged to go out, be better paid, and given more authority. Thirdly, that to superintend the ministry of these clergy, the Bishop must have a representative on the spot in America—hence the need for a commissary.

A commissary has been defined as 'an officer whom the bishops of the Church of England are accustomed to appoint to exercise ecclesiastical jurisdiction in particular parts of their diocese where owing to distance or other causes, they cannot attend in person'. Compton had no wish, of course, that such an officer in America should exercise any of the civil authority which a bishop in England still possessed.

The ideal which Compton had in mind, though he was never destined to realise it, was a commissary in every colony. He wisely decided, however, that the first territory on the mainland to benefit in this way should be the crown colony of Virginia, where the Church of England was legally established. The Bishop's choice fell on a vigorous, pious and able Scotsman, James Blair (1656-1743). Compton was not always a very good judge of character, but on this occasion he could hardly have chosen to

---

[1] Sainsbury and Fortescue, *Calendar of State Papers, Colonial Series, America and West Indies*, 1677-1680, 1896, no. 1448, p. 590.

better advantage. An American has well written: 'The story of the
life of James Blair is a story of pure and tireless labours. . . .
He was a man of great simplicity and force of character, very
positive, very persistent, with an abundance of Scottish shrewdness, as well as Scottish enthusiasm, actuated by a lofty and
apostolic determination to be useful to his fellow creatures
whether at the moment they liked it or not.'[1]

James Blair was some thirty years of age, and in the employ of
the Master of the Rolls, when Compton first made his acquaintance in 1685. The Bishop was immediately impressed with his
ability and religious zeal, and he took the initiative in suggesting
that he might go as a missionary to Virginia. It was a challenge
which the young Scotsman felt that he must accept, and with
a licence from the Bishop of London, he went out that same
year as Rector of the Parish of Varina, later known as
Henrico. His first impression of this new country convinced
him that there was work to be done, for he was horrified 'not
only at the disorderly and ineffective condition of the Church
but the almost universal neglect of education'.[2] Already
when Compton appointed him his commissary in 1689 he
had gained a thorough working knowledge of conditions in
Virginia.

Blair remained nine years at Henrico, after which he removed
to Jamestown. His labours among the planters, the government
officers and the colonists were indefatigable. He tried in season and
out of season 'diligently to improve the minds and manners of
the people'.

How to pay his commissaries was always a problem for the
Bishop, but he was fortunate in the case of Blair for he secured an
allowance of £100 for two years (in addition to his other salary)
from the Virginia quit rents. The office made him the highest
ecclesiastical dignitary in the colony, with authority 'to supervise
the clergy in a general way, to preside at the trials of the ministers
charged with offences, and to pronounce sentence when they were
convicted of crimes and misdemeanours'.[3] It gave him, after
1694, a seat on the Council of the colonial government.[4]

---

[1] Tyler, *History of American Literature*, 1879, ii. 260.
[2] E. L. Pennington, *Commissary Blair*, 1936, p. 4.   [3] *Ibid*.
[4] He was admitted to the Council 18 July, 1694. See Bancroft, *English Colonies
in America*, i. 197.

In practice it was clear that Blair's effective authority would largely depend on his powers of persuasion and whether he had a gift for moral leadership. In his original instructions Compton warned him against 'meddling with the laity', advising him to confine himself to 'restrain[ing] the irregularities of the clergy'. 'The chief of my Business', Blair wrote many years later, 'has been when I have heard of any Complaints of the Clergy, first to try to reclaim them by monitory Letters; and when that would not do, I have had a publick visitation of the Church, and upon an open trial of the facts have either acquitted or suspended the Minister, as the case required. I have made in all my time[1] but few examples of this kind; but I find it necessary not to be too slack as on the other hand I am not suspected of too great severity.'[2]

Blair's first concern in Virginia—it was a wise priority—was the educational need, and soon after taking up his office he began a subscription, with the co-operation of the Governor and the Council, to raise an endowment for a college. The response was encouraging and he had soon collected a sum of £2,500. He next placed his scheme before his first Convention of Clergy which forthwith petitioned the Council that the Commissary might go in their name to England to raise money and (equally important) to intercede with the King and Queen for a charter.

Blair arrived in London on 1 September, 1691. It was natural that he should first address himself to his friend and diocesan, but he could hardly have approached him at a worse time. Despite his undoubted interest in the scheme, the Bishop could not at the moment bring himself to go to Court to solicit the Queen (the King was in Flanders)—such was his bitter disappointment at being passed over for the Archbishopric. His advice was that Blair should submit a memorial to the King in Council, which body would almost certainly refer it to the Lords of Trade and Plantations. Blair with his Scottish shrewdness realised that though this procedure might be constitutionally correct, it was not the best way of handling the matter. 'I told his Lordship', he reported to Nicholson, the Governor, 'that I never doubted the obtaining the Charter, but the great difficulty would be in obtaining a gift of such things from his Majesty as we had a mind to ask for the College'. For this purpose, it was

---

[1] This was written in 1714.   [2] Fulham MSS., Virginia Box I. fo. 77.

imperative that he should make a personal approach to the Throne, and this he regarded as the prime reason for his coming to England. 'But all that I could say', he comments, 'could not prevail with the Bishop of London to have the business managed in this manner with the King himself.'[1]

Blair was a man of great determination, however, and the friend he needed proved to be Stillingfleet, Bishop of Worcester, who assured him that the Queen and the Archbishop of Canterbury would certainly interest themselves in the project. And so it turned out. Both Mary and Tillotson were enthusiastically behind it, and the Archbishop and the Bishop of Worcester obtained leave from Compton to bring the matter before the King personally. On 12 November, in the Council Chamber, a very happy James Blair presented, on his knees, his petition to the King, who graciously replied: 'Sir, I am glad that that Colony is upon so good a design, and I will promote it to the best of my power.'[2]

We wonder how grave was the 'fit of the stone' which prevented the Bishop of London from attending this ceremony![3]

The King's warm approval had the effect of enabling Blair to secure a grant from the Boyle bequest. Certainly his visit to England had been well worth while.

The great pioneering work of the College, appropriately named after William and Mary, in educating the colonists and the native Indians, and in providing ministers for the Church, lies outside the scope of this work. Despite his unhelpful attitude at the beginning, under great emotional stress, Compton always took a personal interest in the work of the College, and was its first Chancellor, an office he held for four years.

When Blair returned to America he found a new Governor in office. His predecessor, Sir Francis Nicholson, had given Blair his enthusiastic support, even issuing an order to all justices of the peace 'to enquire into and present all parishes . . . that have no legal vestries and Churchwardens, and that keep not their Churches and Churchyards in repair'. Sir Edmund Andros (1637-1714), his successor, displayed such a consistently violent hostility to the Commissary as to make harmonious relations impossible. The Governor resented Blair's efforts to use royal funds to augment the salaries of the clergy, and he managed to

---

[1] Pennington, *Commissary Blair*, p. 8.   [2] *Ibid.*, p. 10.   [3] *Ibid.*

block a bill to this end. He put all kinds of obstacles in the way of building the College, and did his best to oppose the Commissary's exercising any ecclesiastical jurisdiction whatever. In language which knew no restraint, he accused Blair of filling the Church with Scotsmen, and of misapplying funds which ought to have gone to the College. Finally—it was the climax of his displeasure— he suspended Blair from the Council.

Such a wanton attack on the Bishop's representative was, in effect, an attack on the Bishop of London himself, for the Governor had made it almost impossible for Blair to discharge his duties as Commissary. Blair was not the kind of man to take this treatment lying down, and he decided to come in person to England to put his case before his diocesan. Before leaving Virginia, Blair wisely met a group of prominent citizens, who drew up a letter, dated 16 April, 1697, in which they commended his work in the College. On 30 April, Francis Nicholson, with questionable wisdom, also wrote to the Archbishop of Canterbury, asking him to give 'entire credit' to Blair, and deploring the policy of his successor. 'If it please God that Affairs be not better settled for the Interest of the Coll[ege] in Virginia, I fear that they will go very right to be ruined', he commented.

Both Compton and the Archbishop of Canterbury saw only too clearly that this clash in Virginia represented a serious attack on the whole status of the Church in America. A hostile Governor was using his office to deny to the Church of England any real jurisdiction. They decided to hold an enquiry and to hear Blair in person, and Sir Edmund Andros through counsel. Thus on 27 December, 1697, at Lambeth, they met for over two hours in the Palace. The Commissary made the most of his opportunity, and brought thirteen charges against the Governor, all of them indicative of a rivalry between two different parties each with its own attitude towards colonial responsibility—the one reactionary under Sir Edmund Andros, which stood for making quick fortunes through exploitation, the other more liberal of which the Church, despite all its shortcomings, was the inspiration.

Of the charges brought by Blair against the Governor, it may suffice if we mention three: that he deliberately kept livings vacant and refused to induct ministers; that he would never assist in augmenting their salaries; and that he put every possible obstacle in the way of building the College.

As to Andros's complaint against Blair that he was filling the country with Scottish clergy, Compton here accepted full responsibility. To the Archbishop he said:

My Lord, whatever there is in this, I must take it upon me; your Grace knows the circumstances of these poor men in their own Country, and I must confess it both a charity to the men, and that it was a piece of good service to the Plantations, to send them thither and I think it in unkindly done in Sir Edmund Andros to make a noise about this, for I wrote a full account of all that I sent and told him the characters I had of them, and told him that if any of them did not behave himself well, he should be as easily turned out as ever he had been put in; he makes me no return to this, but raises a clamour against these men only on account of their country.[1]

The Archbishop on his part expressed himself in no uncertain terms concerning the Governor's attitude to the clergy in their parishes. 'This seems to me', he complained, 'a very strange way they have here, that their ministers are not inducted, but may be removed, like domestic servants, by a vote of the Vestry.'[2]

The findings of the enquiry were never really in doubt. The Archbishop of Canterbury and the Bishop of London came down emphatically on the side of Blair, and, as a result of Compton's influence on the Committee of the Lords of Trade and Plantations, Sir Edmund Andros was recalled in 1698.

It must not be thought, however, that the Commissary had behind him the unanimous support of all the episcopal clergy in Virginia. There certainly was a great deal of anti-Scottish feeling. Nicholas Moreau, for example, wrote somewhat cryptically as follows to the Bishop of Lichfield and Coventry in April 1697: 'Though the whole country hath a great Respect for my Lord Bishop of London, they do resent as a high affront made to their Nation because his Lordship has sent here Mr. Blaire, a Scotchman to be Commissary.'[3]

Andros was succeeded by Nicholson who returned to the scene of his former labours. He at first worked zealously for Church and College, but unfortunately his relations with Blair

[1] Fulham MSS. Virginia Box III, fo. 187. The Earl of Bellamont complained to the Committee of the Lords of Trade and Plantations of the Bishop's 'vein' for preferring Scotsmen, and the consequent depopulation of Caledonia.
[2] *Ibid.* fo. 187.
[3] Moreau to Bishop of Lichfield, 1697, *ibid.*, fo. 59.

later deteriorated, and he too began to obstruct the Commissary in his task of reform. This unhappy breach introduced a serious division into the ranks of the clergy in Virginia. Blair once again complained to his diocesan, and in a letter to the Archbishop of Canterbury protested that Nicholson 'governs us as if we were a Company of Galley Slaves by continual roaring and thundering, cursing and swearing, base abusive Billingsgate language to the degree that it is utterly incredible to those who have been the Spectators of it'.[1] It is difficult in this intemperate language to recognise a man who undoubtedly did a great deal to further English colonisation in America.

Compton was at first reluctant to intervene, and in fact he secured the renewal of Nicholson's patent on the accession of Queen Anne, when some of the Governor's enemies hoped that he might be superseded. The Bishop probably did not feel easy in his own mind as to the rights and wrongs of the dispute, particularly since he had received a petition from twenty of his clergy in Virginia (some of them Scotsmen) all testifying to the merits of the Governor. These men deplored the 'sly insinuations' which had been levelled against him, and confessed their 'joy unspeakable' that he was still in office. Particularly did they complain of the hard words used by Blair in a sermon on the death of William III, and they bewailed their own plight in these words: 'We are entangled in a kind of dilemma under two rival authorities, the Governor . . . and Mr. Commissary.'[2]

Once again Blair's persistence won the day, and in 1708 Nicholson was replaced by George Hamilton Douglas.

Despite these unfortunate controversies, however,—they are a fair reflection of colonial life at the time—no one can deny the contribution which Blair made towards a more orderly and settled church life in Virginia. Under the stimulus of his activity, religion and education prospered as they had not done hitherto. The powers and duties of the vestry were defined, the position of the parish priest was determined, and his salary was regularly provided for at the public expense. Episcopally ordained ministers were encouraged to go out from Scotland.

This tribute to Blair is indirectly a tribute to his diocesan. It was Compton who appointed him, and sustained him in office.

[1] Blair to Tenison, 13 July, 1702, Fulham MSS. Virginia Box II, fo. 78.
[2] Fulham MSS. Virginia Box III, fo. 48.

The establishment of a commissary in Virginia encouraged the Bishop of London to extend this method of control to other colonies. The next territory to receive the benefit of such supervision was the island of Barbados where the Reverend William Walker was appointed in 1691. Walker seems to have exercised more authority than any of his successors in the office, for he certainly held 'several visitations and did many judicial acts'.[1] He was followed by Cryer, who unfortunately (it was all too common) quarrelled with the Governor, and was thereby prevented from doing much effective work. The Bishop of London seems to have suspected that the fault lay rather with the Commissary, since he was forced to admit that the Governor 'was a man of too much honour and conscience to wrong any man wilfully [being] a true friend of the Church'. Apparently Cryer had 'engaged in a faction against him'.[2]

The next Commissary was the Reverend William Gordon, but in his hands the office became even more ineffective, for he confessed years later to Bishop Robinson that he 'never held any visitation nor called any Convention, nor indeed ever did any judicial Act except one in Lowther's Government and one in Mr. Cox's Presidentship'.[3]

The Bishop next turned his attention to Maryland, where, as we have already seen, the Church of England was legally established in 1692. The Act which effected this was certainly unpopular in many quarters, being bitterly attacked by the Quakers, so much so that its operation was suspended from time to time, and an appeal against it lodged with the Committee of the Lords of Trade and Plantations in 1699. But the establishment of the Church of England remained a legal fact, and the Bishop of London determined to make it a spiritual reality. This meant a two-fold policy, to encourage more clergy to go out, and to secure effective supervision over them through a Commissary. Hitherto the Bishop's authority in Maryland had been largely non-existent, and the few resident Anglican clergy were very conscious of their isolation. In a petition to the Bishop in which they expressed their appreciation of Nicholson's period of office as Governor, they represented 'the great and urgent necessity of an Ecclesiastical Rule here, invested with such ample power and Authority from

[1] Compton to Gordon, 28 Nov., 1704, Fulham MSS. Barbados Box, fo. 101.
[2] *Ibid.* [3] *Ibid.*, fo. 152.

your Lordship as may capacitate him to redress what is amiss; and to supply what is wanting to the Church'. Only such support would prevent their being 'wholly discouraged from staying in these p[ar]ts of the English Empire, and preach the Gospel here, as well as the papists and presbyterians & Quakers do after their manner'.[1]

The Bishop's choice of a Commissary was once again very wise, for it was none other than the excellent Thomas Bray, (1656-1730) a man of indefatigable industry, and a life-long enthusiast for the spread of the Christian Gospel.[2] Compton was also fortunate in that the much maligned Francis Nicholson welcomed the Commissary and gave him every support. In fact so much was this the case that some of the colonists later complained to the Lords of Trade and Plantations that the Governor was so 'furiously zealous for building of Churches and Colleges that the country is not able to bear it'.[3] In 1694-5 the Assembly passed an Act vesting the office of judge in testamentary causes in such ecclesiastical person as the Bishop of London might appoint as his Commissary, allocating to him no less than £300 a year.

After many delays, Dr. Thomas Bray arrived in the Plantations in 1699. He soon discovered that his task was no light one, and it was made more difficult from the beginning by a discreditable intrigue which deprived him of the salary previously assigned to him. To offset this disappointment, he endeavoured to buy a plantation but without success, with the result that during his stay in Maryland he was always in financial difficulty. His genuine enthusiasm, however, was obvious, and during his short sojourn in America he established thirty-nine libraries, attempted to evangelise the American Indians, and made a careful investigation of the whole religious situation. He nominated three clergy to hold visitations, and generally to see that their brethren observed the canons, but he was regretfully forced to admit that the clergy 'would not submit to them'.[4]

The Bishop did his best to support Bray from London, and to see that new Governors of Maryland went out with definite instructions. In August 1699, he wrote to Sir Philip Meadows

---

[1] Fulham MSS. Maryland Box, fo. 145.
[2] An interesting life of Thomas Bray by F. W. Thompson has recently been published (S.P.C.K., 1954).
[3] Fulham MSS. Maryland Box, fo. 144.
[4] See *ibid.*, fo. 152.

(1626-1718) a member of the Committee of the Lords of Trade and Plantations, urging that something be put in the Governor's orders as to collations to benefices. It was one of the most persistent problems with which the Bishop had to deal. What happened all too frequently (even in Virginia) was that the vestry took their minister on trial and never presented him for institution, so that he had no legal claim on his dues, and his whole position remained precarious. The Bishop now proposed to Sir Philip that the Governor, in virtue of the King's supreme ecclesiastical jurisdiction, should immediately collate ministers to their livings. As to the Commissary—'who will, I am sure, give no offence, but do what good he can'—the Bishop expressed the hope that he might 'continue to be of the Council [which] gives him more consideration among those people who are too apt upon the smallest occasions to contemn his slender authority'.[1]

But Bray found the obstacles in the way of his task insuperable and he became convinced that he could do more to serve the work of the Church in Maryland, and throughout the Plantations, by returning to England. He was right, as we shall see later, for it was from this decision that the Society for the Propagation of the Gospel was born.

Bray came home in August 1700, but he realised that it was essential for the good of the Church in Maryland that a successor be appointed. To ensure this he waited on Compton, and to quote his own words 'represented to him the Great Necessity there would be that his Lordship should forthwith send a Commissary to Preside over the Clergy of that Province if it were but to prevent their falling into any Disorder'. The Bishop recognised the need but still hoped that he might persuade Bray to return, preferring in the meantime to appoint a surrogate to act for him. The real difficulty in the way of such a compromise, or of appointing another Commissary, however, was 'the total Want of Means to support one with either Character'.[2]

However ineffective on occasions might be the authority of the Commissary, it is significant that in Maryland discipline soon began to suffer from the lack of any ecclesiastical supervision. In 1702 Bray was informed by a correspondent in America

---

[1] Fortescue, *Calendar of State Papers, Colonial Series, America and West Indies,* 1697-1698, 1905, no. 737, p. 372.
[2] Fulham MSS. Maryland Box, fo. 60.

(we quote this letter as typical of many others) that a 'wretch' named Holt, previously degraded by the conscientious William Blair in Virginia for 'Adulteries, Drunkeness and Fightings', had been appointed to one of the wealthiest livings in Maryland.[1] News like this was most distressing, and Bray paid another visit to Fulham, laying before the Bishop 'the most pressing Necessity there was of sending a Commissary there', with power to induct, though of necessity the right of presentation must remain with the Governor. The Bishop now realised the urgency of the need, and that he could not count on Bray's returning. He therefore asked his former Commissary to look round for the right man, and as a result Bray commended Michael Huetson, Archdeacon of Armagh, whom he described to the Bishop as a 'Person of as clear a Character as I ever met with and to my own Knowledge of excellent Piety and Exemplary Life, of a prudent Conduct and grave Deportment'.[2] The Bishop saw the Archdeacon and approved.

So far all was satisfactory but there still remained the same old problem. How was the Commissary to be supported? This could only be solved through the co-operation of the Governor and the settling upon the office such a position as judge in testamentary causes. Nicholson was now back in Virginia, and the new Governor, Nathaniel Blakiston, was reported to be unfavourable to the appointment of another Commissary. Such rumours, however, appear to have been unfounded, for in 1700 he assured the Archbishop of Canterbury that 'concerning the settling the Commissary office here, notwithstanding what some people may suggest, I am always ready and willing to settle that office upon any person my Lord of London shall appoint to come over here to reside some time in the Province'.[3]

Nathaniel Blakiston, however, was not long in Maryland, being succeeded by John Seymour, a forthright, blustering colonel, very jealous for the rights of his office, and determined to resist what he regarded as any encroachments by ecclesiastical authority. Compton, realising that there would probably be difficulty, arranged for the Governor (while on a visit to England) to dine with him at Fulham in company with Bray and the Archdeacon. When the meal was over, the two latter tactfully

[1] Fulham MSS. Maryland Box, fo. 60.   [2] *Ibid.*
[3] Blakiston to Tenison, 12 June, 1700, *ibid.* fo. 132.

withdrew, and the Bishop informed the Colonel of his intention to nominate Mr. Huetson as his Commissary, asking that he might be appointed judge in testamentary causes. What Seymour said to the Bishop has not been recorded, but on rejoining the two ecclesiastics and entering with them into the coach, he broke into an ungovernable fury. He had been made the victim of 'a trick and a cheat', he shouted: he should have been told all about this before, and turning upon the unfortunate clergymen he protested that if they had not been protected by their gowns 'he would have had satisfaction with his sword'.[1]

In face of this implacable hostility, it was impossible for Compton to make any appointment, and for the rest of his episcopate, the Bishop was without a Commissary in Maryland.[2] Seymour's immediate anger may be accounted for if we assume, as seems possible, that Compton suggested that the new Commissary be given power to induct, an authority which had hitherto been vested in the Governor. But both Bray and Compton recognised that his real objection was to any effective ecclesiastical jurisdiction in the Colony exercised by the Church. This is further suggested by the fact that the Assembly in Maryland proposed to remedy the defect of being without a Commissary by establishing its own spiritual court to consist of the Governor and three laymen. Its jurisdiction was to be extensive, none other than 'to superintend the conduct of the clergy, to have cognisance of all cases of immorality on the part of a clergyman, and of non-residence in his parish for thirty days at one time . . . to deprive from livings and to suspend from their ministry'.[2] A Bill to this end passed both houses of the Assembly, but even the Governor felt that he could not give it his approval without instructions from England and these he never succeeded in obtaining. The clergy on their part were filled with alarm, and protested to Compton that 'it would be establishing presbyterianism in the Colony upon the neck of the Church, and raise an effectual bar to the introduction of Episcopacy, which is generally wished for by the Clergy of the Province'.[3] We may be sure that the Bishop of London had something to say on the Committee of the Lords of Trade and Plantations.

[1] Fulham MSS. Maryland Box, fo. 60
[2] Hawks, *Ecclesiastical Contributions*, ii. (Maryland), 129-31.
[3] *Ibid.*

Thus Maryland was left without a Commissary, and in Virginia William Blair dared not exercise his authority to the full. The situation, fortunately, was a little better in South Carolina.

The early history of this colony is largely a story of the struggle between popular and aristocratic interests, between the people and the lords proprietors. The former secured a great victory in 1693, when the popularly elected Commons House gained the right to initiate legislation. Alongside the political struggle for power, there was also a sustained strife between the Church of England and the Dissenters, which culminated in 1704 in an Act of the Assembly which required all its members to receive the Sacrament according to the rites of the Church. This assertion of the supremacy of the *Ecclesia Anglicana* did not in any sense represent, however, a desire to be governed from London, for Governor Johnson proceeded to secure the passing of another Act which instituted a Court of High Commission, consisting of twenty laymen, with power to exercise ecclesiastical jurisdiction and to remove ministers for immorality —and even 'imprudence'. The Dissenters could not but fail to be apprehensive, and they now turned devil's advocate. 'The Governor and his adherents', they said with truth, 'have at last done what the latter often threatened to do', namely, 'to wholly abolish' the Bishop's authority.[1] A deputation of protest was sent over to England, where they found the whigs solidly behind them, and the tory Compton anxious to champion their cause. The petition came before the House of Lords who promptly referred it to the Lords of Trade and Plantations, which body, under the firm guidance of Compton, declared the offending Act of Assembly null and void.[2]

There was now nothing for the Assembly itself to do but to follow suit, which it did on 30 November, 1706, on the same day passing another Act which established the Church of England in the Colony, an Act which remained in force until the Revolution. The Bishop of London now took the opportunity of appointing a Commissary. His choice fell on the Reverend Gideon Johnston, Rector of Charlestown, who continued to hold the office till 23 May, 1716, when he was tragically drowned after saying farewell to Governor Craven.[3]

[1] Hewit, *South Carolina* (Caroll, Historical Collections), pp. 151-4.
[2] *Ibid.*   [3] Fulham MSS. South Carolina Box, fo. 8.

Despite this rather unsettled background in Carolina (perhaps partly because of the stimulus which came from the rivalry of the Dissenters), the Church of England clergy seem to have worked well together under the sympathetic leadership of their Commissary. This kindly man was undoubtedly popular with his brethren, more so perhaps than any other Commissary whom Compton appointed. In January 1713, the clergy wrote to their Bishop telling him how much Johnston 'had endeared himself to them', and they asked his Lordship to place implicit trust in the report that he was bringing over to England. They also took the opportunity of thanking the Bishop 'for the continual demonstration of his Lordship's goodness'.[1]

Most letters passing between South Carolina and Fulham tell the same story. 'We are unanimous in all respects', the clergy wrote at another time, 'and Converse with affectionate and sincere love towards one another: by the Grace of God and with your lordship's blessing we are resolved to continue in that disposition while we live together.'[2] The Bishop's letters to his Commissary often show the warmth of a personal friendship. 'My service to Mrs. Johnstone', he wrote on one occasion, 'and blessing to your Family. Your little boy is like to do very well, of whom I have taken care of for the present.'[3]

There were of course difficult clergy in Carolina as elsewhere, and we must not paint too rosy a picture. Monsieur Giguillet, a Swiss, whom Compton (in his charity) once described as 'an excellent man', was one of them. He deserted his wife, leaving her with a pittance, but the Bishop managed to secure his resignation.[4]

How far was the institution of the office of Commissary successful in introducing more discipline, and in safeguarding the interests of the Church of England in the Plantations? It will readily be granted that a Province with a Commissary was in a more fortunate position than a Province without one, but on the whole results were disappointing and did not come up to the Bishop's expectations. The Commissaries had to contend, in most cases, with the opposition of the Governors, who were able to

---

[1] Fulham MSS. South Carolina Box, fo. 234.
[2] *Ibid.*, fo. 236.   [3] *S.P.G Carolina Papers*, iv. 377.
[4] See Fulham MSS. South Carolina Box, fo. 7.

make life difficult for them, particularly when they were
supported by refractory clergy. Bray in Maryland never received
a salary at all, and the office was even left vacant on his resignation
until revived in the time of Governor Hart. Most of Compton's
Commissaries wrote home at some time or another complaining
of the difficulty of their work. The profits of the office were small
and expenses high. 'As to the Commission of Commissary', wrote
a holder of the office in Barbados, 'I have found it troublesome
and chargeable to me, being obliged in common humanity
sometimes to maintain for weeks three or four clergymen of the
Bishop's sending over in all necessaries till they were provided,
money into the bargain.'[1]

As a general rule these early colonists resented any real
attempt to assert episcopal control, and the Commissary was
essentially the bishop's man. The clergy of South Carolina
reported in 1713 as follows:

> The many hard words that have been frequently bestowed on the
> late most worthy Bishop of London [i.e. Compton] when his
> Right was occasionally asserted and defended by any of us Clergy
> are a further Proof of some Men's Aversion to Episcopacy what ever
> they may pretend to the contrary for at every turn they accused
> him of being a Pope, nay worse than the Pope because (as they said)
> he would fain extend the Diocese and Authority further than any
> Pope ever did, and then they triumphantly added, what have we to
> do with the Bishop of London or he with us? must we go to London
> and the Lord knows where to complain against ill clergymen and to
> prosecute them in the tedious forms of ecclesiastical courts? Wherever
> Christianity was planted then a Bishop was settled in the apostolical
> and primitive time. And since we are thus neglected in this
> Respect, It is but Reason that we should do justice to ourselves.[2]

As a result of this constant opposition the Commissaries
were reluctant to assert their legal authority and preferred to
move by way of private admonition. Even in Virginia, where
the ecclesiastical climate was most favourable to the Church
of England, Blair confessed that except during his first few years
he seldom performed any judicial acts. What was true of Virginia
was more emphatically true elsewhere. A Commissary in
Maryland later complained to Bishop Gibson that 'they will

[1] See Fulham MSS. Barbados Box, fo. 5.
[2] *S.P.G. Carolina Papers*, ii. 423.

scarce allow you judicial authority, unless over the clergy, and those too will dispute it. I never passed but one ecclesiastical sentence, and that was upon a rogue that forged his Orders, and had two wives.'[1]

In these circumstances, it was inevitable that such authority as the Commissary wielded depended largely on his own personal qualities. If he were a good man, sought friendly relations with the Governor, was tactful with the clergy, and possessed ability, then his presence in the colony was a blessing. On the whole, Compton chose his Commissaries wisely. Such men as Blair, Bray, Goodman and Johnstone undoubtedly exerted a steady and healthy influence on the life of their province, though they were unable to achieve what their diocesan had hoped from them.

Where the Bishop had no Commissary he was forced to exercise such influence as he could through cultivating the right relationship with the Governor. Such was the case in Pennsylvania, a Colony which was granted to William Penn by Charter in 1680, the first English settlers consisting of some 2,000 Quakers. When the Lords of Trade and Plantations met at Whitehall on 22 January, 1680, to consider the draft of the patent constituting William Penn absolute proprietor of the Colony, the Bishop of London was successful in securing 'a liberal provision for such Episcopalians as may wish to found a church or churches in the colony'. This he did by making it possible for any twenty inhabitants to 'signify their desire to the Bishop of London that a minister of the Church of England be sent over for their instruction'.[2] 'Thus in consequence of Compton's efforts', writes A. L. Cross, 'the Church of England was at least insured of a definite recognition in the Colony of Pennsylvania.'[3]

Penn's relations with Compton were not unfriendly for he often sought the Bishop's advice through a 'kindly correspondence'. On one occasion in particular, he was guided by Compton into 'buying and not taking away the natives' land'.[4]

Yet in Pennsylvania ecclesiastical discipline was exercised only with great difficulty, and at the end of the seventeenth

---

[1] Quoted A. L. Cross, *The Anglican Episcopate and the American Colonies*, p. 1.
[2] Perry, *American Episcopal Church*, i. 224.
[3] A. L. Cross, *op. cit.* 20.
[4] Perry, *op. cit.*, i. 224.

century—though we must not take the statement too seriously, so strong was the prejudice against the Quakers—the youth of the colony was described as 'very debaucht and ignorant', and the people as 'living in general neglect of the public worship of God, and without the instituted means of grace and salvation'. A new era for the Church of England began, however, when in 1700 the Bishop of London sent out the Reverend Evan Evans to Philadelphia. In February 1702, two ministers, Keith and Talbot also arrived there.

The Bishop of London's steady efforts and frequent disappointments finally convinced him that the only real solution of the problem both of supplying clergy and disciplining them was a resident bishop in America. He was not alone in coming to this conclusion. Writing to the Bishop of Lichfield in 1697, Nicholas Moreau pleaded: 'I wish you to put in your Mind, my Lord, to send here an eminent Bishop, who by his Piety, Charity and severity in keeping the Canons of the Church, might question these base Ministers and force them to mind the Duty of their Charge'.[1]

This question of resident bishops in America was to remain one of the major issues of ecclesiastical politics during the eighteenth century. As early as 1638, Laud had endeavoured to send a bishop to Virginia, and later Dr. Alexander Murray (Charles II's companion in exile) was nominated to this colony, but the proposal broke down, in part through the failure to secure an adequate endowment from the customs.

With the establishment of the Society for the Propagation of the Gospel (1701),[2] this demand for a bishop gained new and militant support, and in 1704 the Society stated a case for the consideration of the law officers of the Crown, in which they asked the following questions: (1) 'Whether under 2 Hen. VIII, Cap. XIII, the Bishops suffragan of Colchester, Dover, Nottingham and Hull might not be disposed of for the service of the church overseas.' (2) 'Whether the Archbishop and Bishops of the Realm would be liable to any inconvenience or penalties from the Statutes or Ecclesiastical Laws should they consecrate Bishops for foreign parts endowed with no other jurisdiction but that of Commissary or the like.' (3) 'Whether by the Act of Edward VI

---

[1] Moreau to Bishop of Lichfield, 1697, Fulham MSS. Virginia Box, iii. 59.
[2] See next Chapter.

for the election of bishops, the Queen might not appoint suffra-
gans for foreign parts within her dominions.'

The Society's efforts were further reinforced by a petition
from fourteen missionaries writing from New Jersey, on
2 November, 1705, begging that a bishop be sent out to them.
Compton was enthusiastically behind them, and in December,
to support their case, he drew up his own *Observations*,[1] a document which is in many respects a strange amalgam of practical
wisdom and ecclesiastical passion.

The necessity for resident bishops in America, Compton
maintained, 'in the present disorders now arising in some of the
Plantations and likely to increase to an entire discouragement of the
Clergy already there established', could hardly be disputed. The
practical question was simply 'what sort of Bishop will be most
proper to settle there'. On this matter, Compton showed a
realistic appreciation of the diverse forces in America which were
hostile to any establishment of episcopacy. He admitted frankly
that any attempt to set up an 'absolute bishop' as in the Isle of
Man, would be most improper. It would cause 'great alarm'
in the Colonies, and would lead to innumerable addresses being
sent over to England. Not so realistic, however, was his contention
that 'the true reason of their averseness to a Bishop, is the great
apprehension they have of being restrained from the Licentiousness they now too often put in practice'. From one end of the
Plantations to another, adultery, bigamy, and incest were rife
which, he said, would receive an effective check if episcopacy
were once established.

The kind of bishop to be sent over to America, Compton
continued, was one 'who had all necessary power to restrain
vice and keep good order but no more'. He could go out to the
Plantations under the same authority as the Commissary, to
whose jurisdiction the colonists were already accustomed,
though he would have the added power of being able to
consecrate churches, to ordain and confirm. 'It will be the
safest way at first', the Bishop wisely added, 'for a proof how
it will take among them, and all the faults and defects may
more easily be corrected and amended: because it will not be
near so troublesome to question and remove a Suffragan
Bishop as another; nor will his being put out of office be

[1] Lambeth MSS. 711, fo. 118.

near so inconvenient. Besides the beginning of any new establishment ought to be carried out gradually which will make all Steps easier and in case of Disappointment the matter will not be so grievous.'[1]

There is much wisdom in Compton's short paper but it was not fair to suggest that the feeling against bishops in America sprang mainly from a desire to indulge in unrestrained vice. The Bishop well knew that there were strong religious and political traditions in America which encouraged independence.

The scheme for American bishops hung fire, despite the support of the bishops in England, the enthusiasm of the Society, and also, it may be noticed, the interest of the Queen. Compton was tireless on its behalf, and refused to let the matter remain in abeyance. In June 1709, he again represented to the Society 'the very great Inconveniencies attending [its] Affairs . . . for want of a Bishop to govern the Church in the Plantations'.[2] Hope for the success of the scheme revived, and it was even rumoured that Dean Swift, whose restless genius sought to reign in worlds other than the kingdom of letters, was to become the first Bishop of Virginia. The Society went so far in 1711 as to negotiate for the purchase of a bishop's house in Burlington, New Jersey, 'in the sweetest situation in the world'; and next year on the motion of Lord Clarendon, it produced a draft Bill for 'the establishment of bishops in America'.

Yet it was not to be. The death of Anne removed a firm friend, and the accession of George I brought other political problems to the fore. True the Society patiently went on with its plans, and petitioned George I on 3 January, 1715, but the rebellion in Scotland, and the fear that many bishops were concealed Jacobites, led to the project being shelved—and so successfully that it was not till 1787 that Charles Inglis was consecrated Bishop of Nova Scotia.

[1] Lambeth MSS. 711, fo. 118.
[2] *Journal of S.P.G.*, 3 June, 1709.

CHAPTER FIFTEEN

THE BISHOP AND THE SOCIETY FOR THE PROPAGATION OF THE GOSPEL

THOMAS BRAY'S return from Maryland in 1700 did not mean that he had lost interest in the work of the Christian Church in the Plantations. He had become convinced that he could serve it more effectively in England; and he was right, for a direct result of his coming home was the founding of the Society for the Propagation of the Gospel.

During the latter years of the seventeenth century people, by and large, became 'organisationally minded', a fact which can be seen in the establishment of the Royal Society, and the Societies for the Reformation of Manners. Reforming bishops endeavoured to secure a more vigorous life in their dioceses by making diocesan machinery work. Parish priests in London founded schools and endowed libraries. More efficient administration at the Navy Board under the painstaking labours of Samuel Pepys was symptomatic of the age.

Bray, in the spirit of the times, conceived the idea of a Society for the Propagation of the Gospel which would assist the Bishop of London in discharging his responsibilities overseas, and encourage regular recruitment to this ministry. Bray had in mind a group of Christian people, representing the best elements in the Church of England, whose constant preoccupation would be the spiritual care of those territories abroad which were under the Crown.

Bray's scheme secured the approval of the Lower House of Convocation on 13 March, 1701, and on 8 January, 1702, a Royal Charter was issued, under which a Society for the Propagation of the Gospel was incorporated. The Archbishop of Canterbury, Thomas Tenison, who declared the establishment of such a Society to be 'of the greatest consequence imaginable', was made its first President, and Henry Compton Vice-President. The creation of this body did not in any way break in upon the Bishop's legal jurisdiction in the Plantations, but it is to the credit of Compton that he welcomed the help which the Society gave him, and despite occasional differences of opinion worked willingly with it for a common purpose. Without such co-operation from the beginning, the intention of the Society might never have been fulfilled.

Before its creation, Compton found ministers for the Plantations by keeping his eyes open for likely candidates. We have already seen how he suggested the possibility of a ministry overseas to Blair, and thus gained a life-long missionary. The episcopal clergy in Scotland, deprived of their livings by the presbyterians, were often only too willing to undertake a ministry in the Plantations. French refugee ministers also, after a preliminary stay in England to learn the language and receive episcopal ordination, often went abroad. As an inducement, Compton sometimes promised good preferment to such as served overseas, on their return to England.[1]

Despite these fields of recruitment, and the inducements which the Bishop occasionally held out, the number of ministers working in the Plantations was small (as we have already seen) and one of the first things that Compton did after the formation of the Society was to draw up a list of all the parishes in the several colonies, including the West Indies, with the number of clergy working there.[2] Compton followed this up by sending a formal letter to the Society on 15 January, 1702, in which he asked that the bishops should direct their archdeacons to recommend to the Society suitable men for work overseas. The Committee agreed that a letter along these lines should be printed. In particular Compton suggested that the Bishops of Hereford and Bangor should try to secure Welsh ministers to go out to Pennsylvania.[3]

In February 1703,[4] the Bishop further sent to the Society a list of all the parishes in the Plantations which were themselves 'earnest for Ministers', and some of which (eleven) were willing and able to contribute towards their salary. In the same letter he enclosed a request from the parish of Burlington which he thought the Queen might be pleased 'in a considerable measure to contribute to'. The parishioners wanted—they were building a

[1] Sainsbury, *Calendar of State Papers, Colonial Series, America and West Indies,* 1675-1676, 1893, no. 784, p. 335.
[2] S.P.G. *Minutes,* 17 Oct., 1701.   [3] *Ibid.,* 15 Jan., 1703.
[4] Compton to Secretary, 19 Feb., 1703, S.P.G. *Letters,* no. 53.

church—'a Book of Common Prayer, a Cloth for the Communion Table, a Cushion and Pulpit Cloth, a barrel of Linseed Oils and colour suitable, and a Bell which may be heard at some distance'.

It is clear that the very fact of the Society's existence brought the needs of the Church in America more forcibly before Christians at home. Many reasons unfortunately discouraged recruits from coming forward. Living in America was hard and salaries precarious—a challenge no doubt to the more heroic, but not an inducement to weaker brethren. A hostile governor or a recalcitrant parishioner could make life almost intolerable.

It was Compton's life-long endeavour to secure an adequate and regular income for these ministers of the Gospel. First he endeavoured to persuade the Crown, through the Committee of the Lords of Trade and Plantations, to settle a permanent income on certain parishes, as he did successfully, for example, in the case of Holy Trinity, New York. From Charles II the Bishop also obtained a bounty of £20 for every schoolmaster or minister going out to the West Indies, a grant which was continued under James II and during the first few years of William III. When 'difficulties put a stop to it', Compton immediately intervened and on 3 January, 1698 sent in a petition to the Treasury that the gift be renewed, particularly in view 'of the great want there is in those parts through the sickness that has carried off many ministers in the Southern Plantations, the scarcity that is in Virginia, and particularly the erection of several new parishes in Maryland'.[1]

Many of the grants which Compton managed to persuade the Crown to give were of an *ad hoc* character and for particular people. For example, in 1677, he secured £20 to pay the fare of six ministers going to the Leeward Islands. James Cruickshank, years after, told Edmund Gibson how Compton by his 'assiduous application' had obtained from the Queen an allowance of £100 per annum while he was in the Islands as Chaplain, until he could be placed in a suitable living. When Mr. Johnston came over to England with his numerous family, he confessed that he 'must have starved had they not been relieved by the Bishop of London'.[2] For Blair, who certainly deserved such consideration, Compton secured £100 a year.

---

[1] Fortescue, *Calendar of State Papers, Colonial Series, America and West Indies*, 1694-1697, 1905, no. 148, p. 79.
[2] S.P.G. *Minutes*, 17 Oct., 1707.

At the meetings of the Society, Compton never failed, with almost monotonous insistence, to bring before its members cases of desperate need. Some of the letters which he received from the missionaries themselves made pathetic reading. Writing from Boston, one Harris expressed himself to the Bishop as follows: 'I have no family at present, but if I stay here, I find a married state will be more convenient, and that I may not bring upon myself ruin and misery, I hope your Lordship will pardon me for my solicitous care about my salary; 'tis now two years behind hand, and the welfare of my whole life depending upon it, I humbly beseech your Lordship to procure an Order from the Queen for the full payment of all my arrears at once; considering the multiplicity of your Lordship's Business, I am heartily grieved that I put your Lordship to this Trouble, and hope your Goodness will excuse me.'[1]

The case of Alexander Adams was also desperate. He had served three or four parishes in Maryland for a number of years, and during that time had received no salary, though the Society had promised him £50 a year. The Bishop took up the case vigorously on his behalf. 'It would be very hard upon me', he complained to the Society, 'and much more upon him to be thus disappointed by that which I am sure must be a very great mistake.'[2] Dr. Le Jau spoke for all his brethren in South Carolina when he protested to the Bishop: 'We live in a place where everything necessary for life is sold much dearer than in London. Our Allowance and Perquisites, whatever the name may be, prove in effect very inconsiderable. And those that have families, far from saving anything, are always behind hand tho' they live but meanly. Which makes us humbly Represent that some Addition to our Salaries would be an Act of Charity. Pardon my Lord my importunity.'[3]

Some of the missionaries—it was only natural—grew bitter as a result of their poverty. The Reverend J. Urmston of North Carolina found himself and his family, in 1711, in manifest danger literally of starving. 'We have', he said, going into details for the Bishop's advantage, 'lived many a day only on a dry crust and a draught of salt water out of the Sound. Such

---

[1] Harris to Compton, 8 Jan., 1712, Fulham MSS., Mass. Box, fo. 10.
[2] Compton to Society, 25 Mar., 1712, S.P.G. *Letters*, vol. 7A, no. 54.
[3] Le Jau to Compton, 23 Feb., 1713, Fulham MSS., South Carolina Box, fo. 2.

regard have the people for my labours—so worthy of the favour the Society have shewn them in providing missionaries and sundry books.'

This unhappy man should have received £100 per annum (with a house) from the parish: in fact he received £30 in five years and this was paid in paper money. No ordinary man could work effectively in such conditions. 'I need not', he continued, 'relate the difficulties and unheard of hardships I've here struggled with. I could not have fared worse at Malabar, and I protest were I in England,[1] I would not come hither again for five times as much as is allowed. I pray your Lordship to make the Society sensible of my misfortunes in being sent to such a wretched place and excite them to consider me whilst here and either provide better for me, or remove me to a Christian country—or else call me home.'[2]

His feelings as he wrote this pitiful letter to Fulham could not have been helped by the thought that he would have to wait at least six months for a reply. It is not surprising, perhaps, to read in the official history of the Society that this unhappy man later 'fell into disrepute'.[3]

Charles Bridges at Narragansett in 1709 found himself facing a similar financial crisis, and communicated his plight to the Bishop of London in the following words: 'I humbly beg your Lordship's favour towards my obtaining from the Society their allowance due to me as from the 25th of March 1708 since which time I have received nothing but have been forced to draw bills payable here, that I might have wherein to subsist hitherto; to this purpose I lay before the Society the state of my case that I may show what title I have to it. I depend in this and my other necessities on your Lordship's Goodness.'[4]

These heart-rending appeals never failed to stir the Bishop into action, and often his generous heart inclined him to forget the financial difficulties in which the Society was undoubtedly placed. Year in and year out he petitioned the Committee to relieve the poverty of its ministers—'for God's sake to shew pity' —sometimes also interceding with the Crown, and often himself

---

[1] He was formerly a curate of Eastham in Essex, in the Bishop's own diocese.
[2] Urmston to Compton, 21 Jan., 1712, Fulham MSS. North Carolina Box, fo. 36.　　　　[3] Pascoe, *op. cit.*, p. 850.
[4] Bridges to Compton, 17 June, 1709, Fulham MSS. Pennsylvania and Philadelphia Box, fo. 154.

volunteering to give money if the parishioners found a like sum. The question of finance sometimes led to a difference of opinion between the Society and the Bishop. It was one of Compton's principles that when a person of exceptional ability volunteered for service overseas he should be given 'more than ordinary encouragement'.[1] Such a person, for example, Compton thought he had discovered in the Reverend Samuel Coleby, 'whose whole intent is to do good', and who had volunteered to go to New Jersey. The Bishop insisted that £100 per annum must be found for him. 'I should be sorry to lose such a man that may do so much credit to the Church, which is not every day to be met with', he commented in a letter to the Society. But the Society would not fall into line, and there followed a 'rubb'. The Bishop let the Committee know how disappointed he was, 'for besides that there is a great Necessity for Missionaries in the Churches of the Jerseys, I look upon him as a person so particularly proper for it that he would certainly do the good of ten others'.[2] In these circumstances, would not the Society think again? It did so and Coleby was soon afterwards dispatched to Jamaica.

In December 1709, the Bishop of Worcester recommended 'an extraordinary man' to the Society, who was able to converse with the natives in their own language. Once again the Society, perhaps with undue nervousness, demurred, and once again the Bishop of London ('expensive Compton') rallied them on their excessive financial caution. There was no danger, he wrote, of having too many such men to provide for, 'but when such men do come our way, I think it ought to be our chiefest care and duty to ensure such an opportunity, cost what it will: especially since we have spread the fame of our Society so gloriously in foreign parts that if they should once see how little we have done in discharging ourselves of that Duty it will be little to our Reputation. I know to whom I write'.[3]

The Society itself was in a difficult position. Its own resources were meagre, though many settlers in America, and some missionaries, thought of it as possessing almost unlimited wealth. Nothing is more pathetic, for example, than a letter which the Bishop received from the parish of Dover in South Carolina,

---

[1] Compton to Society, 19 Dec., 1709, S.P.G. *Letters*, vol. 5A, no. 65.
[2] Same to same, 7 Dec., 1709, *ibid.*, no. 31.
[3] Same to same, 9 Dec., 1709, *ibid.*, no. 32.

on 3 August, 1703, imploring him to send a resident minister (which it had never had): 'We have been informed', so the letter ran, 'that a Society is formed in England for the Propagation of Christian Knowledge in America and a large stock laid in by the Contributions of Several many Good and Pious Persons (in which your Lordship as the Pattern of Piety and Goodness is greatly concerned) and that by this Society £2,000 p.a. is allowed for 40 ministers to be sent to America.'[1]

In fact, the financial situation of the Society, within a few years of its establishment, came to be quite serious. At a meeting in 1708, it was reported that the annual expenditure (i.e. commitments) already amounted to £1,200, and that its guaranteed income was only £762 15s. 6d. Such a situation could not go on, and the Society felt it necessary to inform two ministers, whom the Bishop of London recommended, that they 'could not entertain any more missionaries while the annual certain expenses of the corporation do so much exceed the Income of the same'. Later a resolution to maintain this prudential policy 'during the present state of the Society's revenues' was carried. This decision, however, seems (fortunately) to have been soon forgotten in practice. Nor was the Bishop of London any more happy at another resolution, namely, that the Society would not send out any more married men with families. In fact he continued to recommend such men, sometimes asking that the prohibition should 'be excepted in this case'.[2]

The first problem for the departing missionary was to find the money for the outgoing voyage, and to secure a passage within reasonable time. To obtain this the Bishop often urged the Society to expedite their approval of the prospective missionary. Thus in reference to three Scottish ministers in 1704, he pointed out that 'unless these gentlemen do get their passage in 2 Men of War that are going for the Plantations within a week, they will not meet with another opportunity for a long time'.[3] It was not uncommon for a missionary and his family to find themselves at Southampton waiting for a ship week after week, with the result that the money given them by the Society for the voyage was already spent on lodging before they had left this country.

---

[1] Vestry of Dover to Compton, 30 Aug., 1703, S.P.G. *Letters*, vol. 1A, no. 127.   [2] Compton to Secretary, 15 July, 1707, *ibid.*, vol. 3A, no. 70.
[3] S.P.G. *Minutes*, 4 Feb., 1703/4.

Such a case occurred with Mr. Cordiner and we quote at length his letter to the Society.

We have been five times out at sea, sometimes driven back by contrary Winds and once by the French as we supposed; but now have an order to wait for the Lisbon Fleet which I presume will be a month. I expected to have had a Bill from the Society before now according as they promised when I was in London, viz. that they would consider me next general meeting: my case is very hard and cannot be otherwise expected who has travelled upwards of 300 miles by land with 6 in family, stayed about 6 months in London and has been 3 months in this chargeable place. I came as soon on ship board as I could be admitted, and have been aboard so long that I expended most part of what I provided for my voyage and now have not wherewithall to get a fresh supply; unless being timely relieved by the Hon[ourable] Society I may be able to prosecute the good design, and endure the long wearisome voyage.'[1]

The Bishop took up his case with the Society (which had given him 'no favourable answer') and stressed the fact that this unfortunate man had been forced to sell most of his goods literally to keep his family alive. 'His case is deplorable', Compton wrote to the Society with some asperity, 'and therefore I beseech you to do him what kindness you can and prevail with the Society to pity his condition.'[2]

The difficulties which confronted Mr. Cordiner as he waited in penury for a boat were as nothing to what happened once he and his family got on board. Real adventure then began. On 10 October they left Plymouth on board H.M.S. *Chester*, which was part of a convoy of five men-of-war and two hundred merchant-men. At noon the next day they were engaged by fourteen French warships and H.M.S. *Chester* was in the thick of the battle. It caught fire several times, and thirty-seven men on the quarterdeck were either killed or wounded. The crew was taken prisoner and our missionary, with his family, were landed at Brest on 19 October. 'Then Mr. Cordiner', so he himself wrote, 'was offered provision for his mother, wife and children, if he would betake himself to a convent, and at Faziers and Dinan, Mr. Cordiner administered to his fellow prisoners, holding services on Sundays and Holy Days.' Life was not very

---

[1] Cordiner to Secretary, 3 July, 1707, S.P.G., *Letters*, vol. 3A, no. 60.
[2] Compton to Secretary, 21 June, 1707, *ibid.*, no. 59.

pleasant, however. He was 'several times . . . imprisoned for 2 or 3 hours, and daily threatened with close restraint and confinement'. During his captivity, one of his children died, and another child was born to his wife.

Yet despite all this, our indomitable minister, with his wife and family, eventually arrived in Maryland.

The voyage to America was certainly fraught with peril, and Mr. Cordiner's experience was by no means unique. The Reverend John Mitchell who, in a letter to Compton, said that he arrived in America 'as naked as ever I was born', could claim to have had an equally harrowing time.[1]

No wonder that Compton wrote to the Society: 'This war is a grievous thing to our Missionaries who are forced to be tossed and tumbled, that it costs them and us more for a free passage than if they had taken it in a Merchantman for a price. For God's sake incline as many as you can to have compassion in their next meeting, for if we do not support them under their disagreements we must expect no more good men to offer their service.'[2]

Each missionary once arrived was expected to send to the Society a report every six months, and the Society, through its Secretary, undertook to reply. Compton always recognised that a particular responsibility rested on him as diocesan and Father in God of these clergy working in distant lands. His correspondence with them was vast, and they certainly appreciated his constant concern.

On some occasions the Bishop's generous heart prompted him to think that the Society tended to be a little hard on its missionaries, and was, perhaps, too ready to apply discipline. We quote a case in point.

Two clergymen—Nichols and Rose—changed their parishes without leave of the Society, and the matter came up for discussion at the Committee. The Bishop, in a long letter, made it clear that while he did not wish to justify their actions, he yet thought that certain extenuating circumstances ought to be borne in mind. Finance, he pointed out, was the root cause. Nichols found that he could not subsist in Chester 'and therefore desired that he might have leave to go into Maryland which he

---

[1] J. Mitchell to Compton, 11 June, 1709, Fulham MSS. Jamaica Box, fo. 2.
[2] Compton to Secretary, 4 Sept., 1707, S.P.G. *Letters*, vol. 3A, no. 108.

took to be granted'—'and so did I too', commented the Bishop.[1]
He hoped, therefore, that the Society would not be over anxious
to pass judgment 'otherwise', he warned its members, 'I am
afraid, it will be a great discouragement for those that serve at so
great a distance to be deprived of any part of their subsistence
before they have had a fair time to give an Account of their
proceedings'.

As for Rose, the Bishop could not blame him for moving into
Chester when it became vacant because Jenkins, his Vicar, had
made life so difficult for him in Newcastle that he was 'in a
manner forced to retire for peace sake'. Yet even Mr. Jenkins
was an 'honest but forward young man . . . who may do a
great deal of good in that place where he is, and therefore I
hope you will punish him with a severe reprimand, and not take
his livelihood from him'.

The matter was under discussion at the Committee for some
time, and in a further letter to the Society asking them not to
come to a decision till he could be present, the Bishop again
commented: 'I am afraid that if you should go to this Extremity
for the first fault before you have admonished and reproved
them for this Irregularity, that the discouragement will be so
great as not only to call back those that are faulty but to affright
all those that are to succeed them. For to be so quick upon them,
after they have undergone so great and hazardous a Voyage and
before they know what they have to say for themselves would
make that disorder which is already amongst them become
irreparable.'[2]

This readiness to excuse, and reluctance to take disciplinary
action, was typical of Compton's temperament, and often drew
criticism upon him. When a poor clergyman, Wright by name,
sailed for the Plantations, having sold the books given him by
the Society, it was Compton who assured the Committee that
he would 'be ready to make satisfaction in a little time'.[3] As a
matter of fact, Wright had written to the Bishop from Plymouth
admitting his guilt but pleading that it was 'absolute poverty',
caused by his long delay, which had forced him reluctantly to
take this step. In his distress, it was 'his Lordship's Goodness and

[1] Compton to Secretary, 23 Dec., 1708, S.P.G. *Letters,* no. 67.
[2] Same to same, 18 Jan., 1709, *ibid.,* vol. 4A, no. 72.
[3] Same to same, 15 Apr., 1706, *ibid.,* vol. 2A, no. 14.

Compassion which your Lordship hath graciously pleased to promise me' upon which he depended.

For many missionaries who had safely survived the perils of the outward journey, their troubles began when they took up their duties. Their relations with one another were not always harmonious, and the ineffective authority of the Commissary meant the transference of many problems to Fulham, or to the Society, which by reason of the delays inevitable in such a procedure (and sometimes the pronouncing of judgments based on inadequate knowledge), would have been better dealt with on the spot. A few illustrations will indicate the difficulties.

In Compton's papers which remain at Fulham, the names of three ministers, Myles, Bridges, and Honeyman figure prominently. Bridges is first heard of at Boston, where he was curate to Myles. The relation of vicar and curate has never been found particularly easy, and it degenerated rapidly in this instance. Bridges was energetic and headstrong, a man of real ability, who lived his life in a continual state of emotional excitement and was temperamentally unsuited to work under another man. To quote Compton's own words: 'His spirit is too high [for] that subordination which is absolutely necessary whilst he stays in Boston.' His presence in the town divided the city, and the parishioners, to keep the peace, resorted to the practice of calling a vestry only on the joint summons of the vicar and the curate. It was inevitable that this dispute should eventually find its way to Fulham.

The Bishop immediately recognised that Bridges and Myles could not work together, and that Bridges must go. He therefore wrote a strong letter to the vestry of Boston on 12 February, 1705, which was read to them on 23 September, when the Governor himself was present. In this epistle the Bishop frankly blamed the members of the vestry for putting Bridges 'upon an equal foot with Mr. Myles [since] Mr. Bridges hath nothing more to do in the Church than what Mr. Myles shall direct him, as he is his curate and assistant'. 'Wherefore', the Bishop continued, 'you must pardon me if after all due regard I have for you, I must deal so plainly with you as to tell you that you have been carried too far in this matter by some that have more respect of Persons than for the real good and peace of the Church. I know I shall be forced at last to recall Mr. Bridges and

20

therefore I wish you would persuade him to make his choice to retire to some other place where he shall find me his sincere friend, notwithstanding all that has been said.' The Bishop himself advised Bridges to remove to Narragansett, where he would have 'an hundred pounds per annum stirling, beside what perquisites he may make upon the place, and there he will be his own Master'.[1]

Bridges wisely agreed to leave Boston, and was as good as his word. There was much for an energetic man to do in Narragansett, particularly among the Dutch; but unfortunately the Bishop, in his anxiety to get Bridges out of Boston, had been a little too optimistic about the salary. After six months in his new charge, Bridges was still without any money from the Society, which had not, in fact, officially sent him to this new scene of his labours. On 16 May, 1707, Compton anxiously requested the Committee to do something. Bridges meanwhile was determined not to suffer in silence—he was not that kind of man—and this disappointment, together with the faults of his own temperament, made his stay in Narragansett stormy. Complaints again reached the Bishop at Fulham alleging that Bridges was 'an improper person to be employed as a minister', and that his conduct caused the heathen to despise the faith.

As a result, Bridges suddenly left Narragansett and turned up again at Boston, when he proceeded once more to unsettle the inhabitants and particularly his former vicar, Mr. Myles.[2] From Boston he went on to Newport, Rhode Island, where the minister, named Honeyman, had been sent to the town by Lord Cornbury, as a temporary help, but had proved so acceptable that in October the churchwardens petitioned the Bishop that he might be formally licensed to their city. At the same time they asked the Bishop 'to ignore approaches' which might reach him from 'a set of People whose lives are infamous'.

Mr. Honeyman—not unnaturally—viewed the arrival of Bridges with considerable alarm, for the latter, obviously a forceful personality, was never inactive. Such fears were soon confirmed, for Bridges immediately set up in opposition to Honeyman, and in some extraordinary way ' violently intruded '

[1] Compton to Boston Vestry, 23 Sept., 1706, Fulham MSS. Massachusetts Box, fo. 119.
[2] S.P.G. Letters, vol. 3A. See nos. 3, 7, 15.

himself, turning out the Vicar from his church, and once again dividing the parish into two factions.[1]

We need not detail the long and involved proceedings in this unhappy dispute. In due course the case came before the Society, when Compton immediately protested against any attempt to withhold Honeyman's salary while the matter was *sub judice*. It would leave him, he protested, 'utterly broke'. Even the sympathetic Bishop, however, was now beginning to grow somewhat weary of Bridges and his wanderings. His 'deportment' he told the Society, 'hath been so perfidious and insolent that he may thank himself for the trouble he undergoes'.[2] Yet the Bishop decided to give him one more chance. 'The man can do well if he pleases', he wrote, 'and therefore I shall be humbly of opinion, if the Society so think fit, to send him either to the Jerseys or to Maryland, that the Flames he hath kindled about New England may be extinguished.'

Thus once again Charles Bridges was on the move, but it is good to know that the Bishop's confidence in him was not finally misplaced. In 1709 he went to Rye in New England, where he remained till his death on 22 May, 1719.

We should also like to feel that Samuel Myles of Boston, after he had managed to rid himself of Bridges, passed the rest of his days in some degree of peace. On the whole, this seems to have been the case. In 1708 Compton procured another assistant for him in the person of one Harris, and in view of former difficulties, the Bishop sent a letter to the Vestry on 8 May, 1708, defining his status, this letter being read, in the presence of the Governor, on 1 April, 1709. It is a curious document, however, because in spite of what had previously happened in Boston, it reads very ambiguously.

Yet the relationship between Myles and Harris appears to have been perfectly harmonious, which says a great deal for both men. We quote the Bishop's letter, so that the reader may make his own judgment upon it.

Having appointed Mr. Harris to go over Assistant to the Minister at Boston for his better satisfaction, I have thought fit to declare That as he is not to go under the absolute command of Mr. Myles, yet he is to pay a respect to him in all reasonable things and take an

[1] S.P.G. *Minutes*, 1 July, 1708.
[2] Compton to Secretary, 26 July, 1708, S.P.G. *Letters*, vol. 4A, no. 24.

equal share with him in supplying the Church, but not to meddle in anything that relates to Perquisites whether for Marriages, Burials, or Christenings, and to be content with what is allotted him from hence, and by all means to avoid the Insinuation of any that shall attempt to make matters uneasy betwixt him and Mr. Myles, whom I do likewise require to receive this his Assistant with all fair and good Usage, and that they both conspire with so good an understanding that nothing may creep in to make a breach between them, and that they do agree to relate all stories that shall be whispered to them publicly in the next Vestry, that such little make-baits may be discouraged and made ashamed of such base behaviour; and therefore I desire likewise that this paper may be read in a full Vestry that they may be Witnesses of your sincere Conformity to what is appointed.[1]

Church life in Boston was never uneventful, and a considerable correspondence was kept up with Fulham. In a letter of thanks to the Bishop on 7 July, 1710, Myles complained of 'the unjust censure and malicious calumnies of such turbulent malcontents as are set and rife for any mischief'—but of Mr. Harris, he wrote: '. . . he hath carried well since his arrival and hath moved in his proper sphere, and never attempted any disturbance or to encroach on any of my Rights and Privileges.' There then followed a comment which shows what a zealous letter writer the Bishop of London could be. 'I again renew my request', Myles wrote, 'that your Lordship would resolve against Answering Private Letters from every Makepot Fellow, such notice making 'em conceited and insolent . . . and that your Lordship would please bear in mind the resolve your Lordship made and gave me in a Letter, March 22, 1706.'[2]

We must not exaggerate the effect of these personal disagreements or allow them to loom too large. George Keith, who in 1702 visited the churches in Boston, Rhode Island, New York, and Philadelphia, reported to the Bishop that to his 'great satisfaction and joy I did find great regularity and good order. The Ministers in very good repute among all, and the People devout in the Public Worship of God, and Generally of good morals.' At Philadelphia, he said, he had preached seven times, sometimes to as many as a thousand people, some of whom were Quakers and Presbyterians. 'If in all other places', he commented, 'the

---

[1] Fulham MSS. Massachusetts Box, fo. 118.
[2] Myles to Compton, 7 July, 1710, *ibid.*, fo. 5.

Ministry and People were so pious, so moral and so regular as I have found them in these Places where I have travelled, the Church of England would be in great esteem and greatly prosper."[1]

Compton's unfailing charity, to which we have so often called attention, did not prevent his being severe on occasions, and there were times when he was forced reluctantly to call a missionary home. Pritchard of Rye so 'discouraged' his people, that the Bishop came to regard him as unsuitable for a colonial ministry and he summoned him back to England. In Newfoundland, the religious life was not happy, and it was difficult not to come to the conclusion that this was very largely due to 'the violent temper and scandalous life of Mr. Jackson the minister'. The Bishop accordingly recalled him, and replaced him with Jacob Rice (whose 'sermons and prayers' had very much impressed the Society), thereby earning the gratitude of the inhabitants.[2] It seems that Mr. Jackson remained a problem on his return, though the Bishop in his kindness gave him a small living to prevent him from starving.

One of the great problems confronting the missionary in the Plantations was the difficulty in obtaining books, both for his own private reading and for the parish. The Society often gave a grant when the minister went out, and the Bishop frequently made the Committee aware of the specific need for controversial literature against the Quakers and Dissenters, and (of course) the Roman Catholics: and at other times he urged it to send out Prayer Books, Books of Canons, and Tables of Affinity.

The slave trade to America, one of the most sordid chapters in early colonisation, presented a terrible problem to the more conscientious missionaries. Not that they were opposed to slavery as such, but they were genuinely horrified at the brutality of many planters, and thwarted at every turn by their opposition (for economic reasons) to any evangelisation of the slave population. Many were the letters of protest which Compton received expressing the indignation of the missionaries at the obstructive tactics of the planters. 'Permit me my Lord', wrote the humane

---

[1] Keith to Compton, 26 Feb., 1703, S.P.G. *Letters*, vol. I, no. 103.

[2] S.P.G. *Minutes*, 18 May, 1705. See also Headlam, *Calendar of State Papers, Colonial Series, America and West Indies*, 1706-1708; 1916, no. 192, p. 82.

Francis Le Jau from Gorse Creek, 'to Implore your Favour
and Charity on behalf of the poor slaves that live amongst us.
They are suffered, some forced to work upon Sundays; having
no other means to subsist they are used very cruelly many of
them; the Generality of the Masters oppose that they should
know anything of Christianity. I earnestly beg that those
evils may, if possible, be remedied, but whether this be a
proper time to desire such a Reformation, I humbly submit to
your Lordship.'[1]

Giles Ramsford of North Carolina informed the Bishop (in
1712) that he had managed to baptise some of the negroes, 'tho'
with much difficulty I obtained the leave for so doing from their
Masters'.[2] Thus early was the Christian Faith in the Plantations
having a disturbing effect on the rights of property! The missionaries were certainly concerned that the negroes should receive
the Gospel—as many letters show—and that they should be
treated with humanity, but they did not go so far as to question
the legal status of the slave. So far back as 1680 the Committee
of the Lords of Trade and Plantations had discussed the question
of baptism, and the suggestion was then made that slaves should
be given 'vilein rights'. In 1706 Nicholson wrote to the Society
of the 'vulgar error' which many negroes entertained in Virginia
that baptism meant manumission, and the Society requested the
Archbishop of Canterbury and the Bishop of London to wait
upon the Queen in order to secure such 'declaration laws' as
would make the position 'unambiguous'. The result seems to
have been an Act of Parliament which declared 'that no
Negro or other Servant who shall hereafter be baptised shall be
hereby enfranchised, nor shall such baptism be construed to
be any Manumission of such Negro or Servant'. It is ironic
that the Bill was entitled: 'For converting the Negroes in the
Plantations'.[3]

One of Compton's particular interests was the energetic
evangelisation of the native Indians, and he never failed to exert
himself to this end. Once again it was not popular with the
Planters nor with the Government, for reasons which the follow-

[1] Le Jau to Compton, 27 May, 1712, Fulham MSS. South Carolina Box,
fo. 10.
[2] Ramsford to Compton, 25 July, 1712, *ibid.*, fo. 33.
[3] Lambeth MSS. 941, fo. 72.

ing extract from a letter of Francis Le Jau to Compton
makes clear.

> I don't hear of any Design, nor indeed any Inclination hitherto,
> that Missionaries should be sent among our Indian Neighbours.
> . . . The Indian traders have always discouraged me by raising
> a world of Difficulty when I proposed anything to them relating
> to the conversion of the Indians. It appears they do not care to
> have Clergymen so near them who doubtless would never ap-
> prove those perpetual wars they promote amongst the Indians
> for the only reason of making slaves to pay for their trading
> goods, and what slaves, poor women and children, for the men
> taken prisoners are burnt most barbarously. I am informed it was
> done so this year, and the women and children were brought
> among us to be sold.[1]

In May 1705 the Bishop, on his own authority, granted a
licence to Elias Neau, a schoolmaster, to act as a 'catechist' to
the Indians and Negroes in New York.[2] Compton's own keen-
ness often made him think that the Society was a little too
cautious in its championship of this kind of evangelisation. For
himself, he gave his wholehearted support to schemes for educating Indian children at the College in Virginia, and was enthusiastically behind Mr. Masterman, in his design to labour among
the Chouan Indians, even rallying the Society at their delay in
approving it. 'So good a work', he wrote to the secretary,
'should be Promoted with all Imaginable Speed and Application.'
But the latter scheme hung fire, prudential and financial considerations making the Society hesitate.

In January 1713, the Bishop, now over eighty years of age,
returned to the attack. He writes:

> It is my earnest Request that they [i.e. the Committee] should take
> into their consideration anew what I represented to them from the
> Gov[ernment] of Virginia because I do not believe they have any
> Affaire under their Care that more naturally regards the trust of
> the Commission, when they consider it is most properly for the
> propagation of the faith in Foreign Parts, [than] to bring up the
> Children of the Heathen in the Knowledge of Christianity, & to
> embrace so fair an opportunity of bringing over parents by Building

---

[1] Le Jau, 27 May, 1712, to Compton, Fulham MSS. South Carolina Box,
fo. 10.

[2] Neau was a refugee who had suffered imprisonment in France.

a Church amongst them at their own Request. I should think that we could not too speedily lay hold upon this occasion, especially when it may be done at so easy an Expense, & therefore I hope they will not delay it so long as to refer it to Col. Nicholson to repeat it when he arrives there, since nothing more properly requires a speedy care.[1]

If the Bishop's physical frame was fast decaying, the powers of his mind were still unimpaired.

Around New York there was a considerable Dutch Colony, and it was the Bishop's private hope that these people, with the right kind of encouragement, might be willing to conform to the Church of England. For this purpose, the Bishop ordained a Dutchman, Beyse, and appointed him, as an experiment, to Haarlem in New York. The continuance of his salary was made dependent on the conformity of his congregation. For a time the mission seemed to be successful, and in 1711 it was reported that Beyse 'had gained the most considerable of the inhabitants at Haarlem'. The Society, however, was not optimistic concerning the final success of the scheme, and in May 1713 the Bishop protested against the stopping of Beyse's salary 'without giving him Notice before hand as he ought to have had'.[2] But the mission did not survive the year and was closed.

And so we might go on to quote numerous instances of the Bishop's care for those working in these distant lands. Perhaps, once again, his most significant contribution lay in his making these missionaries feel that they had a Father in God, who had their interests very close to his warm heart.

[1] Compton to Society, 2 May, 1713, S.P.G. *Letters*, vol. 9A, no. 21.
[2] Same to same, 17 Jan., 1713, *ibid.*, vol. 7A, no. 48.

PART III

A UNIVERSAL BISHOP

CHAPTER SIXTEEN

'THE DISTRESSED CHURCH OF SCOTLAND'

O N 2 August, 1709, James Greenshields, writing to the
Bishop of London as a stranger, explained that he would
not have troubled him but for 'the knowledge that I have
of your Lordship's being a chief Supporter of the distressed
Church of Scotland'.[1] The following chapter is a commentary
upon this judgment.

At the time when the bloodless Revolution was taking place in
England, the Scottish bishops met in Edinburgh, on 3 November,
1688, and agreed on a loyal address to King James II. A month
later they commissioned Alexander Rose, Bishop of Edinburgh,
and Andrew Bruce, Bishop of Orkney, to go to London in
support of the King, and for this purpose to confer with William
Sancroft.

Rose (1647-1720) was a man of conservative temperament,
genuinely devoted to the twin causes of episcopacy and monarchy. Unfortunately Andrew Bruce fell ill, and the Bishop of
Edinburgh was left to undertake the journey alone, which
circumstance had the unforeseen result of making him entirely
responsible for difficult decisions, fraught with great significance
for the future. By the time the Bishop arrived in London, James
had fled, and nobody quite knew what was to happen next.
Sancroft, who might have helped him, confessed that he and
the bishops were far too perplexed with their own situation to
be able to advise others. Francis Turner, Bishop of Ely, gave
Rose all the help he could, but others, for example William
Lloyd, Bishop of St. Asaph, were far from sympathetic.

Meanwhile disquieting news was travelling down from
north of the border, harrowing stories of the persecution of the
episcopal clergy by the Presbyterians, and the sudden rising of
the Camerons in the west of Scotland. Rose felt that at least he
must do what he could to stop this 'rabbling' of his fellow
clergy, and he approached Gilbert Burnet, who was then, as

[1] James Greenshields to Compton, 2 Aug., 1709, Bod. Rawlinson MSS. 985,
C, fo. 94.

always, very much in the confidence of William, only to be met with a peremptory reply that Scotsman though he was, he did not presume to meddle with Scottish affairs. After this rebuff Rose approached Compton, who had not long sheathed the sword he had drawn in defence of the Constitution, asking him to use his influence with the Prince of Orange to protect the episcopal clergy in Scotland. The Bishop was at this time full of enthusiasm for the Revolution and not therefore particularly sensitive to the scruples of the conscientious Bishop of Edinburgh, though he was kind and considerate to Rose personally. He could not do anything himself, he said, but he advised a direct approach to William, in which counsel he was seconded by George Mackenzie, first Viscount Tarbat, and other Scottish peers.[1] Such advice presented a real problem, particularly to one of Rose's known views, and he found himself in a genuine dilemma. William was now no longer merely the Prince of Orange summoned to assist in the calling of a free parliament. On 13 February, 1689, both houses of the Convention Parliament had waited upon the Prince and Princess and in their presence had read an address 'that William and Mary, Prince and Princess of Orange, be and are declared King and Queen of England, France and Ireland'.

Accordingly Rose was informed 'that in any approach he now made to the Prince, he must address him in his new style and congratulate him on rescuing the country from popery and slavery'. What was he to do? He had originally come to London to wait upon James II, and even if he could forget his own feelings towards the exiled monarch, he had as yet received no instructions from his brethren how to act in this unexpected situation.

The Bishop of Edinburgh's natural inclination was to return to his own country and thus get out of a situation which pressed heavily upon him. He would have been wise to do so, and in fact made preparations for his journey, but found that a pass from the King was necessary. He therefore again made application to Compton who was insistent that Rose should see the King before he departed. Compton then took the initiative in seeing William, who, though he refused to receive either Episcopalians or Presbyterians as a body, yet agreed to

[1] John Skinner, *An Ecclesiastical History of Scotland*, London, 1788, ii. 520. The exact course of Rose's negotiations in London is a little obscure.

meet two of either party to discuss Scottish affairs. The King on his part took the opportunity of having a confidential talk with the Bishop, leaving him to pass on what he thought fit to the bewildered Bishop of Edinburgh. Compton later confided to Rose:

> You see my Lord, the King having thrown himself upon the water, must keep himself a swimming with one hand. The Presbyterians have joined him closely and offer to support him, and therefore he cannot cast them off, unless he could see how otherwise he could be served. And he bids me tell you that he now knows the State of Scotland much better than he did when he was in Holland. For while there he was made to believe that Scotland generally all over was Presbyterian, but now he sees that the great body of the nobility and gentry are for Episcopacy and it is the trading and inferior sort that are for Presbytery. Wherefore he bids me tell you, that if you will undertake to serve him, to the purpose that he is served here in England, he will take you by the hand, support the Church and Order, and throw off the Presbyterians.[1]

It may be that Compton has here somewhat exaggerated the sentiments of William in order to overcome the hesitancy of the Bishop of Edinburgh. The meaning was perfectly clear, however. There could be no support unless the Episcopalians were as sincere in their attachment to the new government as were the Presbyterians. The Bishop of London did not as yet feel very 'tender' towards the scruples of his brother of Edinburgh. 'All this time you have been here', he complained, 'neither have you waited on the King, nor have any of your brethren, the Scottish Bishops.'[2]

Rose felt that he must offer some explanation, and he replied:

> My Lord, I cannot but humbly thank the Prince for this frankness and offer; but withal I must tell your Lordship that when I came from Scotland neither my brethren nor I apprehended any such revolution as I have now seen in England; and therefore I neither was nor could be instructed by them what answer to make to the Prince's offer: And therefore what I say is not in their name, but only my own private opinion, which is that I truly think they will not serve the Prince so as he is served in England; that is, as I take it, to make him their king, or give their suffrages for his being king.

[1] John Skinner, *op. cit.*, ii. 5, 23.   [2] *Ibid.*, ii. 522, 523.

And though as to this matter I can say nothing in their name, and and as from them, yet for myself I must say, that rather than do so I will abandon all the interest that either I have, or may expect to have in Britain.[1]

Commenting on this interview between the bishops, John Skinner the eighteenth century ecclesiastical historian of Scotland, writes: 'What grounds Bishop Compton had for making such a proposal, or with what propriety of character, a proposal of that kind, and under such an alternative, could come from a Bishop, I shall not take upon me to say. But by this narrative from Bishop Rose's own pen, which none who ever heard of the narrator will doubt the truth of, we may see how matters had been concerted, and what secret encouragements the rabblers had to depend on in their early and illegal attacks upon the Episcopal Church.'[2]

The Bishop of Edinburgh reluctantly agreed to go to White-hall on the day after his interview with Compton. The outcome was tragic indeed. As soon as William saw the Bishop come in, he left his company, walked over and addressed himself directly to Rose, without finesse or introduction. He hoped, he said, that the Bishop would be 'kind' to him, and 'follow the example of England'. It was a dramatic moment, and the issue, in human terms, was immense. The Bishop may have been taken by surprise at the King's directness in raising the one topic he did not wish to discuss. His reply was dignified, formal and correct. 'Sir', he said, 'I will serve you as far as the law, reason or conscience will allow me.' The King's reaction was immediate and characteristic. Without uttering a word, he turned on his heel and went back to his former company.

Rose had certainly discharged his own conscience in the matter and in this respect he could have done no other, but it proved to be an act of ecclesiastical suicide. Whether William could have effectively helped the Episcopalians in Scotland at this time is one of those questions which we cannot answer: but what is certain is that the attitude of Rose, and those who thought like him, made him less inclined to try. There was now nothing more for Rose to do in London, and he returned home, regretful perhaps that he had been persuaded to stay in the south so long.

---

[1] Quoted J. H. Overton, *The Nonjurors*, 1902, p. 423.
[2] John Skinner, *op. cit.*, ii. 522-3.

Compton, as events proved, would have been wiser if he had kept the Bishop of Edinburgh from meeting the King, and if he had advised him to return north some weeks earlier.

The Bishop was not long back in his native country before there was held a meeting of the Scottish Convention of Estates, at which the President, William Douglas, third Duke of Hamilton, informed Rose from the King that 'nothing should be done to the prejudice of Episcopalians in Scotland in case the bishops should by any means be brought to befriend his interest'. William, it is clear, was still reluctant to accept that the whole Episcopal Church would follow the lead of the Bishop of Edinburgh. But Rose did not make matters easier for his brethren. At the opening of the Convention (14 March, 1689) he prayed for the restoration of James II, for which indiscretion he was rebuked by a resolution of the House: and he also refused to sign the declaration (16 March) that the Convention was a free and lawful Parliament. Such a policy proved fatal, because it played into the hands of the Presbyterians, and left William unable, and perhaps somewhat disinclined, to help the Episcopalians.

The King's personal interests (as we have already suggested in another chapter) were not primarily religious, certainly not in any narrow sense, and his main preoccupation in Scotland was to prevent the country becoming a centre of Jacobite disaffection. But so far as was consistent with this over-riding demand of public safety, he was not unwilling to do something for the Episcopal Church north of the border. In the Coronation Oath, for example, he refused to swear 'to root out heretics and enemies of the true worship of God', but on the contrary 'required an assurance that persecution for religious opinions was not intended and himself made a declaration in favour of toleration'. What the King really desired was to unite under his government all Protestant subjects loyal to the Revolution, and to leave to men's individual consciences the question of their exact religious faith.

The unfortunate result of Rose's attitude, however, was to make it evident that many Scottish Episcopalians were not fully loyal to the throne, and that they might at any time become a Jacobite fifth column. This fact had disastrous consequences, for never was there a time when they needed royal protection more, since they were suffering acutely in their parishes from the violence of angry Presbyterians and also from the hostility of Parliament. On 11 April a declaration against Episcopacy was passed, and this was followed, on 13 April, by an enactment enjoining all ministers to take the oaths to William and Mary and inviting parishioners to inform on those who refused to comply.[1]

Many Presbyterians, however, did not need to be encouraged by proclamations or Acts of Parliament. They simply took the law into their own hands, and 'rabbled' the episcopal clergy out of hearth and home. The suppressed emotions of the last fifty years were now released and mob violence was the inevitable result. It is not surprising that the ejected clergy found it almost impossible to secure any legal redress of grievances. The King, on his part, was still anxious to settle upon a formula of subscription which could be taken by the vast majority of Episcopalians. Thus he wrote personally, both to the General Assembly, urging it to accept all who signed the declaration, and to the Episcopal clergy, instructing them to make their addresses to this body, after which he would take them under his protection. The Assembly, however, was more eager to revenge the past than to concern itself with securing a toleration of this kind, and it decided that political loyalty was not enough: only those Episcopalians were to retain their livings who subscribed to the Confession of Faith and the Presbyterian form of government.

No matter how intolerant the Presbyterians might be, no one could deny that they were intensely loyal, and that their legal establishment worked for the security of the throne. A few episcopally ordained ministers, who were willing to subscribe to the Confession of Faith and acknowledge the Presbyterian form of Church government, managed to retain their benefices, especially in outlying districts which remained Episcopalian in sentiment; and others officiated in private meeting houses: but the Episcopal Church as such was both unofficial and illegal.

The position was the more complicated because, as we have seen, this Church now contained two parties. One consisted of those clergymen who had taken the oaths of allegiance to William and Mary, and were thus loyal supporters of the Revolution of 1688. Their quarrel was not with the Government but with the

[1] Bod. Rawlinson MSS. 985 C, fo. 18.

Presbyterian Church: they believed in Episcopacy, and since they could not conform to the Kirk, they fell under the civil and religious ban of the Presbyterian authorities. The other party, which included most of the Scottish bishops, and a majority of the episcopal clergy, consisted of those who opposed both the Revolution in England and the Presbyterian form of Church government. These men could not in conscience take the oath of allegiance, and some of them quite definitely associated themselves with the 'King over the water'. They thus fell under a legal disability in both countries.

English churchmen, however, could not but regard with sympathy the sufferings of their brethren in the northern kingdom, and even such a good whig as Thomas Tenison drew up a *Memorial concerning the Episcopal Clergy in Scotland*, which was designed in their interests.[1] Henry Compton's warm heart inevitably went out to them, and his real concern made him come to be regarded as their special protector among the English bishops. Many were the letters which came to him throughout the later years of his episcopate recounting the sufferings of these dispossessed clergy.

Perhaps a few typical cases of hardship, particulars of which found their way to Fulham and are preserved amongst the Bishop's papers, may best illustrate the general situation.

James Gordon was ordained in 1689 by the Bishop of Aberdeen and in 1692 went to Foveran. In 1694 he was declared an intruder by the Committee of the General Assembly. Against this decision he appealed to his Majesty's Council in London, which sustained him in office until April 1696. This assertion of jurisdiction from Westminster, so far from protecting him, added to his misfortunes, for the Presbyterians did their best to break up his services, and on one occasion armed dragoons were employed for this purpose. In disgust James Gordon left his home to help his father in a parish some twenty miles distant, but even this move did not secure him peace and tranquillity, for the Presbyterians now threatened to eject the father for befriending the son. In his extremity Gordon appealed to the Bishop of London.[2]

---

[1] Lambeth MSS. 929, fo. 10.
[2] Bod. Rawlinson MSS. 985 C, fo. 26. *A brief account of the severe maltreatment which Mr. James Gordon, an episcopal minister, did meet with from the Presbyterians in Scotland.*

George Dunbar, minister of Haddington, came home from taking a funeral to be confronted by a Presbyterian clergyman, armed with a commission from the Presbytery at Glasgow, declaring the living vacant and himself the minister—a declaration which all Dunbar's efforts could not undo. He accordingly addressed himself to the Bishop of London.[1]

James Hay, 'a true genuine son of the Church, a modest humble presbyter and an excellent preacher', was living in 1698 at Gogar, about twenty-four miles from Edinburgh, in solitude with his 'poor family'. Both the Archbishop of Glasgow and the Bishop of Orkney urged him to make the journey south to seek an audience with the Bishop of London since he was distinguished for his 'generous goodness to all such as can be useful to the Church'.[2] So Mr. Hay called upon the Bishop, who not only promised to do something for him individually, but also assured him that he was as active as possible on behalf of the Scottish clergy generally. Andrew Bruce, Bishop of Orkney, acknowledged the Bishop of London's interest in a warm letter. 'I was exceedingly pleased', he wrote, 'with the account Mr. Hay gave me of your Lordship listening so patiently to what I had given him Commission to Represent concerning me, and that your Lordships did not only with Compassion regret the hard circumstances those of our Order in the Church, and particularly myself, were in but fully signified your design to interpose for procuring to us all the favour [that] is now possible.'[3]

The irregular proceedings described in these letters indicate what was going on all over Scotland. A large number of episcopal ministers were as a result penniless, and their families suffered real hardship. Most of them had no possibility whatever of exercising their ministry in their own country, and they were thus forced to look elsewhere. Here Compton did his best to help them and not without some measure of success, both in finding them work (i.e. those who would take the oaths) and also in raising money for the support of their families. Such help as he gave proved at times an embarrassment to him, for so energetic was he, that unkind critics used to accuse him of 'taking much more care to

[1] Dunbar to Compton, 8 Dec., 1702, Bod. Rawlinson MSS. 985 C, fo. 45.
[2] Patterson to Compton, 31 May, 1698, *ibid.*, fo. 32.
See also Bruce to Compton, 3 June, 1698, *ibid.*, fo. 24.
[3] Andrew Bruce to Bishop of London, 30 Aug., 1698, *ibid.*, fo. 36.

prefer Scotchmen than the honest clergy of the Church of England'.[1]

An obvious territory where clergy were needed was the American Plantations. James Blair, the Bishop of London's Commissary in Virginia, was a Scotsman, and Compton was only too ready to encourage him in his willingness to surround himself with men from his own country.[2]

To other Scotsmen he gave parishes in England, as for example, Robert Falconer, who became Vicar of Dunmow, and Thomas Dunbar, Rector of Kelvedon, both parishes being in Essex.[3] Nor can we think that the fourteen Scottish clergy reported to be in London in February 1695, went away empty handed.[4]

Yet though Compton applied himself diligently to providing a ministry for these dispossessed clergy outside their own country, this did not remove the poverty with which many of them continued to be oppressed. The only practical way to relieve their discomfiture was to provide hospitality for them in England, or to raise money to support them in Scotland, until such time as they were able to resume their ministry elsewhere, or secure government help along the lines indicated by Tenison's *Memorial*.[5]

The immediate problem, therefore, was money, and Henry Compton took the initiative in organising a public subscription and in securing collections in the parishes. In 1694 various people seem to have taken charge of these money raising efforts in different parts of the country. Mr. Lauder, for example, accounted to the Bishop for monies he had received from 14 March, 1693 to 19 November, 1694—a sum which included donations from Lord Nottingham, Sir William Godolphin, Dr. Beveridge, Dr. Gouge and the Duchess of Monmouth.[6] Mr. Lauder hoped himself to obtain some pickings, in return for 'the incredible pains and trial of my collecting'.[7]

[1] Thomas Hearne, *Remarks and Collections,* ed. C. F. Doble, Oxford, 1889, i. 304.   [2] See p. 267.

[3] Anthony Wood, *Athenae Oxoniensis*, 1691/2, ed. John Gutch, col. 969.

[4] Bod. Rawlinson MSS. 985 C, fo. 30, *List of the Scots Clergy at present in London.*

[5] Tension suggested that certain revenues out of the endowments of the Episcopal Church be legally devoted to them. See Edward Carpenter, *The Life & Times of Thomas Tenison,* p. 388.

[6] Princess Anne gave £44 to this collection.

[7] Bod. Rawlinson MSS. 985 C, fo. 28.

Unfortunately—as so often happened in the case of the French refugees—there were protests by some of the Scots clergy who thought that Mr. Lauder had already had more than his fair share. They complained that the funds had been misapplied and that the expense sheet was too heavy. Compton wisely ordered an investigation which was undertaken by Dr. Lancaster and the Dean of Windsor. They reported that Mr. Lauder had received in all some £84, and that of this he had disbursed £35 11s. 6d. to four poor clergy, leaving him with over £48, part of which he had sent to his own family.[1]

It is not surprising that some of the Scottish Episcopal clergy, faced with such poverty—that is, those who were willing to acknowledge William and Mary—began to feel that they were having the worst of all possible worlds. They were persecuted by the Presbyterians as Episcopalians: they were despised by their brethren, the Jacobite Episcopalians, as time-servers and traitors. Alexander Cairncross, Bishop of Raphoe, writing to Henry Compton from Edinburgh on 4 January, 1698, expressed their feelings of frustration as follows:

> The Loyal, regular Clergy in and about the City having again sent up (as frequently before) their humble Address to the King's Majesty expressing their sincere and constant loyalty and imploring his protection and favour, to be tendered by your Lordship's hand & Moderation, I cannot [but add] both my certain knowledge & Christian compassion for their sufferings. They and their families, . . . are slighted by the Jacobites for their Loyalty & affection to the present Government; they are hated by the Presbyterians for their serving under episcopacy . . . and whatever may be the inclinations . . . of the Government towards Episcopacy in the Church at this juncture, yet I hope the poor subordinate suffering clergy may be put in a capacity to serve the Church under the King's immediate protection, they giving all the assurances of their Loyalty unto the King's Majesty that the law may require of them.[2]

A few days later these same clergy themselves despatched a pathetic petition to Compton which contained the following words:

> If these happily come to your Lordship's hands either by Mr. Alexander Loish our Reverend Brother or otherwise, we can make

---

[1] Bod. Rawlinson MSS. 985 C, fo. 31.

[2] Alexander Cairncross to the Bishop of London, 4 Jan., 1698, Bod. Rawlinson MSS. 985 C, fo. 38.

no apology for our present presumption but absolute necessity that enforced us. Our sad and long sufferings have so disabled us that we are not in a capacity to send one of our number to offer our address to his Majestie. My Lord, the known sympathies you have always had for poor suffering Churchmen hath prevailed with us humbly to beg your assistance that our address may reach his Majesty's hands. The number of those that have formerly addressed with us are about four score, most of which are necessitated to seek for bread among their friends, a few only now residing in and about the city.[1]

William, as we have said before, had no personal desire that the loyal Episcopalians in Scotland should suffer from the animosity of their Presbyterian countrymen. He was never a religious bigot, and the repeated stories of what was going on north of the border induced him to hold a Conference at Whitehall. As a result of this meeting he agreed that 'the whole Episcopal Clergy in Scotland at present in the exercise of their Ministry should be preserved, without any restriction or distinction betwixt such as had entered their Churches before the Revolution, or such as have entered since the establishment of Presbytery'.

But the King was forced to face political facts. The opposition against such a policy was too strong and such resolutions remained a dead letter.

The accession of Anne raised fresh hopes in many episcopalian breasts, for she was known to be eager to do something for them, and was regarded as less of a statesman than William, and consequently not so inclined to consult political expediency. But the old difficulty remained—the division in the episcopalian ranks between those who would, and those who would not, own the present Government. This division had crippled William's efforts on their behalf for it had encouraged Presbyterian intolerance and thus made persecution more easy. The nonjuring right wing had consistently prevented any effective approach to the throne, and this at a time when many Englishmen regarded the return of James as highly probable.

The death of this exiled King, however, in 1701, seemed to offer an opportunity for even the more sensitive of Episcopalians to overcome their scruples. At least their oaths to James could no longer stand in the way of Anne, unless they were

[1] Bod. Rawlinson MSS. 985 C, fo. 100. 8 Jan., 1698.

committed to the principle of hereditary succession, and even here the fiction of the warming-pan might well come to their aid. So thought the Archbishop of Glasgow, who wrote to Compton on 15 October, 1702, recalling the indulgence granted to Presbyterian ministers by Charles II, and suggesting that a like tolerance should be given to the episcopal clergy. 'What the Queen may do in the present circumstances as to any favourable Indulgence to suffering loyal episcopal clergy and to broken subjects of the episcopal persuasion, I presume not to prescribe.'[1] But protection, he recognised, must depend on loyalty. Nor was the Archbishop of Glasgow alone in thinking this way.

Soon after the death of William, the Bishops in Scotland had received a petition from a large number of their clergy asking for guidance as to what they should do now that Anne was on the throne.[2] As a result, the Bishops met, but they could not come to a common mind. The Archbishop of Glasgow was definitely in favour of petitioning the Queen,[3] but the Bishops of Edinburgh and St. Andrews protested 'that it was not then seasonable to move in that affair'.[4] So they dispersed, Alexander Rose summing up to Compton what he understood to be their final decision in a sentence which is quite masterly for its lack of definition. 'So soon as we found a proper juncture', he wrote, 'we should then give the best directions we possibly could.'[5] Yet a decision of this kind could not but leave behind it a certain ambiguity, in spite of the fact that Bishop Rose affirmed emphatically later, again to Henry Compton, that the Archbishop of Glasgow agreed that the present was not a propitious time to petition the Queen.

Subsequent events, however, hardly support the story in quite the form in which Bishop Rose told it. He himself admits that he had not returned more than six days from this meeting before he was surprised with the news that an address was going forward. What had happened is now clear, namely, that the Archbishop of Glasgow (John Paterson) determined not to be put off by the doubts of his brother bishops, whom he regarded as concealed Jacobites: but encouraged, it would seem,

---

[1] Paterson to Compton, 15 Oct., 1702, Bod. Rawlinson MSS. 985 C, fo. 43.
[2] *Ibid.*, fo. 51.
[3] Paterson to Compton, 26 Jan., 1703, *ibid.*, fo. 49.
[4] Rose to Compton, 12 Jan., 1703, *ibid.*, fo. 51.
[5] *Ibid.*

from England, by the Archbishop of Canterbury, he drew up an *Address to the Throne* on his own initiative, and circulated it among his clergy. His intention was to present the petition in person to the Queen in London, and thereby to see if something could not be done at least for the loyalist episcopalian clergy.

The Archbishop's intention undoubtedly came as a great shock to the Bishops of Edinburgh and St. Andrews, and of course, to the Jacobite Episcopalians generally.[1] These non-jurors were naturally suspicious of the *Address*, and since the Bishops of Edinburgh and St. Andrews had been 'ignored', they refused to sign it. 'There are some of our Clergy', Robert Mackenzie wrote in reply to a letter of enquiry from Compton, 'that scruple to take the oaths to her majesty, upon the account of their being bound up by former oaths, but there is none of the episcopal clergy, but are very well pleased, and does heartily congratulate her majesty's [*sic*] accession to the throne.'[2]

The fact, of course, was that the nonjurors feared lest concessions granted to the 'loyalists' by the Crown, should have the effect of making their own position even more difficult. As the time approached for the Archbishop of Glasgow to leave Scotland with the petition, so did the Bishop of Edinburgh grow more anxious, and on 5 January 1703 he sent off a bitter letter to Compton. 'This matter', he complained, 'has been transacted all along without so much as any acquainting me (or other) of it: for neither my Lord Glasgow whom I have lately seen, nor any of our presbyters concerned in it, have so much as [indicated] that they were ever upon such a Design, much less to ask my opinion about or concurrence with it; & as my Lord St. Andrews has been likewise so treated, so far as I know none other of our order have been consulted in it. So what's the meaning of this I do not know but this is not the first instance of a certain person his taking separate measures both to the diminution & prejudice of his Colleagues.'[3]

---

[1] In using the term Jacobite, we do not wish to infer that all the nonjuring Episcopalians were actively engaged in furthering the interests of James. Many, of course, did nothing of the kind, and had no desire to do it: they were passively loyal to William or Anne, but felt that they could not in good conscience take the oaths.

[2] Robert Mackenzie to the Bishop of London, 6 Mar., 1703, Bod. Rawlinson MSS. 985 C, fo. 53.

[3] Alexander Rose to the Bishop of London, 5 Jan., 1703, *ibid.*, fo. 47.

It is clear that personal relations between the two bishops were going from bad to worse, for Rose goes on: 'My Lord, I know that of late to colour over his Grace's unbrotherliness, and that the reason we were not advised with, is that they believed we were against addressing. . . . My Lord this is all sham & stuff invented only to serve the forenamed purpose[1] without any solid ground, as your Lordship shall (God willing) within 2 or 3 posts clearly see by [my] transmitting to your Lordship a Double of a letter of mine I shall send to my Lord Glasgow.'[2]

As promised, a few days later (12 January) Bishop Rose despatched a long letter to the Archbishop of Glasgow which gave his version of their consultations and expressed surprise that the Archbishop should have acted independently of his brethren.[3]

It was evident to such a man of affairs as Henry Compton that there was a clash here, both of principles and personalities. The Archbishop of Canterbury had for years been urging all Scottish Episcopalians to take the oaths to the Government in order to qualify them for protection—and it was precisely this which the Archbishop of Glasgow was anxious to lead his clergy into doing. On 26 January, therefore, John Paterson sent off an indignant letter to Fulham, giving a far different picture of what had happened. It was quite untrue, he protested, to say that 'the address of our Clergy was carried by me in such clandestine manner that neither the bishops or clergy were made parties to it'. He had not 'trepanned' anyone. Rather, soon after King William's death, he himself had told the Bishop of St. Andrews that 'our case was far altered that I wondered that now all parties did not come in without scruple to own & serve the Church.'[4]

The Bishop of London was at one with the whig Archbishop Tenison in maintaining the principle—no taking of oaths, no protection. Sooner or later there must come a 'show-down', and

---

[1] I.e. 'to distinguish himself by signal service which the circumstances don't merit'.
[2] Alexander Rose to the Bishop of London, 5 Jan., 1703, Bod. Rawlinson MSS. 985 C, fo. 47.
[3] Same to same, 12 Jan., 1703, *ibid.*, fo. 51.
[4] John Paterson to the Bishop of London, 26 Jan., 1703. *ibid.*, fo. 49.

on 8 March, 1703, Archbishop Paterson wrote another letter to Compton, which was very frank and to the point. 'Let your Lordship be pleased', he suggested, 'to write to them [i.e. the Bishops of Edinburgh and St. Andrews] desiring to know that supposing her Majesty should find ways to recognise Episcopacy in Scotland, whether in that case they are clear and free to own her title and to give their allegiance to her; and to desire a plain & categorical answer from them to that question.' If this were done, he wrote, then his lordship would really know whether the bishops' caution, and the misgivings of some of their clergy in respect of the Address, were really due to the unpropitiousness of the times or, as he himself suspected, to the fact that they were not able with a good conscience to acknowledge the Queen. 'Glad shall I be', he commented (and we must in charity believe him), 'if they answer your Lordship by one affirmative.'[1]

Henry Compton saw the point only too clearly: sooner or later the Bishop of Edinburgh and his friends must commit themselves on this all-important question. If it were possible for a united petition to come from Scotland in the name of all the bishops and clergy, then no time could be more 'propitious' than at the beginning of Anne's reign. If this were not possible, it were better to know how the position stood.

The Bishop of London did not waste much time. On 6 April he sent a letter northward to Edinburgh, asking very kindly, but equally firmly, whether the Bishop and his brother of St. Andrews were prepared to accept Anne without reservations.

Faced directly with the question, the Bishop's reply, sent off on 24 April, amounted to admitting that they could not take the oaths to the Queen without reserve. 'As for the Question & case', he said, 'that so far as I know is put to none of our Order save two and which your Lordship very justly calls nice, I did not expect to be interrogated upon it, even for that very reason.' He confessed that he had always regarded himself 'as bound in point of prudence to avoid the making any discovery of my thoughts upon that subject', but since his Lordship had promised that his reply would not 'operate any manner of way to my prejudice', he was prepared to give his answer which was : 'I

[1] John Paterson to the Bishop of London, 8 Mar., 1703, Bod. Rawlinson MSS. 985 C, fo. 55.

cannot, neither dare I assert, that I am clear to come entirely into the interest which your Lordship wrote of: and that is likewise my Lord St. Andrews sense and answer which I hope is in the very strain your Lordship desires without any evasive ambiguity which I do assure your Lordship is none of my inclination to practice.'[1]

The information contained in this letter proved decisive. It was now apparent that there could be no point in delaying the Address if it were to be presented, since there was no immediate possibility of the Bishops of Edinburgh and St. Andrews associating themselves with it. So far as Alexander Rose was concerned, the Bishop of London was not without sympathy, for he himself had moved a long way from the militant whiggery of the Revolution. What the Bishop of London said in his reply to Rose, written on 26 June, we do not know, except that the Bishop of Edinburgh described it as 'very acceptable to me and so expressed as to encourage me to open my mind most freely'.[2]

It is disappointing, after this long preamble, to record that the petition went forward from the loyal Episcopalians in the name of the Archbishop of Glasgow, but that results were meagre. A Bill was introduced into the Scottish Parliament to grant a legal toleration for all loyal protestants, but once again the Presbyterian opposition was so strong that it had to be withdrawn.

The Episcopalians in Scotland were therefore forced to accept the bitter fact that for the time being they could hope for no legal security. Their main preoccupation turned, therefore, to the more mundane problem of preventing themselves from starving. The practical difficulty here was to see that orders for their benefit, issued in England, were respected north of the border.

This may be seen in connection with the bishops' revenues. It was certainly the Queen's wish that at least part of this income should be used for the advantage of the Scottish clergy, and many were the occasions on which Bishop Rose begged Compton to move the Queen to secure this. These revenues, he wrote on

---

[1] Alexander Rose to the Bishop of London, 24 Apr., 1703, Bod. Rawlinson MSS. 985 C, fo. 58.
[2] Same to same, of London, 20 July, 1703, *ibid.*, fo. 60.

14 September, 1703, were being dissipated, and unless something were done soon, they would be 'totally exhausted' and the
clergy consequently 'left destitute'.[1] The only solution was a
peremptory order from the Queen warmly expressing herself
'against the undue misapplication of sacred things '. Yet even
this support would still leave 'some difficulty in getting our rents
rightly applied to the important purposes of piety and charity'.

In their desperate financial plight, it was to the Bishop of
London that the episcopal clergy uniformly turned, a fact which
is strikingly illustrated in the number of letters which reached
Fulham. Nor was their confidence in his genuine desire to help
them misplaced. On 12 October, 1703, Bishop Rose said grate-
fully: 'I am so perfectly satisfied of your Lordship's care of us,
that I write not this from any apprehension of your unmindful-
ness of us, but lest my silence should occasion your Lordship to
think that our affairs might perchance be now more favourable,
than when I wrote my last.'[2]

When the Archbishop of Glasgow returned home after
presenting his Address in London, where he was indeed grateful
to Compton for his consistent kindness, he continued to keep
up a correspondence with the Bishop. Whatever differences
might divide him from Alexander Rose on the thorny question
of oaths, they were at one in their concern to do something
about this business of the bishops' rents. On 8 March, 1704,
the Archbishop of Glasgow wrote to Compton: 'By my last
I presumed to beg of your Lordship as I did of my Lord
Archbishop of York that you with him jointly may apply to
the Queen to mind her Majesty to order her pious designs for
the upkeep & sustenance of us, the surviving Bishops, and our
Clergy out of our own Rents, to be made effectual in the respective proportions which by advice of her two Secretaries of State
she hath approved & signed under her Royal hand.'[3]

It is sad to record that when the Queen was prepared to do
something about the bishops' rents, there was dissension amongst
the episcopal clergy as to how the monies should be allocated.
We shall, unfortunately, notice precisely the same situation in
the case of the French refugees. Persecution does not always

---

[1] Alexander Rose to the Bishop of London, 12 Oct., 1703, Bod. Rawlinson
MSS. 985 C, fo. 64.   [2] *Ibid.*
[3] Paterson to Compton, 8 Mar., 1704, Bod. Rawlinson MSS. 985 C, fo. 68.

ennoble. It often makes those who suffer from it bitter and unreasonable. With the Scots, as with the French, there were the
same complaints of unfair distribution, and the neglect of the
really poor.

The Archbishop of Glasgow, to quote one example, managed
to secure from the Queen £60 per annum for his 'numerous
children', to be paid up to fifteen years after his death. When
knowledge of this grant got abroad, the Archbishop was subjected to bitter attacks from many of his own clergy, particularly as it was popularly reported that he enjoyed a private
fortune worth some £3,000 per annum. The Archbishop undoubtedly fell in general esteem. Even his old friend, the Bishop
of London, was said to be 'offended'—avarice was never one of
his vices, and he would give to others even when he had to
borrow to do so. The result was an embarrassed epistle from
Glasgow to Fulham, written on 30 October, 1705, in which the
Archbishop recalled his 'great sufferings', and 'the many good
services I did to the Church & Crown . . . in bringing over
by my example & influence, some . . . of the Clergy and laity
to their duty and allegience'. He had been 'maliciously misrepresented', he complained, and he hoped that his Lordship would
'be satisfied that I have done nothing mean or unbecoming in
this matter'.[1]

Though the Queen had issued instructions about the rents,
it was difficult indeed to secure that her commands be obeyed.
In commending the Dean of the Orkneys[2] to the Bishop of
London in May, 1707, John Paterson commented: 'Had our
Queen put us and our clergy in possession of what her Majesty
graciously appointed and signed in my presence for our subsistence and release out of our Bishops' rents she would have
been saved from much trouble and particularly from this new
application'—but the fact was that her Majesty's bounty was at
the moment being 'stopt'.[3]

No man was more appreciative of the Bishop of London's
strenuous exertions on behalf of the Scottish clergy than the
Bishop of Edinburgh, and his letters breathe an atmosphere of

---

[1] John Paterson to the Bishop of London, 30 Oct., 1705, Bod. Rawlinson
MSS. 985 C, fo. 70.
[2] A Mr. Pitcairne whom Compton had helped before.
[3] John Paterson to the Bishop of London, 15 May, 1707, *ibid.*, fo. 74.

genuine thankfulness. 'My Lord', he wrote in February, 1707, 'I delayed to make my thankful acknowledgments to your Lordship for the late special favour done to me until, together with that, I should be in a condition to acquaint your Lordship of the Queen's most gracious present being made effectual to me here, which is now fully and faithfully done.'[1]

While these letters were being sent to and fro, the whole position of ecclesiastical politics was changed by an event which represented the triumph of reason over the passions of centuries. Scotland, Presbyterian in religion, particularist in sentiment, and (in the north) Jacobite in allegiance, was united with an un-friendly England, Episcopal in religion. Compton seems to have been, on the whole, in favour of this act of wisdom, and he, with Archbishops Tenison and Sharp, was one of the Lords Commissioners appointed on 25 August, 1702, 'to treat for the union between England and Scotland'.[2] This Commission met from 10 November, 1702, to 3 February, 1705, but its proposals miscarried through its unwillingness to grant free trade between the two Kingdoms. In 1706, however, the English Parliament sanctioned the appointment of new Commissioners. 'I do not find my Lord Bishop of London's Name in the New Commission', writes Compton's anonymous biographer, 'granted by her Majesty in April 1706, on the side of England as before, for treating on that important affair. The Reason of this, unless it was that Whiggery had the Ascendancy at Court, I cannot pretend to assign and yet both the Archbishops are in, and no other of the Order, whereas the Archbishop of York was not in the other Commission issued out in the first Year of her Majesty's Reign.'[3] But if Henry Compton was left out, another of his family was put in, for Spencer Compton, Earl of Wilmington, a strong whig, was appointed Chairman of the Committee for settling the Articles of Union.

The debates in the English House of Lords on these terms of union began on 10 January, 1707, when it soon became obvious that the Act was to have no easy passage, though the opposition was careful to divide only on subordinate issues. The position of the English bishops was certainly beset with difficulties (Compton

[1] Alexander Rose to the Bishop of London, 22 Feb., 1707, Bod. Rawlinson MSS. 985 C, fo. 72.
[2] *S.P.D.* Anne, 23 Aug., 1702.   [3] *The Life of Dr. Henry Compton*, p. 69.

was probably not sorry to be 'off' the Commission) and drew forth a malicious comment from the Earl of Nottingham (now head of the High Church tories), who maintained that their Lordships were abandoning the principle of episcopal ordination which 'has been contended for between them and the Presbyters these thirty years'. The Bishop of Bath and Wells declared that the Union had come a hundred years too late, but Archbishop Tenison affirmed boldly that 'he had no scruples against ratifying, approving, and confirming it within the bounds of Scotland [since] he thought that the narrow notions of all Churches had been their ruin, and he believed the Church of Scotland to be as true a Protestant Church as the Church of England though he could not say it was so perfect.'[1]

Compton seems to have kept very quiet while these debates were before the House, and to have taken little or no part in them. The reasons for this silence are, perhaps, not far to seek. The Bishop was regarded, north of the border, as the protector *par excellence* of the episcopalian clergy. Yet he was sufficient of a statesman to realise the advantages of union, and had served on the first Commission, albeit not enthusiastically. His heart was with the Archbishop of York, and the Bishops of Durham, Chester, and Rochester when they entered a protest at what they regarded as the inadequacy of the Bill (appended to the Act of Union) 'for the Security of the Church of England' —but on the whole he preferred to keep silent.

Compton was now an old man, and his relationship with Scottish affairs seems to have become less political and more confined to doing what he could to relieve the financial embarrassments of the Episcopalians. In this respect he was not entirely unsuccessful for he gave liberally from his own resources, and frequently solicited the Queen. In 1708 he was instrumental in securing collections throughout all England on their behalf, which he supported with energy. To stimulate more enthusiasm he wrote a strong letter to his Archdeacon of London, who in his turn exhorted all the clergy of the diocese to co-operate. 'Dr. Scott tells me', the Bishop wrote, 'that the late Collections go very slowly on in London for the poor Scotch ministers, and therefore I would entreat you to further them as much as you can, especially since several of them have been put to great hardships

[1] Carstairs, *State Papers and Letters*, 1774, p. 760.

of late by Arraignments and Imprisonments who had notwithstanding owned the Queen and Her Government, by praying
heartily for her in public and private, ever since she came to the
Throne, and others by taking all the usual Oaths and Assurances.'[1]

The clergy in Scotland, to their credit, were not unapprecia-
tive of this constant remembrance, and in May, 1709, Alexander
Rose thanked the Bishop once again for his 'assistance & countenance to these contributions that are making for our poor
clergy'. In the same letter he asked him to help the son of Lady
Kilragok, who was a slave in Algiers: and also Mr. John Hog
'whom the late Archb[isho]p of Glasgow presbyterated in order
to serve as a Chaplain on a frigate called the Marmaid.'[2] In the
next month Rose wrote again: 'I take the opportunity to give
your Lordship my most hearty thanks and the humble acknowledgments of our poor clergy who are deeply sensible how much
they owe to your Lordship both for soliciting the Queen &
giving such countenance to these Collections as are going on
for their relief & support.'[3] Right up to the end of his days the
Bishop remained active and on 3 September, 1711, he ordained
and befriended one Glas, a Presbyterian member.[4]

If Compton (of legal necessity) could find ministerial work
only for those Episcopalians who would take the oaths, he yet
extended his charity to all without distinction.

[1] *A Copy of my Lord Bishop of London his Letter,* 1708.
[2] Alexander Rose to Compton, 28 May, 1709, Bod. Rawlinson MSS. 985 C,
fo. 90.
[3] Alexander Rose to the Bishop of London, 30 June, 1709, 985 C, fo. 92.
[4] *H.M.C.* App. ii, Rep. XIV, p. 476 (Portland MSS.).

CHAPTER SEVENTEEN

THE FRENCH REFUGEES

THE Church of England, in Compton's day, occupied a unique position in Europe among the Protestant churches, because of the manner in which it had achieved its Reformation. Though it retained episcopacy, it had certainly broken away from Rome, and its anti-Roman vitality was one of its distinguishing characteristics. In the eyes of foreign Protestants struggling to maintain themselves against the full blast of the Counter Reformation, the Church in England was *Sancta Ecclesia Anglicana omnium Protestantium Ecclesiarum praecipua et florentissima*, whose protection and hospitality were eagerly sought after. 'The Church of England hath been a shelter to other neighbouring Churches when the storm hath driven over them. It was such in former times, it hath been so of late, and I question not but it will be so in this instance'—so wrote Archbishop Tenison in 1709.[1] Not even the fact that Protestantism expressed itself in the pattern of national churches—*cujus regio ejus religio*—prevented its ministers cultivating a sense of unity, if not union, alongside their new found national loyalty. A common enemy, of course, was a powerful stimulus bringing them together.

The influence of the continental reformation on English Churchmen went right back to the middle years of the sixteenth century. Under Mary, many of her subjects were driven across the Channel by her persecution of Protestants. This was followed by the religious wars in France which turned the tide the other way. England became the asylum for God-fearing Huguenots, who settled here in small communities, consequently enriching the economic life of the towns. Most of them remained even when Henry IV of France secured a legal toleration for them in their own land. In 1618, King James sent a delegate from the Church of England to the synod of Dort, who subscribed to the Profession of Faith that was drawn up at this assembly, though not to the synodical declaration on church government.

[1] T. Tenison, *Letter to the Clergy of the Convocation of Canterbury*, 1709.

John Milton was so moved by the persecution of the Waldensian Christians that he wrote, in bitter protest, one of the noblest sonnets in the English language. During the Commonwealth, many members of the Church of England fled from these shores to France and Holland.

There were, of course, inevitable differences of faith and order within the various Protestant churches of Europe, particularly between those who had deliberately dispensed with episcopacy and the Church of England which had retained it. Yet the *Ecclesia Anglicana* did not unchurch those who preferred to organise their religious life without bishops. Doubtless they were rendered thereby less perfect, but compared with the corruption of Rome, they were pure indeed.

Henry Compton's first acquaintance with foreign Protestantism, as was the case with many Englishmen in his day, resulted from his sojourn in France during the Commonwealth. In that same country during those years was John Cosin (1594–1672), later Bishop of Durham and already an ordained priest in the Church of England. His relations with the Huguenots of Paris, and in particular with their worship at Charenton, may help us to infer (it cannot be more than an inference) the general attitude which Compton adopted towards them—that is if at this stage of his career he was in any way interested. 'I never refused', Cosin writes, 'to join with the Protestants either here or anywhere else, in all things where they join with the Church of England. Many of them have been here at our Church, and we have been at theirs. . . . I have baptized many of their children at the request of their own ministers. Many of their people . . . have frequented our public prayers with great reverence, and I have delivered the Holy Communion to them according to our own order which they observed religiously.'[1]

Relations, in other words, were friendly and co-operative, though the difference of orders was respected.

After the Restoration, Compton appears frequently to have visited Paris, and thereby to have made the personal acquaintance of some of the leading French Protestant ministers. As for the Roman Catholic Church in that country we know that he thought it in a most unhappy condition, oppressed by the throne and the

[1] N. Sykes, *The Church of England and Non-Episcopal Churches in the 16th and 17th Centuries*, 1918.

22

Papacy. The jurisdiction of their bishops, so he informed Sheldon, was rendered ineffective, because the Pope interfered with it and the King insisted that any appeal from ecclesiastical excommunication should go to his own Court.[1]

The policy of Louis XIV towards his Protestant subjects reflects the essential littleness of his mind. To this proud monarch a Gallican form of Roman Catholicism was the only religion compatible with absolutism, and early in his reign he declared his intention 'to reduce [the Protestants] gradually, not imposing any new hardships upon them, and observing the liberties granted by his predecessors, but granting them nothing beyond those liberties'.[2] In the eyes of *le roi soleil*, the very existence of the Huguenots, professing a faith different from his own, seemed a deliberate personal affront, defying both his religious and his political authority. Many of these Protestants who could read the signs of the times sought refuge in flight years before the King's Revocation of the Edict of Nantes in 1685 converted the trickle into a stream. By this act of folly—both a crime and a blunder—'all privileges granted to the Protestants by Henri IV and Louis XIII were suppressed; public worship was forbidden to them except in Alsace; their ministers were to leave the realm in fifteen days; and lay Protestants were forbidden to follow them under pain of the galleys and forfeiture.'[3]

Such was the religious background in France during the first years of Compton's episcopate. It was not only a feeling of religious solidarity which made the English people so kindly disposed towards the fleeing French Protestants. Fear of Louis XIV was as widespread in England as on the Continent. Determination to resist absolutism, which Charles flirted with and Louis expressed to perfection, brought English Protestant and French Huguenot together. These refugees from across the Channel were both religious and political exiles whose enemy was a common foe.

Such 'foreigners' were allowed to make a home in England solely through the Royal mercy. They came, of necessity, under no diocesan jurisdiction, but were answerable direct to the Crown. What Charles did was to depute their oversight to the

---

[1] Compton to Sheldon, 23 July, 1664, Bod. Tanner MSS. 47, fo. 184.
[2] Duruy, *History of France* (Everyman ed.) ii. 169.
[3] *Ibid.*, ii. 170.

Bishop of London, not so much because of Compton's particular interest in their affairs, but because of the indefinite overseas jurisdiction which had become associated with the Bishop of that See. The presence in this country of a number of Protestants whose traditions were not those of the Church of England was bound to cause difficulty *vis à vis* the national church and the Dissenters, and therefore they often stood in need of Royal protection. As Secretary Jenkins wrote to Compton in 1682: 'The King looks on himself as concerned that foreigners, who have a liberty of using a way of public worship and discipline not altogether conform[able] to what is established here by law, be by their ministers well principled in the duty of obedience they owe to the Government they live under, and be particularly instructed that no pretence of liberty to use foreign forms and discipline might carry them to uncharitable censures of us, and separation from us, which cannot be without prejudice not only to the reformed religion but also to the public peace.'[1]

Compton shared to the full the feelings of the more enlightened of his countrymen, and the interest which he consistently took in the French refugees, helping them individually and fostering the life of their communities, was life-long. This enthusiasm shows him at his best, and so much was this the case that he came to be regarded as their special protector. The Bishop was himself thoroughly convinced that the Church of England must accept a real responsibility for the welfare of these unfortunate people, particularly for their ministers who, of course, had no trade to fall back on. Here the problem was a practical one, namely, to find a means whereby they could continue to discharge their ministry either to their fellow-countrymen or within the Church of England—and in the meantime to prevent them from starving.

The year 1681 undoubtedly saw a considerable increase in the number of Huguenots flying from France. 'The poor French ministers still come over in great numbers and under great necessities', wrote a member of the Admiralty at the time.[2] The Protestant feeling of the nation forced the government to do something, and Charles entrusted Compton, in July, with their 'speedy care', commanding him 'to represent the sad state

[1] Jenkins to Compton, Dec. 1682, *S.P.D.* Car. II, E.B. 53, p. 84.
[2] *S.P.D.* Car II, 20 Oct., 1681, Admiralty: Greenwich Hospital, i. 45.

of these poor people' to the clergy, who in their turn were to 'excite their parishioners to contribute freely to supply their necessities'.[1] On Monday, 19 October, Compton led a deputation to the King consisting of a few 'considerable' representatives of the Dutch Church and two French ministers (Messieurs Lambert and Primrose) who made short orations in which they 'blessed God for his Majesty and gave him the thanks and prayers of all those afflicted members they represented and more particularly for his late merciful protection of them'. The King knew how to be gracious when occasion demanded and his heart was not nearly so hard as his brother's. He received them, an eye-witness reports, 'with great kindness, telling them that they might rest assured of all imaginable protection and favour he could do them'.[2]

Many were the stories of great suffering which the refugees poured into the sympathetic ear of the Bishop, particularly after the Revocation of the Edict of Nantes. In April 1686, there came into his hands a letter smuggled out of a prison in Paris written by a Huguenot to his mother.[3] He was confined, the young man said, in a dark and narrow cell, and was lying in water, being allowed neither bed nor straw. At one time he had been thrown into a deep dungeon, without any daylight, and among dead dogs and cattle. In this condition he was manacled, fastened to a post, strung up and flogged.

A few years ago we might have been inclined to dismiss such a story altogether as a propagandist exaggeration.

This letter is typical of others which the Bishop received. Equally harrowing was an epistle from Sir Thomas Bureau sent out of Niort in Poitou to his brother a merchant in London. It contained a most distressing account of the outrages to which his fellow Protestants were being subjected by the French dragoons.[4]

No one in England, therefore, knew more of the conditions of the French Protestants in their own country than did Henry Compton, particularly as he kept in touch with some of the

---

[1] Bod. Rawlinson MSS. 984 C, fo. 43. The letters patent for the collection were issued on 10 Sept., 1681.

[2] *S.P.D.* Car. II, Oct. 1681, Admiralty: Greenwich Hospital, i. 45.

[3] René Guybert to his mother, 20 Aug., 1685, Bod. Rawlinson MSS. 984 C, fo. 62.

[4] Bureau to his brother, 20 Aug., *ibid.*

ministers whose acquaintance he had made on his earlier visits to France. One such correspondent was Monsieur Lortie of La Rochelle, whose book, *Traité de la Sainte Cène* the Bishop found time to translate into English in 1677 under the title: *Treatise of the Holy Communion*—a work which has often been mistaken for an original theological study by the translator. Three years passed before Monsieur Lortie discovered his debt, when he hastened to thank the Bishop for 'bringing [his work] out of the obscurity of its first birth to give it a second which is more illustrious and which promises immortality'.[1]

In 1681 the same correspondent wrote informing the Bishop that things were so bad that he had been forced to leave his ministry at La Rochelle and was now in Paris. He was reluctantly coming to the conclusion that the chances of discharging an effective ministry in France were small and that he must consider escaping to another land. Soon he hoped to be able to preach in English, a language he had known since boyhood. 'I would regard it', he assured the Bishop, 'as a singular honour to serve the Church of Jesus Christ under your direction.'[2]

With Henri Justel, another Protestant minister in Paris, the Bishop also kept up an interesting correspondence, and since both were keen horticulturists, it was not only theology (the Bishop sent him the works of Cudworth)[3] which formed the substance of their letters. Justel was a friend of Marchant, the King's gardener, and this enabled him, on one occasion, to promise the Bishop a *thlaspi semper vivens*, and whatever else he might choose, in exchange for a Bermuda cedar or tulip tree. It is, perhaps, rather pleasant to read of the Protestant Bishop 'swapping' specimens with the gardener of the despised Roman Catholic monarch.[4] At one time Justel, like Lortie, contemplated settling in England, and wrote to the Bishop asking for assistance for himself and his young family since they could no longer live under the rule of Louis XIV.

So we might go on to enumerate many others with whom the Bishop corresponded, whom he helped to rescue out of France (like Madame Regnier),[5] interceded for through the

[1] Lortie to Compton, 2 July, 1680, Bod. Rawlinson MSS. 982 C, fo. 17.
[2] Same to same, 21 Apr., 1681, *ibid.*
[3] Justel to Compton, 5 Feb., 1678, *ibid.*, fo. 5.
[4] Same to same, 28 May, 1681, *ibid.*, fo. 27.
[5] Bod. Rawlinson MSS. 982 C, fo. 21 and fo. 25.

English ambassador in Paris (like Madame de la Bar)[1] or ordained into the Church of England (like Monsieur Barbat).[2] Typical of his great pains was his effort to persuade Bishop Morley in 1682 to recommend a Frenchman for election as a demy of Magdalen College, a request which the Bishop of Winchester said that he must refuse, even if he were not already committed to a grand nephew of his 'dear friend Dr. Hammond'.[3] Equally typical was the zeal with which in 1684 he pleaded with the Council on behalf of a poor Huguenot fisherman who because of national prejudice was finding it difficult to follow his livelihood:[4] and the pains that he took to provide a minister for the French master mariners settled at Rye.[5]

Such incidents may serve to remind us that refugees are never universally popular, and some Englishmen, with their insular outlook, refused to believe that many of them were genuine exiles. In some parts of the country, it was readily believed that these Frenchmen were Roman Catholics in disguise, whose task it was to create a papal fifth-column against the day when Louis should launch an invasion. It was a plausible story, particularly calculated to play upon the fears of the man-in-the-street. Some were taken in by it, for it seemed consistent with the tortuous foreign policy of Charles II. So disturbed was Compton lest such absurd stories should gain ground—he feared their effects on his money-raising efforts—that he himself wrote to the Government protesting against 'these foolish rumours [and] groundless suspicions'.[6]

We need to remember, and it is but fair to remember this, that the background of such myth-making was the Popish Plot and the lies of Titus Oates. In such an atmosphere charges of this kind against the refugees might easily seem reasonable. Nor, in fact, were such rumours without that little grain of truth which is necessary to give substance to even the most bare-faced fabrications. In January, 1679, for example, the Bishop of London received a letter from a certain Bonvallet at The Hague

[1] Preston to Compton, 30 Sept., 1682, Bod. Rawlinson MSS. 983 C, fo. 57.
[2] Lortie to Compton, 21 April 1681, *ibid.*, fo. 21.
[3] Morley to Compton, 16 June, 1682, *ibid.*, fo. 54.
[4] Compton to Jenkins, 20 Mar., 1684, *S.P.D.* Car. II, 437, n. 41.
[5] Bod. Rawlinson MSS. 984 C, fo. 72.
[6] *S.P.D.* Car. II, 19 Dec., 1681, 417, no. 275.

informing him that there were some pretended converts in London who had obtained tutorships in families of rank with the intention of making their pupils Papists.[1] It is just possible, therefore, that a few Roman Catholics may equally have assumed the guise of Protestant refugees, and this is actually suggested in a letter written by Monsieur Primrose, a refugee minister in London.

The best way to refute these rumours, so the Bishop thought ('if it be possible for any to be in earnest that pretend it'), was to let the people know the real facts of the religious situation in France. To this end a little treatise had been drawn up by Monsieur Claude, a French minister, under the title: *The Present State of the Protestants in France*. Compton read it with great interest,[2] and his opinion of it may be seen in his comments to the Secretary of the Council:

> Whatever is there quoted as Edicts or Acts of Council, I have seen Authentic Copies of, except one or two, which likewise I have all reason to believe to be true, as any as we have here printed in our Acts of Parliament or Proclamations. Besides, will any one believe that even any merchant on the exchange can be imposed on in the manner of these proceedings from a country so near and where so daily a correspondence is held. 'Tis true the usage is more cruel in some parts than others, as in Poitou, Saintogne and about Rochelle, which is the reason we do not receive informations of these barbarities from all places alike but what we have received comes from so many and unquestionable testimonies, that there is little doubt of their facts as of the orders by which they are committed, nor have we a thousandth part of those cruelties to these poor Protestants abroad yet related to us, besides what are in daily execution.[3]

It was therefore Compton's intention to publish a translation of *The State of the Protestants in France*, and to add a preface from his own pen; but he had become so *persona non grata* at Court of late that he thought it prudent to find out in advance how such an action would be received in this quarter. He accordingly consulted Secretary Jenkins, asking bluntly whether this would 'give an offence'.[4] The reply must have been unfavourable for

[1] Bonvallet to Compton, 15 Jan., 1679, Bod. Rawlinson MSS. 982 C, fo. 11.
[2] Compton's own copy is in the Bodleian. See Rawlinson MS. 984 C, fo. 254.
[3] Compton to Jenkins, 19 Dec., 1681, *S.P.D. Car.* II, 417, no. 275.
[4] *Ibid.*

the Bishop certainly went no further with the project at the time.[1]

As the inflow of refugees was steady and continuous, so it became obvious that they could not immediately on arrival be self supporting, and must therefore for a time be a charge on the towns where they settled. Hence the need to raise money through royal briefs which ordered collections in all the parishes throughout the country. By this means immediate help was provided for many penniless exiles before they were able to earn their own living. But money was not the only problem, and Compton's constant preoccupation was to decide where these French Protestants were to settle.

The Channel Islands seemed to provide an obvious territory for their ministers, because it was largely French-speaking, a great advantage seeing that many of them knew no English. Guernsey and Jersey were peculiars of the diocese of Winchester, and each island had its own dean. The Governor of the former during the first years of Compton's episcopate was Christopher Hatton (1632-1706), an intimate friend of the Bishop's brother, the Earl of Northampton. Doubtless this personal link helped the Bishop in his good intentions, and many were the letters which passed between Compton and Hatton in the interests of the French refugees. Early in 1680, for example, the Bishop examined personally Alexander de Souliers and then sent him off to Lord Hatton at Northampton to solicit preferment.[2]

It would be tedious, however, to quote at length the names of those whom Compton commended in this way, and we must be content to give a few typical examples. In 1680 he petitioned the Governor that Monsieur Gomarsh might be appointed to the parish of St. Peter, Guernsey;[3] that a relative of Monsieur Bourdeaux, 'an extraordinary character', might go to the parish of St. Saviour;[4] and Monsieur Breuvet to a parish which is not named.[5]

The Channel Islands could only take a small proportion (and these mainly ministers) of those that poured in, and most of

[1] This work was published a few years later by Thomas Tenison when Vicar of St. Martin's.

[2] Compton to Hatton, 29 Feb., 1680, B.M. Add. MSS. 29, 584, fo. 18.

[3] Same to same, 12 Apr., 1680, *ibid.*, fo. 22.

[4] Same to same, 5 Jan., 1680, *ibid.*, fo. 32.

[5] Same to same, 8 Jan., 1680, *ibid.*, fo. 34.

them were forced to seek a haven, at least temporarily, in English
towns. The embarrassment of some civic authorities at these
incursions was clearly stated in a *Memorial* presented to the
Bishop in 1681, which stressed the 'absolute necessity there is to
free the towns from the great number of Protestants who arrive
daily from France, and to procure them a settlement for gaining
their livelihood'. They must not be left in idleness, the *Memorial*
continued, since it was impossible to maintain them long by the
alms of the country. They must be set to work, but as this could
not be done in London, they must be established where there
was land to be cultivated and commodities to allow them to
pursue their trades. The collections from the briefs should be used
to support them only for an interim period.[1]

There can be no doubt that there was a definite fear among
some of the English lest these refugees should take away their
livelihood. Compton, in his desire to help them, had constantly
to overcome an unreasoning prejudice, a fact which may be well
illustrated from his letter to the clergy which accompanied the
King's brief in 1686. These French Protestants, he here pointed
out, had not escaped from France simply to save their own
skins, 'but what is ten thousand times more dear, their
Conscience'.

When we reflect upon that Desolation which has been made before
their Eyes, of all their Goods and Stores, the Barbarity of Usage
both to their Bodies and Estates, and their quitting their whole
Subsistence with their Native Soil, through all Sorts of Peril, one
would imagine it the greatest Hardship. But when we come to
examine that Anguish, which is brought upon their Minds, it is
incomparably greater: their Wives, Children and Relations imprisoned, clapt down into Monastries, put down into Dungeons,
inhumanly tormented and afflicted, till they renounce their faith
or perish in the Trial. All men are not required to be wise enough
to judg[e] of the Secular Consequences of this accident in the
peopling of our Country, increasing Manufactures, Industry,
Trading, and the like: But God excuses no man from being good
and charitable. They who have no Mite to give have Hearts to
pray; and this occasion requires, with an equal Necessity, our
prayers for those who still lie in Misery and Irons, as it does our
Benevolence for such as are escaped. Exhort then your People,
whilst they have time, to do good.[2]

[1] *S.P.D. Car. II*, 1681, 417, no. 279.   [2] Bod. Tanner MSS. 30, fo. 7.

The reception given to the refugees varied, of course, from town to town in accordance with the good sense of the local authorities, and the size of the incursion. We propose to quote a few typical examples.

In Ipswich the refugees, who established themselves there in the reign of Charles II, seem to have conformed from the outset to the national church, and to have constituted a model community. Compton always took a particular interest in their welfare, and was delighted at their 'continued loyalty and adherence to the Church of England', which he felt was largely due to the wisdom of their minister. Caesar Benalieu. So impressed was the Bishop with his tactful leadership that in July 1682 he made him his quasi-personal adviser in matters relating to the French in England, consequently relieving him of his responsibilities in Ipswich.[1]

Even in Ipswich, however, the French exiles were faced with economic difficulties, and it was fortunate for them that the civic authorities proved singularly enlightened and sympathetic. When the news of the Huguenots' unhappy financial plight reached the Bishop of London, he immediately wrote to the Mayor asking for more information, and received a reply dated 8 June, 1685, signed by twenty-five prominent citizens. They admitted that the linen manufacture was 'like to be in time very advantageous, not only to our Town, but also to the whole Kingdom', but at the moment it was 'in danger of falling down for want of a necessary fund for supporting it'.[2] They therefore expressed the hope that everything might be done to encourage this industry, particularly as the French 'heartily and willingly conform to the Government established in Church and State'.

The plight of these refugees attracted the sympathy of that charitable and loveable man Thomas Firmin. whose theological unorthodoxy did not prevent his consistently showing forth the Christian virtues of charity and compassion. He proceeded to organise a collection on their behalf, and received a donation from Compton, to whom he wrote on 29 August, 1685, acknowledging that the Bishop 'had been in a world of pain for these poor distressed Protestants of France, for which, I doubt not, the God of mercys will reward you in due time'.[3]

---

[1] Bod. Rawlinson MSS. 984 C, fos. 57, 59.   [2] *Ibid.*, 599.
[3] Firmin to Compton, 29 Aug., 1685, *ibid.*, fo. 64.

Rye was another town which distinguished itself by consistent charity to the refugees who had established themselves in its midst. In 1681, Compton appointed as their minister Monsieur Bertrand, 'an honest man, firm to the Government', a refugee whom he had himself ordained, and who he was convinced would 'not go a hair's breadth less than the service of the Church of England'. The Bishop was delighted with the manner in which the town authorities 'preferred them their Church at vacant times', so much so that he urged the Secretary of State to acknowledge publicly this act of civic generosity in order 'to encourage this charity [which] might conduce to their establishment'.[1] It is sad to notice that some three years later Bertrand was accused of neglecting his ministerial duties, and had to defend himself vigorously to the Bishop.[2]

Not all corporations, much to Compton's distress, took the sensible view of the people of Ipswich and Rye. In fact, many towns refused the refugees the use of their church altogether, a lack of charity which induced the Bishop of London to draw up a strong letter of protest, which he sent to the Secretary of State suggesting that it might be dispatched to all such inhospitable authorities. 'I am very sorry', the letter ran, 'that the poor French Protestants met with such cold entertainment from you. I should be loath to complain to his Majesty, but to deny them the use of your Church and such conveniences as may encourage their conformity to our Church and fidelity to the King is so great a disservice to the Government and the established religion that I beg an answer that may stop further complaint.'[3]

In Norwich the refugees seem to have had a bad time, and in 1683 the trouble came to an unfortunate and sudden climax. Some citizens seem really to have believed that the French were disguised Papists, determined to ruin their trade. As a result, so an eye-witness reported, 'the rabble of the town made a regular riot, dragging the French about, sacking their houses and actually killing a woman'. It was up to the civic authorities to take firm action, but unfortunately though 'at first some effort was made to check them and the worst rioters were put

---

[1] Bod. Rawlinson MSS. 984 C, fo. 72.
[2] *S.P.D.* Car. II, 1681?, 417, no. 280.
[3] *Ibid.*, 19 Dec., 1681, 431, no. 88.

in prison', the judges on circuit did not follow this up and there was 'much reason to fear that [such] impunity may make the people more insolent, and that they may finish entirely what has been only half begun'. For a few weeks the French in the town lived in fear and trembling, and one of their number wrote a strong letter to Sir John Charden asking that they might be protected, and allowed 'peaceably to enjoy their ancient privileges'. Only an express injunction from the King to the Lord Mayor, he suggested, would 'put our nation for a good while out of anxiety, and will reassure them here as well as others who intend to come'. The letter to Sir John concluded: 'I am not ignorant that you have the ear of the Bishop of London, who takes a great interest in all our affairs, and that by that means or others which your dexterity will suggest to you, you will be able to give repose to this flock'.[1]

The prejudice felt by some Englishmen towards the refugees —a prejudice at once economic, religious and national—was not confined to the uneducated. When Compton wrote to the Bishop of Winchester urging him to do what he could for a Monsieur Brevet, Morley replied that he would do his best but that he wished the Huguenots, instead of coming to England, where they offered a great deal of encouragement to the Non-conformists, would retire into Germany and Holland. In fairness to Morley it must be admitted that the presence of refugees in his diocese had led to difficulty in some parishes. To persuade the Bishop of London that he was not unreasonably prejudiced, he forwarded to Compton a letter he had received from the Mayor and two prominent citizens in Southampton, requesting him, as their Bishop, to insist that the minister of the French Church in the town should conduct his services in French since they were attracting so many Dissenters.[2]

Compton, on his part, was convinced that if only the civic and religious authorities were sympathetic, then a great many refugees would become members of the Church of England, particularly as a number of them intended to make this country their permanent home, though, for the time being, the difficulty of language necessitated their meeting separately. The Bishop of London's policy was to persuade the English

[1] *S.P.D.* Car. II, 4 Sept., 1683, 431, no. 88.
[2] Bod. Rawlinson MSS. 984 C, fo. 48.

towns, by encouragement, or if need be, by reprimand, to be reasonable.

The faults, of course, were not always on one side. It was not to be expected that men who had been suddenly forced to leave their own country would find it easy to settle happily in another. Their bitter experience in France often left its mark, and made some of them disillusioned. Persecution does not always bring out the best: more often it leads to unbalanced religion; and some of the exiles, like the Camisards in France, three of whose 'prophets made a visit to England',[1] displayed all the symptoms of mental disease. Their visions and speaking with tongues did not make settled government easy, and the French themselves had to exercise discipline over their fellow nationals.[2] This tendency to eccentricity long remained a problem, even when the most violent persecutions in France were long past. As late as 1706 Compton received an account, attested by ministers and elders of the French Church in London, of the activity of certain 'pretended prophets', with a graphic description of their convulsive movements— all which, it was claimed, were very 'unworthy of the Holy Ghost'.[3]

Behind such eccentricities there often lay the grim fact of poverty. Many of the French refugee ministers, since they (unlike their flocks) had no trade to fall back on, were so badly off that they could see no way out unless they became ordained ministers of the Church of England, or schoolmasters in America. They could not be all employed in ministering to their own countrymen, as they themselves pointed out in a letter to the Bishop of London.[4] The French minister at Plymouth, for example, complained bitterly to Compton of the inadequate income he was receiving and promised that he would learn English as soon as possible in order to qualify himself for an English benefice.[5] The French pastor at Thorpe was only per-suaded to remain at his post by Compton's assuring him of

---

[1] Bod. Rawlinson MSS. 984, C, f. 246. Voltaire relates (*Siècle de Louis XIV*) that one of them, Marion, attempted to raise a dead body from St. Paul's Church-yard.

[2] *Ibid.* fo. 242, 'Declaration of a French congregation signed by—Braquiers, the secretary, against the impostures of the French Cevennes prophets'.

[3] *Ibid.*, fo. 152.   [4] *Ibid.*, fo. 244. See also *ibid.*, 984 C, fo. 219.

[5] *Ibid.*, 982 C, fo. 33.

'cheese etc. towards his subsistence'.[1] In 1685—the year of the Revocation of the Edict—many refugees were penniless, and Sancroft, doubtless with the support of Compton, wrote to all the bishops urging them to be active in collecting money in their diocese since 'the interest was so low at present'.[2]

Such poverty was also, at times, the indirect cause of some of the difficulties which the refugees experienced in organising their common life. Frequent were the complaints made to Compton of misappropriation of funds. One example, perhaps, will suffice, and may be taken as typical of many others. In 1705 Jean Thoué des Essars brought charges of maladministration against the French Committee which was responsible for allocating the monies raised from various collections, and Compton was called in to undertake the unpleasant task of holding an enquiry. He decided against the complainant, being influenced, doubtless, by the fact that a group of refugees swore an affidavit before Sir John Houblon testifying that 'the French Committee have discharged faithfully the trust laid on them'. As for des Essars, the defendants alleged that he was 'a common Liar', 'a self confessed murderer'—and what was even worse, a Roman Catholic in disguise![3]

The distribution of the monies raised in the collections was bound to cause embarrassment exactly as it did with the distressed Scottish ministers. Of course, the revenue obtained in this way was not enough to go round, as may be seen in the letters which Compton and Sancroft wrote to their brother bishops urging them to support the appeals as much as they could. In fact, it was one of the Bishop of London's constant preoccupations to keep his episcopal brethren active and interested. In apologising for the smallness of one of his contributions, the Bishop of Winchester assured Compton that he had done what he could by letters and personal example, but that he was greatly handicapped by the illness of his archdeacon.[4] The Bishop of Hereford confessed that he had lost all the briefs for one deanery, and that most of the money from his diocese (£26) was bad.[5] In writing to Lloyd, Bishop of St. Asaph, in November 1681,

[1] Bod. Rawlinson MSS. 983 C, fo. 145.
[2] *Ibid.*, 984 C, fo. 61.
[3] Reneu to Compton, 2 Aug., 1705, *ibid.*, fo. 140.
[4] Morley to Compton, 19 Aug., 1683, *ibid.*, 983 C, fo. 55.
[5] Bishop of Hereford to Compton, 24 May, 1684, *ibid.*, 982 C, fo. 67.

the Bishop of London was forced to confess his disappointment. 'It is so long since the encouragement his Majesty's Brief has given us hopes of a full return of the charity in behalf of those persecuted protestants of France', he wrote, 'who have hitherto subsisted by it: that the want of returns from several Dioceses have in a great measure discouraged the hopes that might justly have been entertained for their relief'. 'For mercy's sake to poor souls, daily perishing', complete your collection—so he begged Bishop Lloyd.[1]

The response to the financial appeals, we repeat, was not ungenerous. Between the dates 15 November, 1682, and 10 February, 1683, a sum of £1,569 5s. 3d. was paid into the Chamber of London upon the King's brief and later the total reached £6,684 17s. 8d.[2]

Money was not the only problem which concerned Compton. Difficulties of another kind which developed in some communities may perhaps be best illustrated if we take a glimpse at two French congregations in London, both of which experienced a great deal of stress and strain in the daily ordering of their religious life.

Compton had not long been Bishop of London before he was made painfully aware that there were sharp differences of opinion between the Consistory of the French Church in London and one of its ministers, Dr. Herault. Herault's crime was to have supported the King's nomination of the late Sieur Michaeli, an unpopular minister, for which act the congregation branded him 'a cheat, an incendiary, and a traitor', putting him off the consistory, taking away his pension, and inhibiting him from carrying on his ministry.[3] The accused pastor appealed to the Crown, and it fell to the lot of the Bishop of London to hold an investigation, as a result of which he reported that 'Dr. Herault has behaved as a true and faithful minister of the Gospel and a

---

[1] Compton to Lloyd, 12 Nov., 1682, Bod. Tanner MSS. 35, fo. 24.

[2] The sum was made up as follows, though it must be remembered that the figures quoted for each diocese simply represent the monies paid in during the period stated. Lincoln £346 6s. od; Ely £64 5s. 3d.; Durham £144 15s. 9d.; London £95 9s. 10d.; Winchester £382 6s. od.; St. David's £50 19s. od.; Hereford £120; York £105; Llandaff £63 18s. 3d.; Peterborough £23 11s. 2d.; Archdeaconry of St. Albans £8 11s. od.; Lichfield £42 7s. 3d.; Rochester £60; Norwich £50; Gloucester 7s. 6d.; Chester £11 7s. 5d. See Bod. Rawlinson MSS. 984 C, fo. 209.

[3] *S.P.D.* Car. II, June 1676, 382, no. 194.

good and loyal subject'.[1] The King accordingly informed the
elders and deacons of the French Church in London that 'they
must make good their agreement between them and Dr. Herault,
and publish this royal command in the church the next Lord's
day'.

This assertion of Royal authority, through the Bishop, did
not serve to make Herault any more popular with his fellow
religionists; particularly since he unwisely tried to follow up
his success by securing from the Crown 'some reprimand for the
persons who have ill treated him for his deference to orders'.[2]
When another minister, Monsieur Primrose, advised his brethren
on the consistory to make their peace with Dr. Herault lest these
continued wranglings should again come to the ears of the King,
they promptly turned on him also with the words: 'Are you one
of those who run after and adore the beast?'[3]

The fact was that the refugees, though they welcomed the
protection which the Crown provided, yet resented the assertion
of any effective external jurisdiction, whether by King or Bishop,
over the religious life of their community. Dr. Herault seemed
half a traitor because he was a King's man. The unfortunate
disagreements in this French community in London were not
soon disposed of.

The French Church in the Savoy, which had been settled
there by an order of Charles II, dated 11 March, 1661,[4] also had
its up and downs. This community regarded itself as pre-eminent
among French churches, and one of its former ministers was
made a Canon of Canterbury in 1680. Yet its corporate life
suffered sadly from much internal upheaval.

The year 1679 was a particularly troubled one. Two of its
non-resident ministers, de l'Angle and Breval, were presented
by the Bishop of London to English benefices, and this raised
the thorny question of their arrears of pay. Compton was again
called in and, under his guidance and in the presence of the
churchwardens and 'housekeepers', the whole matter was
thrashed out. The Bishop decided, and for once both parties
seem to have acquiesced in his decision, that the arrears of

---

[1] *S.P.D.* Car. II, 22 May, 1676, E.B. 27, fo. 84.

[2] *Ibid.*, June 1676, 382, no. 195.

[3] Primrose later had his difficulties with the Consistory. See Bod. Rawlinson
MSS. 984 C, fo. 225.

[4] *Ibid.*, fo. 5. The order was entered into the Bishop of London's register.

Breval's income—some £60 for a period of eighteen months—should be paid to him at the rate of £10 a year.

The system of non-resident ministers at the Savoy does not seem to have worked very well, and the secretary of the consistory wrote to Compton asking for permission to elect a minister who would constantly reside with them.

About the same time another minister, D'Allemagne by name, was suspended from office, though on expressing penitence he was restored by the Bishop of London.[1] His restoration, however, caused some misgivings in the congregation, in spite of the fact that Compton had acted in accordance with the wishes of the consistory, and most of the French had declared that they 'were quite content to leave the matter in the Bishop of London's hands'.[2]

These matters may appear trivial and in themselves unimportant, but they represent the psychology of the dispossessed the world over and the irritation which persecution breeds. A balanced Christianity does not easily flourish in a people who have suffered oppression in their own country and have been forced to fly to another. The refugees certainly needed tactful handling.

The Church of the Savoy was situated in the Parish of St. Martin-in-the-Fields, and relations with the vicar became somewhat strained in the reign of Anne. This arose out of an Act of Parliament which required parents to inform their parish priest within five days of the birth of a child. The refugees at the Savoy were reluctant to do this, and this meant a loss of income to the Vicar of St. Martin's, since a fee was charged for baptism. He therefore let it be known that although he had no desire to exact money from 'poor distressed French Protestants', yet he was determined to insist upon his rights in respect of 'such as live Plentifully and [are] thought rich'. The French, on their part, maintained that the King had given them a Church in the Savoy so that 'all English rites shall be administered there', and that the registration which the Act required applied only to those who desired baptism in their parish church.

The dispute was inevitably referred to the Bishop of London.[3]

---

[1] Bod. Rawlinson, MSS. 984 C, fo. 15. [2] *Ibid.*

[3] St. Paul's Cathedral, Lord Mayor's Vestry, Bundle II. It is interesting to notice that Claude Denise wrote to Compton in 1679 concerning the settlement of the Savoy congregation: 'It pleased his Majesty to establish the French Church assembled at the Savoy on condition that it conformed to the discipline of the Church of England' (Bod. Rawlinson MSS. 984 C, fo. 37).

If the Church of Savoy had its troubles within, it was certainly united in not regarding with too friendly an eye the establishment of other refugee congregations in London, each claiming to manage its own affairs. Perhaps it was natural that the more influential membership of the Savoy congregation, and its royal foundation, should encourage the assertion of a quasi-supremacy. Particularly did the consistory at the Savoy disapprove of the building of other churches for their fellow countrymen in or near London. When the French in Hungerford Market, for example, petitioned the Bishop of London that they might be allowed to have their own church, they were met by stern opposition from the Savoy, and a counter-petition was sent to Fulham.[1] Nor was this an isolated case for Compton received a memorial from another group of seventy-two refugees, one of whom was R. Garric, grandfather of the famous actor, praying for permission to build a church.[2]

The French in Windsor found themselves in the expensive predicament of having to travel up to the Savoy to receive any settled pastoral care, and they requested the Bishop that they might have their own minister. The petition came with more force since the community in Windsor was miserably poor, and in 1680 its members were living almost entirely on the charity of others.[3]

It is quite clear that the authority that the Church in the Savoy tried to exercise over younger communities was strongly resented. In a Memorial sent to the Bishop ('Réponse des particuliers qui demandent d'établissement d'une nouvelle église aux representations de messieurs de la Savoye à My Lord Evêque de Londre') the writers repudiated in no uncertain terms any such claims to authority over them, and they alleged that it was simply the desire to keep power in their own hands which made those of the Savoy always oppose the building of new churches.[4]

If it was the policy of the refugees at the Savoy to prevent the erection of other churches, and the setting up of new congregations, they were certainly unsuccessful. In fact, the rapid establishment of refugee churches alarmed even the Bishop of London, and he decided to make enquiries as to their number

---

[1] Bod. Rawlinson MSS. 984 C, fo. 250. The French in Hungerford Market replied to the counter petition with another document sent to the Bishop.
[2] *Ibid.*, fo. 223.   [3] *Ibid.*, fo. 258.   [4] *Ibid.*, fo. 274.

and location. He found that there were in all eight 'comformable' churches in London under nineteen ministers, and seventeen 'non-comformable' under twenty-six ministers. The intelligence was alarming, and the Bishop sent to each congregation a citation, 'upon his Maj[es]tie taking notice of so many new Churches erected of late without his Consent or Licence'. 'Such as they have erected upon their own head', he threatened, would be 'prosecuted according to law'.[1]

We must remember, of course, as the background of these and similar disputes, that very real problems relating to the status of these French communities were involved in their relations to each other, to the Church of England, and to the Crown. The Archbishop of Canterbury and the Bishop of London did not lack advisers as they tried to wrestle with these questions. The Bishop of Winchester tried to make things easier in his own diocese by ordering that the French in Wandsworth (then in his See) should henceforth organise the life of their Church under two wardens acting with the minister, rather than by means of a consistory.[2] The problem was simplified when the refugee ministers were ordained into the Church of England, and this was what Compton preferred. Yet even then the community was still regarded as standing in a unique relationship to the Crown by whose favour its members were allowed to settle in England—and this in practice meant being under the general superintendence of the Bishop of London. It was the Crown which through the Bishop licensed them, regulated their internal life, and protected them from the occasional malice of the English.

The French were themselves conscious of their difficult situation, and one of their number drew up, for the benefit of the Bishop of London, a paper *Avis pour l'établissement d'un bon gouvernement dans les églises étrangères de ce royaume* which contained, however, little that was new.[3] In another document which found its way to Fulham, *Memoire touchant la manière de recevoir et employer les proselytes et protestans qui se refugient en Angleterre*, it was suggested that to meet fresh incursions temporary building should be constructed, and that those who could

---

[1] St. Paul's Cathedral, Lord Mayor's Vestry, Bundle III.
[2] Bod. Rawlinson MSS. 984 C, fo. 213.
[3] *Ibid.*, 984 C, fo. 261.

not be so housed should be sent off in groups of twenty or thirty
to Carolina.[1] As a matter of fact, many French Protestants were
only too pleased to avail themselves of the opportunity to go to
America, and Compton ordained some of their ministers in
order that they might take charge of congregations, not exclusively French, in the Plantations.

One scheme of a rather novel character—that the Bishop of
London should meet the Marquise de Reigne, who owned 'a
town in Poitou, and that together they should petition the King
of France for permission to establish the Huguenots in this one
place—does not seem to have got beyond the tentative stage.[2]

Compton's period of most active labours on behalf of the
Protestant refugees came in the reigns of both Charles and
James. It is not surprising that James did not regard these French
men and women with too favourable an eye[3] and that Compton's
energies, therefore, during his reign were devoted to shielding
them from royal malice and protecting them in their rights.[4]

After the Revolution there was still need to help persecuted
Christians, but partly owing to the initiative of Archbishop
Tenison, the Bishop of London's role was less dominant. The
Prince of Orange had not long been on the throne before events
in Europe drove more refugees over to England, particularly
Vaudois and French speaking Protestants from Switzerland. In
November 1695, the King, in his speech to Parliament, stressed
the need to make provision for these unfortunates, and £15,000
was voted out of the civil list for their relief.[5] The feelings of the
nation were once again stirred, and a special appeal for the
support of their ministers and schoolmasters enabled £10 a
quarter to be paid to a majority of them.[6]

In January 1699, there was a renewed outburst of persecution
which brought fresh incursions of the Vaudois and French
Protestants from Switzerland. William received a letter from
the States General on their behalf, and replied that 'he would
gladly do what he thought fit for their relief'. Henry Compton's
experience was recognised to be invaluable and he, with the Arch-

---

[1] Bod. Rawlinson MSS. 984 C, fo. 228.   [2] *Ibid.*, fo. 243.
[3] Yet amongst Compton's papers (*ibid.*, 983 C, fo. 89) there is a declaration
from the French minister and thirteen refugees at Thorpe-le-Soken that they
will assist the King, against 'James Scott, late Duke of Monmouth', with their
lives.
[4] See p. 85.   [5] Lambeth MSS. 1122, fo. 1.   [6] *Ibid.*, 930, fo. 42.

bishop of Canterbury, was consulted, and it was left to them 'to propose the methods they judged the most proper'. They met forthwith and decided on a national collection which the Archbishop supported by a letter to the clergy. The money thus obtained was paid into the Lord Chamberlain's Office, and to secure a just allocation of funds a commission for the relief of the Vaudois was appointed on 12 March, 1699, under royal licence. The Bishop of London was most assiduous in his attendance at its meetings, and he was active in rallying his own clergy to support the collections: but as we have suggested, the initiative was largely taken out of his hands through the personal interest of the Archbishop, and also by the Bishop's estrangement from the Court.

There can be no doubt of Compton's deep and genuine concern for the welfare of the Protestant refugees during the whole of his episcopate. Large was the number with whom he corresponded, and for whom he obtained financial help. Many, again, were the refugees upon whom he laid his hands and for whom he found benefices either in England or America. It was his constant practice, by sympathetic understanding of their problems, to encourage the French ministers to seek ordination in the Church of England and to use its liturgy: but he was careful not to push this policy to extremes and resisted James's efforts to abuse it. It was the Bishop's wish that his own countrymen should be better informed as to the sufferings which these French Protestants were undergoing in their own land, and he constantly tried to overcome the prejudice which so many entertained against them. The interest of the Bishop of London was certainly the keener because of his opposition to the unconstitutional policy of James: but it would be unfair to regard his concern as a political game with the refugees as his trump card.

CHAPTER EIGHTEEN

THE CHURCHES OF SWITZERLAND

THE close communication between the various churches which the refugee problem, and the consequent provision of relief, made necessary, inevitably produced an early manifestation of what may be called an ecumenical spirit, that is a brotherly awareness by Protestants in one country of their fellows in another. There was a half guilty feeling that divisions among those churches which had broken away from Rome were not only dangerous, but in a measure sinful, and consequently that there ought to be a move towards some kind of union. In the early years of the eighteenth century, this ideal almost (but not quite) became practical politics, the reasons for which may be briefly summarised.

First the successes of the Counter Reformation placed the Protestant bodies definitely on the defensive. The avowed aim of the Jesuits was none other than the re-incorporation of all those lands lost to the Roman See, and already much territory had been restored to the bosom of the Roman Catholic Church. Moreover, the military aggression of Louis—though his assertion of power was in reality more nationalistic than religious—undoubtedly bred a common opposition to a common foe. There is nothing so effective as fear to produce unity, though a unity so gained usually proves to be very temporary.

Secondly the reformed churches were in some respects more consolidated internally in Compton's day, and thus could begin to look outwards. They had never forgotten, emotionally, the universality of the mediaeval church, but so long as they were fighting for their very existence, they had of necessity to insist on the right to dissent. They were now free to work out some of the implications of their faith, although they possessed this freedom only within the framework of the national state which protected them. Paradoxically the fact that some of the Protestant churches were forced to deal with the problem of dissent within their own communions also made them anxious to gain prestige by seeking some wider union.

Thirdly, the very existence of a refugee problem inevitably tended to bring the Protestant churches nearer together, particularly the English, French, and German branches. When the Commission on which Compton served was sending money over to Brandenburg for the settlement of refugees in that country, the Bishop, and those who worked with him, could hardly help being brought into contact with the heads of the Lutheran Church. Certainly many reformers on the Continent desired some kind of union among Protestants, and Leibnitz wrote to Burnet, in 1698, suggesting that a small committee be formed in England to discuss their common faith. A year later, Dr. Erastus Jablonski, Chaplain to the King of Prussia and superintendant of the Protestant Church in Poland, sent a letter to Tenison, Archbishop of Canterbury, asking whether they might consider together this question of unity. We are not concerned here, however, with the failure of these negotiations, which was due in part to the timidity of the Archbishop and his fear of alienating the High Church section within the Church of England. Compton certainly took no part in them, but he became intimately involved in a correspondence along similar lines with the Protestant churches in Switzerland.

As a background to this correspondence, it is well to remember that this was a most unhappy period in the history of the Swiss Confederation. The Cantons were distracted by the religious division between Roman Catholics and Protestants, and further divided by the tensions between the Zwinglians in the German, and the Calvinists in the French speaking Cantons. It is little wonder that in such a religious *milieu*, feeling should often run high, and that the churches should be most sensitive to criticism.

The Bishop of London's casual contacts with the Swiss churches began early in his episcopate. In 1684, for example, he received a very profuse tribute to his Protestant zeal from Philip Mestreynt, doctor and senior professor of theology at Geneva, who had recently had long conversations with two of the Bishop's nephews.[1] Compton's correspondence with the Swiss churches took on a more definite character, however, in 1700, due to the following circumstances.

---

[1] Mestreynt to Compton, 25 Sept., 1684, Bod. Rawlinson MSS. 982 C, fo. 29.

To 'high Anglicans' the very name 'Geneva' was anathema. It conjured up the militant figures of such Protestant heroes as Calvin, Knox, and Beza. It was in Geneva, moreover, that Christopher Goodman, and other English exiles, during the reign of Queen Elizabeth, had drawn up a 'body of Articles concerning Discipline, which caused great Troubles within Church and State'.[1] Perhaps nowhere was this stronghold of Calvinism held in more abhorrence than at Oxford, and at no time more so than during the early years of the eighteenth century. So much was this the case that it found expression in a poem written by a former member of the University to commemorate the sad death, in 1700, of the Duke of Gloucester. In the course of this laboured composition, the author made a vehement attack on the Swiss churches for using a translation of the Psalms by the Frenchman Conarbus. News of this criticism eventually reached Geneva, whereupon two Professors in the city wrote to the Bishop of London, on 26 November, 1700, explaining the precise circumstances under which this translation (with 'its pure and native simplicity') had been admitted into their church.

Compton acknowledged their letters with politeness and cordiality. ''Tis with a great deal of satisfaction on my Side', he wrote, 'I embrace the Occasion you have given me of your dear Correspondence, looking upon it as a happy Omen of a more strict Alliance at this Conjuncture; when the Common Interest of our most Holy Religion is most furiously attacked on all sides.' The Church of England, he reassured them, 'made not the least scruple of admitting New Translations, provided they are very well examined beforehand'. As for the offending verses, Compton explained that they were written by a young student, and unfortunately signed by the Dean of Christ Church without his reading them. 'Be satisfied', the Bishop concluded 'that the Prejudice conceived against you has been much abated a considerable time ago, amongst those of our Church, and this Reflection must be attributed to nothing else, than the indiscreet reading of some Author or other of the last Age: For I can assure you that our present Church is absolutely disposed to recognise your Friendship and to live with you in the Communion of Charity in our Lord Jesus Christ. I therefore beg of you to

[1] *Several Letters from the Pastors of Geneva*, 1707, p. 3.

assure the rest of your venerable Partners, your Brethren, of my Affection and Services.'[1]

This little storm in a teacup seemed to have blown over, but most unfortunately, in 1705, another attack was made on the Church of Geneva, once again in a poem 'approved of the University and under its Name offered to the Queen by the Title of *Strena Oxoniensis*'. The distress of the pastors in Geneva was understandable, and on 5 May, 1705, they complained bitterly both to the Archbishop of Canterbury and the Bishop of London at this renewed hostility. 'There is not so much as one single Person among us', they wrote somewhat pathetically, 'but what has very honourable Sentiments and speaks accordingly of your Episcopal Government.'[2]

The Bishop of London, himself not a little aggrieved, got into touch with the University immediately and sent them a copy of the letter he had received. Their reply to the Pastors, sent on 12 February, 1706, and signed by George Cooper, Notary Public, is not without interest in its ambiguity. In it they assured the Church of Geneva of their 'benevolence' towards them, and stated that the author of the poem had not meant to attack their Church, but rather Schismatics in England who used the authority of Geneva to absent themselves from the established worship. They wrote:

> Your worthy approbation of our Church will at all times be highly esteemed among us which would soon put an end to the Schisms in this Country, if your Authority had in reality the same Weight with those that dissent from us as they pretend it has. Most illustrious Friends, concerning the difference of Rites used in the divers Churches, we have always been of the same Opinion with you, for this you will find expressly laid down in our Liturgy and in the Articles of our Religion; That it belongs to every Church to make use of her Right of prescribing certain Ceremonies, and that it is not allowable for one Church to upbraid another because she does introduce different Ceremonies. Far be it from our Charitable Intentions, to be so rigorous as to condemn those of the Reformed Churches, which by an irresistable Necessity, were forced to recede from the primitive form of Episcopal Government, as if they were destitute of true Pastors and Sacraments. Those of our most Celebrated Divines, who in their Travels abroad have made no Scruple

[1] *Several Letters from the Pastors of Geneva*, pp. 4 and 5.
[2] *Ibid.*, p. 6.

to resort to your Congregations had certainly quite a different opinion of your Church.[1]

On 30 April, 1706, the Bishop himself replied to the Church at Geneva in a further letter breathing charity and sweet reasonableness. He admitted that 'among a sort of People, either for Want of Time, or of penetrating rightly into all the Qualifications requisite', the name of Geneva was associated with the theology of such extremists as Christopher Goodman and his like. But, Compton assured them again, 'I dare give you my Word, that there is scarce a Person deserving to be taken notice of, either by you or us, who is not lately satisfied with those obliging words you have made use of in regard to our Church; I can assure you, in particular in the behalf of the University of Oxford, that the Governors and Heads of Colleges are much dissatisfied with the Indiscretion of those that made use of such odious Reflections'.[2]

This statesmanlike epistle was well received in Geneva, and it evoked a letter of gratitude, 'for the Goodness you have had to lay our Interests to Heart, and to reconcile us to some Members of the Church of England who had received sinister impressions about us concerning the Discipline and Liturgy of our Church'. Particularly were they satisfied with the accommodating spirit of the University of Oxford, and the opportunity the contretemps had provided of entering into a friendly correspondence. 'Yet if these Steps on both sides were to produce any wholesome Effect', they affirmed, 'it will be owing to your Lordship, in whose Power it is to make us enter into all the Engagements you shall judge proper for the peace of the Churches. Continue, my Lord, your Labours in so good a work. He even will bless your Holy Intentions.'[3]

In a letter written to the University of Oxford at the same time, the Pastors of Geneva went to some pains to explain their ecclesiastical position *vis à vis* other Protestant churches. 'We make use', they explained, 'of such ceremonies as were necessary and suitable to the Government of our Republic; nevertheless we neither neglect nor condemn such as differ from us: for we believe that Faith in Jesus Christ, Love towards our Neighbours, and a Worship free from all Superstition and Idolatry,

---

[1] *Several Letters from the Pastors of Geneva*, p. 9.   [2] *Ibid.*   [3] *Ibid.*

being sufficient to obtain salvation, are not incompatible with those that differ only in Ceremonial. We wish therefore that these bonds of Christian Charity and Communion may not be broken: did we dwell among you we should gladly appear at your Congregations, having nothing so much in view as to contribute our joint endeavours towards the prosperity of all the Evangelical Churches.'

It may be that it was this correspondence, and the charitable and helpful attitude adopted by the Bishop of London, which led to another exchange of letters initiated by J. C. Werndley, who was Chaplain and Secretary to Abraham Stanyan (1669-1732), English envoy to the Swiss Cantons.

Stanyan was undoubtedly a man of considerable ability, whose great triumph it was (in co-operation with the Dutch envoy) to obtain for the King of Prussia the succession to Neufchatel.[1] His wide knowledge of the Cantons is apparent in his *Account of Switzerland* which was published in 1714. In England he was a member of the Kit-Cat Club and the friend of Alexander Pope.[2]

Werndley was one of those active men who delighted in public affairs, and in this respect had much in common with the Bishop of London. Maybe it was at the latter's suggestion that Werndley entered into a private correspondence, sending the Bishop newsletters in which he discoursed at large on military and diplomatic affairs on the Continent. There are in the Bodleian Library no fewer than thirty-eight such newsletters, written in French, all of them dictated by Werndley to his amanuensis, a refugee minister named Clarion.[3] They constitute a valuable source of information on the complicated relationships between the great powers at this time. Compton himself was essentially a man of affairs, interested in the European scene, and he doubtless valued (and paid for) this opportunity of gaining insight, through the eyes of a quick-witted if indiscreet observer, into what was going on behind the political scenes. 'I am glad', Werndley wrote to the Bishop on one occasion, 'your Lordship doth not dislike

---

[1] See Bod. Rawlinson MSS. 984 C, fo. 150. *Copy of a letter from the Archbishop of Canterbury and the Bishops of Ely and Chichester urging the people of Neufchatel to elect the King of Prussia as their Sovereign.*

[2] *D.N.B.* liv. 87.   [3] Bod. Rawlinson MSS. 982 C, fos. 45-141.

the news I send you from impartial hands, and should be the more glad if your Lordship giveth me leave to continue the same.'[1]

Werndley's main preoccupation for some years was his attempt to draw together the Church of England and the Protestant churches of Switzerland. In 1706, therefore, he approached the Bishop to this end. Compton was undoubtedly interested, though obviously cautious, for the days of his militant alliance with the whigs was over, and he was now numbered, if not with the transgressors, at least with the tories. Yet he was not prepared to shut the door outright, but in response to Werndley's feelers replied not discouragingly on 27 March, 1706. We do not know the precise terms of his letter but it certainly served to hearten Werndley for he sent it off immediately to the chief minister at Berne, 'who will be very glad', so he reported back to the Bishop, 'to see your Lordship's mind about the Matter'. He also sent copies of Compton's letter to the Dean of Neufchatel, and the chief ministers of Geneva and Zurich.[2]

Encouraged by the Bishop's interest, the enthusiastic Werndley (perhaps prematurely) felt that the time had come, since there was a definite response in Switzerland, for Compton to be more definite. What was now wanted, and what the Swiss ministers expected, were precise proposals. So far, Werndley had acted purely as a private individual putting out feelers, and he had succeeded in making the two parties, Bishop and ministers, aware of each other's interest. But it must not end there if anything of real value were to come out of it. Also the success of such negotiations depended on 'the pleasure of the Court', and this meant, in practice, that if Stanyan were recalled (so Werndley warned Compton), 'we should be frustrated of our sincere intentions'. The next step must now be taken by the Bishop and it ought not to be too long deferred. 'I can go no further my Lord', he wrote from Berne, 'for hitherto (as your Lordship may guess from the Premises) I did act as a Private Man and so I must put a Stop to it, till I know your Lordship's pleasure and direction how far to proceed for the future'. To assist the Bishop in deciding his

[1] Werndley to Compton, 19 June, 1708, Bod. Rawlinson, MSS. 982 C, fo. 67.
[2] Same to same, 24 Apr., 1706, *ibid.*, fo. 47.

policy, Werndley made the following suggestions which we quote in his own words:

i. That your Lordship in the name of the Church should write a letter of thanks to the Artistes and the rest of the Revd Brethren for their pious Disposition to serve the Crown, the Church established by Law, and the Nation, for a happy Reunion. . . .

ii. That I might be honoured with some private directions and Instructions from England, whether or how to proceed any further in this Affair, so that not altogether as a private man but *nomine publico*.

iii. That the Honourable Mr. Stanyan should be directed from England to give me leave to do a journey to those chief Places that are thus disposed to serve the Crown and the Church. For they all give me a hint that it would be necessary (because of several difficulties that may happen and divers questions that may be moved) I should have some Conference with them by Word of Mouth, and that my Presence (having some private Instructions) would very much contribute to the good Work. And I believe Mr. Stanyan (who is very glad to see me spend my time to such good purpose) would easily give his consent to it, if he were required from the Court or from the Bishops.

iv. That some allowance (suitable for the Purpose) should be allowed me from the Court or elsewhere.[1]

The real difficulty, however, was not in giving Werndley authority to proceed, but in deciding what line to take in respect of some of the thorny problems involved. The Swiss divines had already approached Werndley on some specific points which he now laid before the Bishop in these words:

I have been asked two Chief Questions that have somewhat puzzled me, and I humbly crave for your Lordship's direction about the same, viz.

(1) In case the non-conformists were willing to be Reunited, whether or not they would be obliged to swear that they believe Episcopacy to be absolutely *de jure divino*.

(2) Why are such Priests, as are ordained by Roman Catholic Bishops, admitted into the Sacred Offices in the Church of England, when the French and other foreign ministers are not admitted

---

[1] Stanyan, he added, could only afford to give him £50 per annum.

without a Re-ordination tho' they were ordained by a Protestant Synod.[1]

These two inquiries show how difficult it was—nay almost impossible—for these negotiations to get very far, particularly against the background of the High Church reaction during the reign of Anne. A Church which affirms officially (or in practice takes this line for fear of internal disruption) that episcopacy is an essential and divine pattern, cannot contemplate reunion with other Protestant bodies except on these terms.

Undoubtedly the Church of England insisted on reordination where foreign Protestants were concerned, though it is just possible that a few French refugees may have held English cures without submitting to it, and certainly some theologians of the *Ecclesia Anglicana* regarded episcopacy as more of the *bene esse* than the *esse* of the Church. But 1706, anyhow, was not 1689. A large section of the Anglican Church—and it was the most vocal in Anne's reign, especially in Convocation—were rigid upholders of episcopacy who would brook no compromise. They deplored all schemes for re-union and regarded them as exalting expediency above principle; as but one more example that the church was in danger from latitudinarian whigs who were only too ready to disrupt the Church of England at home, by abandoning its Catholic inheritance, in the interests of a shameful union with Protestants abroad. Nor were the tentative negotiations with the Prussian Church which were then under way any more popular.

It is a great pity that Compton's reply to Werndley is not extant, and that we are left to infer its contents from what later happened. While he was still waiting for instructions from Fulham, Werndley sent off another letter to the Bishop on 1 May, which suggests that it was not only from the side of the Church of England that doubts came: the Swiss themselves were equally cautious and had genuine misgivings. The driving force, it is obvious, was Werndley. We are not surprised, therefore, that the Swiss kept on returning in their discussions to the vexed question of episcopal ordination. Perhaps it was of some help when Werndley explained to them that at an ordination in the Church of England the Bishop was assisted by his presbyters.[2]

[1] Werndley to Compton, 24 Apr., 1706, Bod. Rawlinson MSS. 982 C, fo. 47.
[2] Same to same, 1 May, 1706, *ibid.*, fo. 54.

Compton, despite this further letter, was in no hurry to reply. He was loth to commit himself, and maybe consulted the High Church Archbishop Sharp, and Stanyan himself. Though he must have known that these negotiations would not get anywhere, he was perhaps reluctant to be the one to close the door. Thus he waited, while the more impetuous Werndley grew increasingly impatient, and wrote to him again on 12 May.[1] Interest in Switzerland was now on the increase, he reported, and it seemed that some of the initial doubts had been overcome. The minister of Geneva, for example, had informed Werndley that he himself was most anxious for 'reconciliation and peace', and saw no insurmountable obstacles in the way of a 'rapprochement' since matters of 'discipline or indifferent ceremonies' were local affairs and need not hinder intercommunion. The Swiss churches, on their part, invited those ordained in the Church of England to hold theological chairs at their universities, and they did not themselves find any difficulty in preaching from Church of England pulpits.[2]

Yet though he had received 'kind letters' from a number of prominent Swiss Protestants, Werndley continued, things were now 'at a stand', for he was repeatedly being asked the same question: Was he acting as a 'Private Man or a Public Person'? The minister of Zurich, for example, had gone out of his way to raise this question, and had urged that Werndley be given definite instructions from England, so that he could personally address the Protestant Cantons, 'answer such necessary questions as may be moved', and find out from them 'what in Reason and Honour could be desired or wished towards a happy Reunion'.[3]

The informal negotiations, entered into through the initiative, not of the Bishop, but of Werndley, had obviously reached the point where they must be sanctioned by authority or given their quietus. Even good manners demanded this. Werndley had no real *locus standi*, and it was understandable that the ministers of the Reformed churches in Switzerland should ask themselves whether they were but wasting their time unless they were able to bring the matter officially before some more responsible person in England.

---

[1] Werndley to Compton, 12 May, 1706, Bod. Rawlinson, MSS. 982 C, fo. 60.
[2] *Ibid.*   [3] *Ibid.*, fo. 60.

Compelled at last to say something definite, Compton now made it clear that he was in no mood to go further. In fact he was already nervous lest Werndley, in his zeal, should have committed him to a position which he did not approve, and which might prejudice him with his clergy at home. The question of episcopacy was certainly a difficult one in view of the religious situation in England: and the position of the Dissenters presented embarrassing problems in respect of any proposed union with Protestants abroad.[1] Could they be left out, if those abroad were brought in?

The Bishop's eagerly awaited reply to Werndley—again not extant—closed the door as firmly as possible consistently with Christian charity.

In acknowledging it on 19 June, 1706, Werndley nervously 'assured' the Bishop that he had 'engaged' himself no further in the matter than was 'proper for a private Person'; and that 'his chief Design' was simply 'so to feel the pulse of the Churches in Switzerland . . . as might be instrumental to a Reunion'. 'But all is now superseded', he wrote, and without positive orders from the Bishop or from the Court, he would 'do nothing but keep up a good Correspondence with those worthy Gentlemen'. 'I was invited by the President of the Synod of Grisons', he wrote, 'to appear at their synod, if possibly I could: but I made my civil excuses, as having no orders from England. I have only laid such a foundation as some good structure may be made upon it, when Providence shall find fit.'[2]

It is in no way surprising, as we have suggested, that these negotiations broke down. So far as the Bishop of London was concerned they came at the wrong end of his career. He was now well over seventy. Changed political circumstances and personal disappointments had made him forsake old loves. Even had he been enthusiastically behind Werndley, it would not have altered the attitude of Convocation, nor overcome the scruples even of some 'liberals' who, as practical men, feared schism at home as the price of 'reunion' with those abroad, and thus

[1] Monsieur Calendrin, the minister of Geneva, confessed to Werndley that he could not understand why there was not a perfect union between the members of the different churches in England.

[2] Werndley to Compton, 19 June, 1706, Bod. Rawlinson MSS. 982 C, fo. 67. At the instigation of the Bishop of London, the Queen later found preferment for Werndley (*ibid.*, fo. 145).

recognised the need for caution. No man, for example, had greater sympathy for his continental Protestant brethren than Thomas Tenison, Archbishop of Canterbury, yet even he thought it necessary to be prudent, even dilatory, in his response to the approaches of the Prussian Church. The Archbishop, again, was over seventy: but the younger men, in the main, were orthodox and tory, and did not entertain feelings of excessive charity towards their Swiss Protestant brethren. In fact, quite the reverse, as the affair between the University of Oxford and the Church of Geneva showed only too plainly. There had already been one disastrous separation—that of the Nonjurors—which had drawn a vast treasury of piety away from the Church of England. Most contemporaries did not wish for another.

The Bishop of London's correspondence with Werndley and the ministers of the Swiss Churches did not suddenly cease with the breakdown of these tentative negotiations but it became more occasional and lacking in significance. When the Swiss ministers met together in October 1706, they particularly asked Werndley to assure the Bishop of their 'hearty Respects, and of their Good Inclinations to serve [his] Lordship upon any occasion, especially to serve the Church of England according to the Emergency of Times and Affairs':[1] and a year later they informed the Bishop that it was a particular joy to them in Geneva that Mr. Stanyan, her Majesty's Envoy, had received the sacrament at their altar. 'We regard this', Osterwold wrote, 'as an authentic sign of the sentiments which are felt in England towards our Churches, and as a happy augury for that union so much desired.'[2]

Unfortunately increasing age often made the Bishop a lax correspondent. On one occasion Werndley felt it necessary to write anxiously to Fulham, suggesting tactfully that the ministers of Zurich would be grateful if his Lordship could answer their last two letters and assure them of his continued protection. 'Our worthy Artistes of Zurich', he commented, 'having had no news of your Lordship this great while would be glad to hear something'—if it were only the condition of his health.[3]

---

[1] Werndley to Compton, 9 Oct., 1706, Bod. Rawlinson MSS 982 C, fo. 84.
[2] Osterwold to Compton, 21 Oct., 1707, *ibid.*, fo. 143.
[3] Werndley to Compton, 27 Oct., 1706, *ibid.*, fo. 95.

24

We know that the Bishop did eventually write to them, but what he said has not come down to us. We may be fairly safe in assuming, however, that he was content to express the most charitable sentiments.[1]

[1] It is a pity that we have no more than a solitary letter from one Cyprian Appia, a Piedmontese, who was ordained by the Bishop of London when in England. Back in his native village, he preached before the synod at Turin and informed Compton of his desire to introduce the English Liturgy to his countrymen, though some of them had declared that it was 'very like Popery'. 'If ever I should be advanced to some authority among you, I'll do what I can to introduce our most sacred Liturgy', he told the Bishop in July, 1709. 'In visiting the sick and in my little Family I make use of no other, and it would be a great Consolation to me to see it established in our Churches', he added. (See Appia to Compton, 1 July, 1709, Rawlinson MSS., 983 C, fo. 162.) As to what happened, we know no more.

CHAPTER NINETEEN

THE GREEK ORTHODOX CHURCH

NO account of Compton's relations with the Churches of Europe would be complete without some reference to his interest in the Greek Orthodox Church, particularly since there was, during his episcopate, a growing awareness on the part of members of the Church of England of the historic place of this ancient Church in Christendom.

During the whole of the Middle Ages, right up to the capture of Constantinople by the Turks in 1453, the East was almost an unknown world (except to such adventurers as Marco Polo, who returned with strange tales) for even the Crusades did little more than lift the curtain for a brief period. But the establishment of Ottoman supremacy, the flight of Greek scholars to Italy and the sufferings of many Orthodox Christians, made Western Europe conscious at last of this outpost of the Christian Empire.

To many convinced Protestants, this increasing knowledge seemed providential. Here was an ancient Church, preserving (or supposed to preserve) primitive traditions, which yet owed no allegiance whatever to Rome, and in fact openly repudiated its jurisdiction. It was but natural, therefore, that high Anglicans should view with particular interest, not unmixed with veneration, this episcopal, apostolic, but non-papal Church. It was equally natural that Greek Christians, suffering from the hostility and aggression of the Turks, should look for sympathy, if not for succour, to the west.

Nor was the interest of some Englishmen in what we should now call the Middle East confined to religion. Many came to think of it as a land of mystery and romance, and set out to explore its secrets, leaving behind them diaries which up to this day have found neither readers nor publishers.

Greek Christians, on their part, began to visit this country, and soon after the Restoration, Papas Jeremias Germanos attracted a great deal of attention, and some vulgar curiosity, when he arrived in England. Nothing could have been more hospitable than the reception which he received in Oxford.[1] This contact between an eminent Greek Churchman and the bishops of the *Ecclesia Anglicana* undoubtedly helped to make the rank and file of the English clergy more alive to the existence of this sister communion, though most of them continued abysmally ignorant of the theological position of the Greek Church, and of the pattern of its worship. In 1670, Dr. John Covel (1638-1722), a thoughtful divine, who in his early years combined a strong urge to travel with an interest in exotic plants, was sent out as chaplain to the English traders in Constantinople. He remained there for some six years, and as a result became intimately conversant with the life and worship of the Greek Church.[2] The fact that there was an English Churchman out there undoubtedly encouraged interest at home, and Sancroft (then Dean of St. Paul's), Gunning, Bishop of Chichester, and Pearson, Bishop of Chester—a great scholar—wrote asking him what were the 'accepted beliefs' of the Greek Church, particularly in those matters which formed the subject of debate between the Church of England and the Church of Rome.[3]

Another Greek dignitary who came to England at this time was Joseph Georgirenes, Metropolitan of Samos, and this visit proved to be important because it led to a proposal to establish an Orthodox Greek Church in London. News of such a scheme immediately attracted the keen interest of Compton, for his warm heart went out to those Greeks who were suffering persecution at the hands of the Turks. The fact that the project was carried through was largely due to his private encouragement, and to his support on the Privy Council. Dr. Smith, in dedicating the English edition of his study of the Greek Church to the Bishop of London, acknowledges his enthusiasm in these words: 'How highly your Lordship has merited of the Greek Church by taking it into your care and by opening a Sanctuary for the poor distressed Bishops and Priests of that Communion to fly unto is not unknown at Constantinople; and whatever the success of it may be, they cannot be so unjust as not to applaud your Lordship's design'.[4]

---

[1] T. Smith, *An Account of the Greek Church*, 1680, p. 46.   [2] *Ibid.*
[3] J. Wickham Legge, *English Church Life*, 1660-1833, 1914, p. 395, quoting J. Covel, *Some Account of the present Greek Church*, 1722.
[4] T. Smith, *op. cit.*, preface, p. 1.

The Church, dedicated to St. Mary, and situated in Crown Street, Soho, was completed in 1677. Over the doorway there was engraved the following inscription in Greek:

In the year of salvation MDCLXXVII
This Temple was erected for the Nation of the Greeks
In the reign of the most serene Charles II
The Lord James being heir apparent.
The Very Reverend Lord Henry Compton, Bishop
At the cost of the above named and the Bishops and Nobles
And with the assistance of Joseph
of Samos, Metropolitan of that Island.[1]

The troubles of the Greek community in London did not end with the consecration of the Church, for there were problems connected with its life and worship which goodwill of itself could not solve. Joseph, Metropolitan of Samos, seems to have understood the position of a refugee community far from its own country better than some of his brethren at home, and the fact that he was in England seeking favours may have helped to make him more accommodating. His companion in this country, however, a parish priest from Galata (a suburb of Constantinople), returned to Greece soon after the Church was built, and it was natural that he should be asked by the Orthodox Bishops to give a report on what was going on in London. The Bishops seem to have been somewhat disquieted at what they heard, for the result was a summons, in February 1679, to Sir John Finch, English ambassador at Constantinople (and formerly a professor of medicine at Pisa), to meet the Patriarch and five Archbishops in the presence of the synod. The object of the invitation (so Finch reported to Compton) was to 'know of me what I had to communicate to them concerning the establishing of a Greek Church in London'.[2]

The interview, which we are fortunate to possess in an account drawn up for the Bishop of London, does not seem to have come as a complete surprise, either to the ambassador or the Bishop.

It may be, of course, that the priest from Galata had been critical from the beginning and that his return home was expected to have repercussions. Certainly the Bishop appears to

---

[1] G. Williams, *The Orthodox Church of the East in the Eighteenth Century*, 1868, p. lxvi.   [2] *H.M.C.*, Finch MSS., i. 148.

have primed the ambassador as to the general status of the Greek Church in London. Sir John Finch began by explaining that the King 'out of his grace and favour' had been pleased to make a personal contribution to the building, 'but that the Church, being within the diocese of my Lord Bishop of London, his Majesty had left wholly the establishing of it to his Lordship, who both as a Prelate and a Privy Counsellor knew what was fitted to his Majesty's laws and government both in Church and State'.[1]

The four regulations which the Bishop of London laid down to control its life are significant since they indicate how much he was preoccupied at the time with the Roman Catholic controversy. First, there must be no pictures or ikons in the Church. Secondly, every priest who officiated must repudiate the doctrine of transubstantiation. Thirdly, there must be no prayers to the saints. Fourthly, the ministers must disown the Council of Bethlehem.

Sir John Finch therefore informed the Patriarch of the Bishop's orders—the interview was conducted in Italian through the parish priest from Galata—and the Greek ecclesiastics then proceeded to discuss them among themselves. At length they came to a common mind—it was not difficult—and there was no ambiguity about their reply, which we quote from the ambassador's own report to Compton. As to the first, 'they could not without pictures in the Church officiate . . . and they could on no conditions be stript of them'. As to the second, they spoke 'with much heat and indignation'. They did not differ from the Church of Rome on this matter of transubstantiation, and with one voice they 'thundered out . . . the very body of Christ that was crucified on Mount Calvary was after consecration there present . . . and they would never alter the doctrine'. As to the third they declared that 'all their Liturgies were composed of prayers to saints and to the Blessed Virgin Mary in the first place, and that on the eves of the commemorations of the particular saints they always had prayers peculiar to them'. As to the fourth, their reply was brief and to the point. 'They did not know what the import of the Council of Bethlehem was so they could say nothing about it.'[2]

Sir John Finch was too much a man of the world to be overawed by this somewhat shattering reply. He firmly pointed out to the Patriarch that it was 'illegal for any public church in England to express Romish beliefs and that it was just as bad to have them professed in Greek as in Latin'. He even dared to enter into an argument with these ecclesiastics on disputed points in theology. There were no pictures, he maintained, in the early Greek church, no praying to saints in the New Testament, and as to transubstantiation it was clearly contradicted by Christ's bodily presence at the Last Supper. 'But I added', so he reported to Fulham, 'that I should acquaint my Lord of London with these resolutions.'

The interview, however, was not yet finished, for the Patriarch now turned the tables by asking three questions of the ambassador. First, could the Greek priests in London consecrate the Sacrament with unleavened bread? Secondly, might they publicly profess the Holy Ghost as proceeding only from the Father? Thirdly, was it possible for the Greek Church in London to be placed under the general jurisdiction of the Patriarch of Constantinople?

Though not officially briefed, Sir John felt that he was competent to attempt some sort of reply to each of these questions. Concerning the first he said there would be no difficulty at all, as the Church of England was at one with the Greek Church in this practice. As to the second, 'it could hardly be admitted', and in respect of the third, it was 'extravagent and unreasonable, as they could not be exempt from his Majesty's jurisdiction nor would the Bishop of London be deprived of his rights.'[1]

The obvious hostility of these Greek Churchmen to the regulations which the Bishop of London was imposing on their Church in London did not augur well for its future, and it was doubtless this lack of support from home which largely prevented anything of value coming from this promising contact between the English and Greek churches. The Patriarch of Constantinople could not in good faith give the scheme his blessing in view of the *modus vivendi* upon which Compton insisted, and this lack of official backing reacted unfavourably on the whole enterprise from the beginning. Joseph's enthusiasm in England was not enough; support was also needed from Constantinople and this, unfortunately, was not forthcoming. Perhaps nothing is more

[1] *H.M.C.*, Finch MSS., i. 148.

distressing in the history of the Christian Church than the failure of different branches of it to settle their own differences, and to live together in peace.

Joseph, Metropolitan of Samos, remained in England for some years, seeking to interest members of the Church of England in the hardships of the Greek Church. In 1682 he sent a petition to the Archbishop of Canterbury praying 'that about 12 Scholars out of Greece be constantly here to be instructed and grounded to the true doctrine of the Church of England . . . and so to return into Greece to preach the same'.

This idea of establishing a College for Greek Students in England soon gained supporters, and Compton became both interested and enthusiastic, so much so that a contemporary describes him as its 'chief promoter'.[1] Early in 1677 there was 'great talk of converting Gloucester Hall into a College for educating twenty or thirty Greeks in Academical learning and to send them home.'

Many years elapsed before anything practical came of it, and it was only through the constant encouragement of Compton and the hard work of Dr. Woodroffe, Canon of Christ Church, that things finally began to stir. Worcester College was thus assigned for this purpose, and in a letter to the Patriarch of Constantinople (Callenicus) dated 14 March, 1695, inviting students over to England 'in the name of the most godly metropolitan of great London',[2] Benjamin Woodroffe is described as 'President and Head of the Greek College at Oxford'.[3] At Lambeth there is still extant a document headed: 'Model of a College to be settled in the University of some youths of the Greek Church.'[4]

Some young men did eventually come over in October 1698, and they went up to Worcester College, but their residence was brief, largely because not all the charms of a University

[1] 'Union Review' 1863, i. 490. Schemes of this kind were very much in the air at this time. In 1679, for example, Sancroft and eighteen bishops, who included Compton, promised to subscribe annually to educate some young men to Oxford and Cambridge for ordination in the Bohemian Confession 'to provide in some measure for the succession and continuence of the same'. See Bod. Rawlinson MSS. 985 C, fo. 5. Sancroft and Compton promised £8 p.a. Some three years later the indefatigable Bishop of London was obliged to write to the Archbishop reminding him that he was three years behind with his subscription. (Compton to Sancroft, 9 Dec. (no year), Tanner MSS. 36, fo. 187.)
[2] Ibid.   [3] Union Review, 1863, i. 433.   [4] Lambeth MSS. 938, fo. 38.

town could disguise the fact that their accommodation was very poor. The way of the pioneer is often hard and there does not seem, once again, to have been much encouragement for the project from Constantinople. Woodroffe finally lost heart and the scheme flagged.

It found a new supporter, however, in Edward Stephens (d. 1706), son-in-law to Matthew Hale, who conceived the idea of transferring the students 'to a good House well situated with convenient Lodgings for some Greek Clergymen and young Scholars and a decent Oratory here in London'. With the support once again of the Bishop of London, he solicited subscriptions,[1] but the scheme did not prove very practical. There was a general lack of interest, and as a result a serious shortage of money. It was no good not facing the facts, and the whole project finally came to nothing though there was frequent talk of reviving it. In 1700 there were rumours of twenty Greek youths coming over to be instructed in the faith of the Church of England, as 'some of these have already been received into Gloucester [Hall] who by their extraordinary progress have given the greatest helps that the design will answer'.

It would seem from the above that there were still a few young Greeks at Oxford, but a regular Greek College, as originally conceived, was unfortunately not established. Still, a general interest in the Greek Orthodox Church remained, though its expression lies outside the scope of a biography of Henry Compton. It may suffice here, perhaps, to notice that the diarist Luttrell reported, under the date 23 August, 1701: 'A Greek Patriarch is arrived here from Turkey with a considerable retinue, having letters of recommendation from the Lord Paget and Monsieur Collier the Dutch ambassador: he has been splendidly treated of by the Archbishop of Canterbury, and designs to visit the two Universities.'[2] When he went up to Cambridge he was entertained by Dr. Covel, who was able to discourse with him at great length in his own language.

The curtain which separated the East from the West, although lifted for a short time, soon fell again. As the eighteenth century pursued its sedate way, so did intercommunion between churches—despite its obvious appeal to the rationalism of the

[1] Bod. Rawlinson MSS. 564 C, fo. 21.
[2] *Ibid.*, 984 C, fo. 271.

time—cease to attract. The religious interest was not strong enough. The modern national state was emerging.

We have now finished our survey of Compton's relations with the Protestant churches of Europe. Certainly he established for himself an international reputation. Whether it was Matteo Bertando della Lega desiring the Queen's patronage for an Italian translation of the Bible;[1] the reformed congregation at Düsseldorf seeking help for the erection of a church;[2] the chaplain at Algiers—he was appointed to this office through the initiative of the Bishop—angling for a grant to allow him to study Oriental languages;[3] the Baron de Barre asking as to the character of a young Englishman who had proposed marriage to his daughter;[4] or the Churches of Dresden and Leipzig anxious to know how to address the Queen;[5]—it was to the Bishop of London that they all turned for help.

Henry Compton's many disappointments never made him lose interest in the wider church. One of the last letters he ever wrote (4 March, 1713) was to the Earl of Oxford, for the purpose of tracking down what had happened to the communion plate given to the Leeward Islands—a rumour having gone the rounds that it had been 'converted into new plate for the Governor's lady'.[6]

---

[1] Bod. Rawlinson MSS. 984 C, fo. 271.   [2] *Ibid.*, fo. 273.

[3] Holmes to Compton, 15 Oct., 1682, *ibid.*, 982 C, fo. 82. There are extant three letters written by Holmes from Algiers to the Bishop. They show how appreciative he was of Compton's sustained interest. He ministered only to a small congregation, he wrote, which consisted of the consul's family and a few Dutch slaves 'but this will give me more leisure to prosecute other and not unprofitable studies to inform myselfe of the Customs of the Country and to learn Turcick and Arabian languages'. He also related at length the story of a Spanish priest (now a slave) who was anxious to become a member of the Church of England (*ibid.*, 985 C, fos. 78, 80, 82, 88.)

[4] *Ibid.*, 982 C, fo. 25.   [5] *Ibid.*, 982 C, fo. 160.

[6] *H.M.C.* App. ii, Report XIV; p. 269 (Portland MSS.).

EPILOGUE

IT remains only to say something of Compton as a man and to make some estimate of his life's work, a task which devolves as much, perhaps, on the reader as on the biographer.

One fact posterity cannot deny any more than could his contemporaries—that Henry Compton was an extremely busy man, so much so that it is not easy to see how he found time to fulfil all his duties. He was bishop of a large diocese, and himself discharged many functions which others were content to depute to their legal officials. He was for many years a member of the Privy Council, and of the Committee of the Lords of Trade and Plantations, and was assiduous in his attendance at both. He had spiritual charge of the Plantations—a great preoccupation entailing a vast correspondence. He sat in the House of Lords and was on the governing body of the Society for the Propagation of the Gospel. His labours on behalf of French refugees and Scottish Episcopalians were constant, and he corresponded widely with numerous English clergy abroad. He was also for some years Dean of the Chapels Royal and Clerk to the Closet.

In discharging this enormous burden of work he was assisted by a chaplain (of whom we know the names of six) and a secretary, but his letters, short and very much to the point, were often written in his own hand. Such a round of ceaseless activity could only be successfully carried through by a disciplined and ordered daily routine.

Also, above and beyond such duties, there was the Bishop's devotion to botany, which was by no means a dilettante interest. He was a serious and practical horticulturist whose researches proved invaluable to those working in the same field. A few words about this interest may not be out of place.

The seventeenth century witnessed the increasing application of the scientific method to the various branches of knowledge. The mood of the age was experimentalist, and nowhere more so than in the field of natural history. Here the great name is that of John Ray (1627-1705), who attempted a systematic description of the whole organic world in his *Historia Plantarum*. He was not, however, a lone worker. Others, though less well known, were active in the same field—Plukenet (1642-1708), Superintendant of the Royal Gardens at Hampton Court; James Petiver (1663-1718), botanist and entomologist; and Richard Richardson (1663-1741), who dedicated his greatest work to Compton.

The establishment of peace after the troubled years of the Civil War led particularly to an interest in gardens in what has been described as 'The Golden Age of Botany'. Compton caught the enthusiasm and it proved to be life-long. On his appointment to London he entered into possession of an ideal garden at Fulham,[1] and his long residence 'enabled him, finally, to collect a greater variety of Greenhouse varieties and to plant a greater variety of hardy Exotic Trees and Shrubs than had been seen in any Garden before in England'. A visitor to England wrote later of the Bishop: 'There were few days in the year, till towards the latter part of his life, but he was actually in his garden, ordering and directing the Removal and Replacing of his Trees and plants.'

His ecclesiastical responsibilities, if they left him with little time, at least meant that he had acquaintances all over Europe and in the New World, who provided him with specimens. Dr. Henry Newton, at one time his Chancellor, sent him from Italy 'a Box of Mellon Seeds both white and otherwise; & the seeds of several sorts of plants of the best kinds I could meet with here, with Acorns of that kind of Ever Green Oak called Leek which in this place makes a very bountiful tree and shade as your Lordship is no Stranger to'.[2] Henri Justel writing from France on refugee business turned to their common interest, and described at some length a *Narcissus liliareus* of an agreeable odour 'which flowered in September, and was rose coloured until it whitened on attaining its maturity.'[3] Mr. Stevens of South Carolina sent over to Fulham a box with some of the country's products.[4]

Thus the Bishop's garden became well known to all the botanists of the time, and was 'ever open to the curious and scientific'. Ray, Petiver, and Plukenet were regular visitors,

[1] Switzer, *Iconographia Rustica*, 1718. Quoted G. Taylor, *Old London Gardens*, 1953, p. 62.
[2] Newton to Compton, 16 Jan., 1706, Bod. Rawlinson MSS. 983 C, fo. 172.
[3] Justel to Compton, undated, *ibid.*, 982 C, fo. 7.
[4] Fulham MSS., South Carolina Box, fo. 7.

and acknowledged in their writings the debt which they owed to the botanist Bishop. Ray, in his *Historia Plantarum*, refers to the garden as *hortus cultissimus*, while a great number of Plukenet's figures were engraved from its specimens. When William Watson visited Fulham in the middle of the eighteenth century, he still found ample evidence of Compton's care, despite the fact that his successors had been 'more distinguished for their piety and learning than for their zeal in the promotion of natural knowledge'.[1] He was able to list thirty-three exotic trees, some of which were not to be found elsewhere, and others which were among the largest of their kind in Europe.

During his suspension, the Bishop found great satisfaction in suggesting improvements to the gardens at Castle Ashby, and in journeying with Lord Nottingham to visit the estates of Lord Chesterfield, Lord Ferrers, and the Duke of Devonshire.[2]

It was fitting that the Bishop should bequeath his collection of plants to the University of Oxford, for which it was found necessary to build a special house in the physic garden.[3]

This devotion to botany undoubtedly shows an attractive side of Compton's character.

So far as the Bishop was concerned his enthusiasm had one great disadvantage—it was ruinously expensive, and he could not really afford it. In 1709 his chaplain confessed to Dr. William Trumbull that his master seriously intended 'to part with all his curious and exotic plants . . . that he may give away more'.[4]

Such a reference may serve to introduce us to Compton's frequent financial embarrassments which constituted an unfortunate background to most of his life. At the end of his days, in October 1712, he was still in desperate need of money, and he wrote an extraordinary letter (in the middle of a dangerous illness) to Robert Harley, Earl of Oxford, then head of the tory administration which ran as follows:

The world believes me to be on the mending hand and I do not undeceive them in that particular, because if it were spring, I were in all likelihood in a fair way of recovery. But [as] it is my case is dangerous, and I must change my address from desiring a pension

---

[1] *Philosophical Transactions,* vol. xlvii, London, 1753.
[2] *H.M.C.* App. i, Report XIV (Dartmouth MSS. vol. 3, p. 143).
[3] Hearne, *Remarks etc.*, v. 122.
[4] *H.M.C.* Downshire MSS., vol. i, parts I and II, p. 881.

to beg a charity, if ever I deserved anything at her Majesty's hands. The surprise of my indisposition has plunged me in such difficulties that no man but myself knows, nor have I yet discovered it to any but yourself, as my only friend that can help me. In short, I want three thousand pounds immediately to prevent the utmost shame. And therefore if I could have it as secret service by bank bills or otherwise, it would mightily secure my reputation and infinitely increase the obligation.[1]

This is indeed a desperate letter, and it suggests that the Bishop, thinking his end near, is appalled at the thought of creditors who must for ever remain unpaid.

Yet why was Compton in such dire poverty? He was a bachelor without a family to support. The revenues of the See of London were considerable, in addition to which he had an income of £1,000 a year as a member of the Committee of the Lords of Trade and Plantations. In early life we know that his financial worries were largely due to his personal extravagance; but was this still true of his later years?

Contemporaries unanimously ascribe his poverty to his extensive charities. There is, on the whole, no reason to doubt this judgment, for his compassion often made him forget the extent of his financial resources. Various were the causes, and many the people, for whom he accepted a measure of financial responsibility. 'The French refugees have drunk deeply of his bounty for many years', William Whitfield, Rector of St. Martin's Ludgate, said after his death:[2] as had also the Irish, and the Scottish Episcopalians. He was much given to hospitality, and was 'generous and charitable beyond Example. His Table was always furnished, and always free to those whom Respect or Business drew to him'.[3] The poor found in him a constant friend, and he dipped into his own pocket on their behalf (as well as securing royal briefs) with princely generosity. Twelve poor people were his permanent care, and his hall was frequented every morning by petitioners of all kinds, and help was given 'to everyone who could make out (and it was easy to make that out to him) that he was a proper object of charity'.[4] Also there was a number of aged men and widows to whom he gave an

---

[1] *H.M.C.* App. ii. Report XIV. p. 357 (Portland MSS.).
[2] W. Whitfield, *A Sermon etc.*, 1713, p. 19.
[3] T. Gooch, *A Sermon etc.*, p. 15.　　　　[4] *Ibid.*

annual pension; as well as children (especially sons of the clergy) whom he supported at school and university 'at his own cost and charge'. Nor must we forget the money that he laid out on the purchase of advowsons, and on the rebuilding of churches. Certainly we can accept the opinion of a friend 'that he liked nothing that looked narrow or stingy'.

Such lavish giving far exceeded his means, and it is true that he died a poor man. His only real wealth then lay in his magnificent library (half of which went to St. Paul's and the other half to the Corporation of Colchester) and his rare plants.

The Bishop had a warm and affectionate heart, though a certain shyness and reserve seems to have characterised his personal relationships. It was difficult to become intimate with him. Burnet, who did not like him, admits that Compton was essentially a humble man. Others affirm that he was 'courteous and affable, not full of words but very conversable . . . always easy of access'.[1] In his private chaplains—such men as Lancaster, Sill, Ralph Bridges, Hall, Williams, and Thomas Gooch—he seems to have inspired a deep and lasting respect. True on occasions he could give way to bad temper and resentment, yet he did not permanently nourish ill will. His own chaplain relates that of a clergyman who had spoken 'rudely and contemptuously' of his Lordship, Compton said: 'I am glad on't, for he has given me an opportunity of setting a good Example in forgiving him.'[2] Though he disagreed with the principles of the Nonjurors, this did not prevent his going out of his way to help them, as in the case of Bishop Frampton. Like many kindly men, Compton tended 'to trust too much to the recommendation of others', through an excess of charity. But this was the defect of his virtues.[3]

His personal religion was sincere, simple and practical. After he had sown the wild oats of his youth (like his father), he settled down to work hard, and to apply himself, with great seriousness, to his clerical duties. His piety was unostentatious but none the less real. His household went regularly with him to morning and evening prayer : the day was begun with the litany and ended with short devotions.[4]

[1] T. Gooch, *A Sermon.*, etc., p. 15. [2] *Ibid.*, p. 18.
[3] Cockburne, *The Blessedness of Christians*, p. 22.
[4] Gooch, *op. cit.*, p. 20.

His health, right into the seventies, remained amazingly good, and the letters which he wrote up to the time of his death, as well as the amount of business he was able to get through, confirm the words of a friend who was constantly with him that 'he did not feel the Burden of Old Age so much as others commonly do . . . and those who conversed daily and intimately with him were not sensible of any considerable Decay of Memory and other Intellectuals'.[1] In 1711 he was seriously ill, and the next year suffered a fall which brought with it serious complications. Contemporaries thought that this was the end, but the Bishop's strong constitution, despite gout and stone, reasserted itself, with the result that he made such a wonderful recovery that it seemed his 'Youth was renewed'. In the following year he even set about another laborious visitation of his diocese, a most exacting ordeal, but it proved to be more than he could cope with. He was taken ill in the midst of it, and himself immediately recognised that this time his end had come—and so he informed his friends. The clergy of the diocese were genuinely distressed, for long years at Fulham had endeared him to them, and made him almost an institution. Prayers were offered for his recovery in all London churches. On first taking to his bed, the Bishop received the Holy Communion, and 'rose unassisted on his knees to take the Body and Blood'. He talked calmly of dying to those around, and spent a great deal of his time, either having the prayers of the church read to him, or 'silently calling upon God'. He was often in great pain, but was never heard to complain, remaining 'quiet and good natured to the end'. On 7 July, 1713, in the 81st year of his age, while 'hallulaghs for peace were being offered', he died calmly.

He left the most specific injunctions that he should be buried in the churchyard of the parish where he happened to die, for it was an oft-quoted saying of his: 'The church for the living the churchyard for the dead.' He also ordered that his tomb should not be disfigured by any lengthy and eulogistic inscription such as was too common in those days, but that it should simply bear his name, age and the date of his death, with a Greek inscription 'In the Cross only'. Such simplicity was typical of the man, for despite faults of temperament and worldly ambition, he had a real belief in the power of Christ to redeem

[1] Cockburne, op. cit., p. 25.

sinful men. In his spiritual development he may perhaps be numbered amongst the 'twice born'.

He was buried on 15 July, 'attended by his faithful servants and noble Relations', in the churchyard at Fulham, where his grave may still be seen.

It was fitting that he should be memorialised, on 26 July, in the presence of the Lord Mayor and Aldermen, in the great Cathedral of St. Paul's, whose worshipful life he had done so much to enrich. The preacher at the service was a former chaplain, Thomas Gooch, later Bishop of Norwich, who took as his text: 'Faithful is the saying, If a man seeketh the office of a bishop, he desireth a good work.'[1] The sermon was long, but it was not uninteresting, and concluded with these words:

> The greatest loss is to the Public, to the Church, and State. In him the Church has lost a most excellent Bishop, who attended upon, and executed that good work; the Kingdom a brave and able statesman, whose Integrity and Steadfastness had approved themselves in the most trying times; the Queen a faithful subject and wise Counsellor, whose Courage and Constancy has stood her (and She yet trusted would stand her) in the greatest stead; the Protestant Religion at home and abroad, its Ornament and Refuge, who had made (and was ready on any new Attempt to make) the noblest stand against Popery; the whole Christian World (at a Time of the greatest Need, and greatest Declension) an eminent Example of Virtue and Piety, an Unanswerable Instance, and Evidence of the Power and Efficacy of true Religion.[2]

*   *   *

The career of Henry Compton prompts us to ask what place he ought to be assigned in the life of the church and nation.

To the general student of the period, Compton is remembered only as a protestant bishop of whig sympathies, who perjured himself to James in the interests of William of Orange, and after the Revolution, soured by personal disappointment, swung round to violent toryism. This estimate has a foundation in fact, but it is not the whole truth, and stands in need of some revision.

[1] 1 Timothy 3 : 1.   [2] Gooch, *op. cit.,* p. 24.

25

Henry Compton's main loyalty was to the national way of life, as it expressed itself in the ordered pattern of the Church of England, the supremacy of the law, and the government of King and Parliament. In his early years he had seen this balance entirely upset through the political ambitions of the army, and the religious anarchy of the sects, consequent upon the attempted absolutism of the King. Because of these calamities, his father had been killed, the family estates despoiled, and he himself had become a wanderer. He never forgot the experience of these impressionable years. To him individualism in religion, as seen in the sects, made impossible the essentials of law and order. If every man followed his private judgment, anarchy, political and religious, was the inevitable result. Thus this youngest son of a noble house returned to England a tory by instinct and conviction.

He had not been many years in his native land before he was made painfully aware of a new and equally serious threat to the national way of life—a menace which was as great as that which had come from Cromwell. Charles II's sympathies were with Rome, and when he gave place to James, a resurgent Roman Catholicism became wedded to an obstinate assertion of despotic power. Compton had no hesitation in setting himself up in resolute opposition to this royal policy. If the King were successful (so thought the Bishop), it would be the end of the England which he wished to preserve, an England free and independent, with its reformed church and legal constitution. To maintain this inheritance, Compton was anxious to encourage the more amenable Dissenters to conform, and where this was impossible at least to work with them for a common end. He had the good sense not to champion the cause of Monmouth at the bidding of Shaftesbury; but as it was the whigs who were, in the main, in the forefront of the political struggle, so did he find himself more frequently keeping company with them. Also under the pressure of events which induced him to withstand James's assertion of despotic power, Henry Compton was inevitably led to adopt a whig philosophy of government and to hold that the power of the monarch, in certain circumstances, must be subordinated to the will of the people. Compton was the only bishop to sign the invitation to William, and after the Revolution he had no mental reservations. He enthusiastically supported the King and did everything he could to 'bring over the clergy' to the new Government.

The Revolution thus saw the triumph of the cause for which Compton had struggled, and in the interests of which he had perjured himself to James. Its very success tended to take away something of the singleness of political purpose which had hitherto led him on. He was never a doctrinaire whig in the strictest sense, and in fact the period of his greatest political influence coincided with his alliance with Danby, the tory. But it was unfortunate that the moment of national success was followed, for Compton, by the bitterness of personal disappointment. Despite his unparalleled services, William passed him over for the archbishopric; perhaps because he thought him in some ways irresponsible; perhaps because he owed him too much; perhaps because his perjury and quixotic escapade with Anne had lost him respect. The disappointment was extreme, and it made him throw in his lot with those who were equally disgruntled, and who, in the main, were tories. Danby followed the same road.

When Anne came to the throne, however, the 'nursing mother of the church', whose devotion to it was a real loyalty of love, the whole political and religious scene, for the ageing bishop, changed. The monarchy was now as much the patron of the church as it had been its enemy in the days of James: and the old man felt himself back in earlier days when the danger to the church came from the nonconformists and sectaries. Thus as he approached his eighties, and was restored to royal favour, he more and more assumed the character of a rigid churchman. It was, we repeat, a return in some ways to his youth; and a protest against the emergence of a new social and religious class, the trading dissenter. Such men as Thomas Tenison and Gilbert Burnet were convinced whigs, socially, politically and religiously: Henry Compton was not. They regarded the menace of Jacobitism as very real indeed (perhaps more real than in fact it was) and they would not allow their relations with the Dissenters to be prejudiced by such cries as 'The Church in Danger'. It was not so with the Bishop of London. In later years the friendship of Atterbury and the favour of Anne, following upon personal disappointment, undoubtedly clouded his political judgment. Yet at least he was consistent in a life-long devotion to the Church of England, a devotion which did not falter though it was not always informed. Amongst those who helped to preserve English liberties and the English Church, at a time of supreme crisis, Henry Compton may fairly claim a place.

It is a pity, however, that Compton should be known to posterity only by his political activities. As a Bishop of the Church he may with justice claim the gratitude of his countrymen, for he made the office a living reality in his diocese. His conscientious application to duty, his personal superintendence of the lives of his clergy, his visitations, his wide range of interests —all these have been illustrated in the course of this work. The Bishop's main concern, we have seen, was to help his clergy in the practical day-to-day discharge of their responsibilities, and nice doctrinal disputes did not help very much, so he thought, to this end. He had a great fellow feeling for Protestants abroad, which manifested itself in a variety of ways, all of them practical. He was probably the best known of all the bishops on the Continent and deservedly so. Perhaps we cannot conclude better than by quoting the testimony, exaggerated though it may be, of Monsieur Piozet, a minister of the French Reformed Church:

The Care of the Churches of God occupy your spirit day and night. And all the Reformed World sees with Admiration that not only do you govern those in your own diocese with a vigilance truly episcopal and pastoral; but also you receive into your Bosom the sad remnants of our dispersed flock. You gather our wandering and frightened sheep: and you employ yourself with an indefatigable zeal to procure for them spiritual and bodily pasture: so that the faithful in foreign lands are equally the object of your paternal kindliness along with those of your own nation; thus we can say with truth that you are (in effect) bishop of the world.'[1]

[1] Piozet to Compton, undated, Bod. Rawlinson MSS. 982 C, fo. 152.

BIBLIOGRAPHY

MANUSCRIPT AUTHORITIES

Bodleian Library
  Ballard MSS.
  Rawlinson MSS.
  Tanner MSS.
British Museum
  Cole MSS.
  Egerton MSS.
  Leeds Papers
  Additional MSS. 15; 2,803; 27,997; 28,093; 28,879; 29,584; 32,095; 34,268
Fulham Palace
  Fulham MSS. relating to the Plantations (at present with the Church
    Commissioners)
Lambeth Library
  Act Books of the Archbishops of Canterbury 711; 929; 938; 941; 1122
Record Office
  State Papers Domestic, Charles I; Charles II; James II; William and Mary;
    William III; Anne; Privy Council Registers
Saint Paul's Cathedral Library
  Bishop Compton's Register
  Miscellaneous letters, collected by Dr. Newton, Bishop Compton's
    Chancellor
  Liber Visitationis Parochialis Comitatus Middlesexiae, fo. 138
Society for Propagating the Gospel
  Journal
  Minutes
  Letters
  Carolina Papers
  Marquis of Northampton: Family Papers
St. Cross, Winchester
  Records
Parish of Cottenham
  Records
Historical Manuscripts Commission
  Bath MSS.
  Cowper MSS.
  Dartmouth MSS.
  Downshire MSS.
  Finch MSS.
  Kenyon MSS.
  Le Fleming MSS.
  Lindsey MSS.
  Portland MSS.
  Rutland MSS.

Verulam MSS.
Appendix ii, Report xiii
Appendix v, Report xi
Appendix vii, Report xiv
Appendix xiv, Report vii

GENERAL PRINTED AUTHORITIES USED THROUGHOUT

BURNET, G. *History of My Own Time.* Ed. Dartmouth, 1823.

CLARENDON, EARL OF, *The History of the Rebellion and Civil Wars in England.* Oxford, 1826.

COBBETT, W. *Parliamentary History.* 1806, etc.

DALRYMPLE, J. *Memoirs of Great Britain and Ireland.* 1790.

DURUY, J. V. *History of France.* Everyman Library, 1917.

FOSTER, J. *Alumni Oxonienses.* 1892.

FOXCROFT, H. C. *A Supplement to Burnet's History of My Own Time.* 1932.

GRANGER, J. *Biographical History, Continuation by Noble.* 1805.

HEARNE, T. *Remarks and Collections.* Ed. Doble, 1889.

WHITE KENNETT. *A Complete History of England.* 1719.

KIPPIS, A. *Biographica Britannica.* 1778, etc.

LATHBURY, T. *A History of the Convocation,* 1842.

WICKHAM LEGGE. *English Church Life 1660-1833.* 1914.

LINGARD, J. *History of England.* 1819-1830.

LUTTRELL, N. *A Brief Historical Relation of State Affairs from September 1678 to April 1714.* 1857.

MACAULAY, T. B. *History of England.* Everyman Library.

MANT, R. *History of the Church of Ireland.* 1840.

MASTERS, R. *The History of the College of Corpus Christi.* 1753.

OVERTON, J. H. *Life in the English Church 1660-1714.* 1885.
The Nonjurors. Their Lives, Principles and Writings. 1902.

PASCOE, C. F. *Two Hundred Years of the S.P.G.* 1901.

RANKE, L. Von, *History of England.* Oxford, 1875.

SKINNER, J. *An Ecclesiastical History of Scotland.* 1788.

TINDAL, N. *The Continuation of Mr. Rapin's History of England.* 1763.

VENN, J. & J. A. *Alumni Cantabrigienses.* 1926.

WILKINS, D. *Concilia Magnae Britanniae et Hiberniae.* 1737.

WOOD, A. *Athenae Oxoniensis.* 1691-2 edn. Gutch.

Dictionary of National Biography.

Journals of the House of Commons. XVI.

The Life of Dr. Henry Compton. 1713.

OTHER AUTHORITIES ARRANGED UNDER THEIR RESPECTIVE CHAPTERS

Chapter I

COCKBURNE, J. *The Blessedness of Christians after Death.* 1713.

WILLIAM BINGHAM COMPTON, 6th Marquis of Northampton, *History of the Comptons of Compton Wynyates.* Privately printed and circulated.

GOOCH, T. *A Sermon preach'd before the Lord Mayor.* 1713.

LLOYD, W. *Memorials of those that suffer'd.* 1668.

Chapter II

Diary and Correspondence of John Evelyn. 1850.
The Diary of Samuel Pepys. Everyman Library.
PACKE, E. *An Historical Record of the Royal Regiment of Horse Guards.* 1834.
Universal Magazine. June 1770.
WHITFIELD, W. *A Sermon on the late Lord Bishop of London.* 1713.

Chapter III

BROWNING, A. *Life of Thomas, Earl of Danby.* 1944.
CLARKE, J. S. *The Life of James the Second.* 1816.
JANE, W. *A Sermon Preach'd at the Consecration the Honourable Dr. Henry Compton, Lord Bishop of Oxford.* 1675.
SANDFORD, F. AND STEBBING, H. *Geneaological History of the Kings and Queens of England.* 1707.
SPEED, S. *Prison Pietie.* 1677.
Continuation of Roger Coke's 'Detection'. 1718.
THOMPSON, E. M. *Correspondence of the Family of Hatton.* 1878.
Diary of Edward Lake. Ed. G. P. Elliott. Camden Society. 1846.

Chapter IV

The Bishop of London's Seventh Letter of the Conference with his Clergy, held in the year 1686. 1690.
The Bishop of London's Tenth Conference with his Clergy upon the King's Directions to the Archbishops and Bishops for preserving Unity in the Church. 1701.
The Bishop of London's Charge to the Clergy of his Diocese at his Visitation, begun Anno 1693 and concluded Anno 1694. 1696.

Chapter V

CARPENTER, E. *The Life and Times of Thomas Tenison.* 1948.
CORNISH, S. W. *Episcopalia; or Letters of the Bishop of London to the Clergy of his diocese.* 1842.
STILLINGFLEET, E. *The Unreasonableness of Separation.* 1681.
Reliquiae Baxterianae. 1696.
To the Reverend and Merry Answerer of Vox Cleri. 1689.
A Translation from the Italian of *The Life of Donna Olympia Maldalchini, who governed the Church during the Time of Innocent X, which was from the year 1644 to 1655,* written originally by Abbot Gualdi and printed privately at Paris, 1677.
The Jesuites Intrigues; with the private Instructions of that Society to their Emissaries. 1669.

Chapter VI

HART, A. T. *The Life and Times of John Sharp.* 1919.
Life of John Sharp, by his son Thomas Sharp. 1825.
NEWCOMBE, T. *History of the Coronation of James II and Queen Mary.* 1687.
TURNER, F. C. *James II.* 1948.

A true Narrative of all the Proceedings against the Bishop of London by the Lords Commissioners appointed by his Majesty to inspect Ecclesiastical Affairs. 1689.

An Exact Account of the Whole Proceedings against the Right Reverend Father in God, Henry Lord Bishop of London, before the Lord Chancellor and the other Ecclesiastical Commissioners. 1688.

A Vindication of the Proceedings of His Majestie's Ecclesiastical Commissioners against the Bishop of London, and the Fellows of Magdalen College. 1688.

A Letter to the Author of the 'Vindication'. By Philominus Anglicus.

A Letter from the Bishop of Rochester to the Right Honourable the Earl of Dorset and Middlesex. 1689.

The Bishop of Rochester's Second Letter to the Right Honourable the Earl of Dorset and Middlesex. 1689.

The Harleian Miscellany, ed. William Oldys. 1809.

Chapter VIII

BROWN, B. C. *The Letters of Queen Anne.* 1935.

The Correspondence of Henry Hyde, Earl of Clarendon with the Diary of Lord Clarendon from 1687 to 1690. 1825.

HART, A. T. *William Lloyd.* 1952.

HATTON, C. *Correspondence.* 1878.

HEARNE. T. *Remarks and Collections.* 1886.

HICKES, G. *Memoirs of the Life of Mr. John Kettlewell.* 1718.

LUCKOCK, H. M. *The Bishops in the Tower.* 1887.

An Account of the Conduct of the Dowager Duchess of Marlborough. 1742.

Letters of Philip, Second Earl of Chesterfield. 1829.

Memoirs of Thomas, Earl of Ailesbury, written by himself. 1890.

Chapter IX

PERKINS, J. *The Crowning of the Sovereign.* 1937.

The Autobiography of Symon Patrick. 1839.

A Letter concerning Allegiance. 1710.

Chapter X

BIRCH, T. *Life of Dr. John Tillotson.* 1752.

EVANS, S. *Life of Bishop Frampton.* 1876.

D'OYLY, G. *Life of William Sancroft.* 1821.

PENNINGTON, E. L. *Commissary Blair.* 1936.

STILLINGFLEET, E. *Miscellaneous Discourses.* 1735.

The Bishop of London's Eighth Letter to his Clergy upon a Conference how they ought to behave themselves under a Toleration. 1692.

Parliamentary Papers, Vol. 50, 1850. 'Copy of the Alterations in The Book of Common Prayer prepared by the Royal Commission for the Review of the Liturgy, 1689.'

Chapter XI

NICHOLS, J. *The Miscellaneous Works of Bishop Atterbury.* 1789-98.

PAUL, H. *Queen Anne.* 1906.

A Letter concerning Allegiance, written by the Lord Bishop of L – – – –n to a Clergyman in Essex presently after the Revolution, Never before published. 1714.

Memoirs of the Life and Times of the most Reverend Father in God Dr. Thomas Tenison, late Archbishop of Canterbury. 1715.

Some Short Remarks upon the late Address of the Bishop of London. 1711.

Chapter XII

BURN, J. S. *The History of the Parish Registers in England.* Ed. I. R. Smith. 1862.

CORNISH, S. W. *Episcopalia; or Letters to the Bishop of London to the Clergy of his diocese.* 1842.

HICKERINGILL, E. *The Black Nonconformist.* 1709.

The Most Humble Confession and Recantation of Edmund Hickeringill. 1687.

Scandalum Magnatum: or the Great Trial at Chelmsford Assizes, held March 6, for the County of Essex, Betwixt Henry Bishop of London, Plaintiff, and Edm. Hickeringill, Rector of the Rectory of All Saints Colchester. 1682.

Episcopalia; or Letters of the Bishop of London to the Clergy of his diocese. 1686.

The Bishop of London's Seventh Letter, of the Conference with his Clergy, held in the year 1686. 1690.

The Bishop of London's Ninth Conference with his Clergy upon the fifth and tenth injunctions given by the King, 15 February, 1694-5. 1699.

The Bishop of London's Eleventh Conference with his Clergy held in the years 1699 and 1700 upon the King's proclamation for preventing immorality and prophaneness. 1704.

The Bishop of London's Twelfth Conference with his Clergy, in the years 1701, 2, 3; whether set forms of prayer be not very necessary in the publick worship of God. 1707.

The Bishop of London's Charge to the Clergy of his Diocese at his Visitation begun Anno 1693. 1696.

Articles of Visitation and Enquiry exhibited to the Ministers, Churchwardens, and Sidesmen of every Parish. 1706.

Circular Letter to the Clergy of his diocese requesting them to make due presentments of such persons as neglect the sacrament of the Lord's Supper. 1682-3.

Circular Letter to the clergy of his diocese to use their endeavours to recover the peoples from the neglect of the holy Communion. 1683-4.

Chapter XIII

SPARROW SIMPSON. *Registrum Statutorum et Consuetudinum Ecclesiae Cathedralis Sancti Pauli Londinensis.* 1873.

PATERSON, J. *Pietas Londinensis, or the Present Ecclesiastical State of London.* 1714.

Chapter XIV

CROSS, A. L. *The Anglican Episcopate and the American Colonies.* 1902.

FORTESCUE, J. W. *Calendar of State Papers, Colonial Series, America and West Indies, 1681-1685.* 1895.

FORTESCUE, J. W. *Calendar of State Papers, America and West Indies, 1694-1697.* 1905.

FORTESCUE, J. W. *Calendar of State Papers, Colonial Series, America and West Indies, 1697-1698.* 1905.

SAINSBURY, *Calendar of State Papers, Colonial Series, America and West Indies, 1675-6.* 1893.

SAINSBURY AND FORTESCUE. *Calendar of State Papers, Colonial Series, America and West Indies, 1677-1680.* 1896.

HEADLAM. *Calendar of State Papers, Colonial Series, America and West Indies, 1706-1708.* 1916.

PENNINGTON, E. L. *Commissary Blair.* 1936.

PORTEUS. *A Review of the Life and Character of Archbishop Secker.* 1773.

TYLER. *History of American Literature.* 1879.

Chapter XVI

CARSTAIRS. *State Papers and Letters.* 1774.

A Copy of My Lord Bishop of London his Letter. 1708.

Chapter XVII

SMITH, T. *An account of the Greek Church.* 1680.

SYKES, N. *The Church of England and Non-Episcopal Churches in the 16th and 17th Centuries.* 1948.

COVEL, J. *Some Account of the present Greek Church.* 1722.

TENISON, T. *Letter to the Clergy of the Convocation of Canterbury.* 1709.

WILLIAMS, G. *The Orthodox Church of the East in the Eighteenth Century.* 1868.

Several Letters from the Pastors of Geneva. 1707.

Union Review, Vol. I. 1863.

Epilogue

TAYLOR, G. *Old London Gardens.* 1953.

Philosophical Transactions, Vol. xlvii. 1753.

INDEX

26